Syntax

Syntax

A Cognitive Approach

Edward A. F. Gibson

The MIT Press
Cambridge, Massachusetts
London, England

The MIT Press
Massachusetts Institute of Technology
77 Massachusetts Avenue, Cambridge, MA 02139
mitpress.mit.edu

© 2025 Massachusetts Institute of Technology

This work is subject to a Creative Commons CC-BY-NC-ND license.

This license applies only to the work in full and not to any components included with permission. Subject to such license, all rights are reserved. No part of this book may be used to train artificial intelligence systems without permission in writing from the MIT Press.

(cc) BY-NC-ND

The MIT Press would like to thank the anonymous peer reviewers who provided comments on drafts of this book. The generous work of academic experts is essential for establishing the authority and quality of our publications. We acknowledge with gratitude the contributions of these otherwise uncredited readers.

This book was set in Stone Serif and Stone Sans by Westchester Publishing Services. Printed and bound in the United States of America.

Library of Congress Cataloging-in-Publication Data

Names: Gibson, Edward, 1962– author
Title: Syntax : a cognitive approach / Edward A. F. Gibson.
Description: Cambridge, Massachusetts : The MIT Press, 2025. | Includes bibliographical references and index.
Identifiers: LCCN 2025010311 (print) | LCCN 2025010312 (ebook) | ISBN 9780262553575 paperback | ISBN 9780262385046 pdf | ISBN 9780262385053 epub
Subjects: LCSH: Dependency grammar | Psycholinguistics | LCGFT: Introductory works
Classification: LCC P162 .G53 2025 (print) | LCC P162 (ebook) | DDC 415.01/8—dc23/eng/20250519
LC record available at https://lccn.loc.gov/2025010311
LC ebook record available at https://lccn.loc.gov/2025010312

EU Authorised Representative: Easy Access System Europe, Mustamäe tee 50, 10621 Tallinn, Estonia | Email: gpsr.requests@easproject.com

Contents

1 Introduction

Going back to Pāṇini—a logician and scholar from ancient India who lived sometime between 600 BC and 300 BC (Robins, 1967)—people have been trying to figure out the structure of human languages.[1] A **human language** is a conventionalized communication system that is acquired, produced, and understood in a community of people, to be used in their day-to-day lives. For such a communication system to be a human language, it must be able to convey all the meanings that are useful in that community. There are currently approximately seven thousand such languages in the world, from Indo-European languages—such as English, French, Italian, German, Russian, and Hindi—to languages in other families from industrialized cultures—such as Japanese, Korean, Mandarin and Turkish—to languages from nonindustrialized cultures—such as Tsimane' (Bolivia) and Pirahã (Brazil). There are over three hundred distinct language families, such that one language family has no obvious connections with any other language family (Dryer, 2013; Campbell, 2013).

There are three primary components to the structure of a human language: (1) its minimal units: **phonemes** of sound in spoken languages and phonemes of gesture in sign languages; (2) its minimal meaning units: **morphemes** and **words**; and (3) the combinations of its words and morphemes in the **grammar** of a language. There is further structure in language, including the **discourse structure** in a story or in a conversation (e.g., Wolf and Gibson, 2005), but I will not focus on those structures in this book. The main goal of this book is to provide an approach for describing the grammar for a human language, based on aspects of human cognition. First let me briefly discuss the phonemes and morphemes/words, before we get to the primary focus here: the grammar.

Phonemes. The English word *cat* is pronounced using three phonemes from the International Phonetic Alphabet (IPA), /k/ /æ/ /t/, to form a minimal meaning unit—a morpheme or word. There is nothing about the meaning of *cat* in how we pronounce the word, in English or any language: This is what the famous linguist Ferdinand de Saussure referred to as the "arbitrariness of the sign" (De Saussure, 1916, 2006). Indeed, the fact that the word *dog* is translated into very different-sounding forms across languages (e.g., *chien* in French; *inu* in Japanese; *gǒu* in Mandarin) suggests there is little meaning in the sounds.[2]

Morphemes and words. Morphemes are the meaningful subword units, which can be a whole word like *cat* or *giant*; or part of a word like *weasel* and *-s* in *weasels*; or *deliver* and *-ed* in *delivered*; or *happy* or *-ness* in *happiness*. Although the notion of **word** is somewhat hard to define so that it applies to all languages, a useful definition is one of the following: a free morpheme with no affixes (= prefixes, suffixes, or infixes) (like *giant, robot, of, the*), or a root plus affixes (like *weasels* or *delivered*), or a compound plus affixes (Haspelmath, 2017, 2023). A word is the unit that we recognize in writing, made up of one or more morphemes.

The **lexicon** or dictionary in a language is then the set of word forms and idiomatic expressions—common sets of words that co-occur often—each with a meaning (the semantics).[3] The **grammar** then is the set of rules for combining the words (and more complex lexical items like idioms) into higher-level meanings and combining those meanings further, potentially recursively, where each rule has a form (the syntax) and a meaning.

In a growing fraction of the world's languages, we have a pretty good idea of what its **core lexicon** looks like.[4] I define the core lexicon of a language to be the set of lexical items that all fluent speakers of that language would know. For example, the words in the core English lexicon are roughly those in the *Oxford Advanced Learners Dictionary* (https://www.oxfordlearnersdictionaries.com/). A speaker who knows most of those words (and the syntax) would be a fluent speaker of English. Brysbaert et al. (2016) estimates that a literate adult American English speaker knows about forty thousand words, many of which would be in the core lexicon.

Interestingly, this is not all of the words of the language: It turns out that most of the words in a language from an industrialized culture come from narrow semantic domains, such that only a subset of speakers know them.[5]

For example, I have interests in cognitive science, linguistics, neuroscience, hockey (I am Canadian), rowing (I competed for many years, including in the 1984 Olympics for Canada), comic books (particularly Silver and Golden Age, but you will have to look those terms up), among other things. I have rich domain knowledge in these areas, each of which comes with a large lexicon: the **communal lexicon** for the domain (Clark, 1998). Relatedly, names of people and places are also words in the broader lexicon, whose set will differ radically from person to person (Ramscar et al., 2014). So my own lexicon is different from that of almost all other English speakers, even though we share the same syntax and core lexicon. The words in the core lexicon are a small subset of the broader lexicon.

The main goal of this book is to provide an approach for describing the grammar for a human language, based on aspects of human cognition. Because people use human language to **communicate** with each other, there is usually a producer (speaker/writer/signer) and a comprehender (listener/reader/conversation partner). For simplicity here in this book, I will use the word **sentence** to refer to any complete communicative unit transmitted from one conversation partner to another.[6] Perhaps the most fundamental observation about grammar is that it allows us to transmit arbitrary ideas. For example:

(1) Giant robot weasels delivered chocolate piano sandwiches to the Pokémon picnic.

This is a sentence that has never been produced before, and yet a producer and comprehender who know English will be able to discern a similar message in it, which describes an unlikely event involving robot weasels and an unusual picnic. How do humans do this? It's easy to identify a dictionary of all the words and morphemes in this novel sentence:

1. *giant*; meaning: very large
2. *robot*; meaning: a machine resembling a human
3. *weasel*; meaning: a small, slender, carnivorous mammal
4. *-s*; meaning: more than one
5. *deliver*; meaning: an action involving someone giving something to a location
6. *-ed*; meaning: past tense on an action or state
7. *chocolate*; meaning: a tasty substance made from cocoa

8. *piano*; meaning: a particular musical instrument
9. *sandwich*; meaning: a type of food for humans
10. *to*; meaning: marking the goal of an action
11. *the*; meaning: indicating that a thing to be named soon after is already in the context
12. *Pokemon*; meaning: a pocket monster such as Pikachu or Snorlax
13. *picnic*; meaning: an event involving people eating, usually in a park

What are the rules that allow us to put the words together to form a novel sentence like (1)? This is the domain of **grammar**: the rules of how the forms in language combine, also sometime called the **combinatorial** rules of language. Grammar covers **morphology**, responsible for combining morphemes into words, and **syntax**, which deals with combinations of words. This book is focused on syntax—how words combine. So when I refer to grammar below, I am talking about the grammar of the word combinations.

The syntax of a two-word sequence is usually just a link between the two, as below for the sequence *giant weasels*:

Giant weasels

The **meaning** (or **semantics**, or message) conveyed by the syntactic link is obtained by a combination of the meanings of each of the parts (which may be hard to define exactly). Many researchers refer to this property as **compositionality** (Frege et al., 1892; Carnap, 1956; Montague, 1970; Heim and Kratzer, 1998; Steedman, 2001).[7] In this case, the unit formed by composing these words refers to weasels that are giant.[8]

Here, I am interested in describing not only the language but also the mental representations and processes that support linguistic cognition (detailed in chapter 2). Because we are constantly learning new words and ways of putting them together, it is practically impossible to discover a complete and adequate lexicon and grammar for a group, or even for an individual. Further complicating the problem is the fact that each individual in a language community will know a different set of words and combinations (Clark, 1998). We therefore don't seek a complete theory of syntax: We seek to uncover the representations that most speakers of a language community know, and try to understand the generalizations that may underlie them.

For simplicity, I will concentrate initially on examples from English. This is mostly because that is the language that I speak and write well in: a matter of convenience sampling. With luck, the dialect of English that I speak will generalize well for other English speakers of differing dialects.

Some helpful definitions:

- **human language**: A conventionalized communication system that is acquired, produced, and understood in a community of people, which can convey all the meanings that are useful in that community.
- **dialect**: A version of a language, such that a speaker of the dialect can convey arbitrary meanings to speakers of other dialects of the same language. There may be differences in lexicon and pronunciation across dialects. Thus, there are many dialects of English, and they are all mutually understandable. But even though English and German are related languages, speakers of English and German are not mutually understandable. Hence, English and German are not dialects of each other.
- **idiolect**: One individual's dialect. My personal idiolect includes a lexicon encompassing terms from linguistics, cognitive science, neuroscience, ice hockey, rowing, and comic books, among other fields.
- **phoneme**: The minimal unit in a language: sounds in auditory languages, gestures in sign language.
- **morpheme**: A minimal meaning unit in a human language.
- **word**: A free morpheme, with no affixes, or a root plus affixes, or a compound plus affixes (Haspelmath, 2017, 2023).
- **sentence (utterance)**: A complete communicative unit transmitted from one conversation partner to another.
- **lexicon**: The set of word forms and idiomatic expressions, each with a meaning.
- **core lexicon**: The lexical entries that each fluent speaker knows.
- **communal lexicon**: The lexicon associated with a particular semantic domain, used by a subset of speakers of the language more generally.
- **grammar**: The set of rules for combining the lexical items into higher-level meanings.
- **animal communication systems** and their relation to human language: A fascinating question is how animal communication systems relate to human languages. The view that I take is that nonhuman animal communication is likely similar in spirit but likely simpler in terms of its lexicon

and grammar size. Although nonhuman animals have communication systems, they can't communicate anything remotely as complex as arbitrary thoughts. For example, some monkeys have several calls depending on the environment: One call warns of one kind of predator (from the air), a different call warns of predators on the ground, and a third call is used for nonpredator situations (e.g., Campbell's monkeys: Ouattara et al. 2009; Schlenker et al. 2016). This kind of communication is like a simplified human dictionary (lexicon), where sounds are associated with meanings. Monkey calls, and other animal communication systems, are also combinatorial to some degree. It is the size of the lexicon and the range of possible combinations that likely separates human language from animal communication systems (Arnold and Zuberbühler, 2006; Ouattara et al., 2009; Engesser et al., 2016; Suzuki et al., 2016; Townsend et al., 2018).

Methods. The methods to be used in our search for syntax are primarily behavioral:

- **language production data**: What people say in natural speech and texts (**corpora**).
- **language comprehension data**: such as from **acceptability** judgments on sentences.

We are a long way off from being able to figure out syntactic rules using brain data. Behavioral data are currently the primary source. I discuss acceptability judgments in section 2. Other behavioral tasks are discussed briefly in section 2.3. Some neural measures of language processing are discussed in chapter 9.

1.1 A Sentence Is Structured Like a Tree

Remarkably, a sentence of length *n* words in any human language can be structured into a **tree**, starting at a **root** word (marked by the ROOT symbol in my diagrams), connecting to other words via directed links (**dependencies**), with no cyclic links back to previously connected words, and ending at the **leaf** words. The word *tree* here is a graph-theoretic term: a graph with directed links between the words, where each word except one—the root word—has exactly one parent, and there are no cycles. A sentence of length

n words then always has $n-1$ directed links. This is a special case of a directed acyclic graph (DAG).

It's kind of amazing to think for a moment that this is the structure of all sentences, in all human languages (and just as impressive is the fact that many linguists actually agree on this). What this means is that sentences are formed from putting one word together with another, then adding another word to the resulting structure, and doing this repeatedly. The dependencies are the links that connect the words to form the larger compositional meaning of the sentence. Thus, intuitions about **what a sentence means** tell us how to link the words, and these links are the combining rules of language.

Let's consider the simplest structure, between just two words:

(2) Canadian hat

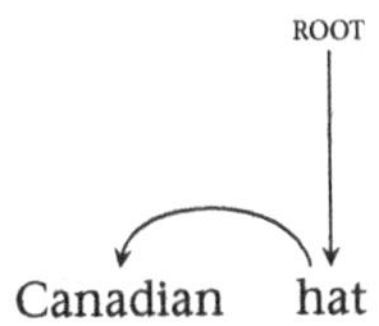

In this structure, a *Canadian hat* is a type of hat, not a type of Canadian, so *hat* is the head: *Hat* determines the semantic category (hats, not Canadians). So *hat* is the root for this structure (the head of the whole structure).

Now let's look at a slightly more complex example, with three words. Here, the phrase *Canadian hat maker* in (3) can be interpreted two ways.

(3) Canadian hat maker

One meaning connects *Canadian* to *hat* and then *hat* to *maker.*

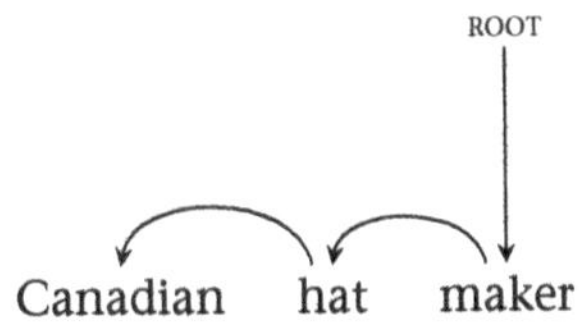

Here, a *hat maker* is a type of maker, not a type of hat, so *maker* is the head of the whole structure. This person is a maker (of any nationality) of a particular kind of hat known as a Canadian hat.

The second meaning for (3) has the connection between *hat* and *maker* (as in the previous one), but *Canadian* is connected to *maker* as well:

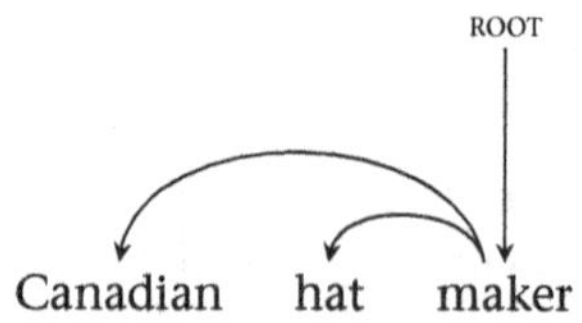

In this structure, a *Canadian hat-maker* is a type of hat maker, not a type of Canadian, so *maker* is the head for the connection between *Canadian* and *maker*. Here, the hat-maker happens to be Canadian and might make any kind of hat.

The connections linking each pair of words are called dependencies: Each of these pairs of words combine to make a larger meaning in the sentence. Following Hudson (1984, 1990, 2015) (cf. De Marneffe and Nivre, 2019 for details on several **dependency grammar** frameworks), I draw the arcs from what we will call the **head** to its dependents, where the head determines the semantic category of the dependency pair as a whole, while the dependent provides some semantic specification.

Most sentences have as their core meaning an **event** or **state**, which is often indicated by a verb. Examples of events are eating, walking, running, sleeping, giving, and sending. Examples of states are seeing, loving, and disliking. The **participants** in the event/state correspond to the **arguments** of the verb and are usually indicated by nouns in the language. The core meaning word—usually a verb—is the head word in the sentence, and some of the other words are its dependents. Let's look at a simple sentence first:

(4) Ollie sleeps.

The meaning of this sentence is a sleeping event indicated by the verb *sleeps* applied to the argument *Ollie*. The head *sleeps* determines the meaning—the semantic category—of the dependency pair as a whole, while the dependent *Ollie* provides semantic specification. So *sleeps* is the head and *Ollie* is its argument. The dependency structure for (4) is given below:

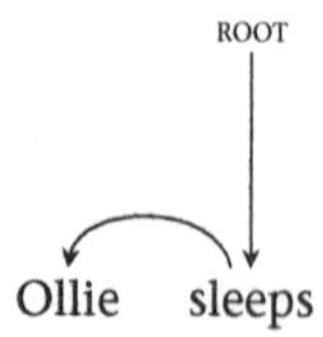

Indicating the ROOT at *sleeps* is just for visualization purposes: We could determine that *sleeps* is the root word, because it is the source of all the arrows in (4).

Now let's look at a few slightly more complex examples:

(5) a. A squirrel awakens.
    b. Ollie chased a squirrel.

The dependency structure for (5a) is similar to that for (4), but now we have to decide what the head of the sequence *a squirrel* is. This kind of sequence—a noun phrase—can replace a name like *Ollie* to give a sentence of similar meaning. Because *squirrel* and *Ollie* both label kinds of things in the world and *Ollie* must be the one connecting to *sleeps* in (4), the noun *squirrel* is the head that connects to *awakens* in (5a). Then the word *a* connects to *squirrel* as its dependent:

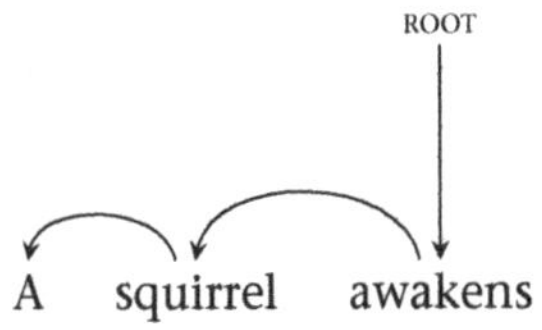

The word *a* is of category **determiner** or **article**: This is a special category of English words that initiates a noun phrase. Its meaning is complex; it relates the noun to the context. Here *a* indicates a new element in the context, whereas the determiner *the* indicates a noun that should already be known or inferred to be in the context.

The dependency structure for (5b) is given below:

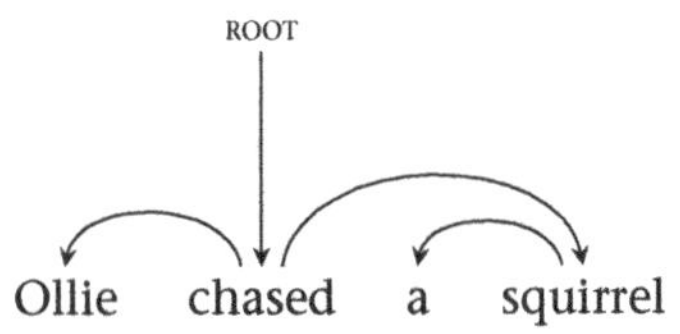

Here, the verb *chased* is the head word for the sentence, with *Ollie* and *squirrel* as its dependents.

As we look at more examples, we will see that there are two very common kinds of content words in English: **nouns** and **verbs**. Most nouns refer to a concrete thing or a kind of thing in the world, such as *girl, boy, animal, rock, dog, squirrel, apple, table, computer, or person*, or a particular person or thing, indicated by a name, like *Ollie* or *Samuel*.[9] Verbs, on the other hand, denote events or states relating the meanings of nouns to other nouns and events/states. Some examples of English verbs are *sleeps, chased, thought,* and *delivered*.

A more complex case is provided by (6), whose dependency structure is provided below it:

(6) The girl thought that Ollie chased a squirrel.

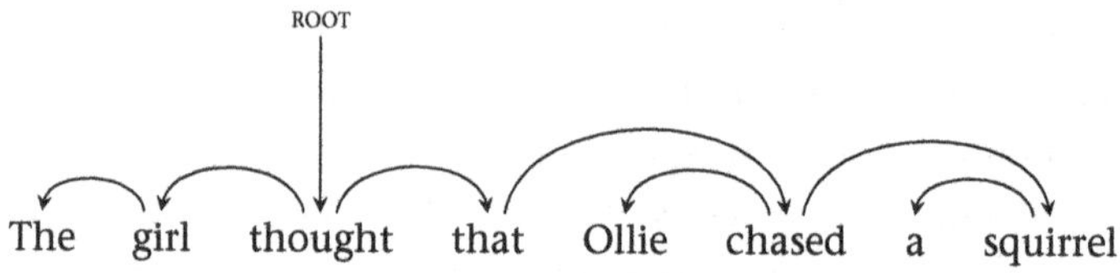

Here, the structure for *the girl thought* is parallel to the structure for *a squirrel awakens* in (5a); and the structure for *Ollie chased a squirrel* is identical to the structure for the same sequence in (5b). The only parts to be added are the connections for the word *that*. The word *that* here is what is called a **subordinator** (or in even fancier linguistic jargon, a **complementizer**): a marker of an embedded sentence. A simple analysis is one where the verb *thought* has *that* as its dependent, and the clause following (headed by *chased*) is a dependent of *that*.

Now we can return to the somewhat complex sentence that we started with in (1). A dependency structure for (1) is provided below:

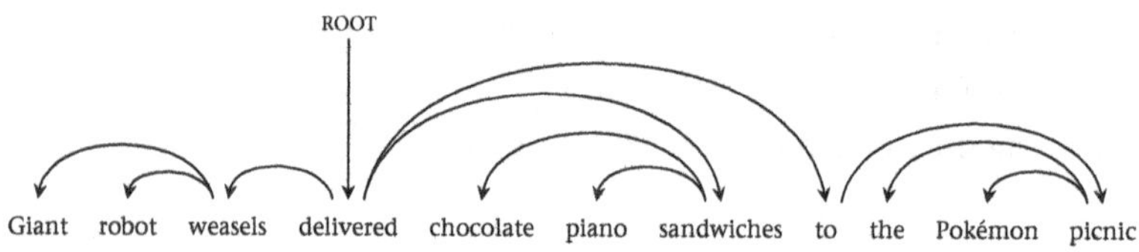

Here, the main event in the whole sentence is *delivered*: This sentence is describing a delivering event. Overall, the basic meaning of (1) is something like *weasels delivered sandwiches to picnic*: This is a structure whose head is *delivered* connected to *weasels*, *sandwiches*, and *to*. This simplified structure is given below:

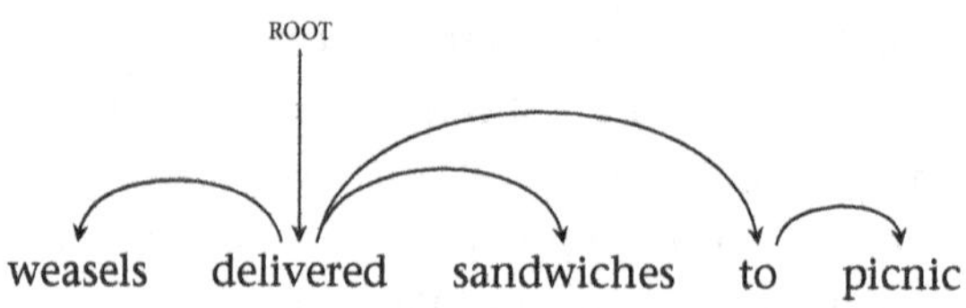

There is a set of event properties that we often need to communicate—such as location, duration, goal, and instrument—and these have typically been grammaticalized in prepositions like *to*, *for*, and *of* in a language like

English. We can work down from *delivered* to its dependents: the word *weasels*, the word *sandwiches*, and the word *to*, which connects to *picnic*. The word *to* is a dependent of *delivered*, because *to* provides a directional meaning specification of where the delivering is happening: not *into*, not *near*, not *beside*, but *to*. The part-of-speech category for *to* is called a **preposition**; this preposition is closely connected to the verb *delivered*. In general, prepositions like *to*, *of*, or *from* are heads for their dependent nouns to follow.

Regarding the modifiers for each of the nouns in the above sentence, English speakers will agree that *giant* and *robot* are semantic specifications of *weasels* in (1). These words function as modifiers of *weasels*, telling us what kind of weasels are engaging in the action to be mentioned later in the sentence. Thus, a noun like *weasels* is the head for its dependents *giant* and *robot*. English speakers will also agree that *chocolate* and *piano* are properties of *sandwiches*, and *the* and *Pokémon* are properties of *picnic*, so there is a similar structure to each sequence within the broader meaning.

1.2 Ambiguity Demonstrates the Existence of Dependency Structure

Evidence for dependency structure is provided by the existence of *syntactic ambiguity*: A string of words can mean two or more very different things. If all of the meaning was contained just in the sequence of words—so that you didn't have to figure out how the words connect—then this ambiguity of meaning couldn't happen. We have already seen an example like this: *Canadian hat maker* in (3), with its two dependency structures. Let's look at another example of ambiguity in the sentence in (7):

(7) The spy saw the cop with the telescope.

Example (7) is a classic example that computer scientists often use to discuss ambiguity in natural language. There are two interpretations for this sentence, notated by their dependency structures below.

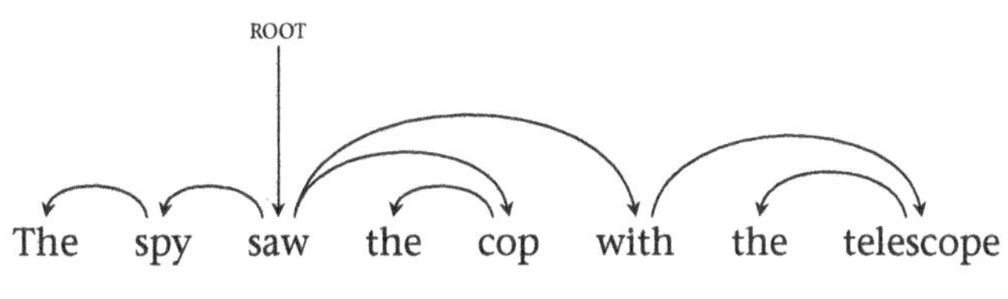

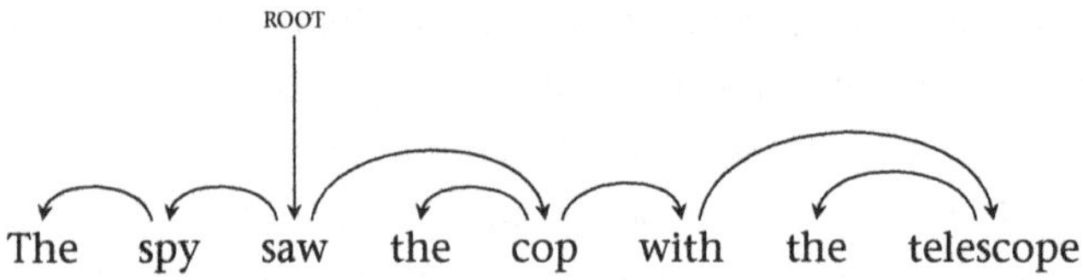

The first structure has the preposition *with* connecting to the verb *saw*. The meaning here then is that the sequence *with the telescope* connects to the verb so that this is the instrument of *saw*. In contrast, the preposition *with* connects to the noun *cop* in the second structure, meaning that it is the cop who has the telescope.

Now consider the ambiguity in the headlines in (8):[10]

(8) a. Rumors about NBA referees getting ugly
    b. Toronto law to protect squirrels hit by mayor

There are two structures for headline (8a):

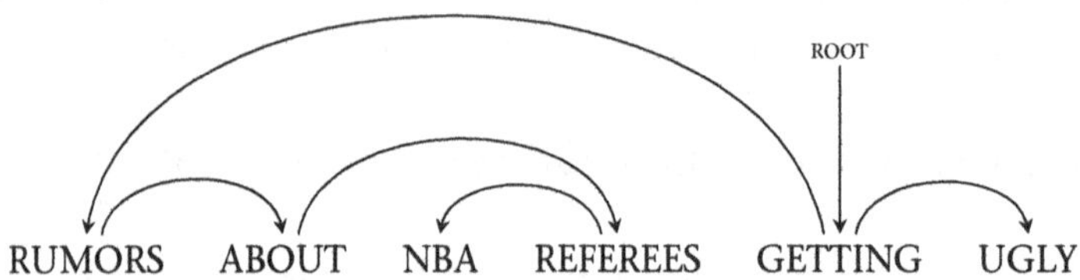

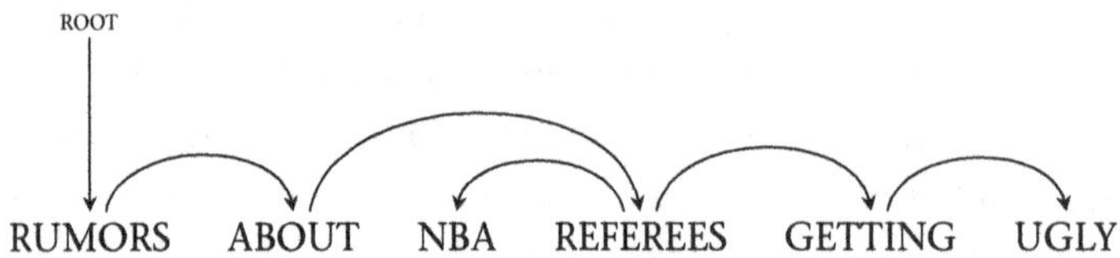

The structure for *rumors about NBA referees* is the same in both: The preposition *about* connects to *rumors*, and the object of the preposition *about* is the noun *referees*, with *NBA* serving as a modifier of *referees*. The difference between the two meanings is how *getting ugly* is connected: in the first (presumably intended) meaning, *getting ugly* connects to *rumors*, suggesting that the rumors are getting ugly. In the second interpretation, *getting ugly* connects to *referees*, suggesting that the referees are the ones getting ugly.

Finally, consider two possible structures for (8b):

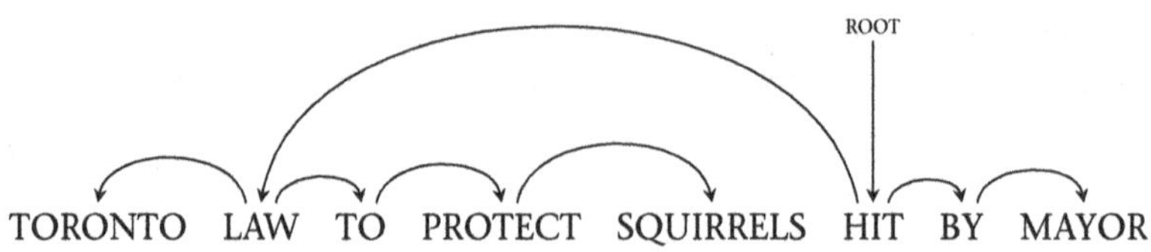

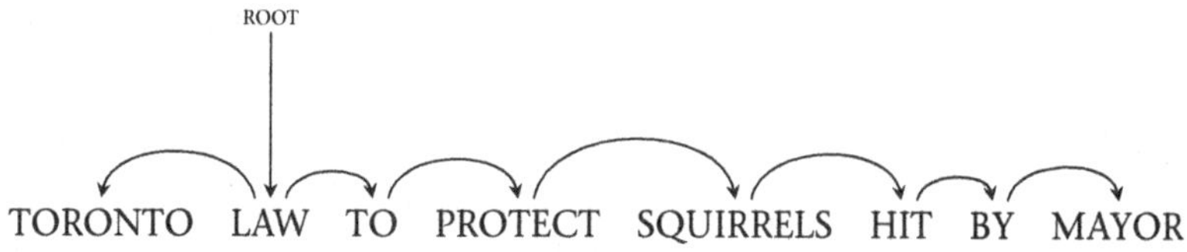

In this case, the structure for *Toronto law to protect squirrels* is the same in both: the meaning of this string is about a law in Toronto that is designed to protect squirrels.[11] The ambiguity involves how to combine *hit by mayor* to this structure. In the first structure, *hit* connects to *law*, indicating that it is the law that is to be hit by the mayor. This is presumably the intended structure: The meaning here is that the mayor is attacking the law, perhaps because the mayor thinks the law is frivolous. In the second structure, the verb *hit* connects to *squirrels*, indicating that the law is in place to protect squirrels who have been hit by the mayor.

The key takeaway here is that there must be a level of description that is *different* than words, which gives rise to two different meanings in each of these cases. The words are identical in each of these cases, and yet there are two distinct meanings for how the words get combined. This is the domain of syntax. We will say more about how people choose among possible interpretations later. Roughly speaking, people tend to choose the most probable interpretation, according to any factor that they might consider, such as the likelihood of the meaning of each in the world, or the frequency of co-occurrences of subsequences of words, or several other factors.

1.3 The Difficulty of Discovering the Grammar

Imagine that you had to figure out the lexicon and grammar of a language that you did not know. How would you go about trying to figure out the structure of that language? It would be enormously helpful to have a bilingual speaker of your language and the new language: With a bilingual, you can agree on rough translations of morphemes and words (although their usages would be potentially different between the languages, and even across speakers). So you might be able to transcribe a lexicon, bit by bit, as long as there was some cultural overlap, such that the two cultures want to talk about the same kinds of things.

But figuring out the grammar is much more difficult. It might help to have some lists of sentences that people say in different contexts, but a long list of such sentences wouldn't bring you much closer to the grammar. In high school physics, we might want to uncover the physical laws explaining how objects move and interact in various ways. We could collect a lot of data of what objects do under different conditions—which might be analogous to having lists of sentences in different situations—but what you really want is the principles underlying such motion.

Figuring out the combinatorial rules is painstakingly difficult work. After first tabulating some sentences, perhaps the fastest way to progress is to ask for intuitions from native speakers as to how each sentence is made up of the minimal meaning units: morphemes and words. Then we can make guesses about how the morphemes and words pattern together in the same categories (e.g., nouns, verbs, and adjectives, if these are the right kind of categories for the language). We can then ask native speakers for their judgments on our categorizations by substituting the new words in an old frame and seeing if the new sequence sounds like a possible sequence from the language. Testing how the combinations go together requires access to a lot of language. If the language is only spoken—with no writing system (which is still the case for the majority of the world's languages)—this is a difficult task.

Even if we restrict our attention to a single language—and even if the language is one that is well documented like English, and even if we restrict our attention to a narrow group of speakers that speak the same dialect and only focus on the most common words and structures—it turns out that the task of tabulating the grammar rules is highly complex. The complexity comes from at least two sources: (1) there are a large number of rules that combine words in some way, certainly thousands, but perhaps many more, depending on how we count the rules; and (2) language is highly productive such that words can be used in novel ways that extend beyond ways in which they have been used before. That is, not only is language productive in that we can use different words in similar locations as they have been used before, but we can also use words in ways that they may never have been used before, generalizing to a different part of speech in a novel way. Adele Goldberg provides many such examples including (9) (Goldberg, 2019):

(9) Can we vulture your table?

The word *vulture* is a noun, with a meaning of a large predatory bird that eats the carcasses left by other larger animals after the more dominant animals are done. The novel aspect of (9) is that this word is used as a transitive verb: this lexical entry of *vulture* is not in any dictionary. So what's going on here?

Goldberg (2019) argues convincingly that we can take important components of the meaning of a word and then use that word in an **abstract syntactic construction**. Here the abstract syntactic construction is the **transitive causative verb** construction, where an **agent** performs an **action** on a **patient**. For example, in *the weasels ate sandwiches*, the agent is *the weasels*, the action is the verb *ate*, and the patient is *sandwiches*. In (9), *vulture*—which is usually a noun—is inserted into the verb position of the transitive construction. The result is that the noun *vulture* is used transitively, with the core meaning of *vulture* being something like "taking left-over things" used in the transitive verb construction.

Overall, then, we have not only words (and their meanings) and the combinations of words with their previously learned parts of speech; we also have the ability to generalize words in constructions they have never been used in before, where a word is used in a novel syntactic way.

1.4 The Advent of Large Language Models as Potential Theories of Human Language

The best current models of human language are large language models (LLMs) such as OpenAI's ChatGPT, Google's Gemini, and Microsoft's CoPilot (Piantadosi, 2024).[12] These models are **deep neural networks** (LeCun et al., 2015), usually so-called **transformers** (Vaswani et al., 2017; Brown et al., 2020; Bommasani et al., 2021). These models are trained on massive texts—typically hundreds of billions of words—in order to predict the upcoming (or missing) word. These models are much better than their recent predecessors, so they can predict material far away from a part of a text (like a word). As we all are probably now familiar, these models can generate **novel perfectly formed English text**, using any construction that you can think of, generalizing in seemingly just the way that humans do (Ahmed et al., 2023). Piantadosi (2024) provides some nice examples of the generalizability of such models, asking one to provide a story of how an ant might sink a battleship. Or you can try your own example. Here, I have given ChatGPT the following prompt:

> Tell me a two-paragraph story about how a young Canadian girl used a hockey stick to eventually become prime minister

ChatGPT can generate any number of stories that satisfy the prompt. Here was the first:

> In the quaint town of Elkridge, Canada, a determined young girl named Sarah Mitchell discovered her love for hockey at an early age. Her days were spent on the frozen pond, practicing with unmatched dedication. One winter afternoon, as she skated across the ice with her favorite hockey stick, a spark ignited within her. Sarah realized the power of unity and community fostered on the rink and decided to channel that spirit into making a difference for her fellow Canadians.
>
> As Sarah grew older, her passion for hockey seamlessly transitioned into a commitment to public service. With her trusty hockey stick always by her side, she entered the world of politics. The symbol of the hockey stick became synonymous with her leadership style, emphasizing teamwork, resilience, and the shared goal of a stronger Canada. Through her unwavering dedication and the lessons learned on the hockey rink, Sarah Mitchell rose to become the Prime Minister, leading the nation with the same grit and determination she once displayed on the ice, proving that sometimes, the most unexpected tools can be wielded for the greater good.

This story is simple in its overall structure, but it has a lot of complex linguistic elements, and it all flows together coherently to solve the prompt question, performing just as well as most humans could do.

Many current researchers are evaluating how models like ChatGPT can generate all kinds of complex components of English grammar. While earlier models had limitations (Futrell et al., 2019; Marvin and Linzen, 2018; Hu et al., 2020; Linzen and Baroni, 2021), current models are much more successful (Warstadt et al., 2019; Gauthier et al., 2020; Warstadt and Bowman, 2022; Wilcox et al., 2023). Indeed, current models seem close to the same as humans in their ability to produce language.

Do we want to call such models "theories" of human language? According to Wiktionary,[13] a theory in the sciences is "a coherent statement or set of ideas that explains observed facts or phenomena and correctly predicts new facts or phenomena not previously observed, or which sets out the laws and principles of something known or observed; a hypothesis confirmed by observation, experiment etc." Do large language models fit this description? I would argue yes: The underlying models are coherent sets of ideas that explain phenomena and correctly predict new phenomena not previously observed. Indeed, it looks like all of a natural language syntax falls out of the particular framework. Are LLMs *good* theories? I think a good theory is one with a good ratio of principles to data that are explained: few parameters to explain many phenomena. There are a lot of parameters in any current LLM—certainly millions and often many more—so it is reasonable to say that the theories aren't particularly good. I think we can do much better. Furthermore, with a simple theory—which doesn't have many parameters—researchers can often work out predictions intuitively, or through simple implementations. Current LLMs are not such theories. Dependency grammars offer such simple theories. The dependency grammar level of description may give researchers insights into predictions that they can't see at a more fine grained LLM level.

1.4.1 LLMs: Construction Grammars Built on Dependency Structures

The kinds of theories of language that LLMs are closest to are so-called *construction-based* theories, which emphasize the memorization of lots of little parts of language, in the form of constructions (Fillmore, 1988; Goldberg, 1995, 2006; Croft, 2010; Steels, 2011, 2012; Goldberg, 2019); for the relation between construction grammars and LLMs, see Madabushi et al. (2020); Tseng et al. (2022); Weissweiler et al. (2023); Mahowald et al. (2024); Potts (2023). Words and morphemes are constructions in the lexicon; additional constructions can be formed from other constructions, usually in a dependency relation with one another. The primary tenet of construction grammar is that it is *usage-based* (Croft and Cruse, 2004): It describes the syntactic and lexical combinations that people actually use. This kind of theory builds on the observation that humans keep track of tens of thousands of words, and we are sensitive to their corresponding exposure frequencies. The hypothesis is that the syntax/grammar is a simple extension of the lexicon: We store not only all the words but the frequent combinations as well (Ellis and Morrison, 1998; Brysbaert et al., 2000; Zevin and Seidenberg, 2002; Juhasz, 2005; Arnon and Snider, 2010; Arnon et al., 2017; Shain et al., 2020, 2022).

An interesting open question is what kinds of representations it is that LLMs learn. An analysis by Hewitt and Manning (2019); Manning et al. (2020) suggests that they at least learn **dependency structures**, at some level (see also Lakretz et al., 2019; Mahowald et al., 2024). Hewitt and Manning (2019) and Manning et al. (2020) analyzed Bidirectional Encoder Representations from Transformers (Devlin et al., 2018) using some fancy math that they called a "structural probe," which extracted simple directed graphs (trees) out of multidimensional vector spaces. They found that the tree-structures that best fit BERT's vector for a sentence were closely related to the dependency trees that researchers had independently hand-coded. For example, the representation for the sentence from the *Wall Street Journal* corpus in (10) was nearly identical to the representation that was provided by annotators. The annotator version is provided below:

(10) The complex financing plan in the S-and-L bailout law includes raising $30 billion from debt issued by the newly created RTC

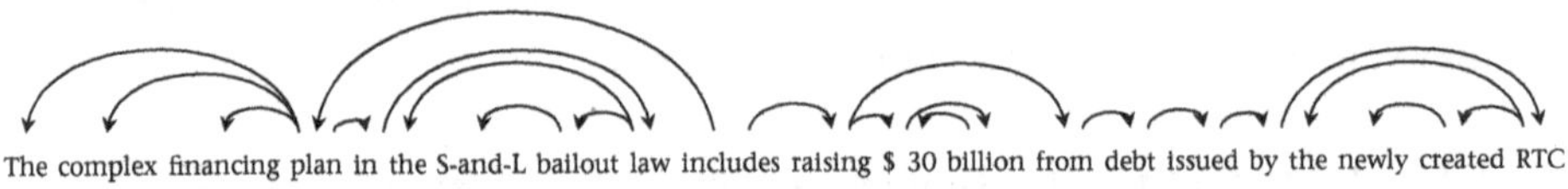

While this representation generally contains local dependencies—between adjacent words—some dependencies are nonlocal, such as the connection between *plan* and *includes*, and between *raising* and *from*. Thus it is nontrivial to compute this structure.[14] Overall the results due to Hewitt and Manning (2019) and Manning et al. (2020) show that LLMs represent dependency structure in their inner workings (cf. Kulmizev and Nivre 2022). Furthermore, work by Papadimitriou and Jurafsky (2023) suggests that adding a prior for dependency structures to an LLM improves the model's ability to learn a new human language substantially.

There are always many different levels of theories or explanations of any phenomena. Marr (1982) famously proposed several levels of explanation for cognitive and perceptual theories. We can think of LLMs as an algorithmic level of explanation for human language. In this book, I seek an abstract level of representational explanation—something in perhaps the computational level—which might help us as researchers of language understand in simple terms what LLMs or the human mind are using in their learning and processing of human language. This is proposed to be dependency structure. The point of the current book is to try to specify the basic representations underlying LLMs and construction grammar: dependencies between words.

1.5 Who Is This Book For? An Outline of the Book

This book is aimed at any interested intelligent person, typically one with little background in syntax research. This is intended as a primer for smart people, possibly from other fields, who may be interested in human language and don't know much about its structure. You may have heard that sentences are tree-structured: What does that even mean? Here, I break it down and explain it from first principles, in what I hope is an accessible way.

But I am not providing a complete theory of any component of any language, not even English. This book is meant simply as an accessible start in order to get people familiar with the kinds of structures in natural languages. The interested reader can adapt the details of the approach I present here in head-driven phrase structure grammar (Pollard and Sag, 1994; Sag et al., 1999), word grammar (Hudson, 1990, 2008, 2015), categorial grammar (Ajdukiewicz, 1935; Steedman, 1996, 2001) or tree-adjoining grammar (Joshi and Rambow, 2003; Abeillé and Rambow, 2000). A detailed summary of each of these theories (and several others) is provided by Müller (2023).

The book takes a novel perspective on syntax compared to any previous syntax primer. In particular, aspects of grammar are motivated in terms of **cognitive processing**: Longer distance connections between words result in structures that are harder to produce and comprehend. The idea is that perhaps word orders that minimize dependency lengths will be more common in the world's languages, a prediction that seems to be true (see section 5.1). Although the motivation for the approach is cross-linguistic, an obvious limitation of the presentation is its Anglocentricity. That is, most of the examples come from English (cf. Blasi et al., 2022; Henrich et al., 2010). In spite of this limitation, I focus on English for presentational simplicity: This is the only language I speak well and can write in.[15]

Before I present the dependency grammar approach in detail, there are some important preliminaries that we need to cover, in chapter 2. First, section 2.1 outlines the difference between what makes sentences acceptable vs. what makes them grammatical. And second, section 2.2 summarizes some of the factors that make language materials easy or complex to process, such as lexical frequency, real-world plausibility of the meaning, contextual fit, syntactic frequency, syntactic complexity leading to memory overload, and temporary or global ambiguity.

Chapter 3 introduces the dependency grammar framework in detail and shows how it can be used to represent the combinatorial structure of some common components of English. Chapter 4 provides some of the best evidence for the value of the dependency grammar framework in explaining aspects of human language. First, behavioral evidence of language processing complexity supports the existence of a cost associated with making long distance connections. Second, it is shown that languages have shorter distance connections than any plausible baseline (Futrell et al., 2015b, 2020b). And finally, dependency length minimization explains word order universals such as the head-direction generalization (Greenberg, 1963; Vennemann, 1974; Hawkins, 1983; Dryer, 2011a). Overall, dependency grammar, under the assumption that longer connections are more costly, explains a wide range of language phenomena. In chapter 6, I discuss one odd exception to the claim that most text in natural language has local dependencies: legal language, sometimes called **Legalese**. It turns out that Legalese has unusually long dependencies.

In chapter 7, I discuss alternative approaches to syntax, including other dependency grammar approaches (Nivre, 2005), construction grammar (Goldberg, 1995, 2006), phrase structure grammar, so-called "simpler syntax" (Culicover and Jackendoff, 2005), categorial grammar (Steedman, 1996, 2001), and X-bar syntax (Jackendoff, 1977). In chapter 8, I discuss perhaps the most well-known kinds of syntactic theories, so-called generative syntactic theories of Chomsky and colleagues. According to these theories, grammar has two critical components: a phrase structure base and "movement," whereby heads and phrases can move elsewhere, up to constraints. Chomsky not only provided such a framework for theories of grammar, but he furthermore suggested that the grammar was unlearnable. Chomsky concluded that aspects of the grammar must be innate: the **universal grammar** hypothesis. I discuss several limitations of such approaches in this chapter.

The final two chapters link syntax to the rest of human language and cognition. Chapter 9 addresses the question of the relationship between language and thought. Brain evidence suggests that much of thought takes place without language: The function of the language system in the brain is communication. Finally, chapter 10 discusses how syntax is embedded within the communication system. This chapter also presents evidence for how communication may shape aspects of grammar.

2 Preliminaries: Components of Language Structure

The goal of a grammarian is to discover the morphemes and words within a language, and to discover how they combine in the grammar. There are many methods that we can use to learn how language is structured and processed in the human mind and brain. Perhaps the simplest method is to transcribe what people say and ask them what each component means. This is what "field" linguists typically do when doing fieldwork on a language. More generally, we might record and transcribe a corpus or text of what people say in natural situations: This is called **corpus analysis** or **text analysis.**

It is difficult to infer the structure of the lexicon and syntax through corpus analysis alone, because language is skewed toward very common words and phrases, and people don't produce most of what is possible. Perhaps the most common method that linguists use is therefore the **acceptability judgment** task, where a linguist provides materials to a speaker and asks them how natural the sentence sounds. I discuss this method in section 2.1.

A critical issue in trying to figure out the structure of language is that there are many factors that reflect how natural a particular sentence sounds in a particular context: The structure of the sentence is only one such factor. No sentence wears its representation on its sleeve: We have to infer the reason why a particular sentence sounds good or bad from a comparison with many other control materials in order to conclude what combination of factors might be relevant for the sentence at hand. The factors include the words and their frequencies, the syntactic rules and their frequencies, world knowledge, the local context, prosody, memory limitations, temporary ambiguity, and the closeness to other nearby possible sentences. I discuss many of these factors in section 2.2.

In addition, we need to think about how all these factors might be put together. Following Chomsky (1965), I assume that the rules for syntax are independent of the other factors. Then, in trying to understand the grammar of a language, we are trying to uncover the syntactic rules that generate all and only the possible structures in the language. We call such a framework **generative.**[1]

In section 2.3, I outline some other methods that researchers use in order to infer aspects of the structure of language. And in the final section of this chapter, I discuss whether the methods that we use as language scientists need to be quantitative, or whether we can rely on our individual intuitions alone. I conclude that current research should always be built on some quantitative evidence, in order to avoid confirmation bias of our own favorite hypotheses.

2.1 The Acceptability Judgment Task

What makes a sentence sound good or bad, or somewhere in between? In an **acceptability judgment task**, native speakers of a language are asked to rate the acceptability (= goodness) of a sentence or language fragment, often with no context. That is, a participant simply uses their own **intuitive judgment** about how good or bad a sentence is.[2]

If there is no context, the participant is asked to imagine a natural context for such a sentence. In a quantitative version of such a task, participants might be asked to rate the sentences on a scale from 1 to 5 or from 1 to 7 (a "Likert" scale, pronounced "Lick-ert"), or on a binary scale (good vs. bad), or even on an unbounded scale.[3] Sometimes this task can be conducted under time pressure: This is called speeded acceptability / grammaticality. In any case, there is a continuity of acceptability, from unacceptable (very bad) to highly acceptable (very good). For example, English speakers will generally agree that the following sequences are acceptable English sentences, and will rate them highly:

(4) Ollie sleeps.
(5a) A squirrel awakens.
(5b) Ollie chased a squirrel.

We can contrast the examples above to some scrambled versions, which are not generated by the rules of English grammar:

(11) a. ∗ sleeps Ollie.
b. ∗ awakens squirrel a.
c. ∗ a chased squirrel Ollie.

Syntacticians notate sentences that violate the rules of the language by prefixing them with a "∗" as in (11), and they call such sentences **ungrammatical**. The proposal is that strings that are generated by the rules of the grammar are **grammatical**, and those that are not generated by the grammar are **ungrammatical**. The nature of the grammar is the focus of this book, starting in the next chapter.

We should keep in mind that acceptability is not a binary construct, even if we force people to give binary judgments (e.g., good vs. bad). While there may be a large acceptability difference between some pairs of materials (like some of those above), this does not mean that there are no materials of intermediate acceptability. Acceptability is continuous.

2.1.1 Descriptive vs. Prescriptive Language

A community of speakers is not fully uniform: There will be differences in what words people know and the rules that they use to combine the words. In our goal to understand the syntax rules of a language community, we must keep this in mind. Furthermore, there is nothing inherently good or bad about any dialect from a scientific viewpoint: None are more "correct" than any other. This is the **descriptive** view of language, as opposed to the **prescriptive** view, which postulates that some versions of a language are better than others. Such a view is not a scientific view: It is advocating a view whereby some rules and words are preferable to others. These biases are often stated as if there were a scientific basis for them, such as the "correct" dialect is better for communication, but there is actually no basis for such a claim. It has never been shown that any naturally occurring dialect of English (for example) is better or worse for communication than any other. There has never been any such evaluation. All naturally occurring dialects of any language have strong communicative value: That's how they came to be.

2.1.2 Predictability or Surprisal as Measures of Word-by-Word Linguistic Acceptability

Because language is produced and processed over time, we get it bit by bit. This allows a measure of the goodness of an incoming word according to how expected it was, given the preceding context: its **expectedness** or **surprisal**. Surprisal and expectedness are inverses: When an incoming word is highly expected, its surprisal is close to zero. We usually measure surprisal in **bits of information**—the negative log probability of the incoming word w_i, given the context $w_0 \ldots w_{i-1}$:

(12) $surprisal(w_i) \stackrel{\text{def}}{=} -\log_2 p(w_i \mid w_0 \ldots w_{i-1})$.

When the surprisal of an incoming word is low (close to zero), the incoming word is highly expected, as in (13a), where most people (Canadians at least), will expect the word *goal*, following the context *Wayne Gretzky scored a*, because Wayne Gretzky was a great hockey player and great hockey players score goals.

(13) a. Wayne Gretzky scored a ... goal.
b. Wayne Gretzky scored a ... chicken.

In contrast, the word *chicken* is highly surprising following this context, because people don't typically score chickens. The word chicken would therefore have a high surprisal in this context, consisting of many bits of information.

People will typically read surprising words more slowly than unsurprising ones (Hale, 2001; Levy, 2008a). In fact, there is linear relationship between the reading time and the surprisal of a word, overall (Smith and Levy, 2013; Shain et al., 2024).

Because large language models are trained on so much text, they provide good estimates of surprisal of words in context. Hence, a surprisal measure usually includes all factors that might affect the acceptability of a sentence, from word frequency to the plausibility of the meaning, to the structural frequency of the material in question.

2.1.3 Acceptability vs. Grammaticality

How do we know that a particular sentence violates the rules of the grammar? Whether a sentence is grammatical vs. ungrammatical is just one part of what makes a sentence acceptable vs. unacceptable. Assessing whether a sentence is grammatical—generated by the syntactic rules of the language—is a theoretical decision made by a language researcher. A language researcher decides that a particular sentence is ungrammatical after they rule out all other potential factors that might make a sentence unacceptable.

It is easy to assess whether a sentence is acceptable or not: This is just how "good" or "natural" the sentence sounds to a group of fluent speakers of a language. The assessment that the badness is likely due to the grammar is a more complex inference. It is easy to construct materials that follow the rules of the grammar but don't make much sense, so that people will rate the materials as unacceptable, as in (14b):

(14) a. The girl kicked the ball.
b. The ball kicked the girl.

A sentence like (14a) gets the highest possible acceptability rating, because it follows the rules of English grammar and says something very simple and likely in the world. (14b) still follows the rules of English grammar but says something very strange: that the ball is the agent of a kicking event, where the girl is the thing being kicked. Because this is such a strange event, people will typically rate (14b) as unacceptable, in spite of the fact that its word order follows English grammar.

Furthermore, we can create materials that are technically ungrammatical—perhaps missing a single word that is necessary according to the grammar but perhaps unneeded for the intended meaning—but close enough to grammatical that people will typically rate them as very acceptable, as in (15a) and (15b):

(15) a. * The girl kicked ball.
b. * The the girl kicked the ball.

Sentence (15a) is missing a determiner (like *a* or *the*), but it's pretty clear what was intended, so people rate such a sentence highly, in spite of the fact that it actually violates the grammar of English: Singular count nouns should have a determiner. Similarly, (15b) has an extra occurrence of the word *the*, which is an obvious error, and people can correct it very easily, so they rate this sentence highly too. This again is technically an error: English nouns cannot be preceded by two occurrences of *the*. Both of these will be rated as better than (14b), which is grammatical but describes a world situation that is very unlikely. So grammaticality and acceptability are distinct.

Note that we can think of grammaticality as a continuous measure, with a cutoff at zero frequency. That is, some structures are more grammatical than others, when the rules that they use are the more common ones. But when a sentence uses an ordering of words that is never part of typical usage, then that ordering is simply ungrammatical. For example, the order of determiners and nouns is rigid in English: The determiner precedes the noun. So *the dog* is grammatical whereas *dog the* is ungrammatical.

2.1.4 The Independence of Syntax: "Competence" vs. "Performance"

Chomsky (1965) proposed a division between the notion of linguistic **competence** and linguistic **performance**:

> We thus make a fundamental distinction between competence (the speaker-hearer's knowledge of his language) and performance (the actual use of language in concrete situations) (Chomsky, 1965, p. 4).

The motivation for this proposal is that there are many factors that can cause a sentence to be low in acceptability, including world knowledge, context, and the memory load associated with different structures, all of which will be discussed later in this chapter. Chomsky's famous "colorless green ideas" sentence (16b) is grammatical under this proposal, but not acceptable (Chomsky, 1957) cf. (Carnap, 1937; Tesnière, 1959; Ogden and Richards, 1927). And a doubly nested relative clause structure like (17b) is also grammatical, but not acceptable.

(16) a. Silly incoherent ideas fade quickly.
b. # Colorless green ideas sleep furiously. (Chomsky, 1957)

(17) a. The boy who the dog bit was upset.
b. # The boy who the dog which the cat chased bit was upset.

Chomsky's (1957) observation is that (16b) follows the grammatical rules of English: This is a sentence consisting of two adjectives modifying a noun, then a verb, and an adverb. This follows the rules of English in a similar way as (16a), which follows the rules of English and makes sense. (16b) follows the grammar rules of English but doesn't make sense. I have correspondingly marked this sentence with a hash-mark (#), which means unacceptable but still following the grammatical rules.

Similarly, (17b) follows the grammar rules of English, but is hard to understand and is not typically acceptable. This sentence uses the same grammar components as (17a), but with a second relative clause—*which the cat chased*—embedded inside another *who the dog bit*. Both of these relative clauses are grammatical on their own. It is just the combination that leads to unacceptability.[4]

Most researchers would agree with the observations thus far. Chomsky (1965) took it a step further and hypothesized that these observations suggest that **there is a system in our minds that computes grammar independent of other factors**: This is what he means by linguistic competence.

This was just an educated guess of Chomsky's back in 1965 based on behavioral evidence. In more recent work, researchers have discovered that the language network in the brain—which is exquisitely sensitive to language material only, and nothing else (see section 9.1)—is just as active for grammatical *implausible* materials like (16b) as for grammatical *plausible* materials like (16a), using frequent rules in the language, which suggests that the costs of processing these inputs are the same for this system (Kauf et al., 2024). Hence, I assume that syntax is independent of meaning to some degree for fluent speakers of a language.

I should clarify that my view here is only a current working hypothesis, which is somewhat controversial. By assuming that there is a syntactic set of rules that are somewhat independent of their typical usage, I am going against the standard view in construction grammars (Goldberg, 2006; Diessel, 2017), where researchers typically assume that usage (performance) effectively *defines* the language. Knowledge of language independent of usage is not a notion in such frameworks. Such frameworks also typically don't try to formalize the grammatical rules, as I am trying to do here. In order to formalize the rules, I need to make some assumptions. The independence of syntax seems to be the best evidence-driven assumption to make at this point. Future research will determine if this is correct or not.

2.2 Factors Other Than Syntax That Affect the Acceptability of Sentences

There are several kinds of factors that can make a sentence less acceptable, leading to unacceptability:

- low lexical frequency
- implausibility: failure to align with our world knowledge
- contextual inappropriateness
- inappropriate prosody/pronunciation
- low syntactic frequency
- syntactic complexity leading to memory overload
- some examples of temporary or global ambiguity

Many of these factors have to do with exposure: lexical frequency, world knowledge frequency, and syntactic frequency (Goldberg, 1995; Bybee, 2006, 2010). Not only does the quantity of exposure to linguistic elements matter in predicting behavioral measures, but the age at which the user was first exposed to such materials also matters greatly (Brysbaert and Ghyselinck, 2006; Kuperman et al., 2012). The age of acquisition effect is generally understudied relative to exposure frequency, in part because getting norms for age of acquisition is much harder than getting frequency data.

In addition, as alluded to above, an important factor involved in sentence acceptability is how close the target sentence is to a sentence that might have been intended, where closeness is determined by the kinds of errors that people might make in typical language production. Thus, acceptability is sensitive to what someone might intend to say in a given situation. I say more about communication-based proposals for language in chapter 10.

2.2.1 Lexical Frequency

Sentences with similar meanings but different word frequencies are shown in (18):

(18) a. The horse bothered the donkey.
b. The zebu aggressed the zonkey.

Example (18a) describes a plausible event and uses frequent English words to do so. Example (18b) is comparable in meaning to example (18a) but uses three low-frequency words (*zebu*, *zonkey*, and *aggress*). People will rate this sentence correspondingly lower than example (18a). They will rate it much lower if they don't know one of the words.

Lexical frequency is a continuous measure of complexity for a word or morpheme: People have less difficulty with words that they are more exposed to and more difficulty with rare words (Brysbaert et al., 2011, 2018).[5] Any task involving words is likely to be affected by word frequency. For example, Howes and Solomon (1951) show that the visual duration threshold necessary for correct report of those words when they are presented via a tachistoscope (an old-fashioned machine that presents visual materials for an exact small amount of time milliseconds) depends on the word frequency: People can do it more reliably for higher-frequency words. Similarly, the speed at which we can decide whether a string of letters is a word is strongly affected by word frequency (see Morton (1969) for one of the first models of word frequency effects; Monsell (1991) for a review of how various word recognition tasks are susceptible to word frequency; Wei et al. (2013) for how word frequency affects saccade length in reading Chinese characters; and Shain (2019) showing word frequency effects in reading times for large naturalistic corpora).

It is often hard to distinguish word frequency effects from age-of-acquisition effects: People are especially fast at processing the words they learned earliest, and these words tend to be the most frequent. We can disentangle the two with words that are learned early but are relatively infrequent (such as fairytale words like *dragon*). Both lexical frequency and age of acquisition contribute to linguistic complexity. In both cases, these are examples of exposure-based factors in complexity: People are sensitive to the amount of exposure or the time of earliest exposure, in a continuous way (Ellis and Morrison, 1998; Brysbaert et al., 2000; Zevin and Seidenberg, 2002; Juhasz, 2005; Braginsky et al., 2016; Frank et al., 2017; Braginsky et al., 2019; Frank et al., 2021).

A generalization of word frequency is word sequence frequency or **n-gram** frequency. (An n-gram is a sequence of n symbols of some kind in a row. Here, we are discussing words, so n words in a row.) Arnon and Snider (2010) show that people read sequences of four words (a four-gram) faster when the sequence was more frequent in the input, even when controlling for the frequency of the words in the sequences. For example, people read the sequence *don't have to worry* faster than the sequence *don't have to wait*, despite the fact that the two phrases did not differ in the frequency of the final word (*worry* vs. *wait*), bigram (any sequence of two words), or trigram (any sequence of three words). This effect was measurably different across three ranges of frequency: high, medium, and low. Arnon et al. (2017) show a similar effect for age-of-acquisition effects. Similarly, Shain et al. (2020, 2022) show that n-gram frequency is a strong predictor of blood-oxygen-level-dependent (BOLD) response in the language areas of the brain (see section 9.1 for information on how the brain has a specialized network for language processing).

2.2.2 World Knowledge

Perhaps the most important factor affecting sentence acceptability is the intended meaning of the sentence. If the event being described is an unlikely event, people will process the sentence more slowly (e.g., Trueswell et al., 1994a), and try to correct it to something more plausible (e.g., Ferreira, 2003; Gibson et al., 2013a). The sentences in examples (19b) and (19d) describe implausible events and would be rated low on an acceptability scale accordingly:

(19) a. The dog bit the boy.
b. The boy bit the dog.
c. The girl ate the pizza.
d. The pizza ate the girl.
e. The peanut was in love. (Nieuwland and Van Berkum, 2006)
f. The banana was an hour long. (Schmidt, 2009)
g. Colorless green ideas sleep furiously. (Chomsky, 1957)

There is a continuum of extremely plausible events—the kinds of events we encounter all the time—to less plausible ones (like a boy biting a dog), to impossible ones (like pizza eating a girl, or a peanut being in love), and to events that semantically are ill-formed and, hence, hard to even imagine, such as Schmidt's case of a banana being an "hour long" (whatever that might mean), to Chomsky's famous example in (19g), which is difficult to imagine.

2.2.3 Contextual Appropriateness

The implausible events in (19) are implausible in any typical context in our world, and hence people will rate them as low acceptability. But an unusual context can make an implausible sentence plausible in that context. For example, if the context was that a dog bit a boy, it's now more plausible that the boy might bite the dog:

(20) a. Context: The dog bit the boy, and then sat on the boy.
b. Target sentence: The boy bit the dog.

Even highly implausible sentences can become much more acceptable in the right context.

(21) a. Context: Some radioactive chemicals were added to the pizza and it came alive, and rolled on its side, approaching the girl.
b. Target sentence: The pizza ate the girl.

A famous example of how context can support unusual events was provided by Nieuwland and Van Berkum (2006), who presented participants with contexts like (22a) for the target sentences in (22b) or (22c):

(22) a. A woman saw a dancing peanut who had a big smile on his face. The peanut was singing about a girl he had just met. And judging from the song, the peanut was totally crazy about her. The woman thought it was really cute to see the peanut singing and dancing like that.
b. The peanut was in love.
c. The peanut was salted.

In the normal world, peanuts can be salted but never in love. In the context that Nieuwland and Van Berkum (2006) provided, people found (22b) not very surprising (as measured by the N400 event-related EEG measure that they used[6]), and they found (22c) very surprising. That is, in the context that Nieuwland and van Berkum set up, it was expected that the peanut might be in love, but not salted, in contrast to the typical world. So an unusual discourse context, unlike something that we find in the real world, can make even the most implausible sentence plausible, and vice versa.

2.2.4 Discourse Effects in Syntactic Constructions

It has been argued that certain syntactic constructions are only appropriate in certain contexts, because of their meaning (Erteschik-Shir, 1973; Kuno, 1987; Goldberg, 2006). For example, a wh-question seeks to get information from the conversation partner:

(23) What would you like to eat?

Erteschik-Shir (1973); Goldberg (2006) suggest that it may be contextually inappropriate to ask a wh-question about an element that is part of background knowledge—for example, part of a relative clause or a presupposed element (Cuneo and Goldberg, 2023). So while it is reasonable to ask someone what they want to eat, as in (23), and it is reasonable to ask about someone's uncertain knowledge or desires, as in (24a), it is is strange to ask about something that is supposed to be known, as in (24b):

(24) a. What does Mary believe that you would you like to eat?
b. ?? What do we believe the fact that you would you like to eat?

The thing that is being asked about in (24b) is part of the phrase *the fact that . . .*, which is stated to be certain (a fact). This is a conflict in meaning: Why would you question something that you also take as a fact, or that you take as part of our background knowledge? See chapter 8.4, Chaves and Putnam (2020), and Liu et al. (2022b) for more on constraints on long-distance dependencies.

2.2.5 Prosody

In spoken language, the same sentence can be pronounced in an unbounded number of ways, just by changing the loudness, duration, and pitch of any of the words in the sentence. These are features of the **prosody** of the language. There are typical **pitch contours** associated with different kinds of meanings for sentences within a language (Bolinger, 1986 cf. Halliday, 2015; Crystal, 1969), and the meanings associated with the contours can vary across languages (Hirst and Di Cristo, 1998). A declarative English sentence is typically produced with a falling pitch contour, whereas a yes-no interrogative English sentence (e.g., "Can I go now?") is typically produced with a rising pitch contour. Furthermore, the discourse context affects which elements are produced most acoustically prominently (i.e., emphasized): Acoustically prominent elements are typically new to the discourse, whereas the words indicating material that has already been introduced are typically less prominent (Fry, 1955; Beckman, 2012; Ladd, 2008).

If a sentence is pronounced with an inappropriate prosodic contour—for example, with large shifts in intensity (loudness) and pitch—then people will find it odd, and rate it as low in acceptability. Throughout the rest of the manuscript, I will put prosodic issues to the side (cf. work by, e.g., Wagner and Watson, 2010; Breen et al., 2010; Jun, 2005, 2014; Cole, 2015 among others).

2.2.6 Syntax Frequency

Current evidence suggests that the grammar rules are accessed probabilistically depending on their frequency of use in the language. For example, Shain et al. (2020) show that brain activation in response to listening to stories is strongly affected by the frequency of the grammatical rules that are involved in the particular materials. That is, when people encounter a sentence that requires the use of a low-frequency syntactic rule, then there is more brain activation in the language network.

An example of a frequent English grammar rule is one that links an initial noun (a "subject") to its following verb, as in (25a).

(25) a. Mary sleeps.
b. That Mary is sleeping is surprising.
c. My shirt needs washed.

This rule is frequent in English because most sentences contain a subject noun and a verb that the subject depends on. An example of a rare rule in English is one that links a sentence-initial clause to a verb, as in (25b). This is much rarer in English. Consequently, people have more difficulty with it compared to a subject-verb dependency between a noun and a verb as in (25a).

Finally, the dependency between the verb *needs* and the immediately following verb *washed* is ungrammatical for most English varieties, but is perfectly fine in Southwestern Pennsylvania, eastern Ohio, and Scotland (according to https://languagelog.ldc.upenn.edu/nll/?p=3422). Its meaning is the same as if *to be* had been deleted between *needs* and *washed*. I first encountered this construction when I moved to Pittsburgh in 1986. It sounded completely ungrammatical to me then, and so I would likely have processed it with much difficulty initially. As I gained more exposure (and even came to use it), its complexity would decrease. Thus we see examples here of the continuity of grammatical rule exposure frequency (and humans' sensitivity to such probabilities) as well as people's ability to learn even aspects of grammar as an adult (Hartshorne et al., 2018).

2.2.7 Syntactic Complexity Leading to Memory Overload

An interesting case arises when structures are repeatedly embedded within the center of other structures so that there are long-distance dependencies. Consider the case of a relative clause, which is a clause that modifies a noun, as in the examples in (26) and their dependency structures:

(26) a. The boy who the dog bit was upset.
b. The book which the author wrote was well-written.

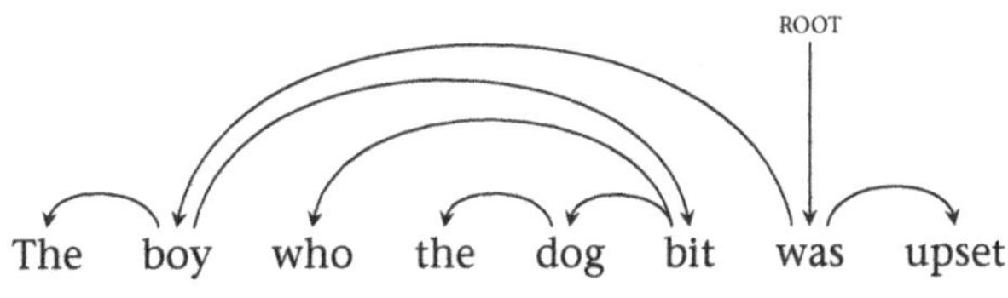

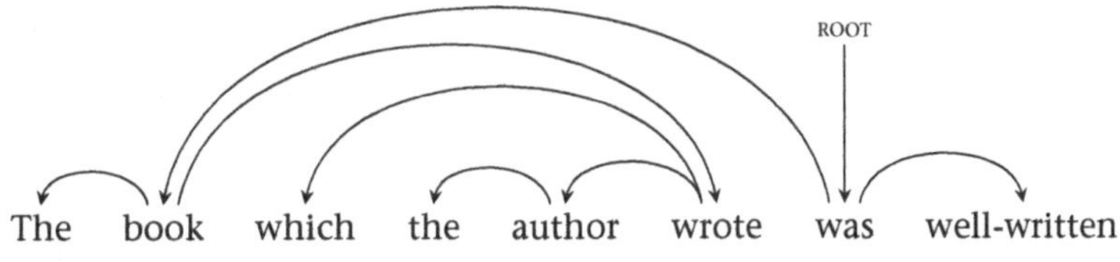

In (26a), the relative clause *who the dog bit* modifies the noun *boy* in (26), giving rise to a clause that is embedded within the noun-verb dependency *boy-was*. Similarly, the relative clause *which the author wrote* modifies the noun *book* in (26b). But now consider what happens when we modify the embedded subject noun *dog* in (26) by another relative clause, as in (27), whose dependency structure is given below:

(27) # The boy who the dog which the cat chased bit was upset.

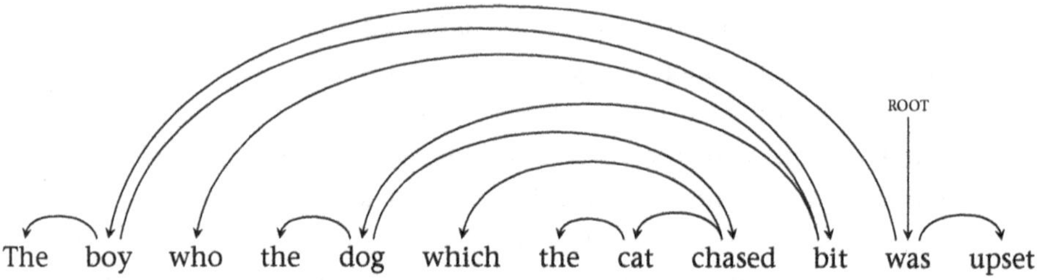

This sentence is difficult to understand. Sometimes researchers prefix this kind of complex sentence with a hash mark (#), as above, to indicate that it is confusing (perhaps even ill-formed for some speakers). I have also included the emoji indicating confusion, but I will stick with the conventional hash mark going forward.

Is it the *meaning* that makes this sentence confusing? Probably not, because we can form sentences with similar relationships between nouns and verbs, but without the nested structure (and so without the long dependencies), as in (28):

(28) The cat chased the dog which bit the boy who was upset.

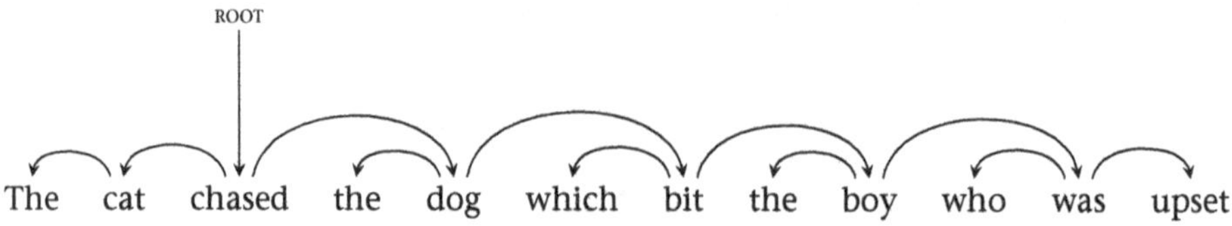

This structure has only local dependencies, and it is perfectly understandable (and produceable, in the right contexts).

It turns out that all structures that have "nested" structures like (27), consisting of one dependency inside another, are difficult to produce and understand, *in any language*, which is kind of astounding when you think about it.

English has subject-verb-object (SVO) word order: In simple sentences like *The girl kicked the ball*, the subject noun phrase is first, followed by the verb, with the object noun phrase last. This is a common word order around the world's languages (see chapter 10). Another common word order across the world's languages is subject-object-verb (SOV), or head-final. Japanese is an example of an SOV language. Some corresponding Japanese examples and their dependency structures are given below. In example (29), all the dependencies are local, and so the sentence is easily produced or understood.

(29) ani-ga imooto-o ijimeta to bebiisitaa-ga itta
older-brother-nom younger-sister-acc bullied that babysitter-nom said
"The babysitter said that my older brother bullied my younger sister"

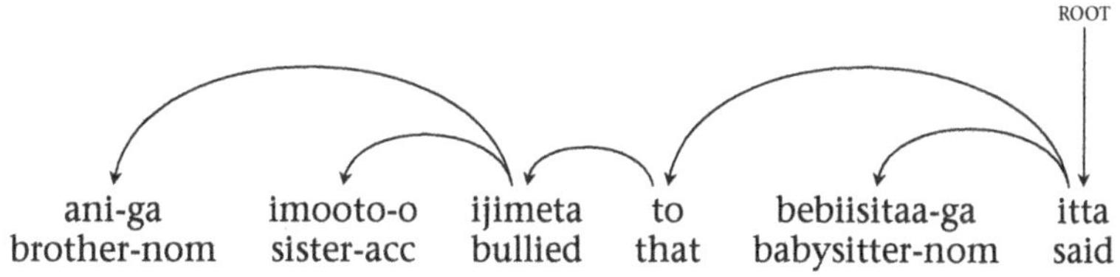

(30) is another way to phrase the meaning in (29): The embedded clause *brother bullied sister* comes between the main clause subject noun *babysitter* and the main verb for the sentence, *said*. This sentence is still processable because the dependencies aren't too long.

(30) Bebiisitaa-ga ani-ga imooto-o ijimeta to itta
babysitter-nom older.brother-nom younger.sister-acc bullied that said
"The babysitter said that my older brother bullied my younger sister"

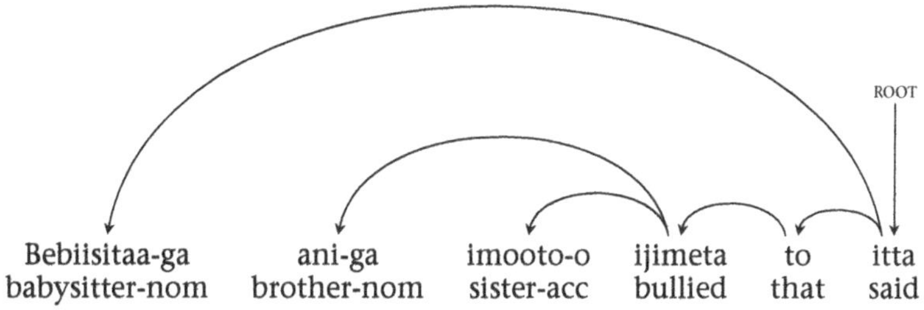

In example (31), we add another clause, at the end of the sentence *aunt thinks*. The dependency distances are no worse, and so this sentence is processable too:

(31) Bebiisitaa-ga ani-ga imooto-o ijimeta to itta to obasan-ga omotteiru
babysitter-nom older-brother-nom younger-sister-acc bullied that said that aunt thinks
"My aunt thinks that the babysitter said that my older brother bullied my younger sister"

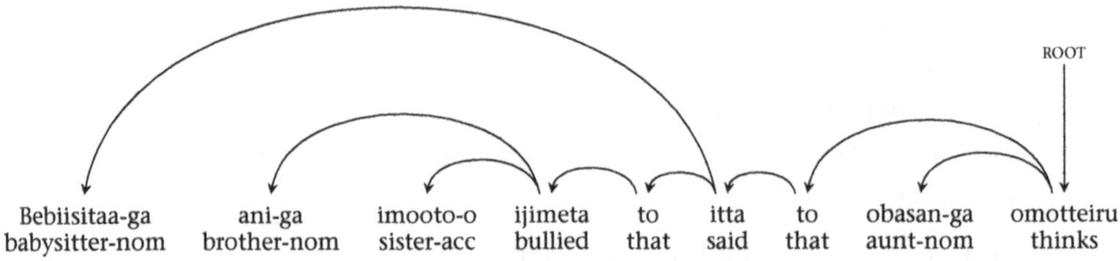

But when we put the clause *babysitter said brother bullied sister* between *aunt* and *thinks* in example (32), the dependency distances are now very long, and the sentence is hard to process:

(32) # Obasan-ga Bebiisitaa-ga ani-ga imooto-o ijimeta to itta to omotteiru aunt-nom babysitter-nom older-brother-nom younger-sister-acc bullied that said that thinks
"My aunt thinks that the babysitter said that my older brother bullied my younger sister"

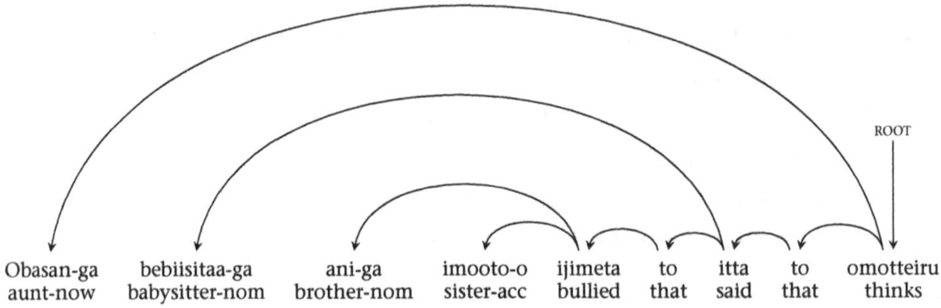

The generalization across languages is that materials like English (33) and Japanese (32) have long dependencies between some of their words. Gibson (1998, 2000) has argued that the complexity associated with processing such structures has to do with understanding (and producing) such long-distance dependencies between words, especially at the end-points where one word has to be integrated way back in the structure (cf. Lewis and Vasishth [2005a] for similar proposals). We elaborate the evidence for this kind of a proposal in chapter 4. Other proposals for the source of the complexity of such examples include the online storage of partial dependencies—for example, Yngve (1960); Chomsky and Miller (1963); Kimball (1973); Gibson (1991, 1998, 2000)—in the nested examples, there are always word positions with many incomplete dependencies. For example, at the point of processing the word *cat* in (27) (*The boy who the dog which the cat chased bit was upset*), there are five incomplete dependencies:

one connecting *cat* to its head verb to follow *chased*; one connecting *which* to *chased*; one connecting *dog* to *bit*; one connecting *who* to *bit*; and finally, one connecting *boy* to *was*. In contrast, there are few dependencies left open in (28) (*The cat chased the dog which bit the boy who was upset*), as we can see in the dependency structure for that sentence.

2.2.8 Are Multiply Nested Structures Grammatical or Ungrammatical?

As alluded to in section 2.1.4, there are disagreements among researchers about whether sentences like (33) are *ungrammatical* or *grammatical but unacceptable* (due to memory limitations of the system). Some researchers have suggested that sentences like (27) may be ungrammatical because they are not in typical usage (e.g., Karlsson, 2007). This comes down to a definitional issue of what it means to label a string as "grammatical." If "grammatical" means "generated by the grammar in normal situations," then such sentences are clearly ungrammatical because we can't generate such sentences in normal language usage. Alternatively, if "grammatical" means "all of whose syntactic components are part of the grammar," then such sentences are grammatical.

Of relevance to the potential grammaticality of sentences like (27) is the fact that materials that are similar to (27), as in (33), are much more processable and are accepted by many speakers (see Gibson 1991, 1998 for references to other similar examples; see also Gibson et al. (2011) for evidence that many speakers produce such materials in certain circumstances).

(33) a. The book which the author who I met at the party wrote was well-written.
b. The book which the author who was on TV today wrote was well-written.
c. The cake which the baker who runs the corner shop baked for my party was delicious.

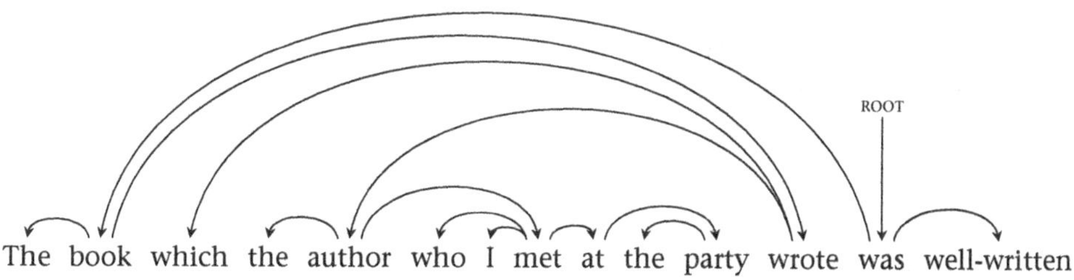

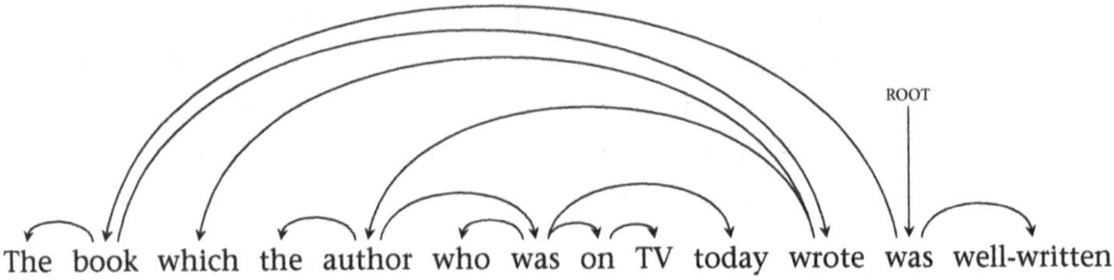

The structure in each of the sentences in (33) is the same in many respects as the structure in (27): All consist of a relative clause modifying the subject of a relative clause, which modifies the main clause subject.[7] Hence, one might argue that (27) is grammatical given that its grammatical properties are identical to those in the acceptable examples in (33). Example (27) is less acceptable than the examples in (33), but that is presumably because of factors other than the grammar—factors having to do with interpreting long-distance dependencies, with intervening material.

2.2.9 Illusions of Ungrammaticality: Strong Temporary Ambiguity

Human languages are highly ambiguous: Words are often ambiguous, and sequences of words are often ambiguous (see Piantadosi et al. [2012a] for an information-theoretic explanation for why human languages have so much ambiguity). For most sequences in normal interactions, the temporary ambiguity doesn't result in any noticeable difficulty:

(34) a. Mary believed the answer. (Frazier and Rayner, 1982)
b. Mary believed the answer was incorrect.
c. The desert trains young people to be especially tough. (Frazier and Rayner, 1987)
d. The desert trains are especially tough on young people.
e. The defendant examined the evidence.
f. The defendant examined by the lawyer turned out to be unreliable. (Ferreira and Clifton, 1986; Trueswell et al., 1994a)

In (34a) and (34b), the noun *answer* can either be analyzed as the object of the verb *believed* or as the subject of the following verb to come. Neither interpretation is difficult to comprehend (Pritchett, 1988). In (34c) and (34d), the sequence *desert trains* can be analyzed as either a noun-verb or as a noun-noun, and both are relatively easy to comprehend. Finally, the word *examined* can be analyzed as a main verb (as in (34e)) or as a relative clause modifier of defendant (as in (34f)), and each continuation sounds ok.

But because of the limitations of human memory, people cannot entertain all possible interpretations for the input (Gibson, 1991, 1998). Consequently, people choose a small set of representations that are locally best (Tanenhaus et al., 1995; MacDonald et al., 1994; Levy, 2008a). This early choice sometimes results in people choosing a representation that ends up being inconsistent with the continuation: a so-called "garden-path" effect (Bever, 1970).[8] Sometimes the local bias is strong, resulting in a consciously confusing sentence, as in the examples in (35):

(35) a. # The cotton clothing is made of grows in Mississippi. (Marcus, 1978)
b. # I put the candy on the table into my mouth. (Gibson, 1991)
c. # The old man the boats. (Ritchie and Thompson, 1984)
d. # The horse raced past the barn fell. (Bever, 1970)
e. # I gave the boy the dog bit a bandage. (Briscoe, 1983)
f. # The granite rocks during the earthquake. (Milne, 1982)

Note that none of these examples are "natural," in the sense that people don't typically say these in most contexts. These examples were all constructed by psycholinguists who knew what the preferred interpretations were at each word position, and then they constructed materials that they expected would be confusing for comprehenders.

In (35a), there is a strong initial bias to take *cotton* as an adjective modifying the noun *clothing*. But when we encounter *grows in Mississippi*, we realize that this interpretation is wrong. Eventually people tend to figure that the sequence *clothing is made of* is meant to be a relative clause modifying the noun *cotton*, but this is difficult (hence the #).

In (35b), the preposition *on* is usually initially analyzed as where *the candy* should be put. But when we encounter *into my mouth*, we realize that this has to be the goal where *the candy* should be put. So the sequence *on the table* is reanalyzed as a modifier of *candy*.

Example (35c) is an interesting case where there is a strong preference for the sequence *old man* to be taken as an adjective noun sequence rather than a noun verb sequence, even though either is logically possible. The preference is probably due to the strong word frequency biases toward *old* as an adjective (over noun) and *man* as a noun (over verb). The consequence is that when we read the whole sentence *The old man the boats* (which might be paraphrased as "the old people look after the boats"), we are simply stumped and don't know what to do, probably because there is no lexical cue in the input to help us fix the initial interpretation (Fodor and Inoue, 1994).

For our purposes here, sentence acceptability can be strongly affected by temporary ambiguity, which results in a high degree of confusion. Such confusion should not be misconstrued as evidence for the confusing sentences as being ungrammatical: Such garden-path sentences are completely grammatical (satisfying the rules of the grammar). They are just hard to understand because of confusing ambiguity.

2.2.10 Illusions of Grammaticality

There are materials that are more acceptable than grammatical controls but are not generated by the grammar, such as the "missing-verb-phrase" examples (Gibson and Thomas, 1999; Futrell et al., 2020a) (example attributed to Janet Fodor) in sentence (36b):

(36) a. The patient who the nurse who the clinic had hired admitted met Jack.
b. * The patient who the nurse who the clinic had hired met Jack.

Sentence (36b) is missing the verb *admitted* associated with the noun *nurse*, yet is often perceived as more acceptable than its grammatical control (36a), which contains the verb.

There also exist examples where the combinatorial meaning of a string is absurd, but whose overall meaning seems plausible, such as so-called "depth-charge" materials (Wason and Reich, 1979; Sanford and Emmott, 2012; Paape et al., 2020; Zhang et al., 2023b):[9]

(37) No head injury is too trivial to be ignored.

This sentence suggests that the normal state of the world is that we might ignore most head injuries but that if a head injury were really trivial, then we might not ignore that kind of head injury. The literal meaning of this sentence is basically the opposite of the true world state with respect to head injuries: We usually treat head injuries (not ignore them), even if they are minor. Perhaps if a head injury was really minor, then we might not treat it. The sentence in (37) is saying something odd, but somehow the sentence sounds reasonable.

Zhang et al. (2023b) suggest that the closeness of the neighboring sentence in (38), which is much more plausible, drives people to interpret (37) as (38):

(38) No head injury is so trivial as to be ignored.

Another famous "illusion" example is the so-called comparative illusion in (39) (O'Connor, 2015; Wellwood et al., 2018; Leivada, 2020; Zhang et al., 2023a):

(39) More people have been to Russia than I have.

When you first read this sentence, it seems like a good English sentence, but when you think about it, this sentence literally means something like *More people have been to Russia than I have been to Russia*. Comparing a bunch of people to the number of times I have been somewhere is incoherent. So although this sentence initially sounds like a good English sentence, it has a peculiar literal meaning.

These kinds of "illusion" examples provide evidence for how the language processor works in constructing meaning. Perhaps the most promising current proposal for explaining these examples is the communication-based "noisy-channel" approach: During comprehension, people try to infer the intention behind what they heard or read. So, people may automatically correct the problematic sentence according to their prior expectations without even noticing that there was any problem (Shannon, 1948; Levy, 2008b; Gibson et al., 2013a; Futrell et al., 2020a). In complex sentences, the closeness of a simpler structure may affect interpretation of the complex sentence: People will confuse a doubly-nested structure for a simpler singly nested one as in (36); and people will confuse a strange meaning for a simpler one, where there is a nearby neighbor as in (37). In (39), maybe what you initially thought was intended was something like (40) (Zhang et al., 2023a), which makes sense:

(40) People have been to Russia more than I have.

See chapter 10 for more details on the noisy-channel approach to language processing.

2.3 Other Methods That Language Scientists Use to Infer Syntactic Structure

While corpus analyses and acceptability judgments are the simplest and most common methods that language scientists use to infer syntactic structure, there are many other methods that are also useful in this endeavor. I survey some of these alternatives briefly, in order to give you a flavor of each. Feel free to skip this section and the next if you want to get right to the dependency grammar. You can do so without any loss of continuity.

There are several dimensions to each method:

- Language comprehension vs. language production.
- Spoken (or signed, for sign languages) vs. written.
- Online vs. offline. An on-line measure is one that measures some aspect of the task in time, as it occurs. So it comes with a time measure of how long the process took. An off-line measure is either a time measure for the whole event, or a measure of properties of the output at some stage. For example, a recall measure and an answer to a comprehension question are off-line measures.
- Naturalistic vs. nonnaturalistic materials (a continuum). Language materials can either be constructed in the process of normal language use (during a conversation; writing a news article, or a fiction story, and so on), and hence be *naturalistic*; or created by the experimenters, and hence be *nonnaturalistic.*
- Naturalistic vs. nonnaturalistic method (a continuum). A method can be something that people do naturally every day (like reading in language comprehension) or something that is less natural (like deciding if word string is acceptable or not).

Most measures that researchers have developed in the experimental literature have targeted language comprehension, simply because such methods are easier to devise. Researchers are often interested in how some unusual or complex structure is processed. In comprehension, we can investigate how arbitrary linguistic materials are processed, just by presenting them to participants. It is much more difficult to devise production methods that result in experimental participants producing targeted kinds of complex structures, without making the task unnatural.

2.3.1 Interpreting Any Task

Behavior on any language task (or cognitive task more generally) is heavily dependent on the materials and the details of the task. Participants will always try to infer what specifically they should be doing in the task by doing a few examples. For example, if the task is to read a text for comprehension, participants will read less carefully (and faster) if the comprehension evaluation is simple (e.g., questions like "Did the word *apple* appear in the sentence?"). On the other hand, if the comprehension questions are difficult, then people will read more slowly and carefully. This is because people are rational with their time: They are always trying to optimize their own time, spending only as much time as needed on any task.

Similarly, if the task is acceptability rating, what counts as "good" or "bad" is always context-dependent. Participants will adjust their use of the scale quickly after doing a few trials. If all the materials are extremely simple, then they will often start using the "bad" end of the scale for materials that might be associated with high ratings if the other materials in the survey were much less natural.

Finally, we should always be aware that no method is the perfect method. Different methods can tell us different things about language structure and processing in different contexts. Furthermore, there is no limit to the kind of method that might be developed: Researchers invent and discover methods that may work better than what we currently have in order to address the questions that they are interested in.

2.3.2 Eye-Tracking While Reading

In an eye-tracking reading experiment, a participant is set up in an eye-tracker and they read normally. Researchers record the time spent on each word, and whether the eye moved left to right (forward in a left to right writing system like English) or regressed backward in the text. The dependent measures include **first-pass reading times** (the time spent for the first time on any word); whether or not there was an eye-movement regression in a region; and other composite measures, such as "go-past" time— that is, the time spent in a region before the eyes moved to a later region.

2.3.3 Self-Paced Reading

Self-paced reading (Just et al., 1982) is an inexpensive method to get online reading times at each region (often single words). In self-paced reading, each non-space character in a text is replaced by a dash "-" as shown below. Participants press a key (usually the space bar) to reveal the next region. The previous region then reverts to dashes and the subsequent region is revealed:

```
Display 1:  --- ---- ------ --- ----.
Display 2:  The ---- ------ --- ----.
Display 3:  --- girl ------ --- ----.
Display 4:  --- ---- kicked --- ----.
Display 5:  --- ---- ------ the ----.
Display 6:  --- ---- ------ --- ball.
```

```
Comprehension question:  Did the girl kick something?
```

The time between button presses indicates the time taken to process the previous region. Thus, the time taken to process the word *girl* above would be the time difference between button presses for displays 3 and 4.

Reading times in self-paced reading are highly correlated with those in the more natural method (eye-tracking), but it is cheaper and easier to gather data using self-paced reading. Moreover, although it may seem like only seeing one region at a time is an odd way to read, participants quickly adapt to it and read approximately as fast as they would in normal reading.

2.3.4 The Maze Task

In the maze task (Forster et al., 2009; Boyce et al., 2020, 2023), participants get a choice between two elements, one on the left and one on the right, over several displays, in order to form a possible English sentence:

```
Display 1:  The     x-x-x
Display 2:  of      dog
Display 3:  pretty  chased
Display 4:  the     eat
Display 5:  go.     cat.
```

The participant presses a key corresponding to the left or right word on each display, to indicate that the word starts or continues a possible English sentence. So the participant would press the key corresponding to the left word "The" in display 1, because "The" is a possible initial word in a sentence, but "x-x-x" is not. For display 2, the participant would press the key corresponding to the word "dog" because "dog" can continue the initial segment "The," whereas "of" cannot. In this way, the participant should press left, right, right, left, right, corresponding to the sentence "The dog chased the cat." Alternative choices at each display are frequency-matched impossible continuations, as selected by a large language model (Boyce et al., 2020, 2023). The time between button presses corresponds to reading comprehension times. If the participant mistakenly selects an impossible continuation, then the trial ends early and the participant is informed of their error.

An advantage of the maze method over simple self-paced reading is that each button press reaction time corresponds to a deep level of processing, because the participant has to decide at that point between an impossible and a possible continuation. In contrast, in the self-paced reading task, people can have a strategy of hitting the key as fast as possible (in order to get paid sooner), or in some rhythmic way, such that they may not fully understand the text that they are passing over. Participants can't do this in the maze task because they will quickly be wrong in a judgment and the trial will end early.

2.3.5 Eye-Tracking While Listening

In an eye-tracking listening study (Cooper, 1974; Tanenhaus et al., 1995; Huettig et al., 2011), participants look at a display and follow auditory instructions given to them. For example, they might be told to *Put the bear on the towel in the box*. If given such instructions, there would be clear referents for the words in the instructions: a bear, a towel, a box, and so on. The method relies on the observation that people tend to look at the referents for the words that they hear in such a task.

Tanenhaus et al. (1995) used this method to investigate what kinds of information are used by listeners when listening to instructions and interacting with a scene. In particular, Tanenhaus et al. (1995) showed that participants use contextual information as early as possible in order to figure out what is intended by the speaker. For example, in a scene with one toy bear, when a participant heard the instruction *Put the bear on the towel in the box*, they would initially assume that the phrase *the bear* does not need further modification, and then they would interpret the phrase *on the towel* as the goal of where the bear needs to go, not where the bear was currently. This would turn out to be incorrect when the phrase *in the box* was encountered, and so listeners would be confused at this point. But in a scene with two toy bears, when a participant heard the same instruction (*Put the bear on the towel in the box*), they would use the phrase *on the towel* to disambiguate which bear was being referred to, and then have no trouble understanding that *in the box* was where the bear was supposed to go.

This work resolved a long-debated question in the language processing literature, whether discourse/context information (like the presence of one vs. two bears in the context) could override a strong lexical bias, for a verb like *put* to prefer that a following preposition like *in* be connected to the verb. This method and experiment showed that the context could guide people's initial interpretations of making syntactic connections. Previous work that had suggested otherwise (e.g., the experiments presented by Frazier and Rayner 1982; Ferreira and Clifton 1986) were shown to be biased by the materials that they used (Trueswell et al., 1994b; Garnsey et al., 1997). Furthermore, the previous research all used reading to make this inference; in reading, participants may not be as engaged with the material as in a task where they are engaging with the experimentalist, and they have to move objects in a scene.

2.3.6 Off-line Reading Measures

There are several off-line reading measures, such as whole text reading time, accuracy on comprehension questions, and recall of aspects of the text. These are off-line measures because there is no time course measure while the language materials are being processed.

- **Sentence completion.** Sentence completion is a language production task where participants are asked to complete some initial sequence of words (a *preamble*), often as a complete sentence. For example, the preamble might be *The girl who ...* and the participant could complete it in any way they like, such as *...was sleeping woke up* or *...was famous signed an autograph for me.* Usually, researchers using this method care most about the distribution of answers, rather than how long people take to do the task.

  Incidentally, the sentence completion task is essentially the task that large language models are trained on. They receive the first part of a sentence from a natural corpus (which someone wrote) and try to guess the next word. They then adjust the weights in the network toward the word that actually appeared, compared to their guess.
- **Picture description / picture naming.** In this task, participants simply say what is going on in a picture. Sometimes this is simple object-naming, and other times this task involves the description of an event (e.g., Bock [1986] had pictures of lightning striking a church). The point of this

method is to keep meaning constant and look at the effect of context on what kinds of descriptions people provide. For example, Bock (1986) used this task to demonstrate effects of syntactic priming: If a previous trial had been described using the passive voice (a low-frequency construction), there was an increased likelihood of using the same construction for the next description.

- **Interactive games.** Perhaps the most naturalistic language production tasks are tasks designed to give a collaborative goal for two partners, so that they must talk (or write to each other) to achieve that goal—for example, Clark and Brennan (1991); Brennan and Clark (1996). While these are the most natural kinds of tasks, it is often difficult to use them to target the production of specific syntactic constructions.

2.3.7 On-line Brain Measures

Both Electroencephalogram (EEG) (Kutas and Hillyard, 1980, 1984; Osterhout and Holcomb, 1992) and Magnetoencephalogram (MEG) (Salmelin, 2007) can be measured as participants are processing language. In EEG, we measure the voltage change on the scalp associated with some cognitive task that the participant is doing, such as reading or listening to a word in a sentence. The dependent measure in MEG is the change in magnetic field, measured near the scalp. In each of these methods, we get a millisecond-by-millisecond reading at each sensor, resulting in a multidimensional on-line measure of the cognitive task as it unfolds over time. One issue with these brain recording modalities is that we don't know what the dependent measure means: Is more voltage, or less voltage associated with a stronger language response? Is a stronger magnetic field associated with a stronger or weaker language response?

You might think that we could use these methods to figure out *where* in the brain language is processed. But it turns out that it is difficult to localize sources of EEG and MEG signals. Thus, although these tasks measure changes in brain activity—in the voltage changes or magnetic field changes associated with the electrical activity in the brain—it is hard to use these methods to understand the relation between brain function and brain localization. Rather, these methods provide multidimensional evidence of cognitive processing but not evidence for what brain regions might be doing what. To figure out which parts of the brain are performing different cognitive functions, we need a method with better spatial resolution, like functional magnetic resonance imaging.

2.3.8 Other Brain Measures: Functional Magnetic Resonance Imaging

Functional magnetic resonance imaging (fMRI) measures local blood flow related to neuronal firing: When cells fire, they use up oxygen and glucose, and new, oxygen-rich blood then comes in to replenish these resources. These influxes of blood are what fMRI measures. fMRI has very good spatial resolution, but its temporal resolution is not as good as EEG or MEG. With its good spatial resolution, fMRI can help us understand which brain regions support language processing or some other perceptual, motor, or cognitive process. This method is well-suited to ask questions like: Do two mental functions rely on the same system? I discuss results from this method in some detail in section 9.1.

2.4 Issues with Nonquantitative Data in Linguistic Theorizing

In this section, I provide a simple proposal to always gather quantitative data, when possible, in a language task, in order to avoid a confirmation bias for your favorite hypotheses. This section is about gathering data, in general, in a cognitive task (or indeed, in any scientific inquiry). This proposal contrasts with an often unstated standard in the linguistics literature, where the intuitions of the experimenter (an expert) are good enough to work with. A reader who is most interested in the details of the dependency grammar proposal can skip this section without loss of continuity.

As discussed at the beginning of this chapter, the easiest method to use in order to infer syntactic structure has proven to be the acceptability judgment task. There has been a bit of a debate in the linguistics community as to what should count as evidence for syntactic theories within a language (see, e.g., Gibson and Fedorenko, 2010, 2013; Gibson et al., 2013c; Sprouse and Almeida, 2013). An old-fashioned view, assumed by Marantz (2005); Phillips (2009); Sprouse and Almeida (2013), is that acceptability judgments from expert native speakers are adequate, without any quantitative data needed. Gibson and Fedorenko (2010, 2013); Gibson et al. (2013c) take an opposing position, suggesting that an acceptability experiment, which includes multiple speakers and multiple instances of each critical condition, can always be informative, even in obvious cases.

A response from Sprouse and colleagues was to evaluate four hundred examples from a linguistics textbook (Sprouse and Almeida, 2012) and one hundred pairs of acceptability judgments from the journal *Lingistic Inquiry* from 2000–2010 (Sprouse et al., 2013). They found that the quantitative judgments overwhelmingly supported the judgments in the syntax textbook (around 99 percent of the time), and strongly so in the *Linguistic Inquiry* examples (around 90–95 percent) of the time. Mahowald et al. (2016) found similar results when they looked at a further one hundred random example judgments from *Lingistic Inquiry*: Around 95 percent of judgments supported the judgments in the literature. Sprouse and colleagues conclude that there is no need to perform quantitative experiments on linguistic judgments, when the current method is so successful with just intuitive judgments from the journal article authors.

While a 95 percent success rate is certainly good, there are several issues to consider before choosing to not adopt quantitative approaches to evaluating acceptability. First, the 95 percent accuracy rate presumes just two categories of acceptability: acceptable, and unacceptable. As discussed below, sentence acceptability is a continuum. Sentence grammaticality probably depends on the frequency of the use of the structures in a sentence, and so may also be a continuum.

Second, even if 95 percent of the judgments are in the correct direction, without a quantitative measure, there is no way to know which ones are correct and which ones are not. Some may be critical ways to tell one theory from another: It's important to be certain that these ones are indeed as predicted by the theory. Theories can be wrong. Allowing 5 percent incorrect data is bad for scientific progress.

And third, as noted by Gibson and Fedorenko (2013), most editors and reviewers of *Linguistic Inquiry* speak English, and hence they can assess the judgments on English syntax provided by the authors. The same is not true for any other language: Most of the editors and many of the reviewers typically do not speak the target language. Most editors and reviewers will thus have to take the authors' judgments at face value. This is not to imply that the authors of papers investigating languages other than English are any different in their psychological biases from those writing about English: Those writing about English simply have their judgments evaluated more thoroughly than those writing about other languages, because of the English bias in the field. Linzen and Oseki (2018) provide some evidence that authors of Japanese and Hebrew papers can be biased and, hence, make many judgment errors, many more than in papers that get through the publishing process based on English. Doing quantitative work would help circumvent this issue.

2.4.1 A Simple Approach: Corpus Data when Available; Judgment Experiments for More Rare Construction Comparisons

In 2010–2013 my coauthors and I argued that one should always do an acceptability judgment experiment for any targeted contrast. Many people have complained that this seems like overkill for many comparisons, because they are so obvious. In retrospect, I agree with this observation, for many purposes. But I still think we always need some kind of quantitative data.

Thus, rather than do an acceptability judgment experiment for all proposed contrasts, I recommend first doing a corpus search for relevant similar examples. If there are many such examples, the contrast can be inferred based on the relative frequency of the two kinds of structures. For example, consider the following three pairs of contrasts from the set of materials that Mahowald et al. (2016) investigated experimentally:

(41) a. * Some cat white was on the porch.
b. Some white cat was on the porch. (Larson and Marušič, 2004)
c. * It is pretty to look at these flowers.
d. It is tough to please linguists. (Hicks, 2009)
e. * They fell him off the stage.
f. They laughed him off the stage. (Nakajima, 2006)

Consider first (41a) vs. (41b), a contrast observed in Larson and Marušič (2004). We need not do an acceptability judgment experiment to evaluate this contrast because it is easily observed in corpora of English: If we search for the string *white cat*, we see that this is far more frequent than the string *cat white* (and the same is true for most adjectives and nouns). Similarly, the string *tough to please* in (41d) is far more frequent than *pretty to look at* in (41c) or another appropriate control. Contrasts like these make up about half of the contrasts in the materials that Mahowald et al. (2016) and Sprouse and Almeida (2012) investigated. The remainder are rare combinations of structures, where an acceptability judgment experiment would be appropriate.

3 Dependency Grammar

The goal of the current endeavor is to find a representation for combinations of words in a human language. The grammar formalism that we will pursue here is called **dependency grammar** (Tesnière, 1959; Hays, 1964; Mel'čuk, 1988; Hudson, 1984, 2015; Tesnière, 2015; Osborne, 2019; De Marneffe and Nivre, 2019; De Marneffe et al., 2021; Nefdt and Baggio, 2023). The notion of dependencies between words dates to Pānini's grammar of Sanskrit, from somewhere between the seventh and fourth century BCE (Vasu et al., 1897; Kiparsky, 1995), and is present in all theories of grammar. Under dependency grammar, there are dependency links between words/morphemes, which themselves have potentially complex features. Most connections are headed, going from the **head** to its **dependents** (Hudson, 1984, 1990, 2006). In these headed relationships, the meaning of the combination of head and dependent is a function of the way that they are linked. Indeed, most syntactic theories include some notion of **headedness** (Bloomfield, 1933; Tesnière, 1959; Hays, 1964; Bresnan, 1982; Hudson, 1984; Mel'čuk, 1988; Corbett et al., 1993; Pollard and Sag, 1994; Sag et al., 1999; Culicover and Jackendoff, 2005), including phrase structure grammars (see chapter 7): A noun is the head of a noun phrase, and a verb is the head of a verb phrase. X-bar theory is a phrase structure theory where a core idea is that every phrase has a head (Jackendoff, 1977).

3.1 Heads and Dependents

As discussed in chapter 1, a sentence of length n words can be structured by $n-1$ dependencies among the words, such that the meaning of the sentence is formed by making these connections. This representation is called a **tree**, which is a special type of **directed acyclic graph (DAG)**. A **graph** consists of a data structure where nodes are connected by edges. In a dependency tree, each node is a word and each edge is called a **dependency**. The graph is directed, because dependencies have a direction: from a **head** word to its **dependent** words. It is **acyclic**: There is a root word, which connects to its dependents, and their dependents, but with no cycles back to words that have been covered initially in the hierarchy. The dependency connections link each word to some other word together to make a larger meaning in the sentence. These dependencies are headed, such that the **head** determines the semantic category of the dependency pair as a whole, while the **dependent** provides semantic specification (Hudson, 1984, 1990, 2015), cf. De Marneffe and Nivre (2019). Recall example (3), which has two interpretations:

(3) Canadian hat maker

According to one, *Canadian* connects to *hat*, indicating a kind of hat, not a kind of Canadian. Therefore *hat* is the head of this relationship. And then *hat* connects to *maker*, indicating that the whole phrase is a type of maker—a maker of Canadian hats—not a type of Canadian or hat.

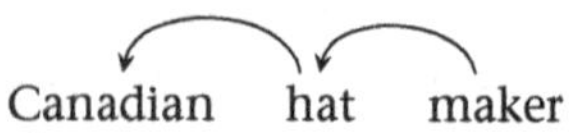

According to a second interpretation, both *Canadian* and *hat* are connected to *maker*, indicating that each marks a type of maker, not a type of Canadian or hat.

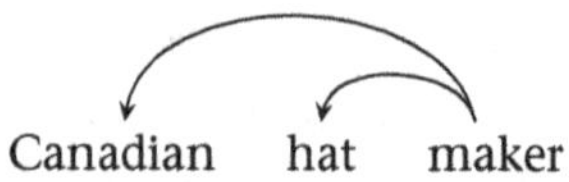

In this section, I will start with a set of simple English sentences—a **corpus**—each describing a simple event or state. I will then propose a **lexicon** and **grammar** that could be used to generate them:

(42) a. Ollie slept.
  b. Lana liked Ollie.
  c. The girl walked.
  d. The cat scratched.
  e. The boy kicked the ball.
  f. Ollie chased a squirrel.

g. Some neighbor ate a pizza.
h. A rock hit the ground.
i. Lana liked the dessert.
j. We liked the pizza.

I will concentrate on the forms, but of course there are meanings associated with most words.[1] Then we will attempt to work out combinatorial rules that could generate these sentences. These rules will often have meanings associated with them, but the focus of this book is the forms.

3.2 The Lexicon: Categories of Words, Each with an Associated Syntactic Structure

First, we categorize all the words by their **parts of speech**, which are categories that indicate how the words are used in the corpus. Two general such categories that have been discussed thus far are **nouns** and **verbs**. Each of these is a broad category, with many subcategories in English and in other languages. Each of these has features that narrow the particular noun or verb to a specific category instance. For example, there are several classes of English nouns, including (a) **names**, such as *Lana, Ollie*; (b) **count nouns**, such as *girl, pizza, rock, neighbor, ostrich, idea*; (c) **mass nouns**, such as *water, sand*; and (d) **pronouns**, such as *I, me, you, she, he, they*. For simplicity of presentation, I will present features of a category as subscripts following the category. So the four classes of nouns I describe here are N_{name}, N_{count}, N_{mass}, and $N_{pronoun}$.

Count nouns refer to countable things, like objects, types of people and animals, and even abstract things and events. Such nouns can be singular or plural. Plural number is typically marked on English count nouns with an *-s* or *-es* on the end of the word, such as *girls, pizzas, rocks, neighbors, ostriches*. There are other features that apply to nouns, such as case-marking (nominative, accusative, genitive, and so on), and person (first, second, third) for pronouns: *I, me, my, you, your, he, him, his, she, her*, and so on.[2]

The second broad category of words in English is **verbs.** Like nouns, verbs have number agreement features (singular, plural) and other features like tense and aspect. In addition, verbs often differ in their **argument structures** (or **subcategorization** requirements), which is a fancy way to refer to the syntactic properties that go with their meaning properties. Initially, I present verbs with only two kinds of verb subcategorizations, which I label as V_0 and V_N. Importantly, these words have dependency structure in their syntax: Each needs a subject noun before, and V_N needs a noun to follow. These structures are detailed in the following section. The labels I give—V_0 and V_N—are short forms here for these dependency structures.

The third broad category in this corpus is **Determiners** (Det) or **Articles**, which include words like *the, a, some, this,* and *every*. The determiner is a very common kind of word in English, but its meanings are complex, indicating aspects of how their head nouns are to be interpreted in context. The word *the* indicates an object that is already assumed to be part of the discourse (the **definite** determiner), whereas the indefinite determiner *a* indicates a new object in the discourse. Not all languages mark this difference in their syntax.[3]

I list the parts of speech that we will cover in this chapter in the box below, along with the features that each uses in my simple grammar, some example argument structures, and some example words in each category. I cover only three of these categories initially—Noun, Verb, Determiner. I will get to other categories in later sections.

Part of speech	**Features, argument structure(s), examples**
Noun (N)	Feature: num (sing, plu), type (count, mass, name, pronoun) *Examples: Lana, girl, girls, you*
Verb (V)	Feature: num (sing, plu), tense (pres, past), person (1sing, 1plu, 2, 3sing, 3plu), aux (+, –) Argument structures: sleep {0}, kick {N}, give {N, N}, give {N, P}, think {C} . . . *Examples: slept, kicked, gave, thought*
Determiner (Det)	Feature: num (sing, plu), count (+,–) *Examples: the, a, some*
Adjective (Adj)	*Examples: tall, green, wide*
Adverb (Adv)	*Examples: extremely, happily*
Preposition (Prep)	Argument structure: {N} *Examples: in, with, of, at*
Complementizer (Comp) (Subordinator)	Argument structure: {V} *Examples: that, whether*

The English parts of speech to be covered in chapter 3.

A lexicon for the above corpus is as follows, with some additional words in these and closely related categories:

$N_{name,sing}$: Lana, Ollie, Susan, Allan, Francine
$N_{count,sing}$: girl, cat, boy, ball, squirrel, pizza, ostrich, neighbor, rock, box
$N_{count,plu}$: girls, cats, boys, balls, squirrels, pizzas, ostriches, neighbors, rocks, boxes
$N_{pronoun,sing}$: I, me, you, he, she, him, her
$N_{pronoun,plu}$: we, us, you, they, them[4]
Det_{sing}: a, every, this
Det_{plu}: these, many
$Det_{sing,plu}$: the, some
V_0: slept, walked
V_N: kicked, chased, ate, hit, liked, ignored

The leaves of the dependency trees that we are going to develop will be the words. The syntactic categories above are the labels associated with the words. Each of these categories is associated with some structure (its argument structure) that we are going to discuss in the following sections. The most interesting of these structures will be the verbs, which have highly variable kinds of argument structures: Some verbs only require a noun to the left (its subject), the intransitive V_0, while others require a noun to the right as well—V_N. Still others require more kinds of arguments, such as two nouns to the right or a noun and a clause to the right. The other words in our corpus also have argument structures, but these argument structures are sometimes empty, such as in the case of many nouns. All this means is that these words don't need other elements to complete them. A noun like *Lana* or *pizza*, for example, doesn't need any other categories to be complete syntactically.

Each lexical item also has a meaning associated with it, but as discussed in section 9.4.1, figuring out how to represent meaning is complex, and beyond the scope of this book. As mentioned in the introduction, when I want to indicate word meanings, I will follow Fillmore (1982) and Langacker (1987) in simply capitalizing the word in order to indicate the meaning. So the meaning of the word *Lana* would be LANA; and the meaning of the word *girl* would be GIRL, and so on.

3.3 Figuring Out the Combinatorial Rules

All words have some syntax associated with them, in the form of dependency structure. To figure out what these dependency structures are, let's start with sentences (42a) *Ollie slept* and (42b) *Lana liked Ollie* from our corpus. The verb *slept* is of category V_0 (**intransitive** verbs), and the verb *liked* is of category V_N (**transitive** verbs). In old-fashioned grammar terminology, an intransitive verb is a verb that doesn't need to be followed by any more words, in order to make a complete sentence. The subscript 0 indicates that nothing needs to follow this verb. And a transitive verb (V_N) is a verb that can be followed by a noun to make a complete sentence. So we use the subscript *N* to indicate this. The dependency structures for these two verb types are as follows:

Rule 1: 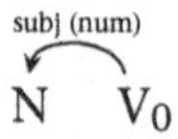

Rule 2: 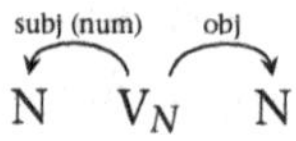

Rules 1 and 2 indicate that the subject (subj) precedes the verb, and is category N. Any of the N types—N_{name}, N_{count}, N_{mass}, or $N_{pronoun}$—will match this rule. Rule 2 indicates that the object (obj) follows the verb, and is also category N.

In general, each rule will have an arrow going from its *head* to its *dependent(s)*: V is the head for the dependent Ns in these rules. There are two different notations for these rules in the literature. I will follow Word Grammar (Hudson, 1984, 1990, 2006) and the Universal Dependencies project (https://universaldependencies.org/; Nivre et al., 2016, 2020; De Marneffe et al., 2021) in drawing the arrows from heads to dependents. The order of the lexical items is given by the linear order in which the items appear in the rule.

In addition, I indicate the dependency type and, in parentheses, the features that need to agree between head and dependent on the arc. In these rules, the dependency type for the subject is *subj*. The number feature **num** is listed in parentheses, indicating that the number (singular = sing, plural = plu) needs to match on the subject noun and verb. Past tense verbs like *slept* and *liked* aren't marked for number in English: They are compatible with both singular and plural nouns when agreement is required. For English verbs, number agreement is primarily marked in the present tense forms (such as *sleeps / sleep, likes / like*).

I will put a star (∗) following a dependent if more than one such dependent of that type can occur there. Here, there can only be one noun (N) for the subject or object nouns, so there is no star in either case. Later, we will see rules where there can be many such dependents of the same type (e.g., adjectives modifying a noun or prepositions modifying a noun or verb).

The dependency structures for sentences (42a) *Ollie slept* and (42b) *Lana liked Ollie* are simply applications of these rules, as follows:

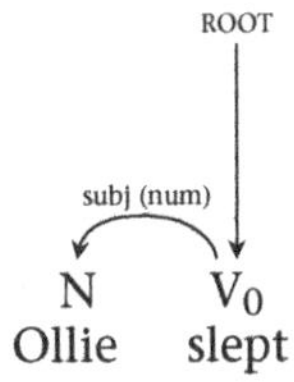

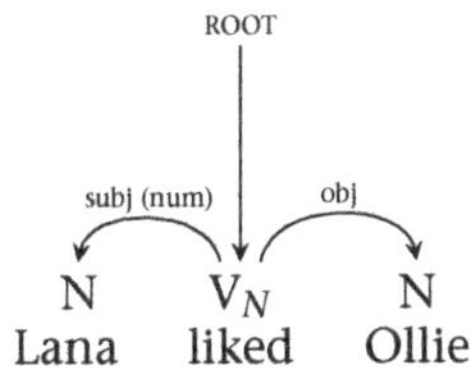

For any sentence, we can indicate its root category, as I have done above. Sentences are trees, which means that there is always one such root. The root of a sentence is simply the word **that does not depend on any other word**. We don't need to mark it in the sentence: We just mark it to make it easy to see in the diagrams.

I will sometimes omit the features that need to agree on the arcs, just to keep the diagrams simpler. I will also often omit many features of the head categories, such as count, mass, name, and number agreement features, again for simplicity of presentation. But keep in mind that all these agreement features are implicitly there.

Next, let's structure (42c) *The girl walked*. The verb *walked* is like *slept*: an intransitive verb V_0. Its dependent is a subject noun, *girl*. The noun *girl* has as its dependent the determiner *the*, forming what is called a *noun phrase* (NP): a sequence of words that is headed by a noun of some kind (including a name or a pronoun). The dependency grammar rule for this combination is as follows:[5]

Rule 3: 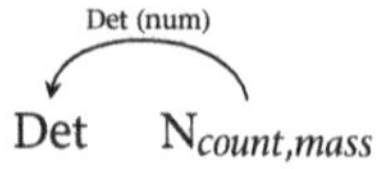

Nouns are the heads of noun phrases in this grammar. The structure associated with rule 3 is therefore connected with the head category, N. Determining the head of a noun phrase is actually complex; some researchers have argued that determiners are the heads. See section 3.7 for more discussion of this issue.

Nouns and determiners are marked in the corpus above with number agreement. This agreement requirement is so that singular-only determiners like *a* and *this* are connected only with singular head nouns like *girl* and *ball*; and plural-only determiners like *these* and *many* are connected only with plural count nouns like *girls* and *balls*. There are also determiners like *the* and *some*, which are listed as $\text{Det}_{sing,plu}$, indicating that they are compatible with either singular or plural head nouns, such as *the girl, the girls*.

Putting rule 3 together with rule 1, we can generate the sentence in (42c) *The girl walked*:

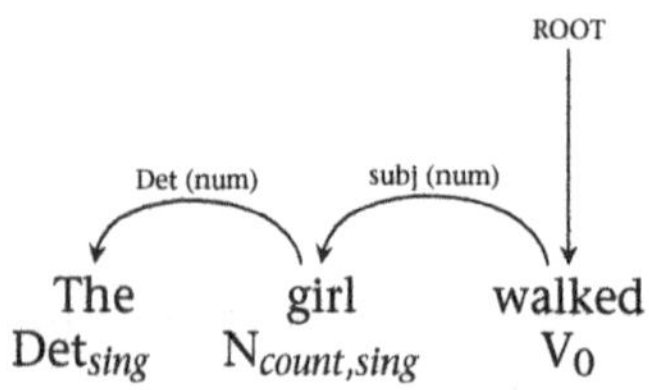

These three grammar rules generate all the sentences in our corpus in (42). For example, (42g) is generated as follows:

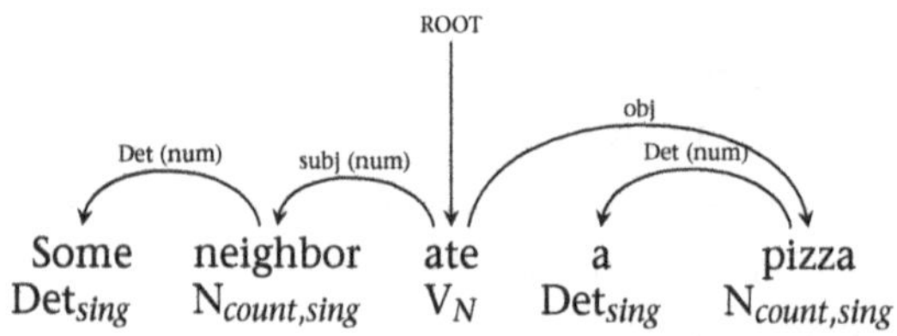

Or more simply, without the agreement features listed:

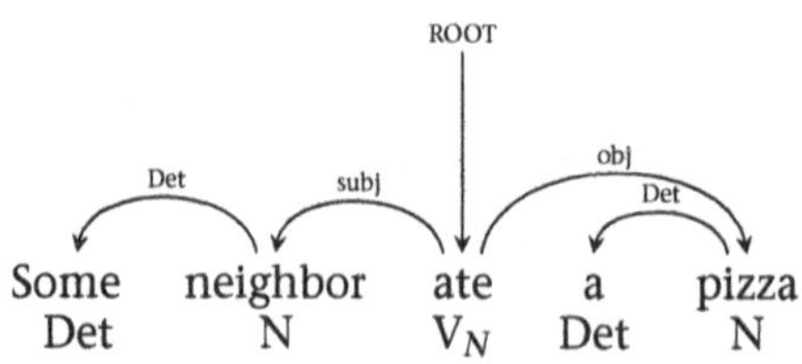

Note that these three rules don't allow all combinations of the words in the lexicon: They only allow the ones that satisfy the dependency rules that we have discovered. So we can't generate the strings in (43):

(43) a. * slept the girl.
b. * girl the slept.
c. * Ollie Susan Francine slept.
d. * The chased a squirrel cat.

Following standard practice in syntax research, we prefix strings that are not generated by the grammar with a star: *. Hence there are two meanings for the * in syntax research: a prefix for an ungrammatical string and arbitrary repetition of a category in a grammar rule.

For example, (43a) is not generated by these rules because the verb *slept* doesn't allow a noun following it; (43b) is not possible because the noun *girl* precedes its determiner *the*; (43c) is not possible because there is more than one name which is part of the noun group; that is not permitted in our toy grammar thus far. Finally, (43d) is not possible because there is no noun to the left of the verb *chased*. Finally, consider (44):

(44) girl slept.

This sentence actually can be generated by the grammar given thus far, as follows:

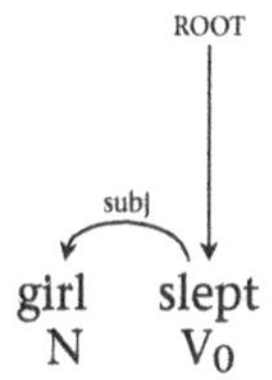

Whereas (44) doesn't sound like a good sentence in my dialect of English, it is still generated by our small grammar. We should also include a constraint such that singular count nouns always have a determiner.

3.3.1 Generating All and Only the Sentences in a Language

A goal of the current grammar framework is to provide a set of rules that generates all and only the sentences of the target language, English. As discussed in chapter 2, we call such a framework **generative**. English prefers certain word orders and allows others in certain circumstances but disallows most others. For example, consider the possible word orders of a subject noun, a verb, and an object noun:

(45) a. Most typical English word order: subject-verb-object (SVO): The girl ate the pizza.
b. Possible in some circumstances: OSV: The pizza, the girl ate.

The most typical English word order for a subject, verb and object is SVO, as in (45a). There are particular discourse circumstances that make **topicalization** of the object at the front of the sentence possible, as in the OSV word order in (45b). These circumstances are usually such that there is background information in the context that the girl ate something, but it's not yet clear what. Then we can topicalize as in (45b). (We can also use a **cleft** in such a situation: *It was the pizza that the girl ate.*)

The other logically possible sequences of subject noun, object noun, and verb are not allowed in standard English, and hence I mark them with an asterisk (*) below:

(46) a. OVS: * The pizza ate the girl.
b. VOS: * Ate the pizza the girl.
c. SOV: * The girl the pizza ate.
d. VSO: * Ate the girl the pizza.

For example, (46a) cannot mean that the girl ate the pizza. The order of words in (46a) is possible, but only with the meaning that *the pizza* is the subject (agent of eating) and *the girl* is the patient of the eating, the thing being eaten. This would be an implausible SVO sentence. Similarly, VOS, SOV, and VSO word order are not allowed in English. All are interpretable somehow, but only as errors where the producer meant something else (see chapter 10 for more on "noisy-channel" inference of what might be intended).

The goal of the current dependency grammmar framework is to provide rules that generate the allowable English word orders, and do not generate the ones that do not occur. A further goal of the framework is to explain human responses to sentence complexity, such as acceptability judgments. I have provided rules that generate the SVO word order above. The topicalization word order would be generated using a topicalization rule, which will be discussed in section 3.19, in general terms. None of the other orders will be generated by this rule system, as desired. Hence, people rate sentences like (45a) as the best of the six orders above. The orders in (46a)–(46d) are rated the worst. In the right context, sentences like (45b) are rated reasonably well, but not as highly as (45a). This is because frequency of use affects acceptability: The most common word orders get the highest ratings due to the probability of the rules that are used.

3.3.2 Dependencies Have High Mutual Information

One way to formalize which pairs of words have dependencies between them is in information-theoretic terms: the ones that co-occur more than chance. These are the ones with highest **mutual information**. This is what Futrell (2019) and Futrell et al. (2020a) call the **head-dependent mutual information (HDMI)** hypothesis.[6] For example, consider a simple sentence like the current one.

(47) For example, consider a simple sentence like the current one.

Pointwise mutual information (PMI) is defined as in (48):

(48) PMI (x,y) = $\log_2 \frac{P(x,y)}{P(x)P(y)}$.

So for two words x and y, the pointwise mutual information of x and y is a measure of the information in x relative to y: Do x and y occur immediately adjacent more than as predicted by simply sampling the two words' probabilities (independent of where they occur)? If this sequence occurs more often than as predicted by the sequence as predicted from independent samples, then it has high mutual information.

Let's consider the word pair *for example*, at the beginning of the sentence in (47): Does this sequence of words occur more often than if the words were sampled independently? The word probability of *for* is pretty high in English: 0.63% according to the Google Books corpus as of 2019 (using the Google Books Ngram Viewer https://books.google.com/ngrams/). The word probability of *example* is also pretty high among nouns, but this probability is much lower at 0.03%. The sequence *for example* (a **bigram** consisting of two words) is where the word *example* occurs most often: 0.01%. This means that for every three times that *example* occurs, the word *for* occurs before it once. The PMI of this sequence is therefore $\log_2(.0001/(.0063 * .0003))$ = 5.72 bits. This is a big number: This says that knowing only the word *for* or only the word *example* would explain much of the information that the bigram *for example* has.

We can do the same calculation for the word sequence *example consider*, the next pair in the sentence. The word probability of *example* is as before 0.03%; and the word probability of *consider* is 0.0096%. The bigram probability of *example consider* is low: only 0.0000029%. The PMI of this sequence is therefore $\log_2(0.000000029/(0.000096 * 0.0003)) = 0.01$ bits. This number says that the probability of the two words occurring together is pretty much the same as if they were picked independently.

The HDMI hypothesis is that the sequences of word categories that occur the most are probably dependencies between those categories. So there is probably a dependency between *for* and *example*, but not necessarily between *example* and *consider*. In fact, what we need to look at is PMI of word categories, not words, in order to figure out the more general word category dependencies. The above calculation is just about the specific words. Futrell (2019) and Futrell et al. (2020a) provide evidence that mutual information does in fact pick dependency pairs, most of the time. So it looks like the head-dependent mutual information hypothesis is a possible explanation for syntactic dependencies.

3.4 Hierarchies of Categories: Category Features and Unification

Linguists have worked out a set of features that allow for a simple, compressed set of rules within a language. And then, for some rules, some features have to **agree** in order for a rule to apply. I have provided two examples like this thus far: Determiners must agree with their head nouns; and subject nouns must agree with their verbs. The process of agreement is a special case of **feature unification** (Shieber, 1986; Pollard and Sag, 1987; Sag et al., 1999), whereby the head and dependent have to overlap on their features in order for the rule to apply. For the examples given thus far, it is hard to see how agreement applies for verbs, because simple past verbs like *chased* and *slept* agree with both singular and plural nouns. We need to examine simple present tense verbs to see how number agreement can apply in English subject-verb agreement, as in *sleeps, chases*, and so on. I also include an example here of a count noun *sheep*, which is both singular and plural. English allows both (49a) and (49b)

$V_{0,sing,pres}$: sleeps, walks
$V_{0,plu,pres}$: sleep, walk

$V_{0,past}$: slept, walked
$V_{N,sing,pres}$: chases, eats
$V_{N,plu,pres}$: chase, eat
$V_{N,past}$: chased, ate
$N_{count,sing,plu}$: sheep

(49) a. Some sheep chases a cat.
 b. Some sheep chase a cat.
 c. ∗ The cat sleep.
 d. ∗ The cats sleeps.

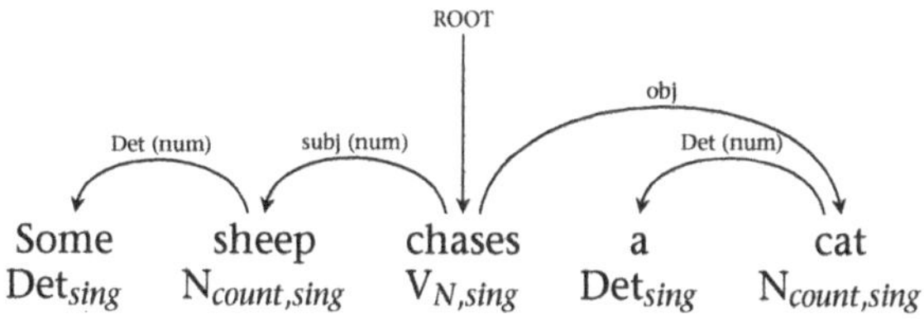

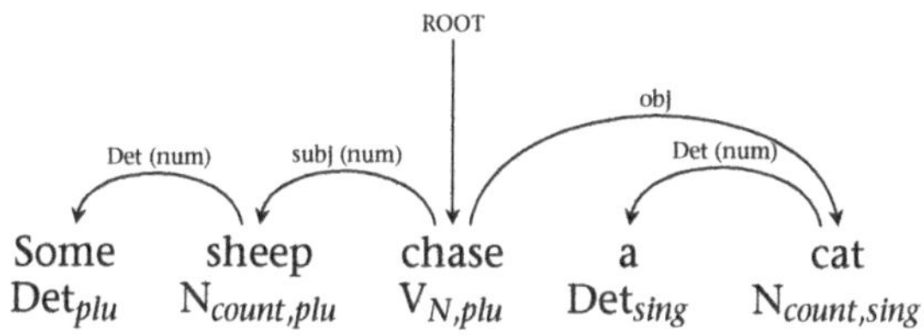

The word *sheep* is ambiguous between a singular noun and a plural noun. Similarly, the determiner *some* can agree with either a singular or a plural noun. The verb *chases* is unambiguously singular in (49a), and hence the agreement matches that on noun and determiner in the first dependency structure above. Similarly, The verb *chase* is plural in (49b), and hence the agreement is plural in the second dependency structure above.

In (49c), *cat* is singular. This word can agree with the determiner *the* (singular), but the resulting singular noun phrase does not agree with the plural verb *sleep* in (49c). Similarly, the plural noun *cats* does not agree with the singular verb *sleeps* in (49d).

3.5 English Morphology: The Structure of Words

Languages have varying amounts of morphology in their words. English is a language with not much inflectional morphology. In this book, I focus on syntax (not morphology), and many of my examples are from English, so I only explain the most basic details of some English morphology.[7]

English words can be broken down into smaller pieces: their **roots** and **affixes** (mostly **suffixes**). English count nouns can be singular or plural: for example, *dog* and *dogs*. The *-s* marks plural for regular nouns. English verbs can have as many as five different forms—for example, for the root *eat*:

Root (infinitive): eat (also the present tense for all but third singular)
Past tense: ate
Past participle: eaten
Third person singular present tense: eats
Present participle: eating

For present tense English verbs in Standard English, the number on the verb must match the number on the subject noun:

(50) a. The girl eats the pizza.
b. The girls eat the pizza.
c. * The girl eat the pizza.
d. * The girls eats the pizza.

Some determiners are marked with singular or plural agreement:

(51) a. a girl
b. this girl
c. these girls
d. * a girls
e. * this girls
f. * these girl

In order to properly cover English grammar, our grammar should have categories of singular and plural determiners, nouns, and verbs, so that only the categories of the appropriate type could unify appropriately to make a sentence. These properties are typically represented as *agreement features* on the categories (N, Det, V) that are required to match (agree) with their dependents (Bresnan, 1982; Gazdar et al., 1985; Pollard and Sag, 1994; Sag et al., 1999; Bresnan et al., 2015).

3.6 Syntax vs. Reference

The kinds of rules that we are trying to discover in this book are syntactic rules: rules of how the forms of language can combine, often with compositional meaning. One component of meaning that is not covered by syntax (as defined here) is **reference**: which syntactic elements refer to which things in the world and whether some syntactic elements refer to the same such elements or not. Pronouns are examples of nouns that refer to other elements, sometimes also mentioned in the syntax and sometimes just referring to elements in the world. The pronoun *I* refers to the speaker/writer, and the pronoun *you* refers to the listener/reader. In (112), the pronoun *she* can refer to *Elizabeth*, or possibly some other person in the context:

(52) Elizabeth thought that she had aced the test.

In (53a), the pronoun *who* refers to *the girl*. And in (53b), the pronoun *which* refers to *the dog*.

(53) a. The girl who aced the test was Elizabeth.
b. The dog which Elizabeth liked was Ollie.

We will discuss the syntax of embedded clauses like those in (53a) and (53b) in section 3.19, but we will not discuss how reference works in any detail here. There are reasons to think that reference and form do not align in human language processing. For example, people's comprehension of referential information is a slow process that has its effects at the end of clauses and sentences in self-paced reading and eye-tracking measures, but not immediately when the referential elements are first encountered. This contrasts to syntactic rule formation, which people are sensitive to as soon as it is encountered. Furthermore, large language models (LLMs) seem to make the same distinction: They are very good at predicting the next words, but they are poor at understanding reference.[8]

3.7 The Head Word of a Noun Phrase Is the Noun, Not the Determiner

While it may seem obvious that in a combination of a determiner and a noun, the noun is the head, some researchers have argued that the determiner is the head: the determiner phrase hypothesis (Abney, 1987; Hudson, 2004). A noun phrase can be introduced by a determiner or consist of a simple or complex name, as in (54):

(54) a. a dog
b. a big dog
c. the big dog

d. dogs
e. big dogs
f. some yellow sand
g. sand
h. yellow sand
i. Lana
j. Lana Gibson

The examples (54a), (54b), (54c), and (54f) are each initiated by a determiner (*a*, *the*, or *some*). But noun phrases whose nouns are plural nouns ((54d) and (54e)) or a mass noun like *sand* in (54g) need not have a determiner. Names are also perfectly good noun phrases, as in (54i) and (54j). As a result, if we wanted to say that noun phrases are always headed by determiners, then we would need to posit an empty determiner in each of these cases. In order to avoid the proliferation of empty elements in the syntax, I assume that noun phrases are headed by nouns of some kind. But this is an open question in the syntax literature; I simply make what seems to be the best current assumption, given the evidence.

3.8 More Parts of Speech: Adjectives, Adverbs, Prepositions

Parts of speech—categories of words—vary across languages (Haspelmath, 2001). The categories that I have listed in the table in section 3.2 are some of the more common ones that exist in English. Hence, this grammar is not intended to be exhaustive. In addition to nouns, verbs, and determiners, we have **adjectives**, **adverbs**, **prepositions**, and **auxiliary verbs**, to be discussed in this section. Some of these categories of words are called **content** words, like adjectives and adverbs: These are **open-class** words, which means that people can invent new examples of such words as they like. On the other hand, there are also **closed-class** words or **function** words, like determiners, auxiliary verbs, and subordinators, which syntactically link the content words in interesting ways. There are a fixed number of these in a language: It's much harder to introduce new function words into a language.[9]

3.8.1 Adjectives

We haven't included adjectives (Adj) in our little corpus, but they are often simple syntactically: They usually come before a noun and after a determiner (if there is a determiner), as in:

(55) a. the tall girl
b. a big apple
c. some green dogs
d. the small yellow rocks
e. a wide house

The dependency rule for adjectives is:

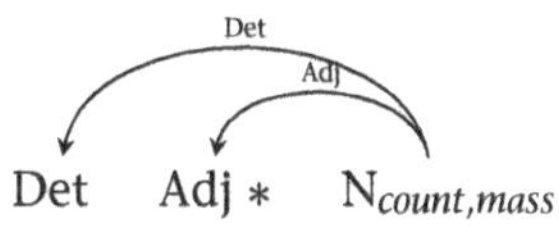

The star following the Adj category indicates that any number of adjectives (including zero) is possible there. The meaning of an adjective is usually a property of the object denoted by a noun. These are simple descriptions that take one argument (the meaning of the noun).

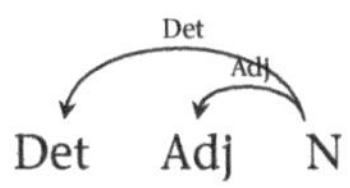

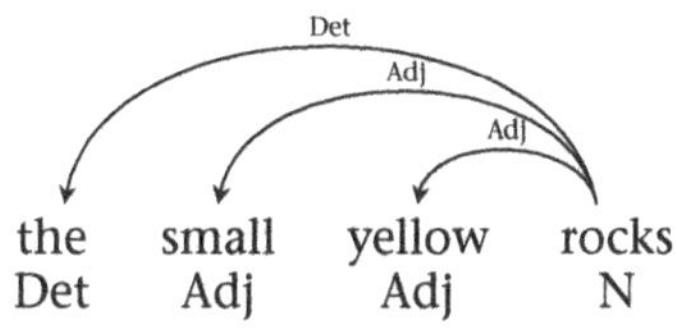

3.8.2 Adverbs

Another category that we don't have in our initial corpus is the **adverb**, which is usually a modifier of a verb. Adverbs include words like *extremely, happily, quietly, brilliantly*, and *excitedly*. They indicate a property of an event or state. There is some morphological syntax to adverbs in English: Many can be formed from adjectives, plus the suffix *-ly*. The adjectives that can do this are ones that make sense as properties of events and states. So *quietly* is an adverb because an event can be quiet, but *greenly* isn't a normal adverb, because green is usually a property of an object, not an event. Adverbs can also modify adjectives, as in *quietly big, happily silent*, or *extremely irrelevant*.

3.8.3 Prepositions

Prepositions are words that link nouns to other nouns or verbs, such as *in, on, of, with, beside, at,* and *to*:

(56) a. The man in the room
b. The girl with the hat
c. The picture of the dog
d. The girl slept in the bed.
e. Lana ate some pizza at the store.

Syntactically, these words always take a dependent noun to follow:

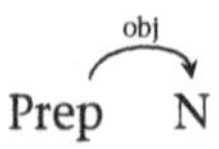

Furthermore, they depend on a count or mass noun, or most any main verb that comes before, and there can be any number of them (hence the star "*" in each rule):

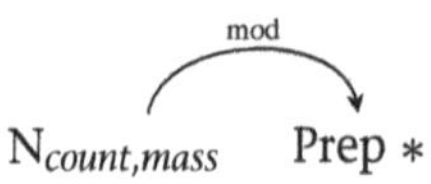

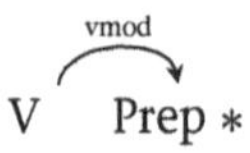

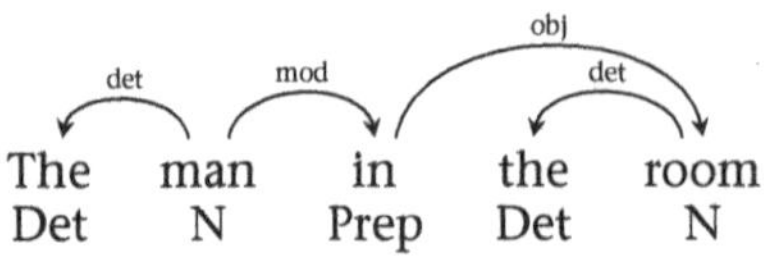

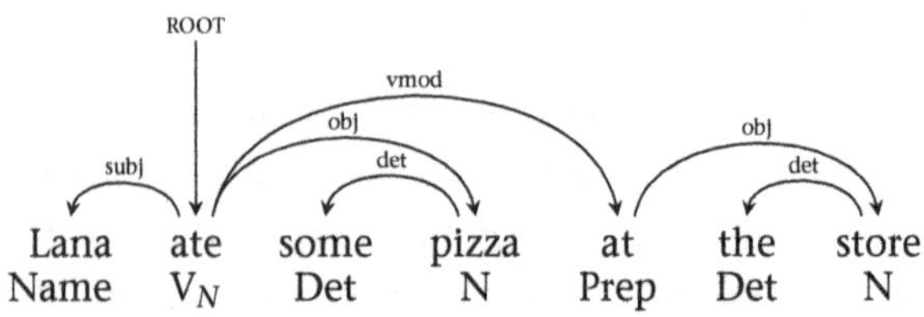

The meaning of a preposition is often a function applied to some arguments (the noun and the head that it connects to). For example, the word *in* in *the man in the room* describes the man's position relative to the room. Sometimes, a preposition like *of* just marks the function from a noun, as in *the picture of the dog*. Here, the function is *picture*, and *of* is a purely syntactic marker of the argument of *picture, the dog*. In this case, there is no semantics for the preposition *of*. Most prepositions other than *of* have a meaning associated with them.

For examples (56d)–(56e), the prepositions link a noun to a verb. In (56d), the preposition *in* states where the sleeping event took place—that is, where the girl slept. In the last example (56e), the preposition *at* links the noun *store* to the verb *ate*, indicating where the eating event occurred.

3.9 Auxiliary Verbs

A subclass of verbs are auxiliary verbs. There are at least six kinds of auxiliary verbs (+aux) in English:

1. modals, whose meanings are about possible events: *might, may, can, might, could, would, should, will, must*. Modals take an infinitive verb complement, as in (57a);
2. progressive copula *be*, which takes a present participle verb complement, as in (57b);
3. passive copula *be*, which takes a past participle verb complement, as in (57c);
4. copula *be*, which takes an adjective, noun phrase, or prepositional phrase, as in (57d);
5. forms of *have* which take a past-participle verb, as in (57e). (The passive and past-participle forms are the same in English.)
6. forms of *do*, which show up in interrogative environments for simple past and present tense, which take an infinitive verb complement, similar to modal verbs.

(57) a. Ollie might / may / can / might / could / would / should / will / must chase the squirrel.
b. Ollie is chasing the squirrel.
c. Ollie was chased by the squirrel.
d. Ollie was a squirrel.
e. Ollie has / had chased the squirrel.
f. Did Ollie chase the squirrel?

The verb following a modal auxiliary must be in infinitival (untensed) form, such as *chase* (and not *chased, chases, chasing*). Here is a possible dependency grammar rule for English modal auxiliaries that implements this idea:

$V_{+aux,modal}$: might, may, can, might, could, would, should, will, must

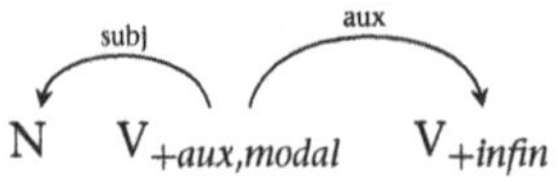

This results in the following dependency structure for (57a):

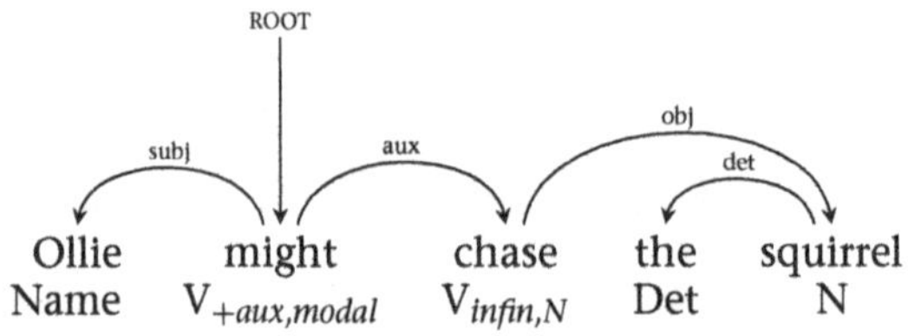

Auxiliary verbs can combine, as in (58). This shows that auxiliaries can take other auxiliaries to follow them, if they are in the appropriate form.

(58) a. Ollie might be chasing the squirrel.
  b. Ollie could have been chased by the squirrel.

The verb following *might* needs to be in infinitival form. This can be a main verb like *chase* in (57a) or a form of *be* in (58a) or a form of *have* in (58b). The verb following progressive *be* in (58a) is *chasing*, which is in present participle form. The verb following *have* in (58b) is in past-participle form *chased* as indicated by the argument structure requirements of these verbs given above.

3.9.1 Auxiliary Inversion in Interrogatives

An interesting feature of English auxiliary verbs is that they can often appear sentence-initially, in an interrogative sentence, as in (57f) above or (59):

(59) a. Might / May / Can / Might / Could / Would / Should / Will Ollie chase a squirrel?
  b. Is Ollie chasing a squirrel?
  c. Was Ollie chased by a squirrel?
  d. Was Ollie a squirrel?
  e. Has / Had Ollie chased a squirrel?

This is sometimes called "inversion," based on the idea that the declarative is the basic form, and the interrogative version inverts relative to the declarative. The analysis of the inversion structures that I use is close to the analysis proposed by Pollard and Sag (1994); Sag et al. (1999); Kim and Sag (2002); Abeillé and Rambow (2000); and Müller et al. (2021) in having a **lexical rule** that generates the interrogative inverted (+inv) form from an auxiliary form (+aux) (cf. the closely related underspecification approach of Sag et al. [2020]). A lexical rule has two components: an input and an output. It targets lexical entries, not rules of the grammar. The auxiliary inversion rule is the following:

(60) $V_{+aux} \Rightarrow V_{+aux,+inv}$
"If a verb is +aux, then there is an auxiliary which is +inv"

All +inv forms have the subject as the first rightward requirement instead of the leftward requirement. The +inv structures that are generated by this rule from the +aux modals are given below:

$V_{+aux,modal,-inv}$: might, may, can, might, could, would, should, will, must

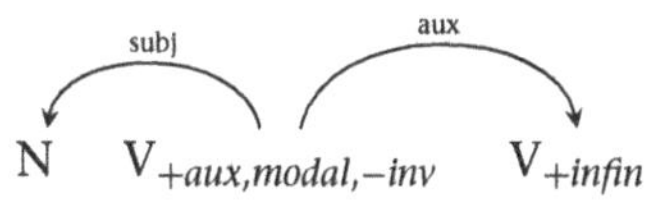

$V_{+aux,modal,+inv}$: might, may, can, might, could, would, should, will, must

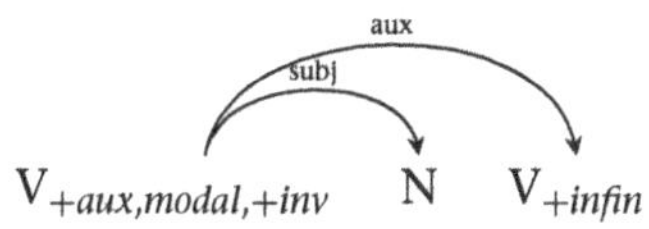

These rules can be used to generate dependency structures for (157a) and (158a):

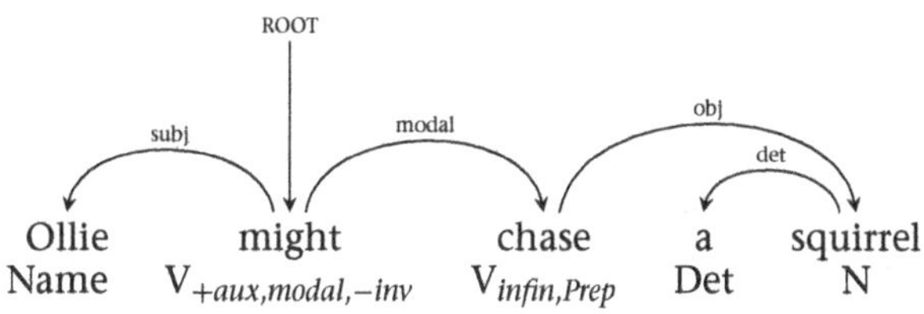

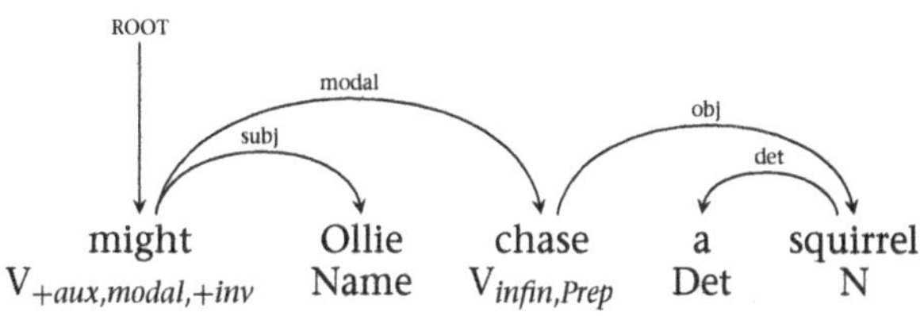

The inversion rule applies to all forms of copula *be*, because copula forms are auxiliaries, as in (61):[10]

(61) a. Ollie is a squirrel.
b. Is Ollie a squirrel?
c. Ollie is happy.
d. Is Ollie happy?
e. Ollie is on the house.
f. Is Ollie on the house?

$V_{be,-inv}$: is, are, was, were

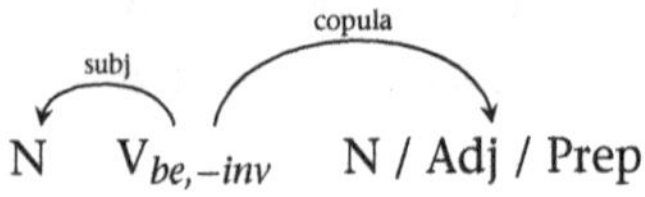

$V_{be,+inv}$: is, are, was, were

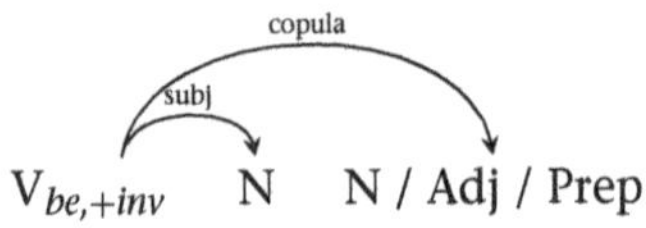

3.9.2 The Lexical Rule Analysis vs. the "Movement" Analysis of Auxiliary Inversion

The auxiliary inversion form generated from the declarative (non-inverted) lexical entry is just one example of a lexical rule that generates lexical items from a lexical item. I will discuss other instances later: the passive rule and filler-gap rules.

In this case, the lexical rule applies to most but not all auxiliary verbs: It depends on whether people use the particular word in the inverted form. If people don't use the auxiliary form in its inverted form, then the rule has not (yet) applied in the English dialect that is spoken. To avoid applying this rule, it is enough to specify some auxiliaries with –inv, like *ought* or *better*. For example, the auxiliary *ought* is somewhat rare in American English, and is used only in the declarative, not the interrogative, and hence is specified with –inv, so that the rule does not apply:[11]

(62) a. Ollie ought to go.
b. * Ought Ollie to go?
c. Ollie better go.
d. * Better Ollie go?

And some auxiliary forms are only possible in the inverted form, like first person-singular *aren't*:

(63) a. Aren't I invited to the party?
   b. * I aren't invited to the party?

So a verb like aren't is listed as +inv in its lexical entry for first person singular. (The other forms of *aren't*—second person singular and all the plural forms—are possible in both the declarative and inverted forms, so the rule applies to them.)

An alternative to the lexical rule analysis of auxiliary inversion is Chomsky's movement analysis (Chomsky, 1957, 1965). In this approach, there is a general rule of "movement" such that certain words and phrases can move elsewhere from where they are generated by the basic rules. The declarative rule is taken as the basic rule in the case of auxiliary movement, such that the auxiliary verb moves to the front of the sentence to form the interrogative.

There are several reasons to prefer the lexical rule analysis of auxiliaries to the movement analysis. The biggest advantage of the lexical rule analysis is that it is learnable. According to the dependency grammar analysis of a language, the words that you hear are the only elements that need to be structured. In contrast, according to a movement theory, the words that we hear are only the surface of what we need to structure: We also have to figure out where these words may have moved from in a deeper structure. This leads to a learning problem that Chomsky has argued makes the system literally impossible to learn (Chomsky, 1971). Chomsky has suggested then that aspects of the auxiliary system (among other complex components of grammar) must be innate, part of a *universal grammar*. Under the lexical rule hypothesis, there is no such concern: The learner can learn the grammar based purely on exposure with the sentences in the language.

A further advantage of the lexical rule hypothesis is that it is highly data-driven: People only make generalizations based on what other people say. So the fact that not all auxiliary verbs are possible in declarative and interrogative versions is not a problem for the lexical rule analysis: people only posit a lexical rule if the usage warrants it. In contrast, it is difficult to have a movement analysis that applies to only some auxiliary verbs. There has to be some constraint on what auxiliaries can move. The auxiliary *ought* in (62b) is one example of an auxiliary that is only possible in the declarative, and does not appear in the interrogative for US and Canadian speakers. There are several other such examples that appear only in the declarative or only the interrogative. While usage might seem to be an obvious solution to this problem, movement theories have traditionally scorned such information (although I am not sure why). I discuss the above and other issues with the movement theory in chapter 8.

3.10 Grammatical Complexity/Simplicity: The Grammar Is a Compressed Representation of Word Combinations

There are two useful properties of the grammar that we have written thus far: (1) It generates many more sentences than we started with in our corpus; and (2) it doesn't generate most possible sequences of the lexical items in our lexicon. Assuming that the generalizations that the grammar provides are correct, this simple grammar is *compressing* the representation of language greatly from just listing the possible sentences, because the grammar is relatively small compared to the language that it generates.

The idea of compression is general in science: We want to find laws to compress/explain the data we see. A way to formalize this idea comes from algorithmic information theory (an extension of Shannon's [1948] information theory: Kolmogorov complexity [Kolmogorov, 1963]). The Kolmogorov complexity of a text is the length of the shortest computer program that produces the text as output, in some predefined programming language. The Kolmogorov complexity is a measure of the computational resources that are needed to specify the text. More recent applications of Kolmogorov complexity to language are provided by Chater and Vitányi (2003, 2007) and Hsu et al. (2011).

One measure of the complexity (or inverse simplicity) of a grammar is the number of rules (e.g., Perfors et al., 2013; Hsu et al., 2011). Another more fine-grained measure is the total number of symbols in the rule set. The total here in our dependency grammar thus far is just seven, but this hides the fact that there are two kinds of determiners (Det_{sing}, Det_{plu}), and five kinds of N ($N_{name,sing}$, $N_{count,sing}$, $N_{count,plu}$, $N_{pronoun,sing}$, $N_{pronoun,plu}$), and many kinds of V.

subj (num)

Rule 1: N V_0

subj (num) obj

Rule 2: N V_N N

det (num)

Rule 3: Det $N_{count,mass}$

If we expand out the types of nouns and determiners, we end up with two rules for the determiner rule, five for the intransitive verb rule, and twenty-five for the transitive rule (five for each N in each position). Even expanded like this, we still have only 2 rules $*$ 2 symbols + 2 rules $*$ 5 symbols + 3 symbols $*$ 25 rules = 89 symbols.

The complexity of the language associated with a grammar is the complexity of the grammar together with complexity of the lexicon for the language: the sum of the number of symbols in the grammar and number of words in the lexicon. For the lexicon, we started with nine categories of words—$N_{name,sing}$, $N_{count,sing}$, $N_{count,plu}$, $N_{pronoun,sing}$, $N_{pronoun,plu}$, Det_{sing}, Det_{plu}, V_N, V_0—and three dependency expansion rules (along with the notion of agreement in each of the rules) to generate our corpus of ten simple sentences. Let's suppose that we have ten words in each of the $N_{name,sing}$, $N_{count,sing}$, $N_{count,plu}$, V_N, V_0 categories (the open-class categories), and five in each of the Det and $N_{pronoun}$ categories, for a total of sixty words, just a few more words than what we currently have.

The complexity of the language generated by the grammar with the lexicon above is therefore 89 rule symbols + 60 words. It turns out that this lexicon and grammar can generate 122,100 distinct sentences. In particular, there are 110 kinds of noun phrases: 10 Names $+10*5$ Singular Count Nouns $+10*5$ Plural Count Nouns. There are $110*10=$ 1,100 intransitive verb sentences $+110*10*110$ transitive verb sentences. This is a ratio of 122,100 / 159 = 768 sentences generated for every symbol stored. This is the point of a grammar for human language: compression.

Without changing the grammar at all, if we had 1,000 singular names in our lexicon, 1,000 singular count nouns, 1,000 plural count nouns, 10 determiners, 100 intransitive verbs, and 100 transitive verbs (3,210 words, closer to what English speakers actually know, but still only a fraction of the real lexicon) then we can generate 441 billion sentences. Now the compression ratio is even better: We have 89 rule symbols + 3,210 words to generate 441 billion sentences; 134 million to 1 ratio of sentences generated to symbols stored.

Some of the sentences that are generated by our grammar other than those in (42) are sentences like:

(64) a. Lana ate a pizza.
b. Lana chased a squirrel.
c. Lana ignored Allan.
d. A squirrel kicked a pizza.
e. A squirrel ate a pizza.
f. A squirrel kicked the neighbors.
g. A squirrel kicked a squirrel.

Many of these sentences are implausible, describing events that are unlikely to happen in the world, such as:

(65) a. Some rock liked Allan.
b. A dessert slept.
c. The squirrel ignored Francine.

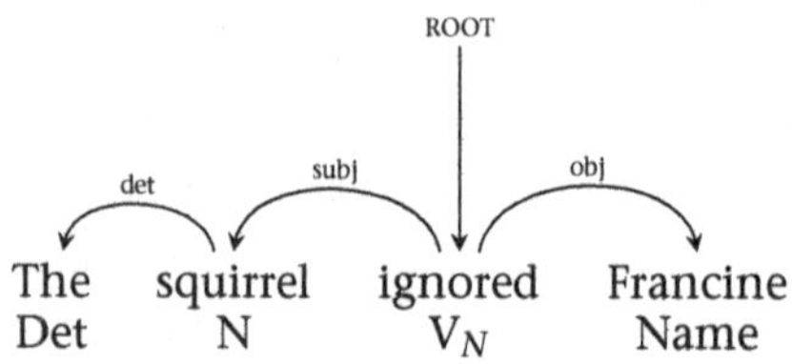

Linguists going back to Chomsky (1957) have argued that it's good that our grammar generates these implausible sentences: These are things that we might like to say, in some possible world. The "badness" (unacceptability) of these sentences seems to be of a different kind of badness than strings that our grammar doesn't generate, like:

(66) a. ∗ Liked Allan rock some.
b. ∗ Pizza neighbors squirrel.
c. ∗ Ate squirrel Lana Allan.

Chomsky's (1957) famous example of an implausible sentence that follows the rules of English is:

(67) Colorless green ideas sleep furiously.

This sequence is generated by an English grammar, although it doesn't really make sense. Chomsky contrasted that example with (68):

(68) ∗ Furiously sleep ideas green colorless.

(68) doesn't conform to the word order rules of English. See section 2.1 for more discussion of the distinction between grammaticality and acceptability, and the proposed distinction between competence and performance.

3.10.1 Compression as an Argument for Headedness Direction

We can sometimes see evidence for a particular headedness direction among head-dependency pairs, in the form of a more compressed grammar. For example, consider the dependency link between an auxiliary verb and a main verb, such as discussed above in section 3.9. While it is clear that there is tight relationship between the auxiliary verb and the main verb, the direction of this link is not obvious a priori. One argument that the head is the auxiliary verb is provided by compression: The set of dependency links to be stored in the lexicon is much smaller when the auxiliary is the head.

This follows from the assumption that what we store in the lexicon is a head together with all its likely dependents (as opposed to the heads that a word can depend on). Most tensed auxiliary verbs in English have two possible argument structures: One for declarative, and one for interrogative word order. There are only about ten such auxiliary verbs in English, so if the auxiliary is the head, then we need to have $2 * 10$ argument structures represented in the lexicon. If, on the other hand, the main verb is the head and the auxiliary verb is the dependent, then we need to represent the two possible argument structures for dependent auxiliary verbs on every main verb in our lexicon, which is several thousand verbs. This results in worse compression. Hence, the more compressed representation is one where the auxiliary verb is the head and the main verb is the dependent.

3.11 More Verbal Argument Structures

All words have argument structures. The argument structure of many nouns—such as names—is empty: We don't need other words to complete them. But singular count nouns need a determiner to the left. And nominalizations of verbs have argument structures to follow. For example, a noun like *destruction* has a similar argument structure as its corresponding verb *destroy*:

V_N: destroy

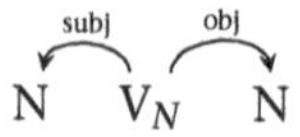

$N_{prep(of)}$: destruction

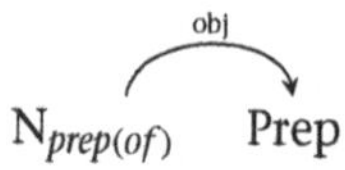

And a preposition has an argument structure consisting of a dependent noun:

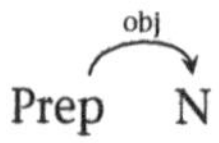

Verbs have the most variable argument structures, because they correspond to states and actions in the world, which can be variable in the types of functions that they indicate. We have divided the verbs in our little corpus into two categories, because we want our grammar to generate all and only the sentences in the English extension of the corpus. If we had a single category for all verbs—rather than V_N and V_0—with all of the argument structures for such a verb, then we would allow strings like:

(69) a. ∗ Lana chased.
b. ∗ Lana ignored.
c. ∗ A squirrel kicked.
d. ∗ A squirrel slept a pizza.

We probably don't want our grammar to generate these sentences, because these verbs don't really fit in these scenarios. The verb *slept* only needs a noun before it (the subject noun): Such a verb is often referred to as being **intransitive** when it has this property. Verbs like *chased* and *ate* also need to have a noun following them (corresponding to the patient of the action in these cases) and are consequently referred to as being **transitive**. There are many classes of verbal argument structures in every language. Indeed, there can be as many as four arguments for English verbs, each with a different type (sometimes nouns, prepositions, and subordinate clauses, initiated by a subordinator). The subject noun always comes first, before the verb. And then there can be zero, one, two, or even three dependents following the verb, of different syntactic types.

Here, we use subscripts on the verbal category labels to indicate each verbal argument structure. We exemplify four here: $V_{N,N}$, $V_{N,prep(to)}$, $V_{N,prep(loc)}$, and V_{Comp}. The verb *gave* is sometimes called **ditransitive**: It can take two nouns following the verb, as in *Lana gave the dog a stick*. Here, the noun *dog* is the recipient of *gave*, and the object or patient of *gave* is the noun *stick*. The first post-verbal noun for ditransitive verbs is sometimes called its indirect object.

$V_{N,N}$: give, send

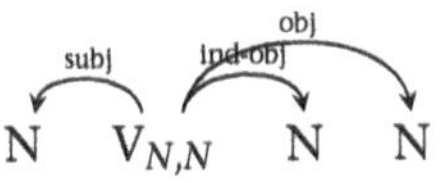

(70) a. Lana gave the dog a stick.
b. Francine sent the boy a pizza.

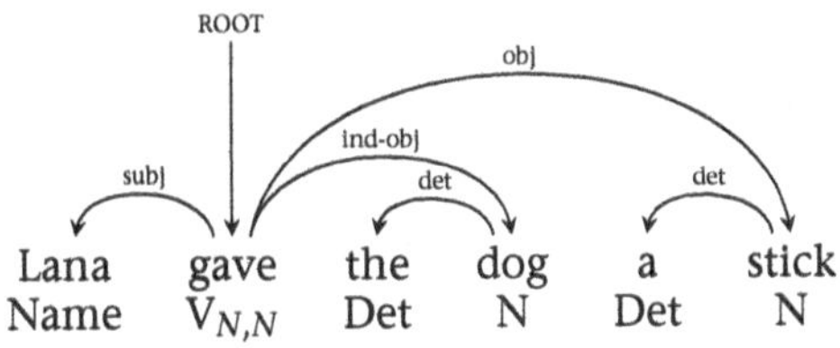

The verbs *gave* and *sent* have another argument structure: a direct object noun, followed by a prepositional phrase indirect object, initiated by *to*:

$V_{N,prep(to)}$: give, send, donate

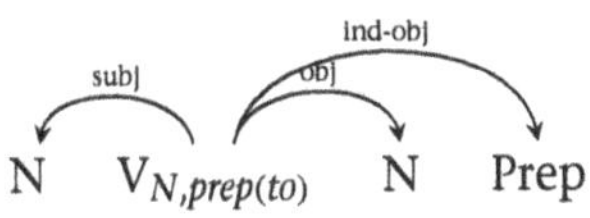

(71) a. Lana gave a stick to the dog.
b. Francine sent a pizza to the boy.
c. Allan donated some money to the charity.

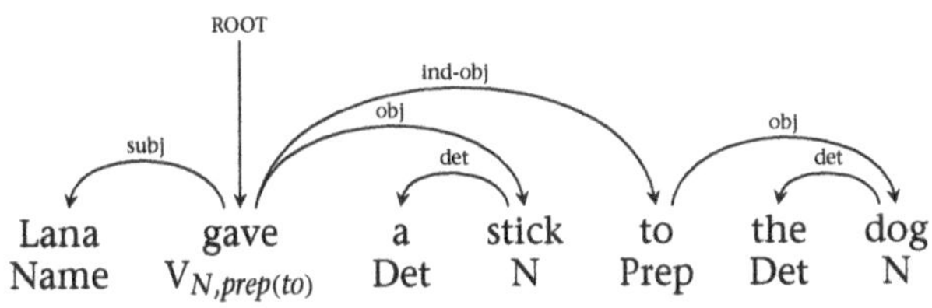

Consequently there are two ways to say the same thing in English:

(72) a. $N_{subject}$ gave N_{object} to $N_{ind-obj}$: Lana gave a stick to the dog.
b. $N_{subject}$ gave $N_{ind-obj}$ N_{object}: Lana gave the dog a stick.

This is the English *dative* alternation, which may be generated using another lexical rule, where a verb taking two nouns ($V_{N,N}$) can generate a verb taking a noun and a prepositional phrase headed by *to* ($V_{N,prep(to)}$). All languages have many ways of conveying the same meaning. This is presumably because of language production pressures: We may want to convey a particular event, and we want to be able to start talking with whatever NP is most salient in our memory at the time. So if I am already talking about the recipient NP *the dog*, then I might say (72b); otherwise I might say (72a). The passive construction is another syntactic alternation, discussed below in section 3.13. See chapter 10 for discussion of other syntactic alternations.

Among the three verbs given as examples of transitive + prepositional phrase recipient, only two of them—*give* and *send*—can also be used as ditransitive verbs. The third, *donate*, does not typically alternate in this way. That is, it is currently not not good to say the following (but a reader points out that this might be changing):

(73) * Allan donated the charity some money.

This shows that verbs that seem to have very similar meanings (like *give* and *donate*) sometimes have seemingly unpredictable usage preferences in their syntax.

Like *give*, the verbs *put* and *place* also take a noun and a preposition[12] as arguments:

$V_{N,Prep(loc)}$: put, place

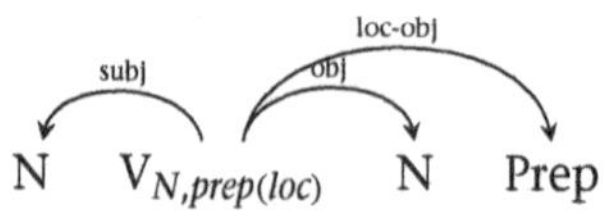

(74) a. Lana put the dog into the house.
b. Francine placed the candle on the table.

The type of preposition required by *put* and *place* is different from that of *give* and *send*, however. The PP that *put* and *place* requires is one that could be a location, like one initiated by *in, into, on, onto*, or *beside* (among others).

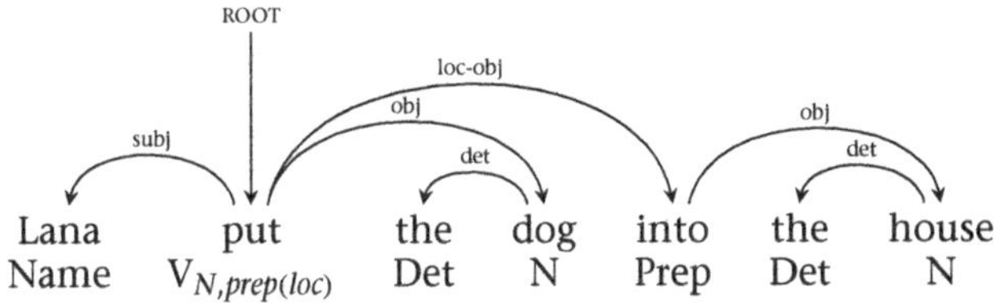

3.12 Complement Clauses

Many verbs can take whole clauses as their arguments. These are sometimes called **sentence-complements** (S-complements) in the psycholinguistics literature, or **complement clauses** in the syntax literature.
V_{Comp}: said, thought, believed

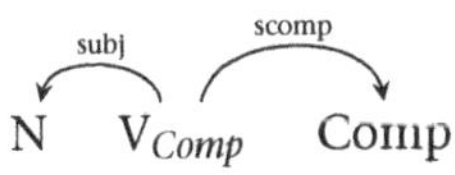

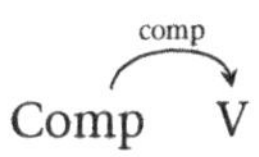

(75) a. Lana said that Francine ate the pizza.
b. Francine believed that Allan liked the pizza.

The verbs *said, thought,* and *believed* all can take a whole embedded sentence as their argument. The embedded clause is initiated with the word *that,* which is referred to as a **subordinator** or **complementizer.**[13] I notate this category as **Comp** (short for complementizer). A verb like *said* or *believed* takes a subordinator following it; and a subordinator takes a tensed verb following it.

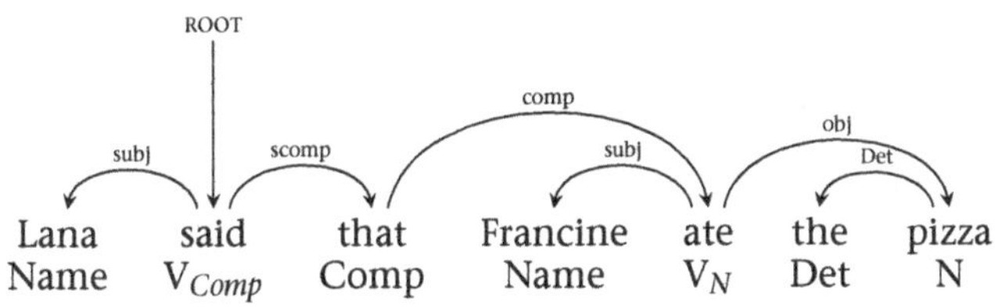

We can see other locations where the embedded clause marker comes with the clause, such as in clause initial positions, where an embedded sentence can be the subject of a verb:

(76) That Francine ate the pizza bothered Lana.

In English, the subordinator can sometimes be left out, without changing the meaning. So we can say:

(77) a. Lana said Francine ate the pizza.
b. Francine believed Allan liked the pizza.

The sentences without the subordinator mean the same thing as the sentences with the lexical subordinator *that* above. One way to treat these is by a lexical rule where a verb that takes a complement clause can simply take a finite verb:

(78) $V_{Comp} \Rightarrow V_{V+finite}$
"A verb that takes a subordinate clause can instead take a finite verb (without the subordinator)"

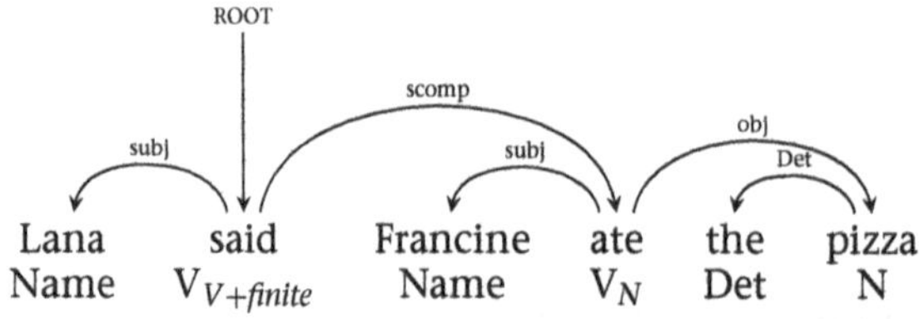

An alternative view is that there is an empty subordinator in these cases. I opt for a theory without such empty elements.

Evidence for this theory is provided by dependency length minimization—to be discussed in detail in the following chapter—whereby people have less difficulty in producing and comprehending structures with shorter distance connections between words. Hawkins (2001) and Jaeger (2010) show that the longer the distance between the main verb and the embedded verb, the more likely that the word *that* is produced:

(79) a. I realized with sadness that he had done it.
b. I realized with sadness he had done it.

There are two post-verbal dependents of *realized* in (79) and (79a), as shown below.

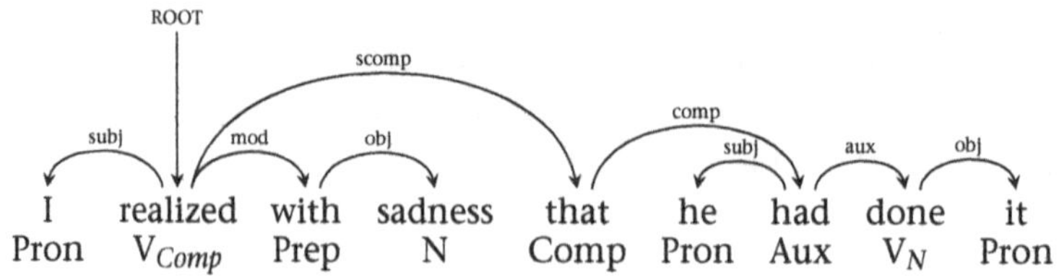

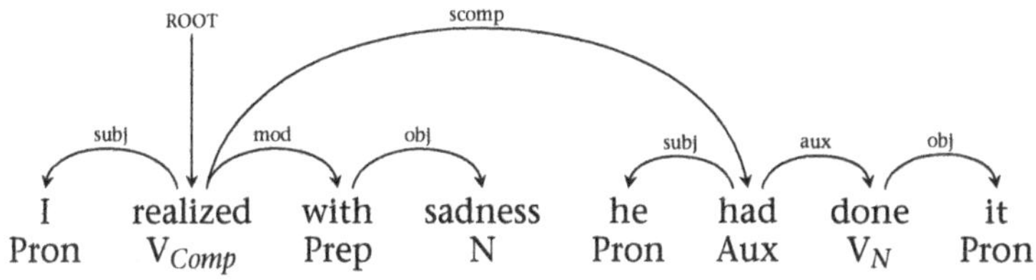

As the connection to the embedded verb gets longer, there is a greater probability of inserting *that*, possibly in order to cut the dependency distance down between the two verbs: (a) a connection between the first verb and *that* and (b) a connection between *that* and the embedded verb. This explanation only makes sense if there is a different argument structure associated with the embedded clause that has no complementizer. Hence I adopt this analysis.

3.13 The Passive Construction

Most verbs that take an object in the active voice can appear in the passive voice, where the noun that was the object in the active is now the subject, and the subject of the active is now an optional by-phrase modifier:

(80) a. Ollie chased the squirrel.
b. Ollie gave a nut to the squirrel.

(81) a. The squirrel was chased by Ollie.
b. A nut was given to the squirrel by Ollie.

One account of these phenomena is a lexical rule (Bresnan, 1982; Flickinger, 1987; Meurers, 2001; Müller, 2003; Müller et al., 2021; Müller, 2023), such as:

(82) $V_N \Rightarrow V_{prep(by),+passive}$

Here are the active versions of the verbs *chased* and *gave* (–passive), and the corresponding +passive versions of each:

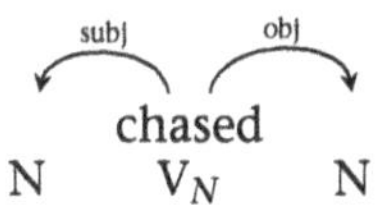

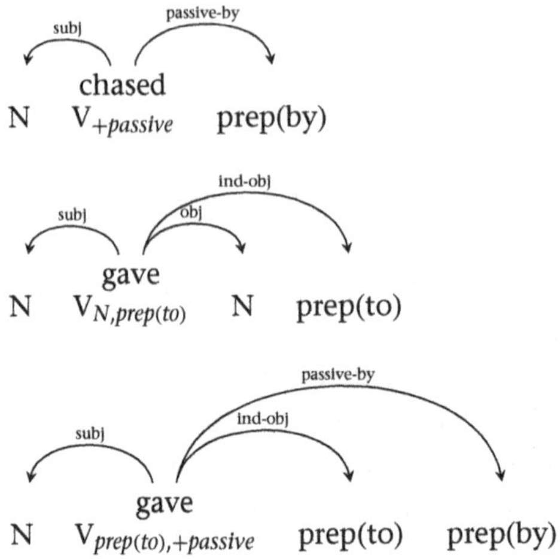

The lexical rule approach of passive contrasts with Chomsky's "movement" theory, where the object noun phrases can move to subject position, up to other grammatical constraints (see chapter 8). I prefer the lexical rule theory because not all transitive verbs can passivize. For example, *have* (own), *lack*, and *suit* each take an object noun phrase as object, but cannot passivize:

(83) a. Ollie had a squirrel.
  b. * A squirrel was had by Ollie.
  c. The house lacked a garage.
  d. * A garage was lacked by the house.
  e. The dress suited Ollie.
  f. * Ollie was suited by the dress.

This is easy to handle in the lexical rule approach: Some verbs may have –passive as one of their features, thus blocking the application of the passive rule. There also may be semantic constraints on whether the rule applies or not.

In contrast, it is difficult for a movement theory to selectively apply to some verbs and not all. The consequence for that approach has been to complicate the syntax of verbs which cannot passivize: It is proposed that they have a more complex syntax that doesn't allow passivization.

3.14 Abstract Constructions

In addition, sets of verbs may have a meaning and usage in common, such that the language includes an abstract construction, corresponding to this syntax and meaning. For example, the double-object construction is a generalization of verbs like *give* and *send*, which takes a preceding subject noun, and two following object nouns (Goldberg, 2006, 2019):

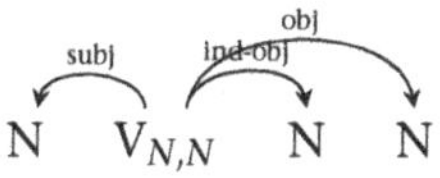

There is also a semantics associated with this construction, such that the indirect object noun gains possession of the object. For example, if you throw me a ball, then I get the ball. The point of the abstract construction is that it can be applied with existing words in novel ways. For example, suppose I am sitting opposite you and I want you pass me a small package at your feet, and you happen to have a hockey stick in your hands. I can ask you to:

(84) Please hockey-stick me that package.

And it's clear what I mean. The noun *hockey-stick* is obviously not often used as a double object verb, but I can do so in the right context. This is similar to the "vulture" example in chapter 1 from Goldberg (2019):

(9) Can we vulture your table?

Here, the more general construction is a simple transitive verb construction, such that the preverbal subject is the actor (causer) of the action, and the post-verbal object is the patient of the action.

3.15 The Syntax of Verbs Has Some Event Semantics

Human languages have a hierarchical structure in their syntax, such that words/morphemes can have head or dependent elements that are not immediately adjacent to them in sequence. Within syntax, there is lot of terminology associated with dependent elements and their positions, often within a clause. First, a *phrase* is a word plus all the words that depend on it, directly or indirectly. A *clause* is a phrase headed by a verb. The subject of a clause (or verb) is just the noun before the verb that depends on that verb for its meaning in a declarative clause. Consider (85) and its dependency structure:

(85) The girl with the dog went to the park.

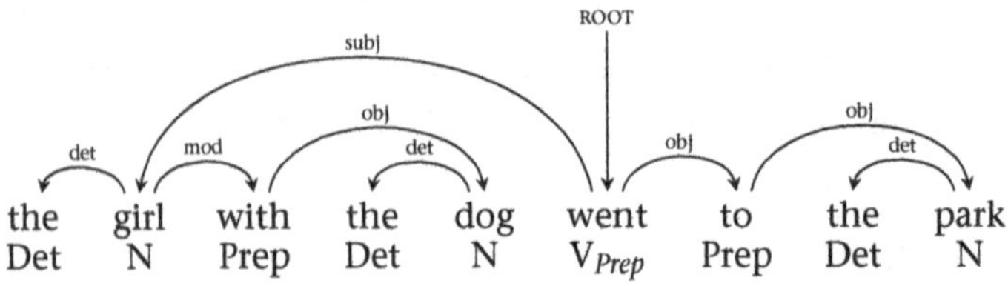

In this sentence, *girl* is the subject noun for the verb *went*. The word *dog* is not the subject of *went* even though it immediately precedes *went*: It is the end of the longer subject phrase headed by *girl*. The notion **subject** is a hierarchical one: the word that depends on the main verb, preceding the verb (in English), and showing agreement with the verb (objects do not agree with the verb in English). The expected dependents of the verb that follow it are often called the verb's **complements**.

The term *semantics* means *meaning*: the conventional meaning associated with a word or combination of words (syntax). There can be many meanings associated with the subject or objects, depending on the words and type of clause. Researchers often call the meanings associated with syntactic positions their **semantic roles** or **thematic roles** (Dowty, 1991). Consider the following examples, along with their syntactic role labels, and the semantic role labels that are often given to them:

The terms *agent* and *experiencer* are terms that are meant to be useful labels for slightly different meanings: An agent has some intention, whereas an experiencer need not intend to do the action in its verb. For example, in eating something, we always have to intend to eat. But we don't need to intend to sleep: It is something that we just do.

These labels are admittedly rough categories. Many researchers don't use such general categories, and prefer to use verb-specific labels like *eater* for the agent of *eat*; *sleeper* for the agent/experiencer of *sleep*, and so on. Always keep in mind that these are rough categories: Semantics is a difficult field, and we don't know what the right categories are, or even if it is useful to think of such categories in semantics.

3.16 Arguments vs. Modifiers

All of the dependents in the above table are **arguments** of their head verbs. A dependent is an argument of a verb if it indicates an essential part of the meaning of that verb. As a consequence, arguments of a verb are a part of

	Lana	*ate*	*the pizza*	
Syntax position	subject	verb	(direct) object	
Semantic role	agent		patient	
	The pizza	*was eaten*	*by Lana*	
Syntax position	subject	auxiliary + main-verb	preposition object	
Semantic role	patient		agent	
	Lana	*slept*		
Syntax position	subject	verb		
Semantic role	experiencer			
	The spider	*annoyed*	*Francine*	
Syntax position	subject	verb	object	
Semantic role	theme		experiencer	
	Lana	*feared*	*Francine*	
Syntax position	subject	verb	object	
Semantic role	theme		theme	
	Lana	*gave*	*the book*	*to Francine*
Syntax position	subject	verb	(direct) object	preposition object
Semantic role	agent		patient	recipient
	Lana	*gave*	*Francine*	*the book*
Syntax position	subject	verb	indirect object	(direct) object
Semantic role	agent		recipient	patient

the entry of the verb in the mental lexicon, while modifiers are not. The nouns *Lana* and *pizza* are arguments of the verb *ate* in (86a), because these indicate core aspects of the meaning of eating:

(86) a. Lana ate some pizza.
b. Lana got some pizza.
c. Lana gave the book to Francine.
d. Lana got some pizza at the store.
e. The girl slept in the bed.

The roles **agent** for *Lana*, and **patient** for *pizza*, are roles that not all verbs assign: These roles are special for a subclass of verbs like *eat*. Hence these are arguments. Similarly, the nouns *Lana* and *book*, and the preposition *to* are arguments of the verb *gave* in (86c), because these dependents are core parts of the meaning of giving. In (86d), the nouns *Lana* and *pizza* are arguments of the verb *ate*, but the preposition *at* is a **modifier** of *ate*, not an argument. This is because the location of where the eating takes place is not a core part of the meaning of eating. Rather, where an event takes place is a property of all verbs, and is not a core part of the meaning of the particular verb. Hence *at the store* is a modifier of *ate* in (86d). Finally, the preposition *in* is also a location where *slept* took place, so it is a modifier of *slept*.

Sometimes English arguments must be present in the syntax. *Modifiers* (or *adjuncts*) are always optional. We can see that *Lana got* (leaving off the object *some pizza*) in (86b) or *got some pizza* (leaving off the subject *Lana*) are not complete sentences in English. The fact that these dependents must be present in the syntax means that they are arguments of the verb *got*. In a dependency grammar, arguments and modifiers are notated in the same way, distinguished only by the labels on the arcs. It is only in phrase structure grammars that arguments and modifiers are sometimes represented differently. See section 7.6.1 for a discussion of how phrase structure grammars represent modifiers.

3.17 Coordination

A common English construction is *coordination*, most often using the conjunctions *and* or *or* as in (87):

(87) a. Mary and Andy are going to the party.
b. Mary or Andy is / are going to the party.
c. Lana was eating, walking, and running while at the park.
d. Lana walked toward the garden, beside the park and near the pond.
e. Lana walked toward and Ollie walked away from the garden.
f. Lana was in the garden and walking to the pond.

Most any sequence of words (including a single word) can coordinate with another sequence that has a similar argument structure. The resulting coordination is the category that matches as many features as possible of its coordinating elements (Sag et al., 1985). Hence a coordinated noun is a noun; a coordinated noun phrase is a noun phrase; a coordinated prepositional phrase is a prepositional phrase; a coordinated prepositional phrase and verbal element is of the same general type; and a coordinated verb plus arguments (traditionally called a verb phrase) is of the same type.[14] One analysis of such structures has the coordinator as the head, and its coordinate phrases the dependents (Sag et al., 1985) (cf. Hudson, 1990; Pickering and Barry, 1991, who propose a multi-headed analysis):

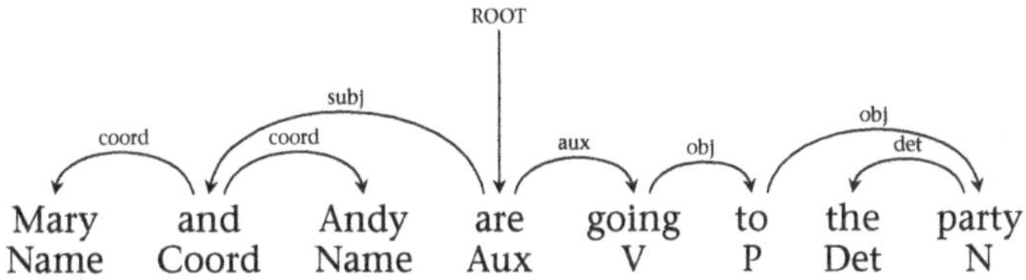

In this analysis, the Coord category matches any syntactic head; and all conjuncts (sometimes called "coordinands") agree with this type, including argument structures to the left and right that are being coordinated. In (87a), we have two names, which are both nouns, and hence they agree in type. A tensed verb (in this case auxiliary verb) will agree with plural for conjunctions, and either singular or plural for disjunctions. For example, either the singular or plural agreement is/are acceptable for (87b) and for the current sentence, for many speakers (Haskell and MacDonald, 2003).

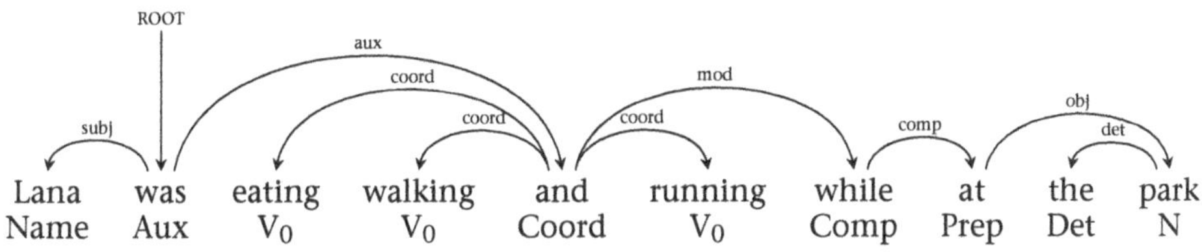

In (87c), the verbs *eating*, *walking*, and *running* all coordinate under the conjunction *and*. And similarly, in (87d), the prepositional phrases *toward the garden*, *beside the park*, and *near the pond* under the conjunction *and*.

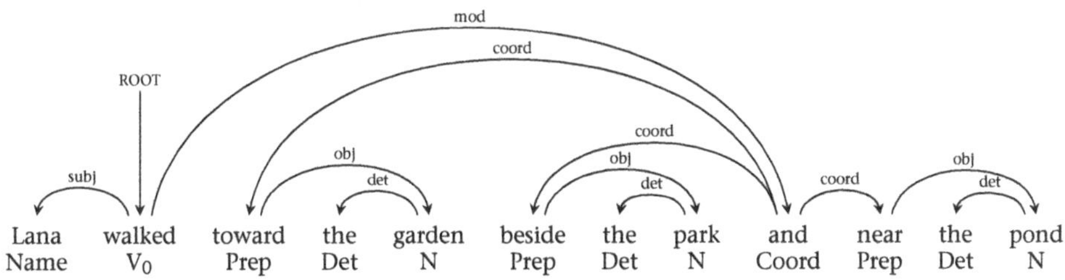

In (87e), the initial segment *Lana walked toward* coordinates with the similar segment *Ollie walked from*. (This happens to be called "Right Node Raising" because initially it was handled by rightward movement, in research under phrase structure grammar. See Chaves [2014]; Shiraïshi et al. [2019] for other data relevant to right node raising.)

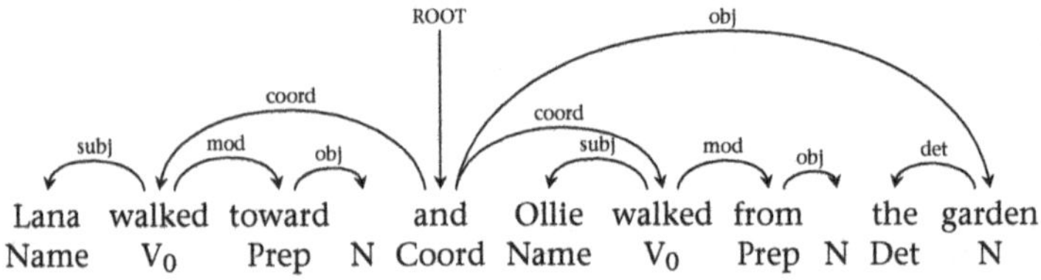

The verbs and their dependents are coordinated in this structure, with a missing N at the end of each. In order to implement this kind of analysis in dependency grammar, we need to pass features of the argument structures that are missing up to the dominating heads, so that they can be matched at the coordinator. One grammar formalism that implements such feature passing in phrase structure grammar is combinatory categorial grammar (CCG) (Steedman, 1996, 2001), discussed in section 7.5 of chapter 7.

In fact, any sequence can be coordinated with another sequence, if the argument structures are matched on the left and right. Some kinds of examples are actually complex to implement in the grammar that we have presented thus far, such as those in (88) (and they are even more difficult to implement in many phrase structure grammars; see chapter 7):

(88) a. Antonia ordered seven and paid for only three pizzas.
b. Mary kicked several larger and juggled a few smaller soccer balls.

A possible dependency structure for (88a) is provided below:

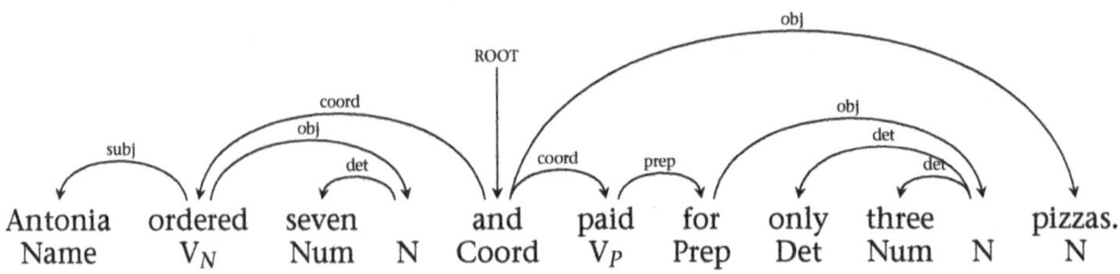

3.18 Lexical and Syntactic Ambiguity

Many words are ambiguous among multiple lexical entries. Common words will often have ten or more interpretations, some of which are related and others that seem quite different in meaning. Some of these will be within syntactic category (e.g., many senses of a verb, like *take*), and others will cross syntactic categories (e.g., most verbs are ambiguous as nouns, such as *report, talk,* and *leave*; *We report that he filed a report*).

A particular verb will often have many different argument structures. Among examples in our small starter corpus, the words *ate* and *walked* have both intransitive and transitive uses:

(89) a. Lana walked.
 b. Lana walked the dog.
 c. Lana ate the pizza.
 d. Lana ate.

The intransitive and transitive verbs have slightly different meanings in the different argument structures: *To walk* intransitively is just the normal sense of walking. But *to walk* something (transitively) means that the first noun has control over the object of the verb. *To eat* intransitively means something like "eat a meal" (e.g., not quite right for a snack), whereas one can eat anything, transitively.

Another common lexical argument structure ambiguity is between a noun object argument structure and a complement clause argument structure—for example, for *know* or *believe*:

(90) a. Lana believed Francine.
 b. Lana believed (that) Francine ate the pizza.

This lexical ambiguity leads to a temporary syntactic ambiguity after encountering *Lana believed Francine*. The comprehender might entertain either the noun phrase interpretation, or the unfinished subordinator one (which might continue *Lana believed Francine ate the pizza*). As discussed in section 2.2, people's initial interpretations are determined by a combination of all relevant factors: the lexical probability of each possibility (according to the comprehender's experience); the syntactic probability of the resulting structure; the meaning of the resulting language in the world; and how well the meaning fits with the current context (among possibly other factors).

A sequence of words often leads to syntactic ambiguity, which is often resolved by the current context. Sometimes there are two salient interpretations, one of which is funny, as in funny newspaper headlines:

(91) a. BRITISH LEFT WAFFLES ON FALKLAND ISLANDS
 b. RUMORS ABOUT NBA REFEREES GETTING UGLY

c. TWO SPIES SENTENCED TO LIFE IN MISSOURI
d. TORONTO LAW TO PROTECT SQUIRRELS HIT BY MAYOR
e. CLINTON WINS ON BUDGET, BUT MORE LIES AHEAD

Consider two possible interpretations of example (91a):

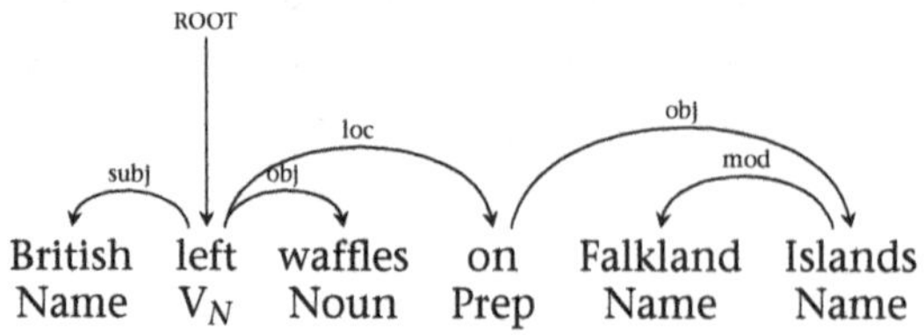

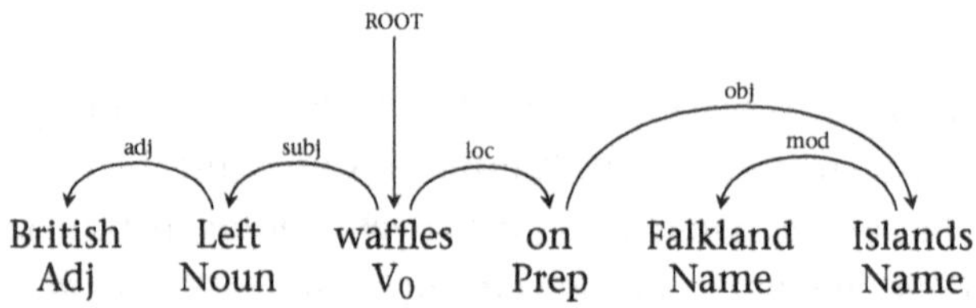

In the first dependency structure, the word *left* is analyzed as a transitive verb, with the noun *waffles* as its object. This meaning indicates that some salient British people left some waffles on the Falkland Islands, which is a strange event for a newspaper story. In the tree structure on the right (presumably the meaning that was intended), the subject noun phrase is *British Left* (i.e., a left-wing group of political leaders), and the sentence states that they—the British Left—are waffling on the topic of the Falkland Islands, referring to the war in 1982.

Example (91c) is a classic case of prepositional phrase attachment ambiguity:

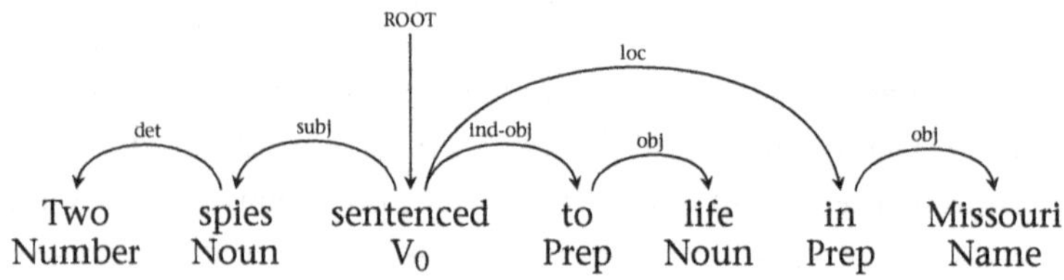

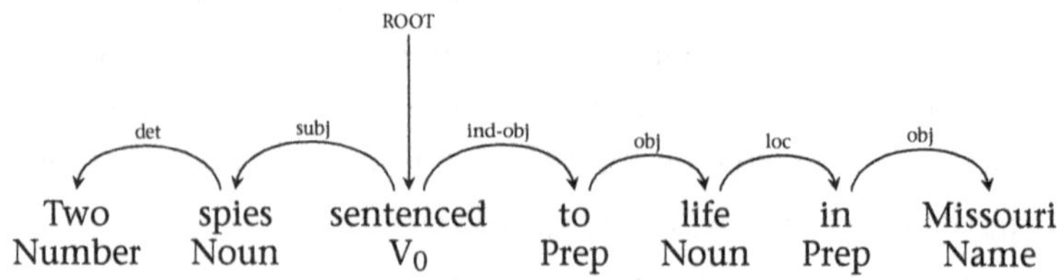

In the first dependency structure, the PP *in Missouri* connects to the verb *sentenced*, indicating that the sentencing event took place in Missouri. In this interpretation, there is no modifier for life, indicating that the sentencing is a life imprisonment sentence. This is the interpretation that was presumably intended. On the other hand, in the second structure, the PP *in Missouri* connects to *life*, indicating that the sentencing consists of life in Missouri. This is presumably not the intended interpretation. It's noticeable because it's funny, for snobs that think that a punishment might consist of living in Missouri.

Finally, consider two structures for headline (91d):

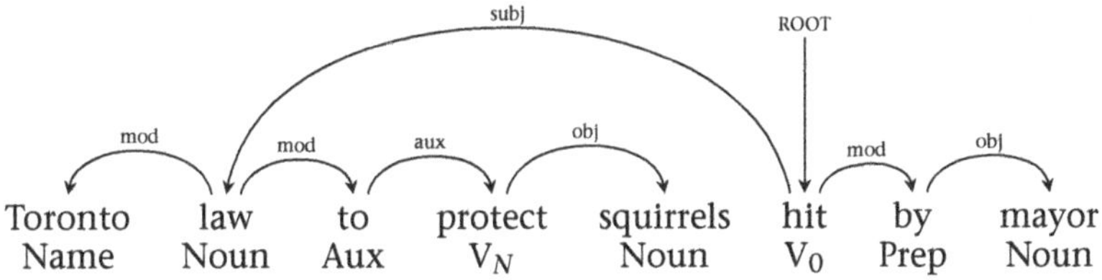

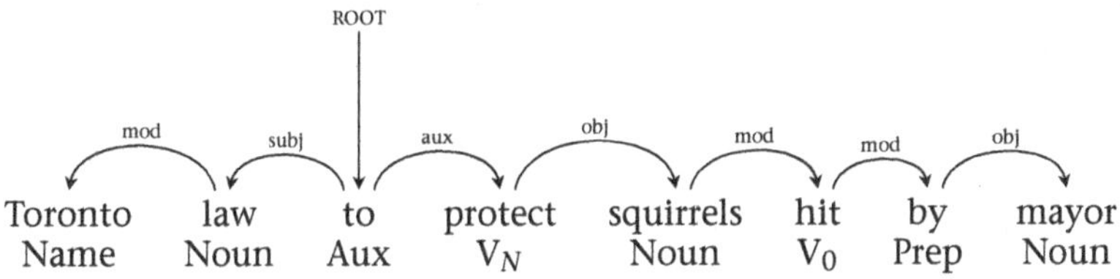

In the first structure, it is the Toronto law that is hit by the mayor. The second structure depicts a meaning where the law exists in order to protect some squirrels that have been hit by the mayor. This is obviously silly, but it makes for a funny headline.

3.19 Long-Distance Dependency Constructions

So far, we have focused on particular word types, and how they are distributed in simple clauses. English and all languages contain many other kinds of constructions that enable us to say more complicated things. One set of constructions that has been important in all theories of language is so-called **filler-gap constructions**, which allow long-distance dependencies. These are constructions that involve a displaced constituent—the "filler"—that appears in a position other than its canonical position in a declarative clause. Filler-gap constructions have been important in language research because of the potential complexity of producing and understanding long-distance connections, which has led to theories of why grammar looks the way that it does. Chapter 4 describes relevant data in detail with respect to dependency grammar explanations. Furthermore, filler-gap constructions have been important in the theoretical development of transformation-based theories, as discussed in chapter 8.

In a filler-gap construction, the canonical position of the filler in a declarative sentence is sometimes called the "gap" site, because some theories propose that there are empty elements ("gaps," "traces," or "copies") in the canonical position, mediating the long-distance dependency (Gazdar et al., 1985; Chomsky, 1965), and so on. I indicate this position with an underscore (__) in the examples below (although the analysis I offer below doesn't actually involve a "gap" in the structure). Such constructions include wh-questions, relative clauses, exclamatives, clefts, and topicalizations in English and many other languages. For example, the declarative form of a simple clause is provided in (92a), along with a wh-question version of this clause in (92b), where the fronted filler (*what*) is the object of the verb *buy*. A corresponding relative clause is provided in (92c), an exclamative in (92d), an it-cleft in (92e), and a topicalization structure in (92f):

(92) a. Declarative: Mary bought an apple.
b. Wh-question: What did Mary buy __?
c. Relative clause: I like the apple which Mary bought __.
d. Exclamative: What an apple Mary bought __!
e. It-cleft: It was Andrew that Mary met __.
f. Topicalization: The apple, Mary bought __.

The feature-based dependency grammar formalism I propose here imports the analyses from head-driven phrase structure grammar (Pollard and Sag, 1994; Sag et al., 1999), closely related to generalized phrase structure grammar (Gazdar et al., 1985), and to the tree-adjoining grammar (TAG) analysis (Vijay-Shanker, 1992; Vijay-Shanker and Schabes, 1992). In these analyses, there is a feature called SLASH that is associated with the noun filler (e.g., *what* in the wh-question in (92b)) and is passed down associated heads until it can be resolved by an argument structure below in the structure, where a noun is needed. This is a process that is called **feature inheritance**, which applies to certain features in the grammar, like SLASH features.

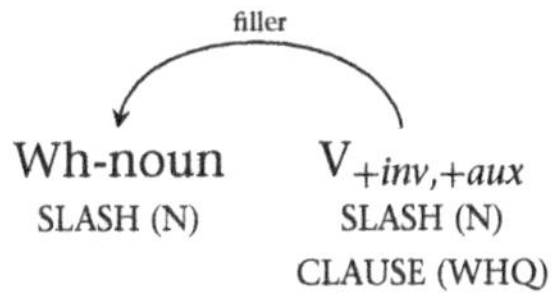

This rule can pass its SLASH feature onto a verb, which can then resolve this feature with one of its noun argument requirements, or it can pass the feature to further lower structures, where it will get resolved eventually.

One way to make this system work is to have a lexical rule (Sag and Fodor, 1994), such that if a word has a noun argument to the right (such as an object), we generate another lexical entry with a slashed version of this argument as a feature of the lexical entry.

(93) $V_N \Rightarrow V_{0,SLASH(N)}$.

So the transitive verbs *bought*, *buy*, *meet*, and *met* would have additional lexical entries, with a slashed object. I present the entries for *bought* and *buy* below:

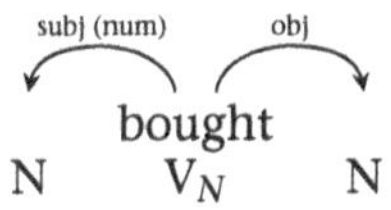

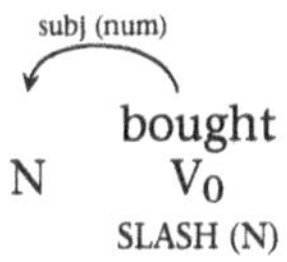

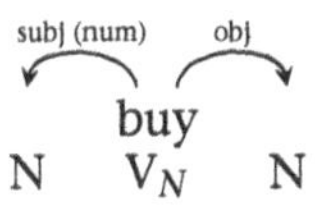

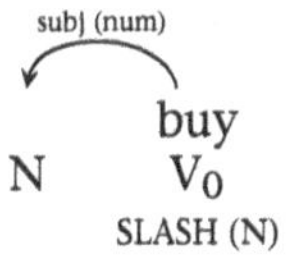

These lexical entries are generated automatically from the lexical rule in (93). For each noun argument in a lexical entry, a new lexical entry would be generated with the argument deleted from the argument structure, but with a SLASH feature of that argument. Additional lexical entries would also be generated for prepositions (which take noun arguments), because nouns can be fronted from prepositional phrases (95a), and for preposition arguments, which can also be fronted (95b).

(94) $P_N \Rightarrow P_{0,SLASH(N)}$

(95) a. Who did you give the book to?
b. To whom did you give the book?

I first present the declarative structure for *Mary bought an apple*, followed by the slash-representation for the wh-question *What did Mary buy?*. I represent the resolution of the slash feature with a red arc in the dependency structure, resolving back to the filler. (This is not a dependency arc of the same type as the others: This just shows how the slash-filler is resolved.)

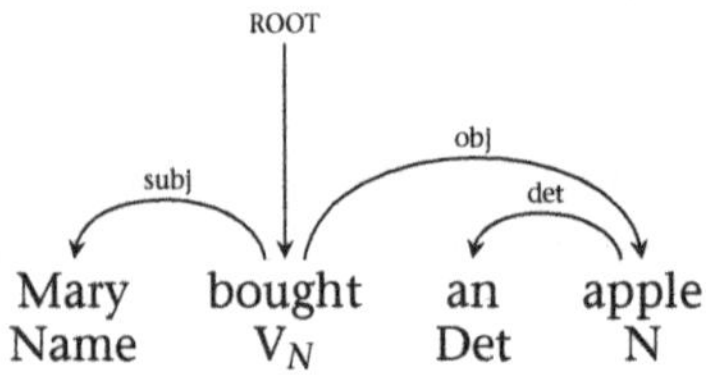

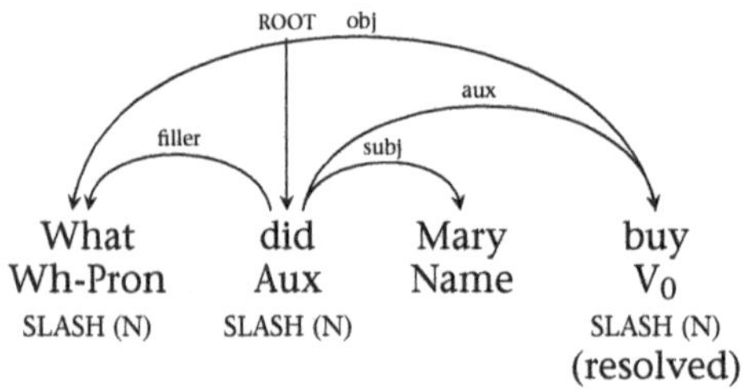

If the slash feature is not resolved, then it can be passed further down the tree, as for (96):

(96) Wh-question: What did Mary think that Lana bought ___?

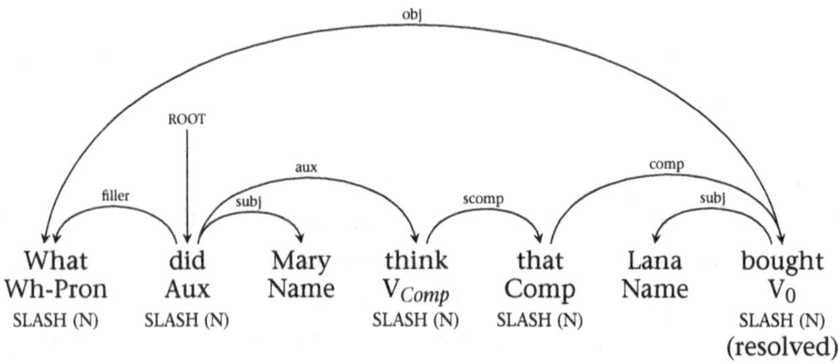

Note that in the slash dependency grammar, there is no empty element that completes the filler's requirement: This requirement is absorbed by the slash feature. I represent these connections using a direct arc (but it passes through the slash feature, down the tree).

Slash representations for (92c)–(92f) are provided below. In each of these, the red arc happens to represent two relations: the dependency arc between the positions and the resolution of the slash feature, which occurs at that verb.

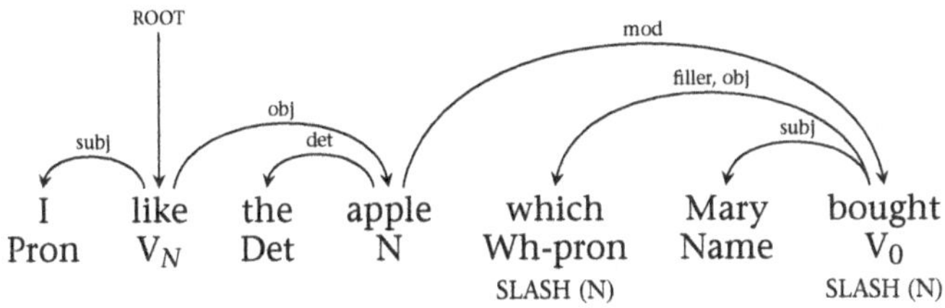

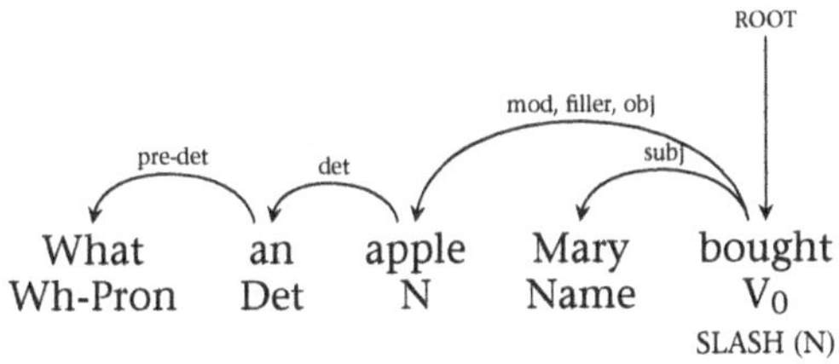

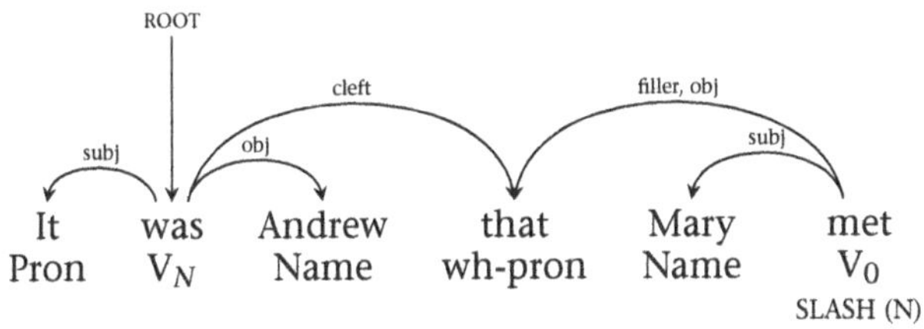

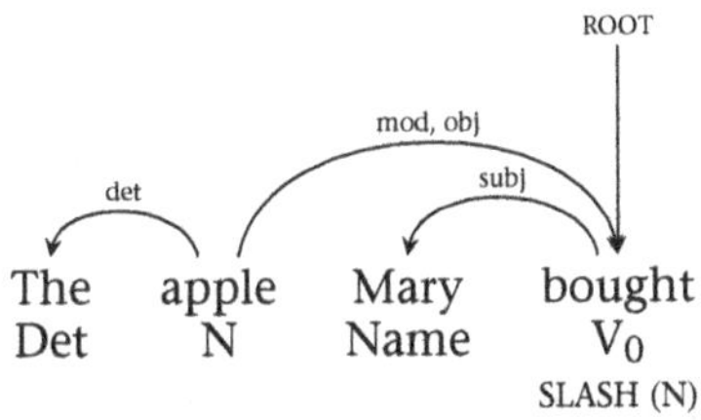

Psychologists interested in structural linguistic complexity have often focused on filler-gap dependencies in relative clauses, across languages (Yngve, 1960; Chomsky and Miller, 1963; Kimball, 1973; Gibson, 1991,

1998; Lewis, 1996; Lewis and Vasishth, 2005a). A relative clause is a clause that modifies a noun, where the noun takes the place of one of the normal noun positions in the clause. There are two kinds of relative clauses: restrictive and nonrestrictive. The meaning of a restrictive relative clause is to pick a subset—often a particular instance—from a set, identified by the head noun. A nonrestrictive relative clause just adds more information about the head noun, but doesn't pick it out of a set. For example, the restrictive relative clause *which Mary bought* in (92c) refers to a particular apple (the one that Mary bought) out of the set of apples (identified by the head noun *apple*). The filler element in an English relative clause can be a wh-pronoun like *who* or *which* (as in (92c)), or the subordinator *that* (as in *I like the apple that Mary bought*), or it can even be absent when it is a non-subject relative clause, as in *I like the apple Mary bought*. These structures are depicted below.

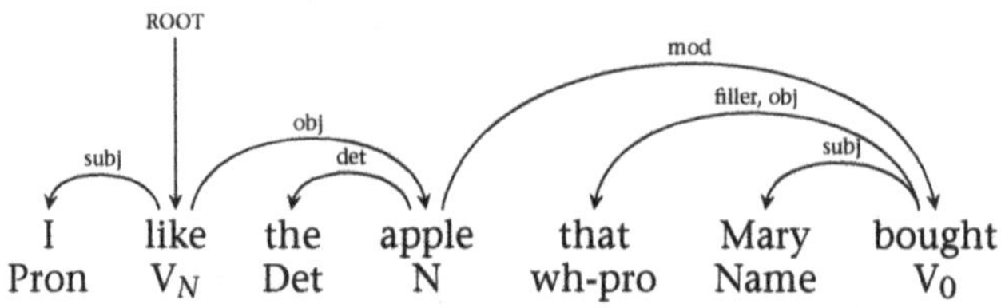

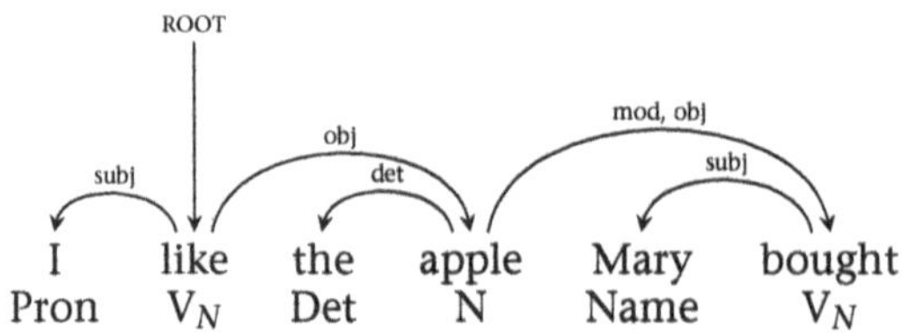

3.20 Summary

This chapter provided a general motivation for dependency structure—high mutual information between words—together with a characterization of many word categories (parts of speech) and their combinations in English. I then described argument structures of various word types in English, and I contrasted the lexical rule approach with the movement approach for several English phenomena, including auxiliary verbs, the passive construction, and long-distance dependency constructions. I will discuss the movement approach more in chapter 7.

4 Dependency Locality in Language Processing

So far, I have provided a dependency grammar analysis of some simple English sentences. The primary idea in dependency grammar is that words join together in a tree structure, to form the ways that we say arbitrary ideas in a human language. Because human languages are often spoken, the structures are linearized in time. That is, we have to say the words one at a time.[1] In comprehension, it is natural to assume that there may be some cost of connecting two elements together that are displaced over time: This is the dependency locality cost hypothesis (Gibson, 1998, 2000; Lewis and Vasishth, 2005b; Lewis, 1996). This is plausibly the case for both language comprehension, and in language production, as we are trying to form sentences. Recall that syntactic dependencies are plausibly just pairs of words with high mutual information, in information theoretic terms (Futrell, 2019; Futrell et al., 2020a). So the dependency locality hypothesis may actually follow from a more general information theoretic idea, the **information locality** hypothesis. Consequently, when I refer to dependency locality in the next couple of chapters, keep in mind that there may be a more general information theoretic motivation. I elaborate this idea a bit more in the final chapter, in section 10.5.

There is a long history of proposals of dependency locality in human languages, going back to Behaghel (1930, pp. 30–31), who proposed two laws relevant to locality in syntactic dependencies:

(97) a. Oberstes Gesetz ("highest law"): That which belongs together mentally is placed close together.

b. Gesetz der wachsenden Glieder ("law of growing constituents"): Of two sentence components, the shorter goes before the longer, when possible.

The law in (97a) is closest to the dependency locality idea. The law of growing constituents follows from dependency locality for head-initial languages, as will be discussed below. Other researchers who proposed similar ideas include Rijkhoff (1986), Hawkins (1990), Hudson (1995), and Ferrer-i-Cancho (2004). See Futrell et al. (2020b) for a good summary of relevant literature.

The current chapter explores evidence—primarily from English—for locality biases in language comprehension and production. In section 4.1, I first provide evidence that people prefer to produce materials with shorter dependency lengths compared to ones with longer dependency lengths, if there is a choice. Second, in section 4.2, I discuss cases of locality biases in language comprehension. Then in section 4.4, I provide evidence that suggests that there is a cost for making longer-distance connections when examining the reading times of unambiguous sentences. Section 4.5 then shows that complex embedded structures of various types can help us figure out how the locality metric works. Section 4.6.1 shows that counting words isn't sufficient as a locality metric; what probably matters more is the similarity of the materials in the intervening region to element that needs to integrate back. Section 4.7 discusses some recent brain-based evidence for locality costs in on-line English language processing.

4.1 Locality Biases in Language Production

Temperley (2007) provides many examples of types of dependency length minimization in English language production. Here, I summarize three cases that Temperley discusses. The first case is quite general: where a head has two or more dependents on the same side. The second case involves English subjects and objects, relying on the observation that noun phrases are usually head-initial; and the third is English quotations, relying on the flexibility of word order for the verb "said": It can come before or after the subject noun phrase (e.g., *said Jane* or *Jane said* are both possible).

4.1.1 Shorter Phrases Occur before Longer Phrases in English

If a word has multiple dependent constituents and there is a choice as to their ordering, the shorter one(s) are generally placed closer to the parent head. Temperley (2007) evaluates this prediction of dependency length minimization in a *Wall Street Journal* corpus that he had access to, and he found that when a verb has two post-modifiers, the length of the first was significantly shorter (average = 3.04 words) than the length of the second (average = 5.96 words) c.f. related discourse reasons for similar results (Arnold et al., 2000; Wasow, 1997, 2002).

For example, consider the two possible ways of ordering the post-verbal argument dependents of a verb like *threw*: the noun phrase *the documents* and the particle *away*:[2]

(98) a. Mary threw away the documents.
b. Mary threw the documents away.

Either way of phrasing the idea results in a structure that is easy to produce and understand. All dependencies are pretty local in each:

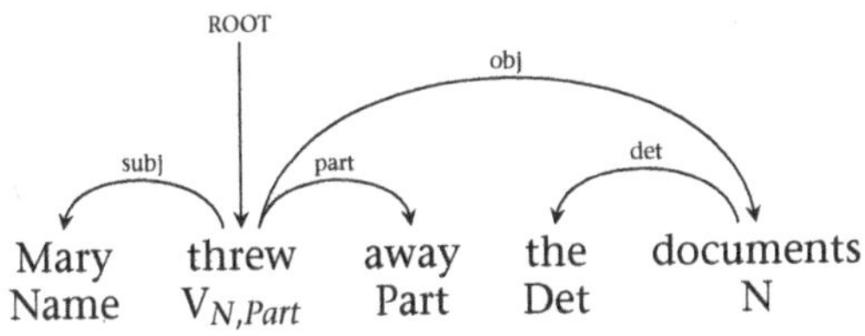

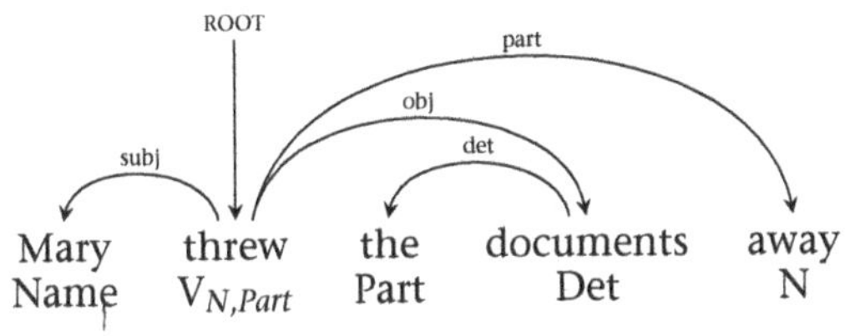

But when the object noun phrase is much longer—such as *the important documents that she brought home yesterday*—suddenly the order with the particle *away* first sounds much better:

(99) a. Mary threw away the important documents that she brought home yesterday.
b. Mary threw the important documents that she brought home yesterday away.

This is plausibly because the dependency lengths in the structure where *away* occurs second are much longer on average than when *away* is placed first. This difference is because *away* is short, whereas the second dependent of threw is long (*the important documents that she brought home yesterday*).

Thus, putting the short thing first means a pretty close connection to the second. But putting the long thing first means a long connection over to the second (*away* in this case).

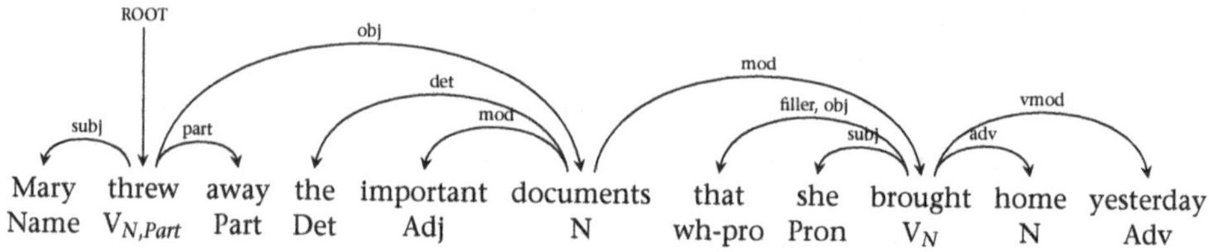

As shown below, the connection between *away* and *threw* in (99b) is long-distance, crossing eight words. Note that there is no ambiguity in where *away* might connect in the structure: The only word that allows *away* to connect to it is the verb *threw*. Thus the difficulty of processing (99b) is not because of a difficult ambiguity; it is probably due to the long distance of this connection.

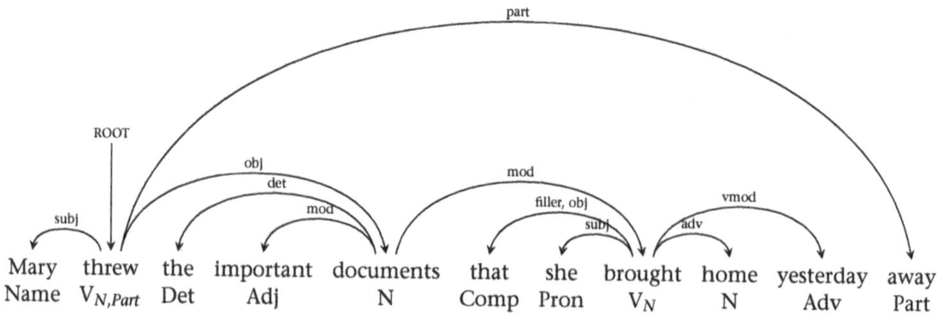

This preferred ordering seems to always be present when there is a choice between a short item and a long item, placed after the verb in any verb-initial language like English. Consider a second example in (100):

(100) a. Alice gave Susan the documents.
b. Alice gave the documents to Susan.
c. Alice gave Susan the very important documents that she brought home yesterday.
d. Alice gave the very important documents that she brought home yesterday to Susan.

As in (98a) vs. (98b), there is no obvious difference in complexity between (100a) and (100b), examples in which all dependencies are local:

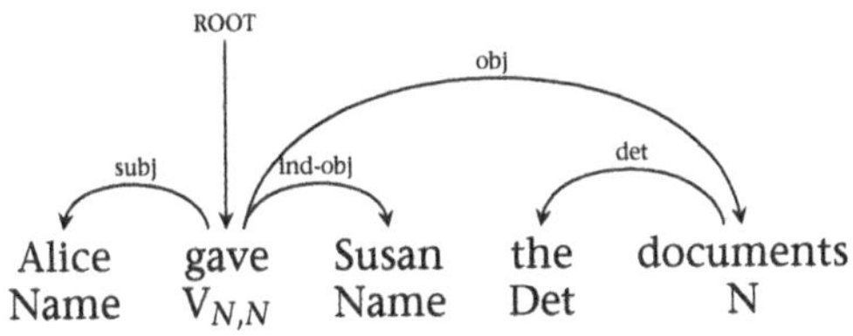

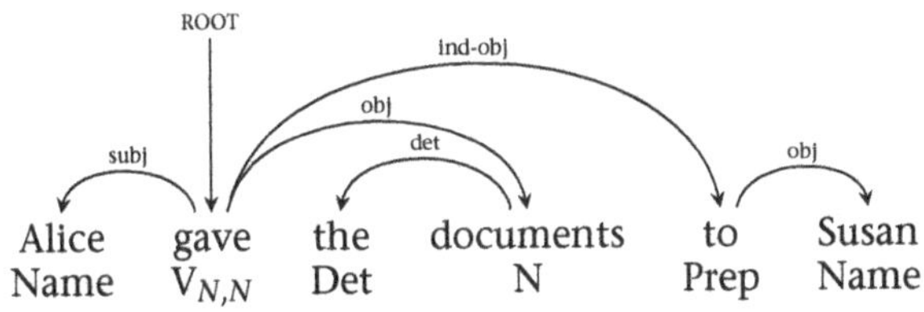

But (100d) sounds more awkward than (100c), plausibly because there is a long dependency between *gave* and *to* in (100d) that is not present in (100c):

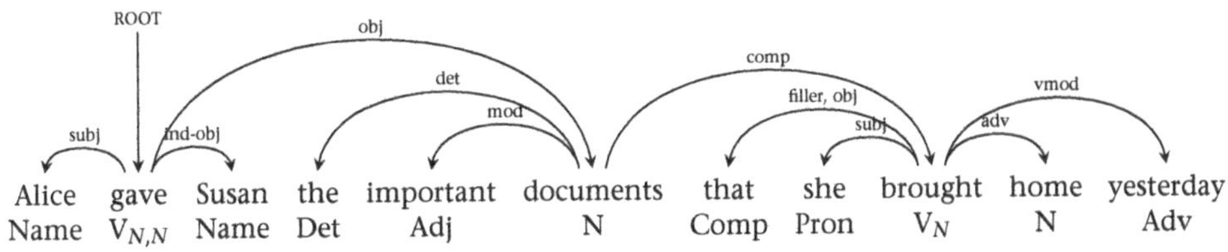

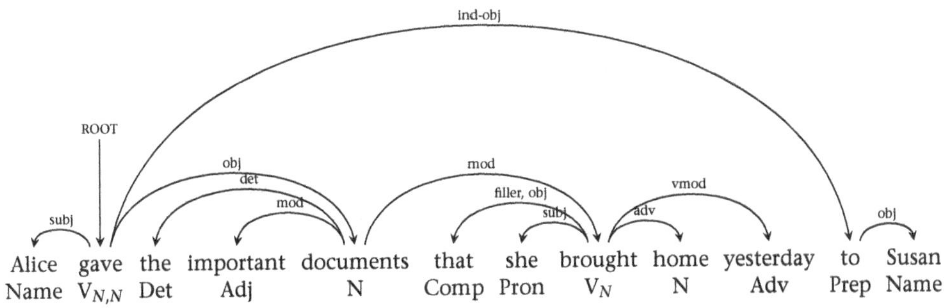

4.1.1.1 Dependency locality applies for two, three, or more dependents to the right. The dependency locality proposal is unaffected by how many dependents there are to the right (or left, in a head-final language): Dependency locality proposal always predicts that dependencies should be as short as possible, up to other constraints. Hawkins (2004) makes a proposal that is closely related to dependency locality—**early immediate constituents.** This proposal makes predictions that are roughly the same as dependency locality except when there are three or more dependents on the same side of a head.[3] In such cases, early immediate constituents predicts that all that matters is the distance from the head to the furthest dependent. This theory predicts no effects on dependency lengths in between. In contrast, dependency locality predicts that all dependencies should be as short as possible, no matter if they are the first, second, or third dependency of a head. Temperley (2007) tested these divergent predictions by looking at verbs with three dependents to the right in English corpora. Dependency locality predicts that the first dependency should be shorter than the second, whereas the early immediate constituents proposal predicts no differences in these cases, only for the dependent furthest from the head. Temperley (2007) found that the corpora supported the dependency locality hypothesis: The first dependent (an average of 2.98 words) was shorter than the second (3.65 words).

4.1.1.2 Head-first vs. head-final word order. The ordering that ends up keeping dependency lengths short in a head-first language like English is short-before-long. But a head-final language like Japanese or Korean, the opposite word order is predicted to be preferred by dependency locality. Some evidence for this prediction is provided by Yamashita and Chang (2001) who evaluate the dependency length minimization hypothesis in Japanese sentence production (cf. Liu (2020).)[4] I will say much more about cross-linguistic word order preferences that are driven by dependency locality in the next chapter.

4.1.2 English Subjects Are Shorter Than English Objects

Whereas some dependents of a noun occur before its head—the determiner and adjectives—most dependents of a noun occur after the noun: prepositional phrases, relative clauses, other clauses. Consequently, the head of a noun phrase generally occurs near its left end. As a result, dependency length minimization predicts that subject noun phrases should be short, in order to keep the head close to the verb. Object noun phrases can be longer, because their head will be close to the verb. Temperley (2007) evaluated this prediction of dependency length minimization in his *Wall Street Journal* corpus. He found that the average length of subject NPs was only 3.13 words, whereas the average length of object NPs was much longer at 5.80 words. He provided example (101a) of an English sentence that has a short subject and a long object, which could have been written as

(101b), with a long subject and short object, using a different verb, or using a passive (101c):

(101) a. For years, a strict regimen governed the staff meetings at Nissan Motor Co.'s technical center in Tokyo's Western suburbs.
b. For years, the staff meetings at Nissan Motor Co.'s technical center in Tokyo's western suburbs followed a strict regimen.
c. For years, the staff meetings at Nissan Motor Co.'s technical center in Tokyo's western suburbs were governed by a strict regimen.

The dependencies are much shorter with the short subject and long object, as demonstrated in these abridged versions of the long sentences:

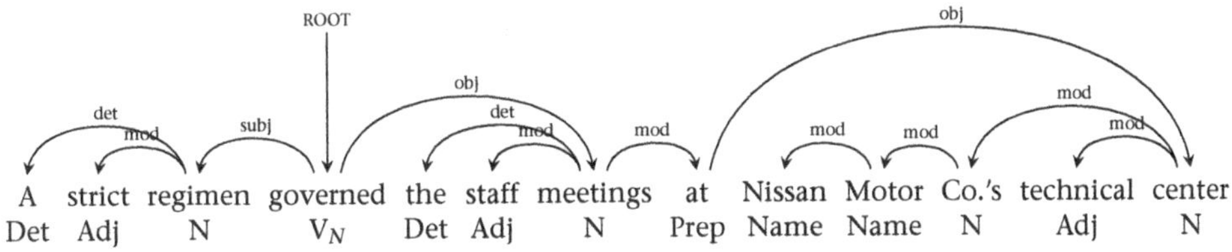

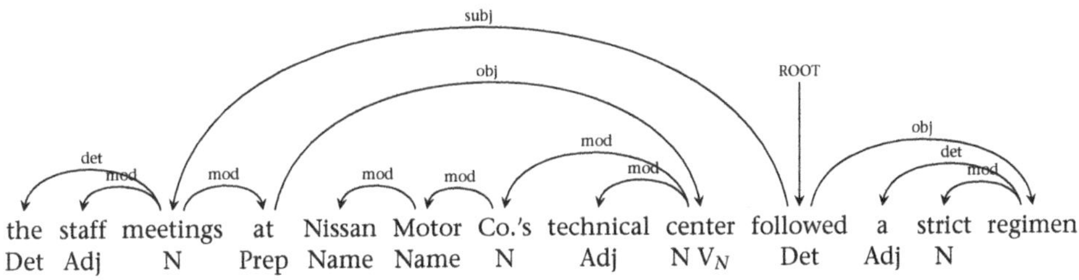

Furthermore, Temperley (2007) observed that there are discourse reasons to put old information first—in subject position—so it may be important to control for the discourse newness of the noun phrases being compared. Consequently, Temperley (2007) also evaluated a narrower version of this prediction of dependency length minimization, by examining only specific indefinite NPs, so that there are no discourse differences among the NPs. Even in this comparison, subject NPs (average length 5.95 words) were much shorter than object NPs (8.95 words).

4.1.3 Asymmetries in English Quotations

Temperley (2007) observed that English quotations in writing can either be subject-verb order (*Jane said*) or verb-subject order (*said Jane*).

(102) a. "I agree," said Jane.

b. "I agree," Jane said.

c. "I agree," said Jane Smith, president of Smith, Brown, and Jones, a consulting firm.

d. "I agree," Jane Smith, president of Smith, Brown, and Jones, a consulting firm, said

Dependency length minimization predicts that the subject NP in the subject-verb order should be shorter than in the verb-subject order. This was as predicted, in Temperley's (2007) analysis: The subject in the subject-verb order was only 2.16 words compared to 9.47 words for the subject in the verb-subject word order. I present dependency graphs for the short and long versions of the long subject in (102c) and (102d):

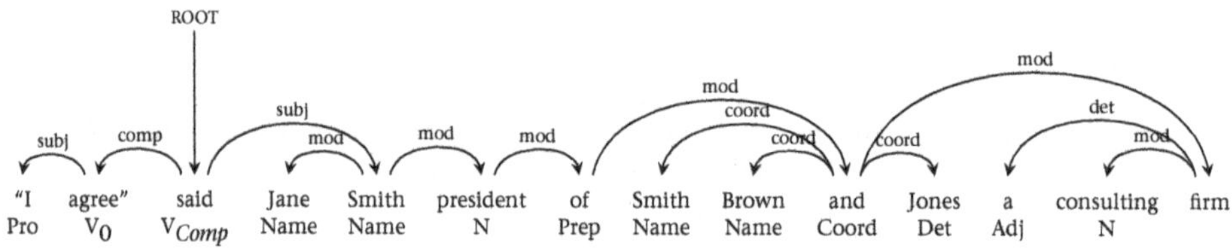

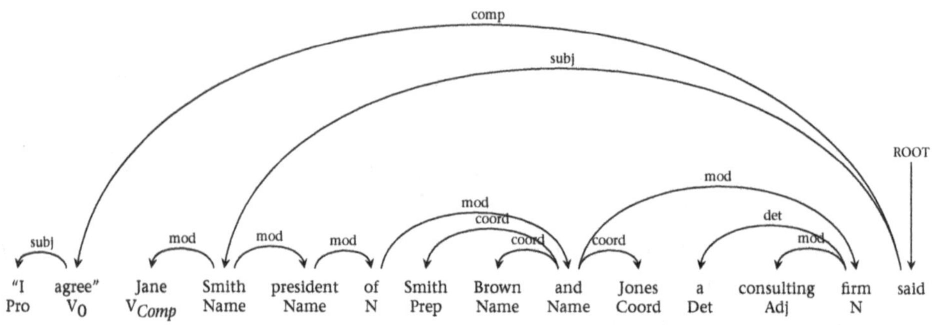

4.2 Locality Preferences in Comprehending Ambiguous Materials

Consider two ways of saying when the bartender told the detective that an event took place yesterday:

(103) a. The bartender told the detective that the suspect left the country yesterday.

b. The bartender told the detective yesterday that the suspect left the country.

In (103a), the adverb *yesterday* follows the clause *that the suspect left the country*, and consequently there is an ambiguity for how to interpret *yesterday*: It could modify the embedded clause headed by *left*, or it could modify the clause headed by *told*:

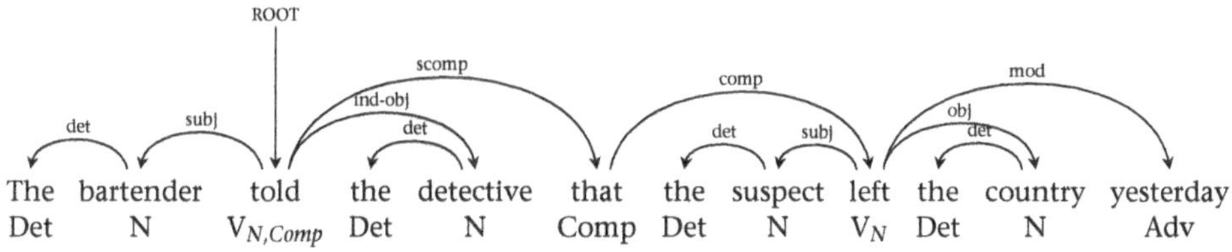

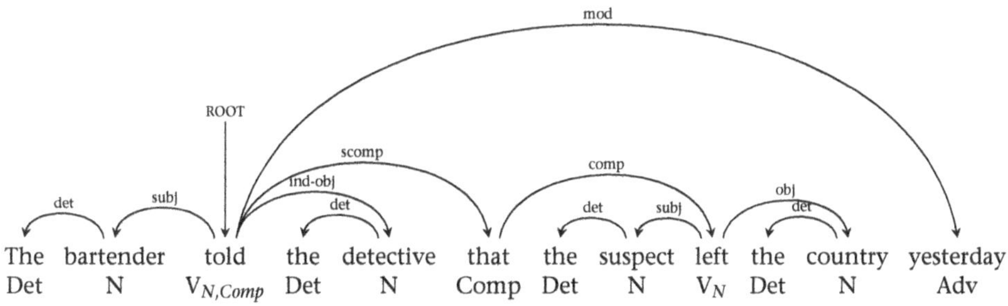

There is a strong preference to interpret this sentence with the more local connection (modifying *left*). Consequently, if we want to convey the meaning where *yesterday* modifies *told*, then it is better to order the words as in (103b):

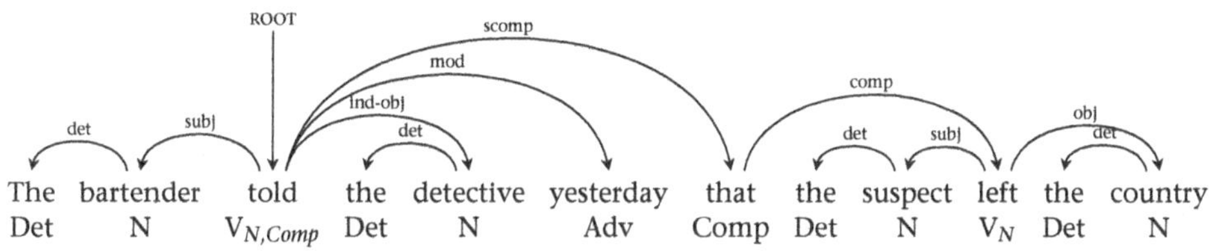

In this sentence, the adverbial *yesterday* occurs immediately following the clause headed by *told*, and hence it preferentially connects to this clause, as desired. Consequently, this is a better way to get the target idea across.

Similarly, a strong locality bias causes the following example to be funny, from a Russian hotel room:[5]

(104) You can visit the cemetery where famous Russian composers are buried daily except Thursday.

The adverbial *daily except Thursday* is intended to modify the verb *visit,* as in the first dependency structure below, but the preferred (crazy) interpretation modifies the verb *buried,* as in the second:

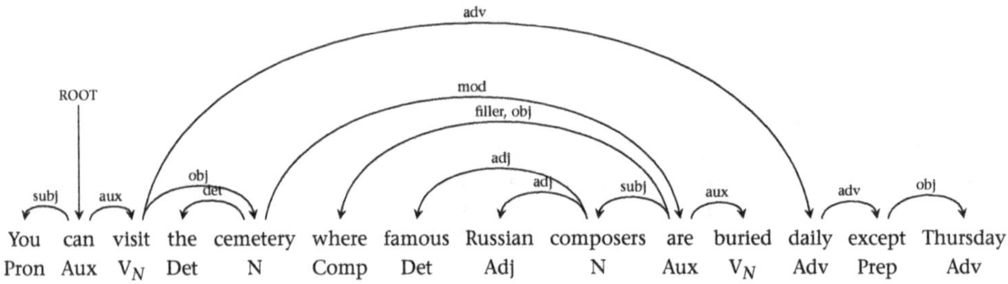

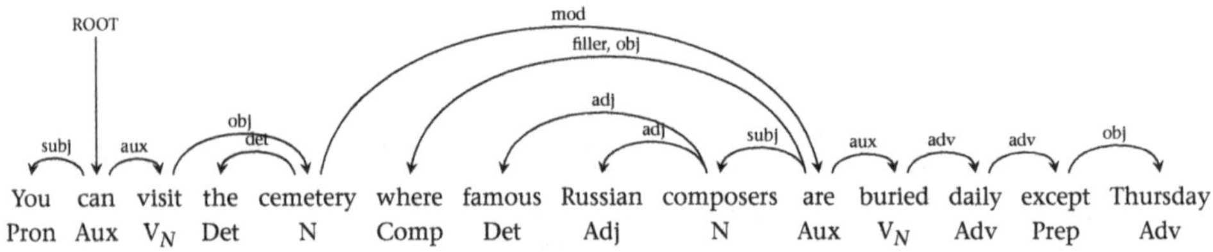

And a locality bias is what makes the headline in (91b) funny:

(91b) Rumors about NBA referees getting ugly

The intended interpretation is one where the rumors are getting ugly:

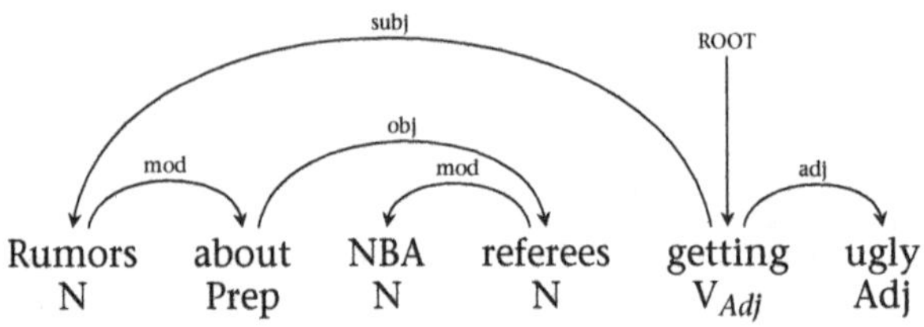

But people often can't help but notice the more local connection of *getting ugly,* where it is the referees that are getting ugly. Critically here, *getting* connects to the most local word *referees:*

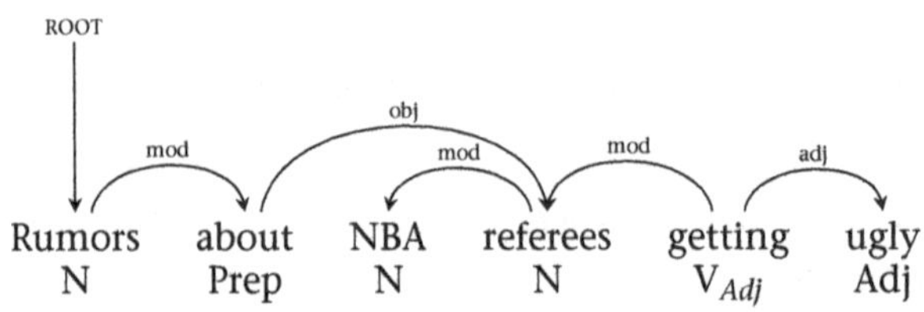

One last temporarily ambiguous example is a report from a doctor about a patient, in a set of released doctor reports:

(105) Patient reports pain starting near his penis which goes down to his knee

Presumably, the intended interpretation is one in which the pain goes down to his knee, but note that this is a long-distance connection between *pain* and *which*:

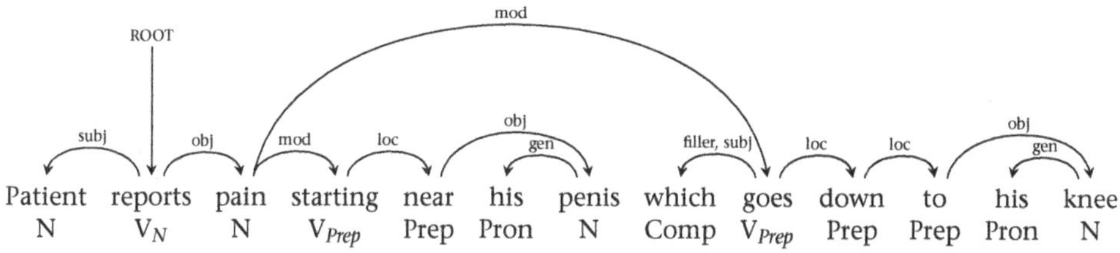

But when *which* modifies *penis*—the most local connection—we get a surprising statement from a doctor. Readers typically can't help but notice this interpretation, presumably because it is so easy to make.

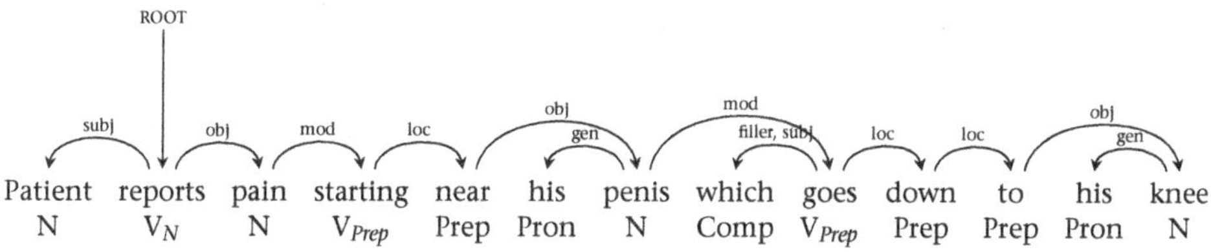

4.3 Locality Preferences in Extraposed Structures

There is a general bias in human languages to avoid crossed dependencies. When a language does allow crossed dependencies, such structures are generally dispreferred, unless the dependency lengths are much shorter for the structure with crossed dependencies (Hawkins, 2004). One experimental evaluation of crossed dependencies was provided by Levy et al. (2012), who showed that materials like (106a)—where the relative clause is directly beside the noun that it modifies—were read more slowly than materials like (106b) where the relative clause crosses the main verb of the sentence:[6]

(106) a. Relative clause in situ:
A performer who had impressed the audience came on.

b. Relative clause extraposed:
A performer came on who had impressed the audience.

The relative clause in (106b) is said to be **extraposed** across the main verb in the sentence. The dependency structures for (106a) and (106b) are given below:

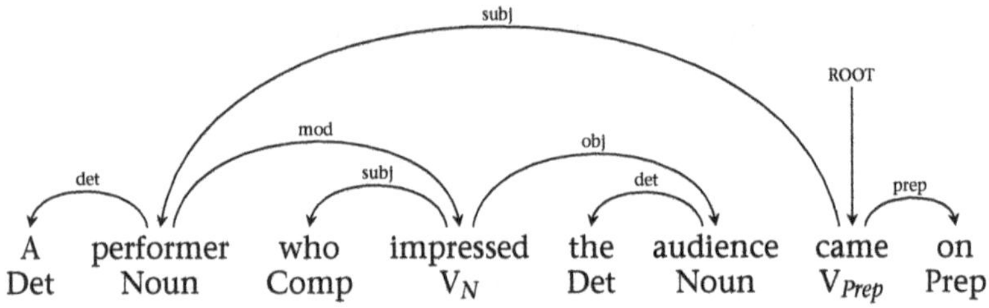

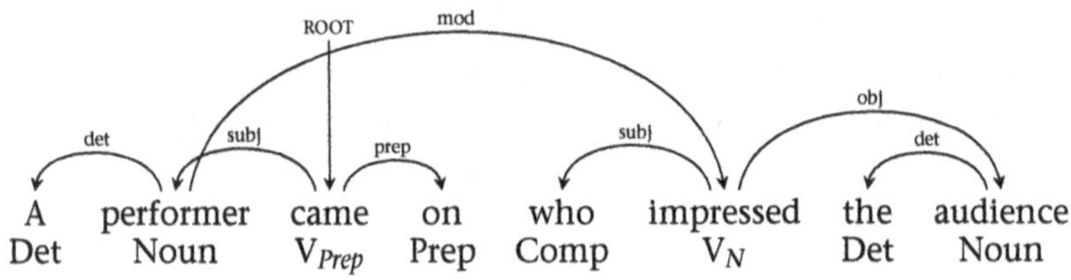

The relative clause *who impressed the audience* is adjacent to its head noun *performer* in (106a). The same relative clause crosses the root dependency coming into the main verb *came* in (106b): a crossed dependency. This structure was read more slowly in Levy et al.'s (2012) experiments, plausibly because of the crossed dependency: the extraposition.

But as dependencies get longer, sometimes human languages favor a crossed dependency when such a crossed dependency leads to much lower average dependency length across the structure (Uszkoreit et al., 1998; Wasow, 2002; Francis, 2010; Francis and Michaelis, 2014, 2017). For example, Francis (2010) had people read sentences with non-extraposed and extraposed relative clauses, of three lengths: short, long, and very long, as in (107):

(107) a. Three people who were from Chicago arrived here early yesterday morning.
b. Three people arrived here early yesterday morning who were from Chicago
c. Three people who were from a northern suburb of Chicago arrived here early yesterday morning.

d. Three people arrived here early yesterday morning who were from a northern suburb of Chicago.
e. Three people who were originally from a far northern suburb of Chicago which is called Lake Forest arrived here early yesterday morning.
f. Three people arrived here early yesterday morning who were originally from a far northern suburb of Chicago which is called Lake Forest.

Participants in Francis's (2010) experiment read the non-extraposed RCs faster than the extraposed RC materials (as in (107a) vs. (107b)) when the RCs were short, but as the RCs got longer (as in (107e) vs. (107f)), the extraposed item was read faster relative to the non-extraposed version, as shown in figure 4.1.

In the non-extraposed structure (107a), the dependency length between the noun and the relative clause head verb is two words, and the dependency length between the noun and the main verb is five words:

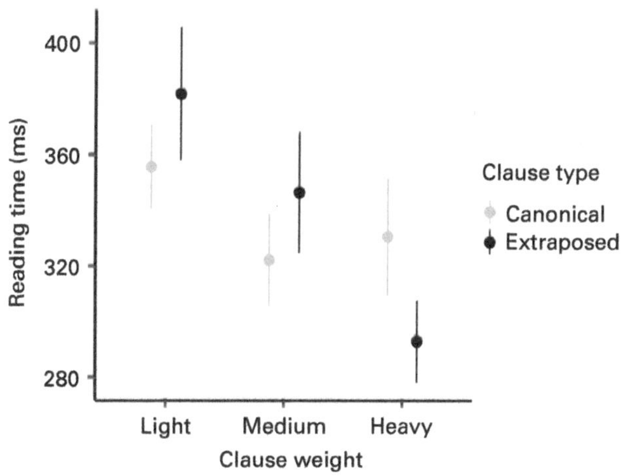

Figure 4.1
Average reading times per word over the course of a sentence for sentences with extraposed vs. non-extraposed relative clause structures, from (Francis, 2010). As the relative clause gets longer, the extraposed structures are read more quickly, compared to the non-extraposed structures.

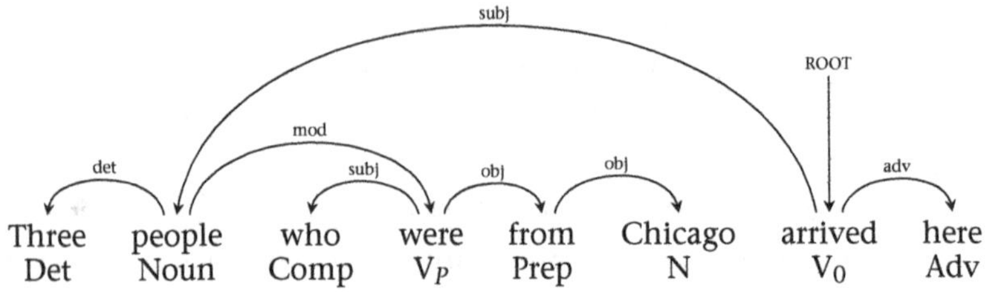

In contrast, in the extraposed structure (107b), the dependency length between the noun and the relative clause head verb is four words, and the dependency length between the noun and the main verb is one word:

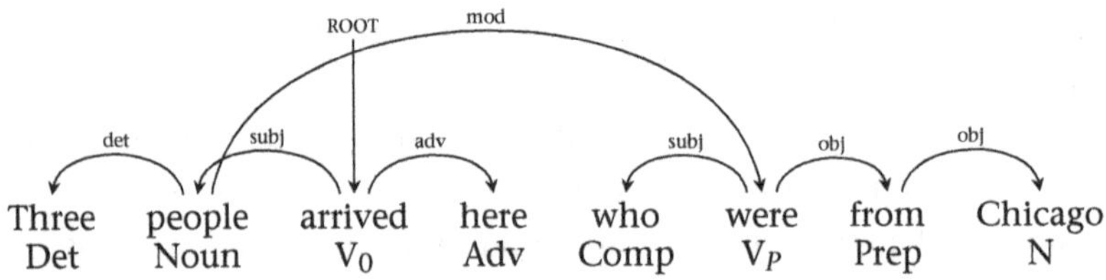

The other dependencies are the same across the two structures. Thus, the extraposed version has shorter total dependency length (4+1) than the non-extraposed version (2+5), although the difference isn't very large: just two words, across the whole structure. Assuming that there is a general cost associated with crossing dependencies, this difference isn't enough to make the crossed dependency cost-effective for the whole structure. As we add more words to the relative clause, the difference between the two structures rises at a constant rate. Consider slightly shortened versions of (107c) and (107d):

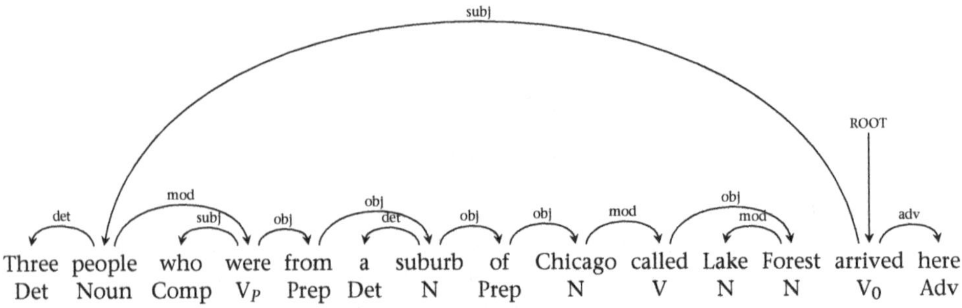

In the non-extraposed structure (107c), the dependency length between the noun and the relative clause is still two words, but the dependency length between the noun and the main verb has increased to eleven words, because the relative clause is ten words long. Consider now the extraposed structure:

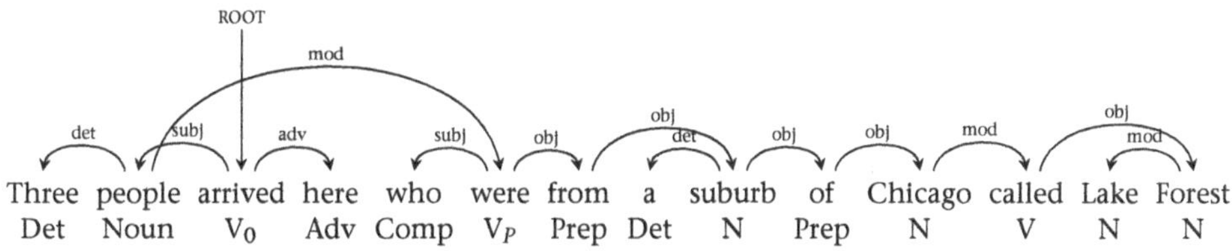

In the extraposed structure (107d), the dependency length between the noun and the relative clause is four words, and the dependency length between the noun and the main verb is one word (the same as for the shorter RC versions). Thus, the extraposed version now has much shorter total dependency length (4+1) than the non-extraposed version (2+11): now eight words difference. As the relative clause gets longer and longer, the bias toward the extraposed structure increases, as the dependency length for that structure becomes much lower compared to the non-extraposed structure (see Hawkins [2004] for a similar theory).

4.4 On-line Locality Effects in English Reading

Grodner and Gibson (2005) investigated the role of locality in on-line language processing in simple and complex English relative clause examples as in (108) and (109):

(108) a. Subject-extracted relative clause:
The reporter who sent the photographer to the editor hoped for a story.
b. Object-extracted relative clause:
The reporter who the photographer sent to the editor hoped for a story.

In (108a), the relative clause *who sent the photographer to the editor* is said to be a **subject-extracted** relative clause, because the relative pronoun *who* is associated with the subject position of the relative clause. Similarly, the relative clause *who the photographer sent to the editor* is said to be an **object-extracted** relative clause, because the relative pronoun *who* is associated with the object position of the relative clause. As we can see in the dependency structures below, the connection between the wh-pronoun *who* and the verb is more local in the subject-extracted version than in the object-extracted version, where dependency lengths are provided on the arcs, in terms of the number of words in between. Furthermore, the connection between the head noun *reporter* for the modifying relative clause verb *sent* is much longer in the object-extracted version than in the subject-exctracted version.

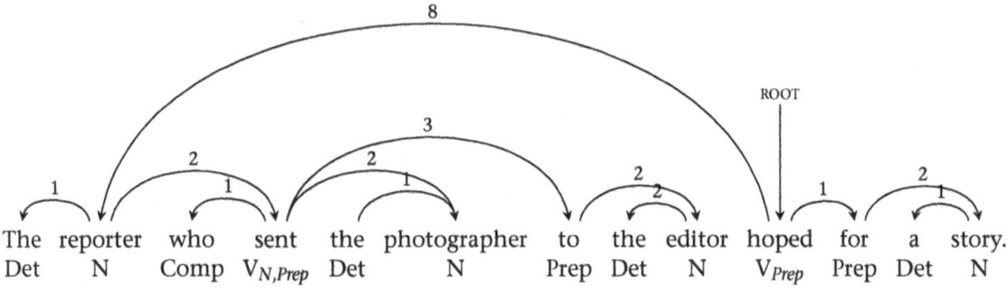

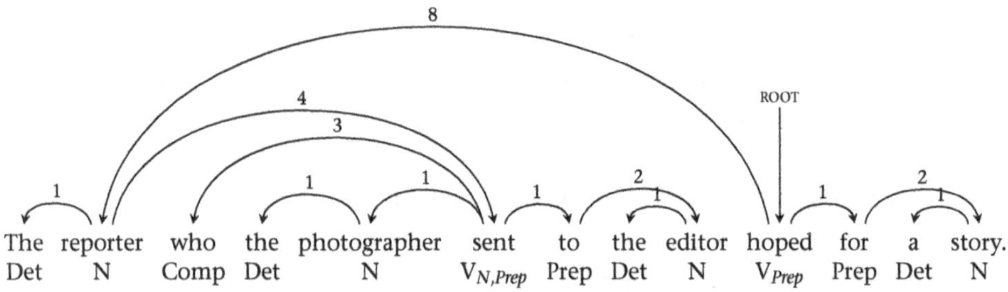

Grodner and Gibson (2005) compared reading times—in a self-paced reading paradigm—with the **integration cost** at each word. The integration cost at a word is defined to be the length of completed dependencies at that word. Grodner and Gibson (2005) actually used a distance metric that only counted nouns and verbs that indicate new discourse referents (following Gibson [1998, 2000]), but these two distance metrics (counting words vs. counting new discourse referents) are highly correlated, so I will use the simpler word-based metric initially here.[7]

Grodner and Gibson (2005) found that reading times were longest at the main verb *hoped* in each structure—the locus of a long-distance integration with the subject *reporter*—and at the embedded verb *sent* in the object-extracted version, where there is one local and one longer-distance connection to be integrated.

Grodner and Gibson (2005) then looked at a wider range of structures, with more variable integration distances, as in the materials in (109):

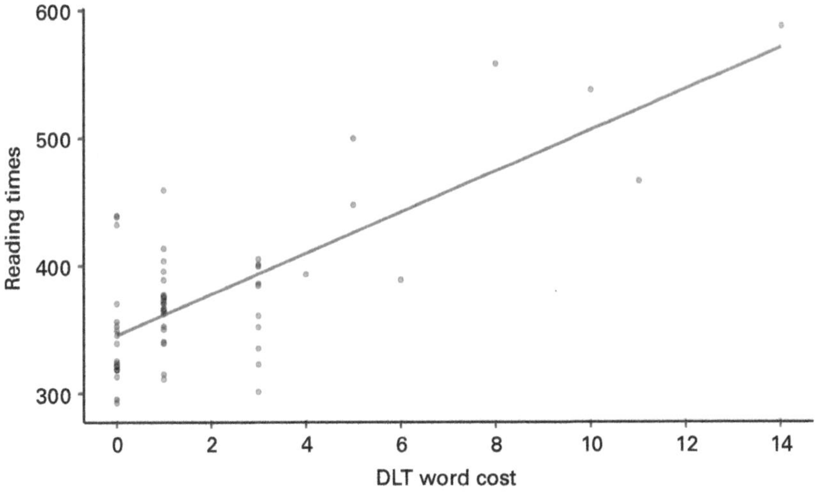

Figure 4.2
A strong correlation between average reading time per word and integration cost, measured by the total length of dependency arcs ending at the current word. Each dot represents a word in each of the six experimental conditions (sentences) in experiment 2 of Grodner and Gibson (2005). Most of the dots have zero or one predicted integration cost. The longer-distance connections tend to be associated with longer reading times. Figure made by Moshe Poliak, based on the data from Grodner and Gibson (2005).

(109) a. The nurse supervised the administrator...
b. The nurse from the clinic supervised the administrator...
c. The nurse who was from the clinic supervised the administrator ...
d. The administrator who the nurse supervised scolded the medic ...
e. The administrator who the nurse from the clinic supervised scolded the medic ...
f. The administrator who the nurse who was from the clinic supervised scolded the medic ...

We can see a close relationship between average reading time and integration cost, measured in words, from Grodner and Gibson's (2005) data in figure 4.2. To understand this in more detail, let's consider the dependency graph for (109c):

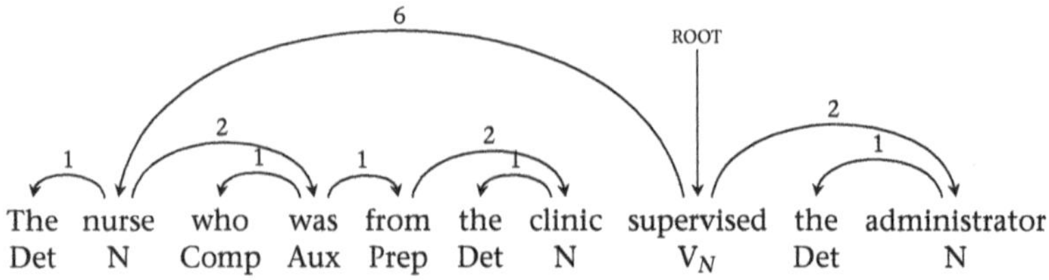

In the dependency structure for (109a) above, the word *nurse* connects to the preceding word *the*, for a cost of 1 at *nurse* (plus a cost of 2 for the relative clause modifier connection between *nurse* and *was*, if we are also counting these). The word *clinic* connects to both the preposition *from* and the determiner *the*, for a total cost of 3 at this position. And *supervised* connects back to *nurse*, for a cost of 6 at this position.

Whereas most word connections in most sentences are local, the relative clause examples that Grodner and Gibson (2005) investigated involved some longer dependencies:

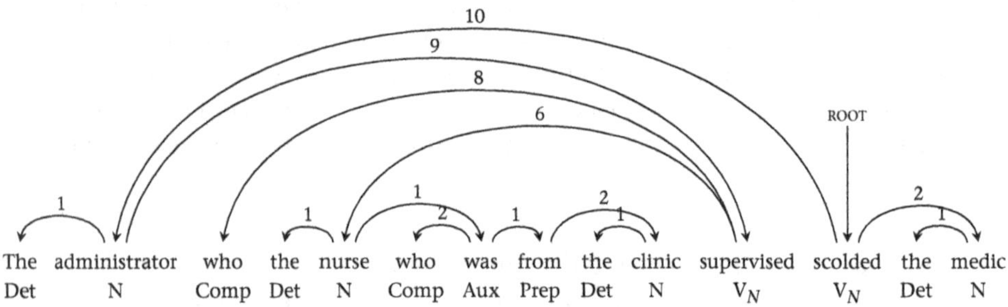

The connection at *supervised* here is 6 words back to the subject noun *nurse*, and 8 words back to the relative pronoun *who* (category Comp in the graph), for a total of 14. (There is also a connection between the noun *administrator* and the head verb for the relative clause *supervised* here, with a cost of 9. As discussed in footnote 45, we are omitting relative clause modifier connections from our counts, because they are somewhat redundant with the connection between relative pronouns and verbs. This means that the differences we observe are conservative.) And the connection at *scolded* is 10 words back to its subject *administrator*. So these positions were predicted to be especially slow. We see in figure 4.2 that most word positions connect to a position immediately before them, and these integrations are typically read quickly. Only when there are long connections to be made do people sometime slow down a lot, at least in these examples.

While the results from Grodner and Gibson (2005) were replicated in eye-tracking measures of reading (Boston et al., 2008; Bartek et al., 2011), the generality to reading typical texts is unclear. For example, Demberg and Keller (2008) found no relationship between dependency length and reading time for people reading simple newspaper texts in eye-tracking measures; and Shain et al. (2016) found no significant relationship for people reading hand-crafted stories in self-paced reading measures. So it's unclear what the relationship is between dependency length and complexity. The materials in Grodner and Gibson (2005) were complex and were presented in a null context. This contrasts to the contextually supported materials that Demberg and Keller (2008) and Shain et al. (2016) investigated. So it is possible that we need very complex examples to really see the effects of dependency locality. Alternatively, there may be a more indirect relationship between reading time complexity and dependency length, such that perhaps people have a harder time *producing* longer connections, but that may not always lead to greater reaction time when comprehending them. Overall, the relationship between dependency length and complexity is not yet an "understood" problem. Rather, dependency locality is a good way to keep track of a lot of language processing effects in a compressed way, but this generalization may not be exactly how the brain organizes such effects. In any case, we do see effects of dependency length in on-line processing for naturalistic materials in brain activation measures (Shain et al., 2022), to be discussed in section 4.7.

4.5 Locality Evidence from Complex Nested Structures

As discussed in section 2.2.7, nested syntactic structures are more difficult to produce and comprehend than non-nested ones, as exemplified in the difference in complexity between (110a) and (110b) (repeated from (28) and (27)):

(110) a. The cat chased the dog which bit the boy who was upset.
b. The boy who the dog which the cat chased bit was upset.

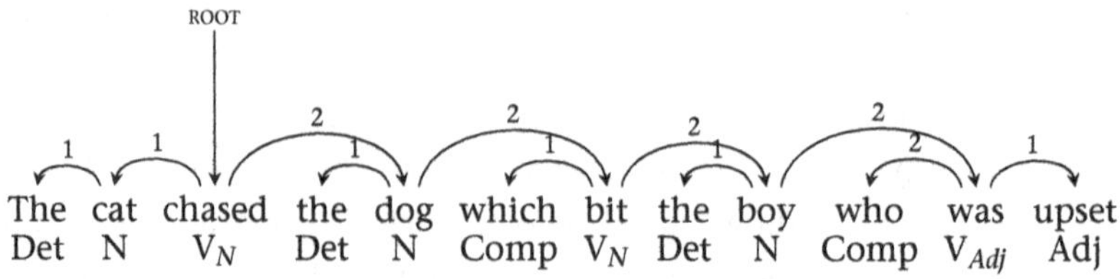

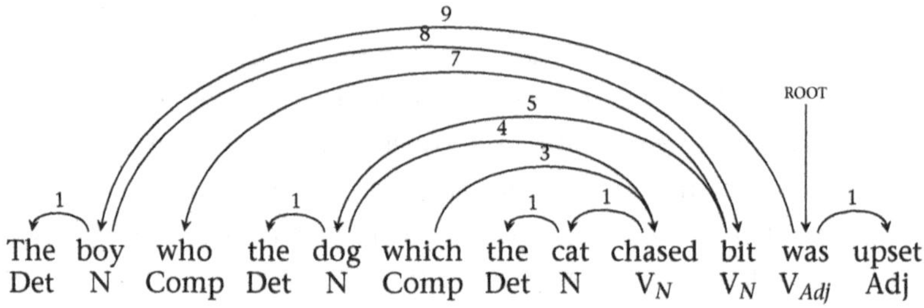

In the first discussion of contrasts like these, Yngve (1960) and Chomsky and Miller (1963) suggested that the complexity of nested structures like (110b) might be due to syntactic storage: keeping track of too many incomplete dependencies, possibly on a stack in an on-line processing mechanism (called a **parser**). For example, at the word *cat* in (110b), there are five incomplete dependencies, whereas there are never more than one or two in the left-to-right parse of a non-nested structure like (110a) (for other storage-based hypotheses, see Kimball [1973], Gibson [1991], Abney and Johnson [1991], Lewis [1996]).

While this hypothesis can account for the complexity difference between the two, it turns out that on-line behavioral measures such as reading times aren't very sensitive to incomplete dependencies, even in lab experiments on materials like these. In contrast, reading times do seem to be sensitive to integration costs in lab experiments on complex materials like these (Grodner and Gibson, 2005; Lewis and Vasishth, 2005a; Lewis et al., 2006) (cf. Chen et al. [2005] for results that appear to provide some evidence for on-line storage costs in English, although these results have never been replicated, and Nakatani and Gibson [2010] for evidence that Japanese is sensitive to on-line storage costs).

4.5.1 Embeddings of Relative Clauses and Sentence Complements

The contrasting pair of structures in (111) was first observed by Cowper (1976) as a problem for the storage-based theories up to that time:

(111) a. Sentence complement then relative clause (SC/RC):
The fact that the employee who the manager hired stole office supplies worried the executive.

b. Relative clause then Sentence complement (RC/SC):
The executive who the fact that the employee stole office supplies worried hired the manager.

(111a) consists of a relative clause embedded within a sentence complement whereas (111b) consists of the inverse embedding—a sentence complement within a relative clause. Both are complex, but (111a) is much easier to process than (111b). On the surface, the difference between these two structures is surprising: They have remarkably similar kinds of meanings, and both are doubly-nested structures (see the dependency structures below). Why would one be so much easier to understand than the other?

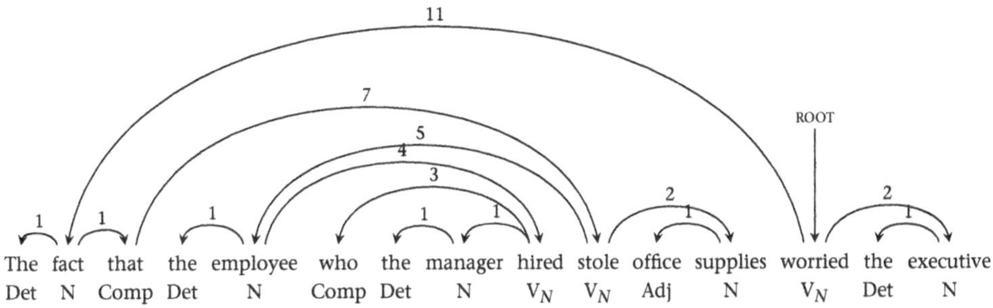

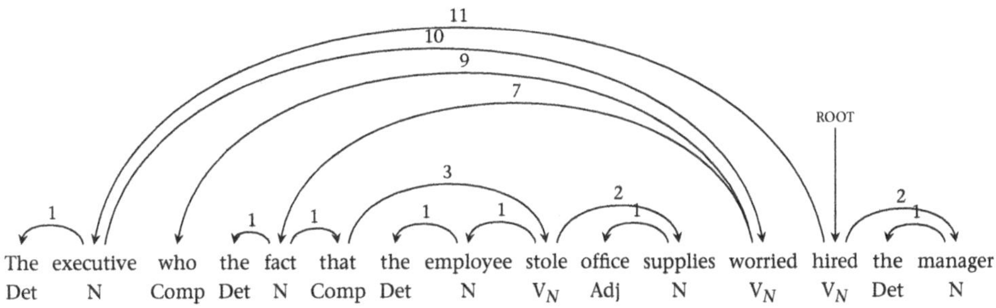

As discussed in section 3.19, a relative clause is a clause that modifies a noun, where the relative pronoun (e.g., *who* or *which*) takes the place of one of the normal noun phrase positions in the relative clause. The clause *who the manager hired* is such a relative clause in (111a): *Who* fills the object position of the verb *hired*. In contrast, a sentence complement is a clause that is lexically specified by a particular noun, like *fact* in (111a) and (111b), and consequently, there is no missing position in the embedded clause. Other nouns with clausal complements include *belief, report, statement, possibility* and many others. These nouns take a clause as part of their meaning. For *fact*, for example, the clausal complement describes the content of the fact. For *belief*, the clausal complement indicates what is believed, and so on.

Most nouns do not take a clausal complement. Only particular nouns specify a clause as part of their meaning, like *fact* and *belief*. Nouns like *table, apple, politician, girl, ball, employee, and manager.* refer to classes of objects and animate kinds in the world that do not have a clause as part of their meaning. Any noun, including these, can have a relative clause modifying it. So any of these nouns can be modified by, for example, the relative clause *which I liked*. But none of these allows a sentence complement, since a clause is not part of the meaning of these nouns.

No complexity difference is predicted between (111a) and (111b) according to storage-based theories of sentence complexity (Yngve, 1960; Chomsky and Miller, 1963; Kimball, 1973). In the dependency graphs above, we can see that the maximal number of incomplete dependencies in each structure is five, while processing the most embedded noun (after *the* or *manager* in (111a) or after *the* or *employee* in (111b)). Consequently, the storage-based theories predict no difference between the two, as discussed by Cowper (1976) and Gibson (1991).

Gibson (1998, 2000) offers a simple explanation of the difference between the two structures in terms of dependency distances. Although there is no difference in dependency length for the longest dependency (at eleven words for each), the second and third longest dependencies are longer in the RC/SC structure—at nine and seven words[8]—than the SC/RC structure, at seven and five words, respectively. Gibson (1998) proposed a distance-based **storage cost** theory of complexity, where intuitive complexity is determined by the length of time (in words or new discourse referents processed) that an incomplete dependency is maintained. In addition, Gibson (1998) assumes a phrase structure grammar as opposed to a dependency grammar. The contrast between these two structures comes out in a similar way as here.

4.6 Figuring Out the Distance Metric

Gibson (1998, 2000) argues that processing complexity may be measured based on dependency distance in terms of the number of **new discourse**

referents between a head and a dependent, and not simply the number of words separating the head and dependent (cf. Hawkins, 1994, 2004). A new discourse referent is part of the meaning that corresponds to a noun or verb that has not already been introduced into the context. Critically, a pronoun can almost never be a new discourse referent, because it refers to something already in the discourse. But names and nouns usually introduce a new discourse referent. And verbs introduce events or states that can also be referred to later.

Intuitive evidence for the idea that dependency distance cost is sensitive to new discourse reference was provided in the form of examples first observed by Bever (1970, 1974); Kac (1981); and Gibson (1991) (repeated from Gibson [1998]):

(112) a. The reporter who [everyone that [I met] trusts] said the president won't resign yet. Bever (1974)

b. A book [that some Italian [I've never heard of] wrote] will be published soon by MIT Press. Frank (1992)

c. Isn't it true that example sentences [that people [that you know] produce] are more likely to be accepted. De Roeck et al. (1982)

These examples are similar in structure to (110b), which is extremely difficult to process, yet somehow these examples are interpretable, despite the fact that they consist of doubly nested relative clause structures. I provide the structure for (112a) below, along with the structure for (110b) again:

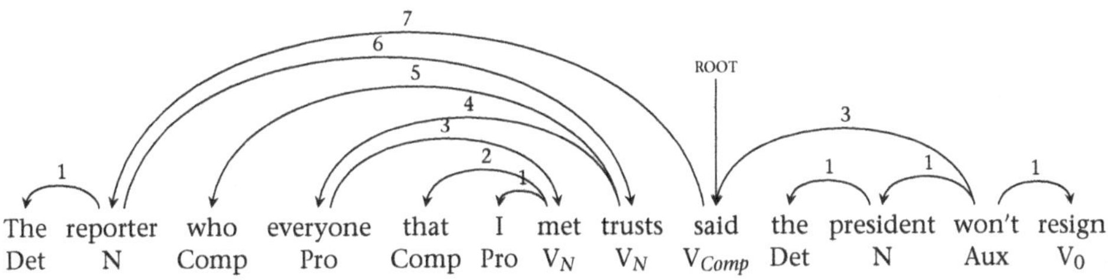

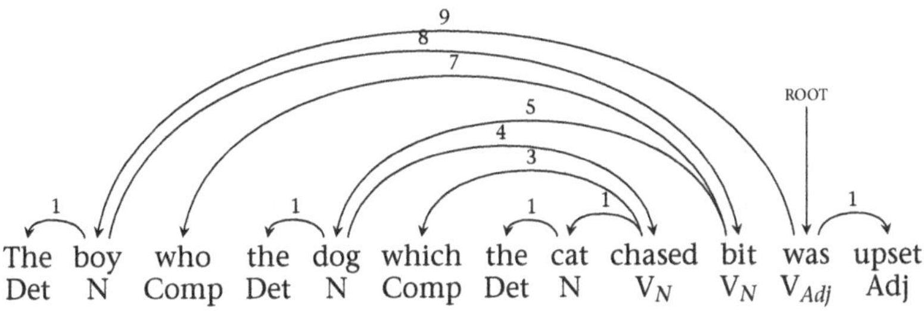

We can see that the nested structures of the two sentences are similar. Gibson (1998, 2000) suggested that if integration cost is computed in terms of new discourse referents—nouns, names or tensed verbs—then the complexity effects would follow. Because first- or second-person pronouns refer to people who are always part of the discourse (the producer and the comprehender), then there would be less cost when such a pronoun intervenes in a dependency than with a noun or name that refers to something not mentioned yet in the context. Above, the arcs count the number of words intervening; when the arcs count new nouns and verbs (new discourse referents), the costs diverge more for the two kinds of materials:

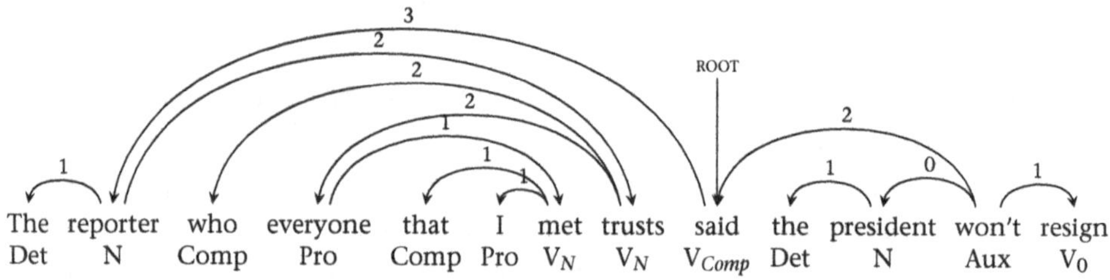

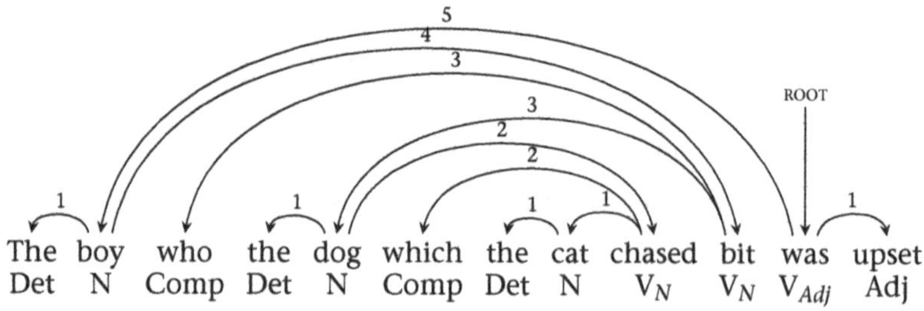

The long connections in (110b) consist of 5, 4, 3, and 3 discourse units; whereas the long connections in (112a) consist of 3, 2, 2, and 2 discourse units. Thus (112a) is less complex to understand and produce.

Warren and Gibson (2002) investigated the discourse-based hypothesis directly in singly nested and doubly nested materials. In the doubly nested materials, Warren and Gibson (2002) compared materials with first or second-person pronouns in the most embedded position vs. materials with a name or common noun in the same position, as in (113):

(113) a. The student who the professor who the scientist collaborated with advised copied the article.

b. The student who the professor who Jen collaborated with advised copied the article.

c. The student who the professor who I collaborated with advised copied the article.

Warren and Gibson (2002) found that participants rated the materials with the pronouns (e.g., *I* in (113c)) in the most embedded position as less complex than the ones with a name (e.g., *Jen* in (113b)) or a definite noun (e.g., *the scientist* in (113a)). Compare the structures for (113b) and (113c), which are identical except for the label on the most embedded subject noun phrase: a name in (113b) and a pronoun in (113c):

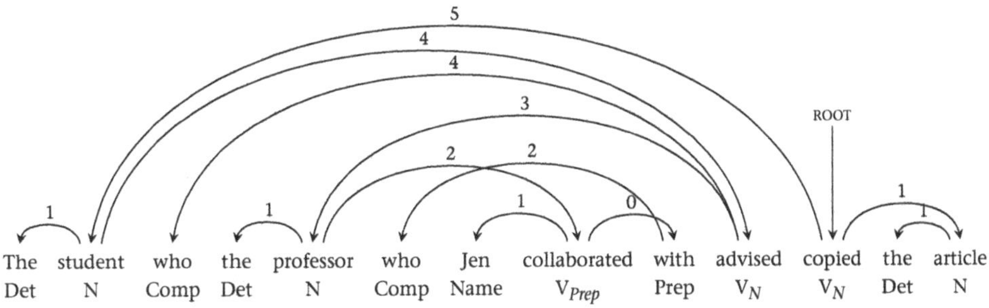

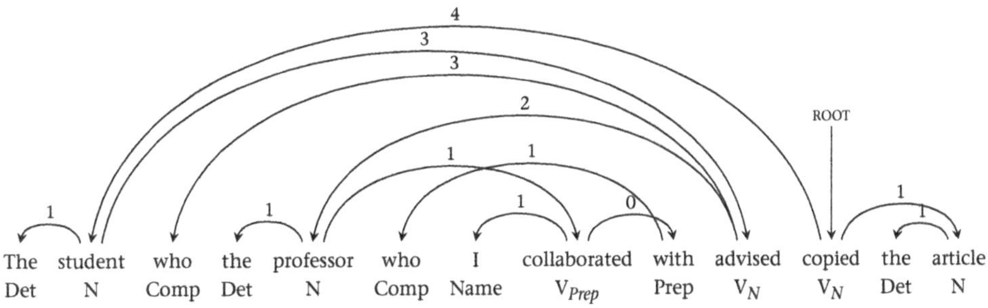

Because the structures are identical, a word-based dependency distance metric predicts no complexity difference between the two. But if we count new discourse referents in our distance metric, then the arcs in (113c) are associated with lower cost than those (113b): The arcs crossing *Jen / I* are 5, 4, 4, 3, 2, 2 discourse units when *Jen* intervenes, and only 4, 3, 3, 2, 1, 1 discourse units when the pronoun *I* intervenes.

4.6.1 Evidence That the Distance Metric Is Interference-Based

An alternative proposal to the discourse is that there may be cost associated with **interference** of similar items in the intervening region at the point of reactivation (integration), and only discourse referents may count for interference. The costs would work out to be roughly the same—only counting discourse referents—but the underlying mechanism would be different. Work by Gordon et al. (2001), van Dyke and Lewis (2003), and van Dyke and McElree (2006) disambiguated theories toward the interference-based approach. For example, Gordon et al. (2001) showed that reading times increase depending on the similarity of the embedded noun phrase subject to the noun phrase that it modifies in a cleft structure, as in (114):

(114) a. It was the barber that the lawyer saw in the parking lot.
b. It was the barber that Bill saw in the parking lot.
c. It was John that the lawyer saw in the parking lot.
d. It was John that Bill saw in the parking lot.

The critical position evaluated by Gordon et al. (2001) was at the cleft verb *saw* in examples like (114). There are two integrations at *saw* in each of these examples: one back to the relative pronoun *that*, and one to the preceding subject noun. The distance back to the relative pronoun *that* is the same in terms of discourse referents in each of the four examples. So the discourse-referent-based distance metric doesn't predict any differences among the four structures. The word-based distance metric predicts more difficulty for the structures with the two-word subject *the lawyer* compared to the one-word subject *Bill*. Consider the dependency structures for (114c) and (114d) below:

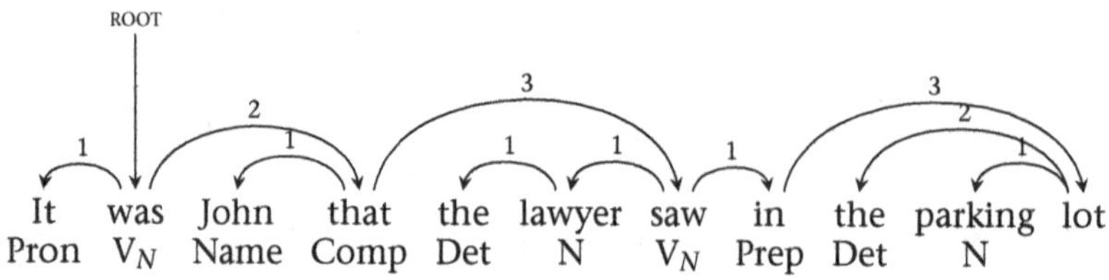

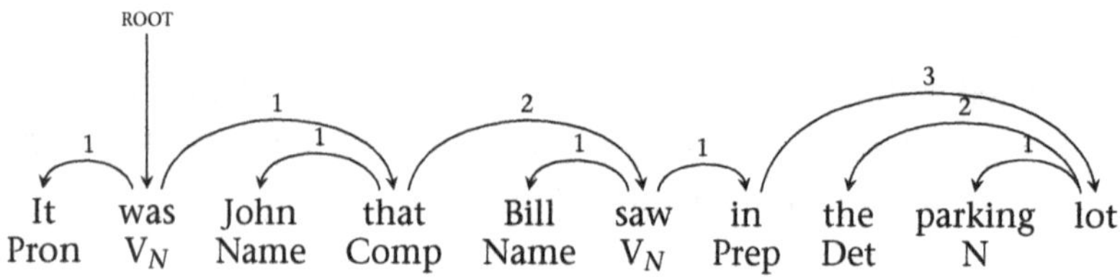

Gordon et al. (2001) found that reading times were much slower at *saw* when the type of noun phrase as subject matched the type of noun phrase in the cleft (coreferenced with *that*). Thus reading times were slower at *saw*

in (114d) than in (114c), in spite of the fact that there are fewer words (one vs. two) for the example with *Bill* as the embedded subject vs. the example with *the lawyer* as embedded subject. These data suggest that the similarity of the noun phrases is part of what makes the integrations back to the preceding site difficult: When both are names or Determiner-Noun sequences, there is increased processing difficulty. Further evidence for similarity-based interference affecting the integrations is provided by van Dyke and Lewis (2003), Lewis and Vasishth (2005a), Lewis et al. (2006), and van Dyke and McElree (2006).

4.7 Dependency Locality in the Brain

Memory-based theories of linguistic complexity go back to Yngve (1960) and Chomsky and Miller (1963) and have continued in all intervening decades (Kimball, 1973; Frazier and Fodor, 1978; Johnson-Laird, 1983; Gibson, 1991; Resnik, 1992; Gibson, 1998; Lewis, 1996; Lewis and Vasishth, 2005a; Van Schijndel and Schuler, 2013; van Schijndel et al., 2013; Rasmussen and Schuler, 2018). While they are intuitively plausible, the evidence for such proposals comes mostly from targeted experiments (Grodner and Gibson, 2005; Bartek et al., 2011), not from the analysis of behavior in response to arbitrary linguistic input. In particular, recent studies of online reading, which control for surprisal (Hale, 2001; Levy, 2008a) have not yielded evidence of working memory effects (Demberg and Keller, 2008; Levy and Keller, 2013; Van Schijndel and Schuler, 2013; Shain and Schuler, 2021).

In a recent large-scale evaluation of fMRI responses associated with people listening to naturalistic English stories, Shain et al. (2022) investigated a range of memory-based theories of language processing and found reasonably strong evidence for the dependency locality theory (Gibson, 2000). In this evaluation, Shain et al. (2022) looked at all current working memory theories of language processing that could be evaluated on arbitrary sentences.[9] There were three classes of theories that Shain et al. (2022) explored, given this constraint: the dependency locality theory (Gibson, 2000), left-corner parsing (Johnson-Laird, 1983; Resnik, 1992; Van Schijndel and Schuler, 2013; van Schijndel et al., 2013; Rasmussen and Schuler, 2018), and ACT-R theories (Lewis and Vasishth, 2005a).

4.7.1 Variants of the Dependency Locality Theory

The original dependency locality theory (DLT; Gibson, 2000) has two components: storage cost and integration cost. We have focused on integration cost here thus far, but there is a second component: storage cost, like the storage cost proposed by Yngve (1960), Chomsky and Miller (1963), and Kimball (1973). According to the DLT storage cost proposal, there is a cost associated with keeping track of an incomplete dependency. Thus, in a complex sentence like (113b), there are maximally five open dependencies at the most embedded location, when processing the most embedded subject noun *Jen*, which can be seen as the dependency arcs above the word *Jen*.

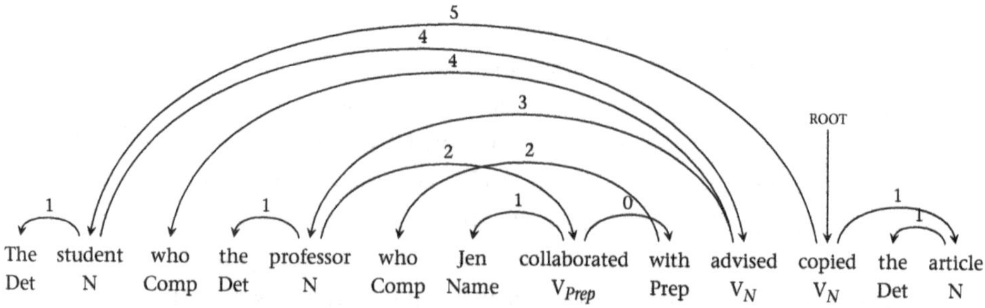

As discussed above, Gibson (2000) proposed that the cost of a retrieval arc was determined by the number of new discourse referents—nouns indicating discourse referents (names and nouns, not pronouns) and tensed verbs—in the interim. Since that work was proposed, several researchers ran into several kinds of examples that motivated potential ways in which this proposal might better model human-perceived difficulty. Cory Shain, William Schuler, and I discussed three kinds of cases where dependency distance might be modulated from the original proposal, each of which was discussed in Shain et al. (2022):

1. Verbs (+V): Gibson (2000) proposed that integrations across tensed verbs are associated with more cost than integrations across untensed verbs based on complexity effects from Gibson and Thomas (1997), such as the difference between (115a) and (115b):

   (115) a. The colonial settlers who the sun god protecting the tribe had frightened were not taken seriously by the government.
   b. The colonial settlers who the sun god which was protecting the tribe had frightened were not taken seriously by the government.

While both (115a) and (115b) are complex, Gibson and Thomas (1997) found that (115b) was rated more complex. The two mean the same thing; one of the main differences between the two is that the modifier *protecting the tribe* in (115a) is extended to include tense, as in *which was protecting the tribe* in (115b).[10] Thus, it appears that tensed verbs in embedded positions incur some extra processing cost, beyond the untensed verb version.

Rather than assigning one unit of cost for finite (tensed) verbs and zero for all other verbs, it is just as plausible to give all verbs (tensed or not) a cost of one unit, and then an extra cost of one for the tensed verbs. Under this proposal, there is a cost of one for the verb even with underspecified tense (Lowe, 2019) and one extra for the tense information (Binnick, 1991). Hence, under this +V proposal, nonfinite verbs receive a cost of 1 (instead of 0), and finite verbs receive a cost of 2 (instead of 1). Of course the precise weights are not known: The costs that Shain et al. (2022) used here were simply approximations, as were the costs in Gibson (2000).

2. Coordination (+C): Examples like (116) motivate the proposal that the cost of integrating across a coordinated structure is the cost of the most expensive of the set of coordinated structures, not the sum of all of them. If all six noun phrases in a conjoined noun phrase like *a cake, streamers, balloons, party hats, candy, and gifts* count in integration cost, then the costs are as in the dependency structure below, which results in very high costs at the conjunction and at the preposition *for*:

(116) I bought a cake, streamers, balloons, party hats, candy, and gifts for my niece.

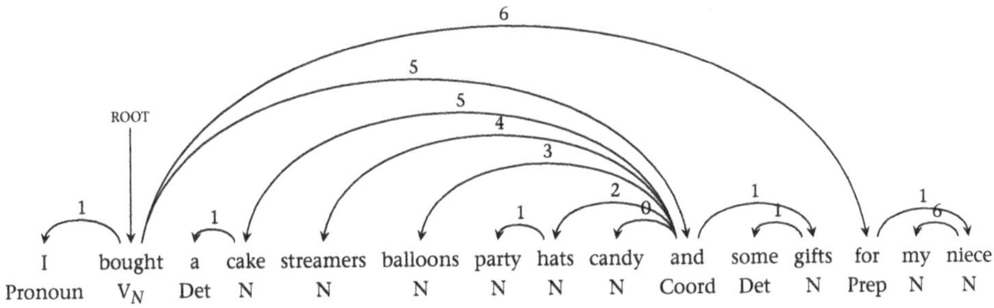

This is similar in magnitude to that of some of the most difficult dependencies explored in the study by Grodner and Gibson (2005). Alternatively, if conjuncts are incrementally integrated into a single representation of the coordinated phrase (a complex discourse referent), and thus their constituent nouns and verbs no longer compete as possible retrieval targets, then the integration costs are much lower as in the representation below:

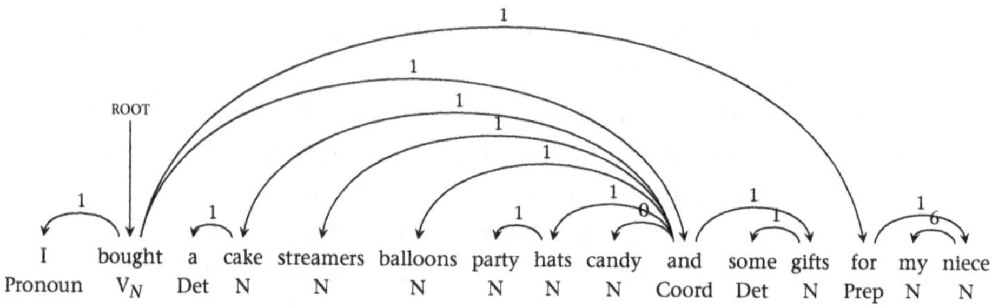

In this example, the dependency from *for* to *bought* does not intuitively seem to induce a large processing cost, but it crosses six coordinated nouns, yielding an integration cost of six. The +C variant treats the entire coordinated direct object as one discourse referent, yielding an integration cost of 1 at the preposition for.

3. Modifiers (+M). Under the original DLT proposal, the integration cost of all dependencies count in the same way. Anecdotally, Shain et al. (2022) motivate the low complexity of preceding modifiers by the following sentence:

(117) Yesterday my coworker, whose cousin drives a taxi in Chicago, sent me a list of good restaurants.

The dependency costs according to the original DLT proposal are as given below:

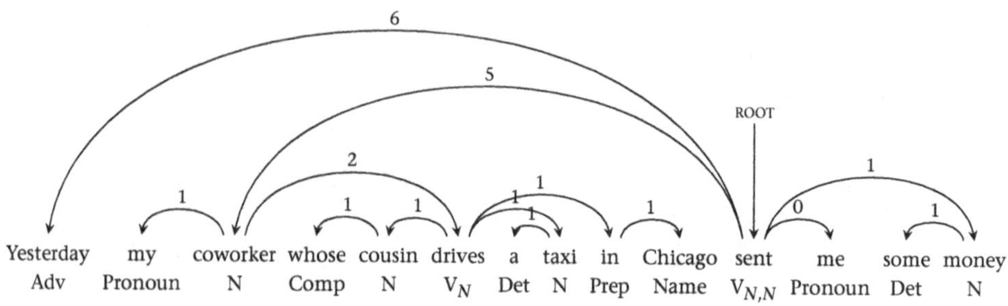

The dependency between the verb *sent* and the subject *coworker* spans a finite verb and three nouns, yielding an integration cost of 4, plus a cost of 1 for the discourse referent introduced by *sent*, for a total of 5 on the arc. If the sentence includes the pre-sentential modifier *yesterday*, connected to the main verb *sent*, then the DLT predicts that it should more than double the structural integration cost at *sent* because the same set of discourse referents intervenes in two dependencies rather than one. Intuitively, this does not seem to be the case.

Alternatively, Shain et al. (2022) suggested that since there is only one retrieval at the head in cases like this (at the verb *sent* in this example), there should only be one cost-bearing retrieval dependency arc associated with processing this verb. The idea is that in cases where two or more dependent words both predict a coming head word, the language processor can collapse its predictions for the upcoming head together with other dependent words also predicting the same head, such that there is only one retrieval at the head. The cost of this retrieval is then the cost associated with the most recent connection. Under this proposal, there is also a cost of connecting each prediction to the next pre-head dependent. In the example above, this connection of predictions is shown in red between *yesterday* and *coworker*. There is no direct connection between *yesterday* and *sent*: This is shown as a dotted dependency, because it is implicit in the connection between *coworker* and *sent*.

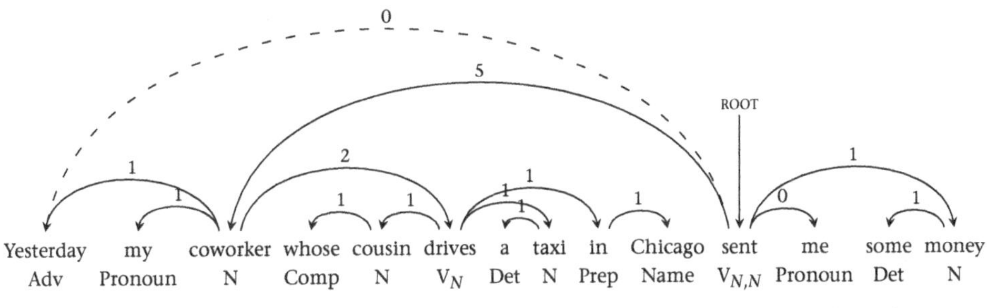

(Note that the name +M (for modifier) from Shain et al. (2022) is a bit of a misnomer: It should probably be called something like "pre-head" for more perspicuity.)

4.7.2 Other Theories That Shain et al. Evaluated

Shain et al. (2022) evaluated two other classes of theories: left-corner parsing variants (Rosenkrantz and Lewis, 1970), and a memory-based theory called

ACT-R based on general-purpose "unified" theories of cognition by Alan Newell (Newell, 1990; Ritter et al., 2019).

Left-corner parsing predictors Going back to Johnson-Laird (1983), Resnik (1992), Van Schijndel and Schuler (2013), and Rasmussen and Schuler (2018), researchers have proposed that human language parsing resembles **left-corner parsing** from the programming languages literature (Rosenkrantz and Lewis, 1970). Under this kind of proposal, working memory is a **pushdown store**, and partial structures representing the hypothesized parses of the sentence are put together as the sentence unfolds one word at a time, usually using a context-free grammar representation of the language (see section 7.3 for a discussion of context-free phrase structure grammar). The working memory does three things: (1) pushing new derivation fragments onto the stack in storage; (2) retrieving and assembling the fragments from the store; and (3) maintaining the incomplete derivation fragments in the store (Rasmussen and Schuler, 2018). Shain et al. (2022) investigated eleven potential ways in which these kinds of frameworks could be associated with working memory costs, including costs like those in the DLT corresponding to retrieval and storage, but in left-corner parsing terms.

I won't go through the details of these proposals here, because they are somewhat complicated, and it turns out that these particular memory proposals weren't correlated with brain activity in Shain et al.'s (2005) analysis.

ACT-R theories In ACT-R theories of sentence processing, representations are constructed through a content-addressable retrieval operation that is subject to similarity-based interference (Gordon et al., 2001; McElree et al., 2003; van Dyke and Lewis, 2003; Lewis and Vasishth, 2005a; Lewis et al., 2006). The grammar for the first ACT-R parser (Lewis and Vasishth, 2005a) was constructed so as to handle a particular set of target materials, from the psycholinguistics community. This implementation was not designed to handle arbitrary sentences from a corpus. However, a recent implementation constructed by Dotlačil (2021) is an ACT-R model with broad coverage. Shain et al. (2022) evaluated the predictions of this model. In this model, activation decays on both time and degree of similarity with retrieval competitors, and is highest when the cue strongly identifies a recently activated target. ACT-R target activation was predicted to be correlated with retrieval, such that higher activations meant easier retrieval.

4.7.3 Materials and Participants in Shain et al.'s Experiment

In order to evaluate these language processing theories, Shain et al. (2022) had seventy-eight participants listen to naturalistic stories while lying in the MRI scanner. The texts were from the naturalistic stories corpus (Futrell et al., 2018): ten stories about one thousand words each, each recorded by one of two speakers (one of those speakers was me). Each participant listened to some subset of the stories in the scanner. Forty-one of the participants answered questions about the content of the stories that they heard, while the remainder (n=37) listened passively. The stories were naturally occurring short narrative or nonfiction materials that had been edited in order to overrepresent rare words and syntactic constructions without compromising perceived naturalness. An example from Futrell et al. (2018) is given in (118):

(118) *If you were to journey to the North of England, you would come to a valley that is surrounded by moors as high as mountains. It is in this valley where you would find the city of Bradford, where once a thousand spinning jennies that hummed and clattered spun wool into money for the long-bearded mill owners. That all mill owners were generally busy as beavers and quite pleased with themselves for being so successful and well off was well known to the residents of Bradford, and if you were to go into the city to visit the stately City Hall, you would see there the Crest of the City of Bradford, which those same mill owners created to celebrate their achievements.*

This example component of one story includes rare structures such as an it-cleft (*it was in this valley where...*); a sentential subject (*That all mill owners ... was well known*); and an object-extracted relative clause with a full noun phrase as its subject (*which those same mill owners created to celebrate*).

4.7.4 Analysis and Results from Shain et al.'s Experiment

Because so many theories were being investigated, Shain et al. (2022) first evaluated the theories in a subset of the data (the exploratory data) and then tested the theories that were successful in making predictions beyond all the controls in that dataset, in the held-out data (the test data). The exploratory data consisted of half of each participant's data in the training, using a method that didn't bias the materials in the training or test. The remaining half formed the test data.

Overall, only the DLT predictors were reliable in the exploratory data: Six of the eight integration cost proposals were significant in a conservative test, with a twenty-two-way Bonferroni correction. The other two were also correlated with the remaining six but were not significant under a 0.001 level of significance. The DLT storage cost proposal was also reliable in this exploratory set. None of the eleven left-corner parsing predictors was reliable nor was the ACT-R predictor ($p = 0.70$).

In the test data, Shain et al. (2022) evaluated the DLT storage cost hypothesis together with the best of the DLT integration cost hypotheses: the one that explained most variance. The best DLT integration cost hypothesis was the one with all three parameters set: extra cost for tensed verbs; a cost of only one for a conjoined NP, independent of the number of NPs that are conjoined; and no cost for initial modifiers. The results of the analysis on the test set are presented in panel A of figure 4.3. There, we can see that the DLT integration cost is significantly activated above baseline in the regions predefined as language areas of the cortex, but not in regions predefined as multiple demands areas of the cortex (Fedorenko et al., 2013), all as predicted.[11] However, the DLT storage cost was not significant in either the language areas of the cortex or the multiple demands areas of the cortex in these test data. Furthermore the DLT integration activations were comparable in size to those associated with the best surprisal measure, adaptive surprisal. This experiment thus provides evidence for (a) brain activation associated with working memory demands in the language regions of the cortex, above and beyond syntactic or lexical surprisal; and (b) the DLT integration cost hypothesis as a measure of linguistic working memory demands in the brain over other theories of working memory in language.

4.8 Summary of Dependency Locality Effects

In this chapter, I have provided evidence that there is a cognitive cost associated with making a longer-distance dependency connection relative to making a shorter one. This observation leads to a simple explanation of many cognitive effects, including the greater cognitive complexity of nested dependencies compared to non-nested dependencies, among many

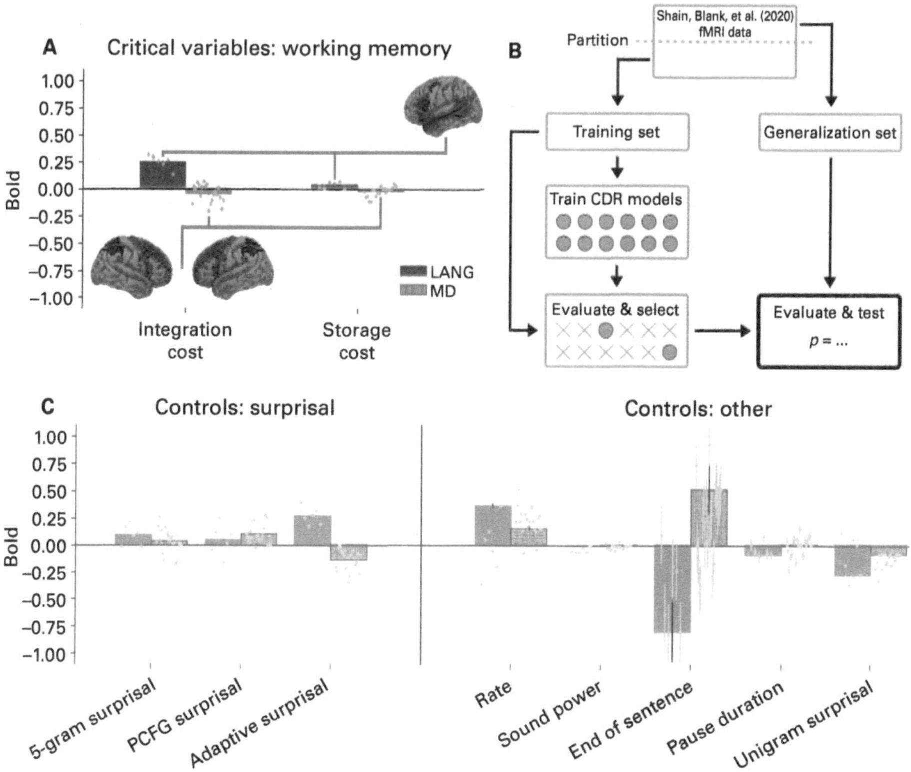

Figure 4.3
In panel A, we can see that that the DLT integration cost is significantly activated above baseline in the regions predefined as language areas of the cortex, but not in regions predefined as multiple demands areas of the cortex, all as predicted in Shain et al.'s (2022) analyses of the training data. The DLT storage cost was not significant in either the language areas of the cortex or the multiple demands areas of the cortex. These activations were comparable in size to those associated with the strongest surprisal measure, adaptive surprisal, as shown in panel C (where the language network activations are shown in the more solid color, on the left of each pair of bars). This experiment thus provides evidence for (a) brain activation associated with working memory demands in the language regions of the cortex, above and beyond syntactic or lexical surprisal; and (b) the DLT integration cost hypothesis as a measure of linguistic working memory demands in the brain over other theories of working memory in language.

other observations in language production (from corpus analyses, mostly in English) and language comprehension.

While the existence of locality effects is robust, the details of the distance metric are still very much under investigation. It appears that the effects are interference based, such that the similarity of material in the intervening region matters for complexity.

Finally, there appears to be evidence of dependency locality in brain activation in the language cortex, but many more experiments in this domain need to be carried out before we can be certain of theoretical details.

5 Dependency Length Minimization as a Constraint on Grammars

Chapter 3 provided a dependency grammar analysis of some simple English sentences. And chapter 4 provided evidence that there is a cost of connecting two elements together that are displaced over time: This is the dependency locality cost hypothesis (Gibson, 1998, 2000; Lewis and Vasishth, 2005a).

In this chapter, I explore whether dependency locality cost might affect how languages order their words. The hypothesis to be explored here is that languages will tend to use word orders that minimize dependency distances between words. I first describe results from Futrell et al. (2015b) and Futrell et al. (2020b), which showed that the fifty-three languages in the Universal Dependencies Corpora (Nivre et al., 2016, 2020; De Marneffe et al., 2021) all minimize dependency lengths relative to a conservative baseline.

In the remainder of the chapter, I work through some of what are sometimes called **harmonic word orders**, from Greenberg's word order generalizations across languages (Greenberg, 1963). According to these generalizations, there is a bias for word orders in different kinds of constructions to align within a language in the same head direction (also called the **head-direction generalization**; Dryer 1992). In particular, languages with head-first word order in one kind of dependency relationship (such as a verb-object dependency) tend to have matching head-first word order in other dependency relationships, such as in prepositional-object word order or subordinator-verb word order. I show how dependency length minimization leads to a bias for these effects within a language.

5.1 Dependency Length Minimization across Languages

Futrell et al. (2015b) and Futrell et al. (2020b) evaluated the hypothesis that languages might generally minimize dependency lengths by examining corpora from thirty-seven languages from the initial Universal Dependencies (UD) corpora in 2015 (Nivre et al., 2016, 2020; De Marneffe et al., 2021; Futrell et al., 2015b), and fifty-three languages from the UD corpora in 2020 for Futrell et al. (2020b) (see also Liu 2008; Temperley 2007, 2008; Gildea and Temperley 2010) (there are currently 148 languages in the UD corpora, as of 2024).[1] For each dependency structure in each corpus, Futrell et al. (2015b) computed the total dependency distance in terms of words. So for (99a) (repeated below, an example that Futrell et al. [2015a] created for illustration purposes), the total dependency distance is eighteen words, as you can see from its dependency structure to follow:

(99a) Mary threw away the important documents that she brought home yesterday.

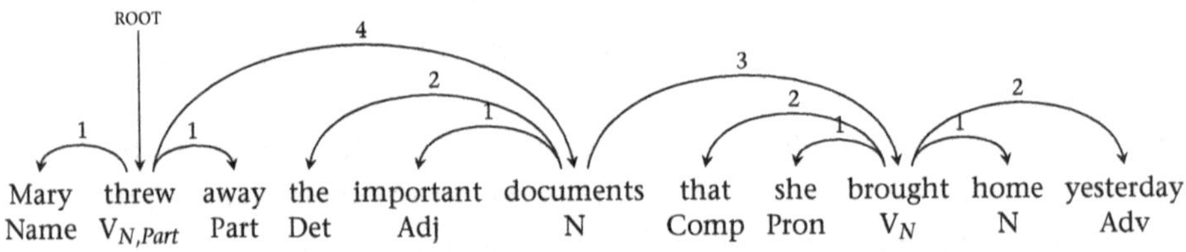

Futrell et al. (2015b) and Futrell et al. (2020b) computed several baseline structures on which to compare dependency lengths. Perhaps the most obvious baseline structure is to simply keep the dependency structure the same and scramble the words. This keeps the meaning the same but results in a non-English word order as in the following:

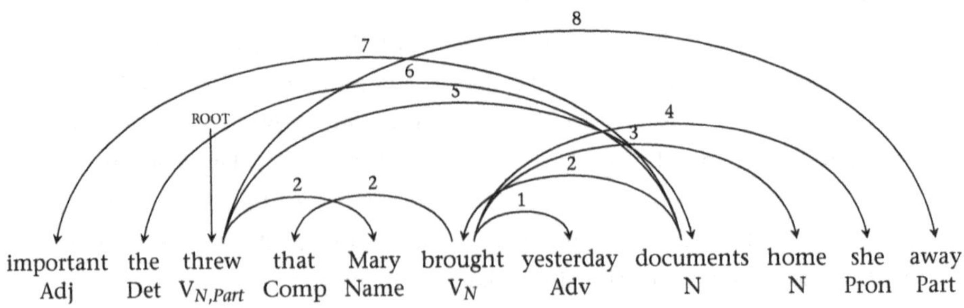

We can see that the random word order above is kind of bizarre, in part because it has many crossed dependencies. And its total length is forty, much more than the eighteen that the source sentence started with. Human languages tend to have few crossed dependencies (Kruijff and Vasishth, 2003; Levy and Manning, 2004; Levy et al., 2012). Absence of crossed dependencies is called **projectivity**: Human languages tend to be projective. Allowing non-projective structures allows for much longer possible dependencies in the baseline on average. Indeed, Ferrer-i-Cancho (2006) has argued that perhaps human languages have evolved to having fewer crossed dependencies because of a pressure to minimize dependency distances (see also Ferrer-i-Cancho, 2015, 2016; Yadav et al., 2021).

A more constrained baseline is therefore a projective one. In order to create a projective baseline, Futrell et al. (2015b) started at the head word of each structure, and randomly ordered this word with its dependents below. So for (99a) they would choose some order of *threw*, *Mary*, *away* and *documents* here. Then they repeated this step all the way down the structure, choosing a random order each time. An example projective control for (99a) is provided below:

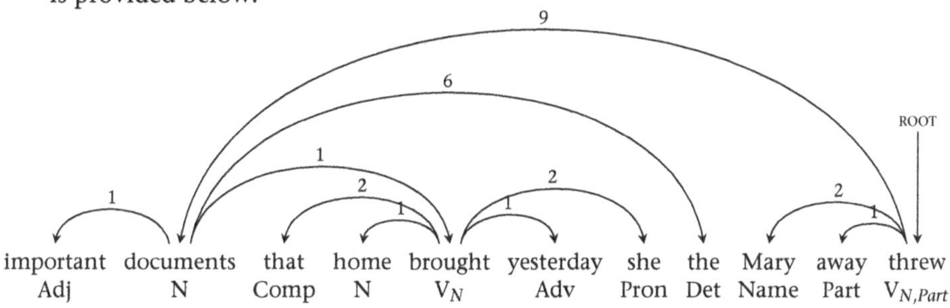

We can see that, like the fully random ordering, this word order also has long dependencies, but not so many as the non-projective one. The total length on this one is twenty-eight, much less than the fully random, but much more than the source structure. In order to get meaningful baseline dependency comparisons for each sentence, Futrell et al. (2015b) and Futrell et al. (2020b) created one hundred random versions of each (non-projective or projective) on which to compute dependency lengths. These results across fifty-three languages are presented in figure 5.1. We can see that, for all languages, the real sentences have shorter dependency lengths than either the non-projective or the projective baselines. The non-projective baselines have very long dependency lengths. But even the projective control sentences are much longer than the sentences that people actually produced.

For example, let's look at English, in the second row of the figure, five columns over from the left. We see that the actual dependency lengths in English are much lower on average than either the non-projective baseline

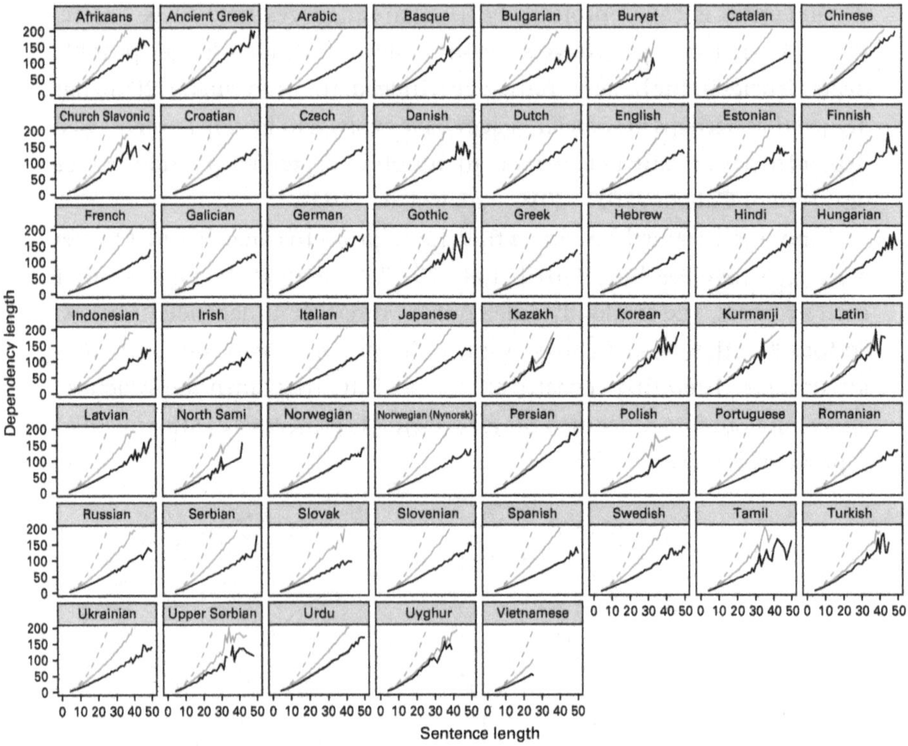

Figure 5.1
Dependency length as a function of sentence length for fifty-three languages. The x-axis is sentence length, and the y-axis is the mean of total dependency length for all sentences of that length. The black line represents the average dependency lengths of the sentences in the corpora. The dashed lines represent non-projective random baselines, and the grey lines represent projective random baselines. The attested orders are shorter than either baseline, for all languages, as sentences get longer (from Richard Futrell, working with the materials discussed in Futrell et al. [2020b]).

dependency lengths (which are very long) or the conservative projective dependency lengths.

While most languages have much shorter dependencies than the baselines, there are some languages that are much closer to the baseline than the others. Latin, Korean, Chinese, Kurmanji, and Uyghur are examples that pop out when we look at figure 5.1.[2] The case of Chinese is not well understood: In this corpus, the dependencies are barely above the baseline. The corpus that Latin is evaluated on consists of a lot of poetry, which is probably not the right kind of language to evaluate a communication-based hypothesis (because the function of poetry is much more than simple communication of the literal meaning of the language). The word order in Latin is relatively free, so poets can move the words around to make sentences that fit desired rhythms and rhymes. The result of the poetry is language with lots of long-distance and crossed dependencies. It is possible that Latin language that is constructed for the purposes of simple communication only (without the other poetry constraints) might have more local dependencies on average, but this cannot be tested any more, because Latin is a dead language, with no current native speakers.

Regarding Korean, this SOV language genuinely has many long-distance dependencies, often between the subject and verb. Hence its dependency distances are not much above the baseline. Japanese—a language with similar structure to Korean—also has many long-distance dependencies, but its analysis shows it to be well above the baseline dependency length. Both of these languages have cases for their nouns: morphological endings on the nouns to tell us what their grammatical role is in the sentence. For example, the ending *-ga* is the nominative ending for Japanese, indicating that the noun is the subject in the clause. And the ending *-o* is the accusative case-marker in Japanese, indicating that its noun is the object in the clause.

The difference between Korean and Japanese dependency lengths here is probably due to a difference in what counts as a token in the Universal Dependency structures for each language: In Japanese, the case-markers are counted as separate tokens, whereas in Korean the case-markers are part of the head nouns. This accidental difference in the way that the languages have been coded likely leads to the observed dependency length difference between the two languages in their control structures. Kurmanji and Uyghur are also head-final (SOV) languages, but the datasets are small in the Universal Dependencies corpora, so it is possible that the results are not fully representative of the languages. It is also possible that these results are similar to those from Korean.

Futrell et al. (2015b) also did some probabilistic grammar modeling, such that they pick the most likely order of a head and its dependents, in the rules that are given by the parses in the treebank for a language. So, under this analysis, they find subject-verb-object rules in SVO languages like English, but subject-object-verb rules (head-final) rules in SOV languages like Japanese or Korean. Then Futrell et al. (2015b) looked to see if samples from this grammar have lower dependency lengths than the random baselines. If so, then that's evidence that the grammar minimizes dependency lengths. And if real dependency lengths are shorter than samples from the grammar, then that's evidence for dependency length minimization in usage. Their analyses found evidence of both types of minimization. This suggests that human grammars are constrained by memory limitations: We want rule systems that allow more local dependencies compared to longer ones.

5.2 Harmonic Word Orders across Languages

A fascinating generalization across languages is that if a language has head-initial verb-object word order, then its head-argument word order rules tend to be head-initial, as in English and in lots of other subject-verb-object (SVO) languages such as Mandarin, Spanish, French, or Swahili. But if a language has object-verb word order, then all of its head-argument word order rules tend to be head-final. This is true for subject-object-verb (SOV) languages in general, such as Japanese, Korean, Turkish, Persian, and Hindi. This is the **head-direction generalization**, leading to **harmonic word orders** (Greenberg, 1963; Vennemann, 1974; Hawkins, 1983, 1990; Dryer, 1992; Temperley, 2007; Dryer, 2011a; Hahn et al., 2020).

In this section, I first show what it means for a language to be head-first, or head-final across different dependency relationships. Then I evaluate some of Greenberg (1963) harmonic word order generalizations, using word order data from the World Atlas of Linguistic Structures (WALS) (Dryer, 2013) (see Hahn et al. (2020) for related by different potential explanations for these word order phenomena). I show how dependency length minimization leads to a bias for these effects within a language.

5.2.1 Word Order Rules in English, a Verb-Object Language

So far, I have provided a dependency grammar analysis of some simple English sentences. Below I provide many of the rules that we have seen thus far. A key observation has been that, whereas subjects come before the verb, all other arguments of a verb come after the head.

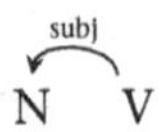

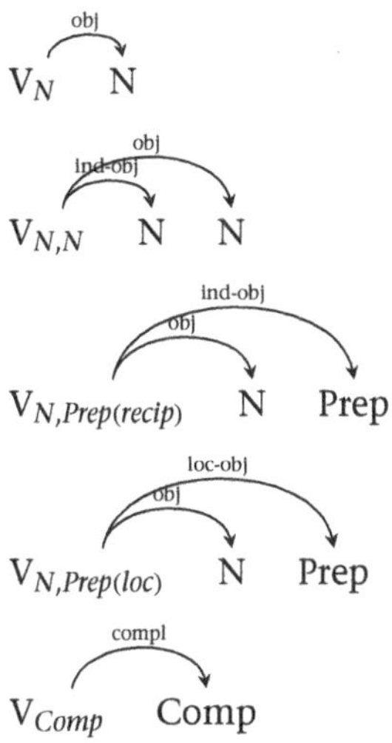

There are several other head-initial rules in English that we have identified, including the subordinator-before-verb rule and the preposition-before-noun rule:

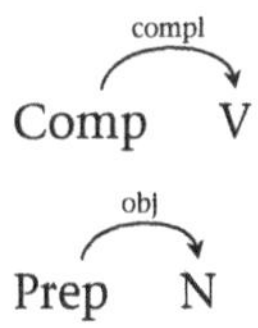

There are also modifier rules, most of which are head-initial, like prepositions following nouns and verbs:

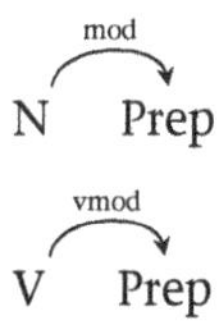

We have also identified three head-final rules: Subject nouns come before their head verbs, for all main verbs (the first rule give above)[3]; determiners come before their head nouns; and adjectives come before their head nouns:

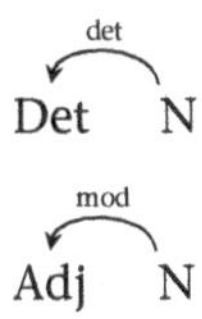

5.2.2 Word Orders in Subject-Object-Verb Languages

We can form the verb-final rules for a head-final language like Japanese by inverting the right-hand side of all the rules:

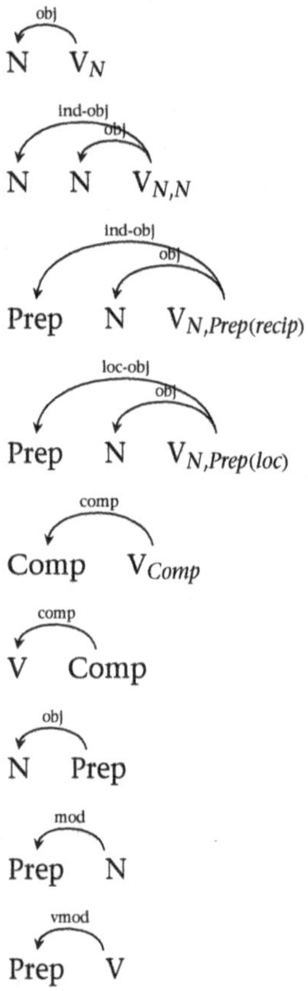

The subject-verb rule in an SOV language is unchanged from that of an SVO language: This is already head-final. The determiner rule is not so general across languages. Many languages don't mark words like *a* and *the* in the way that English does, so I will ignore this rule for head-final languages.

Consequently, the structures for some English and Japanese sentences are effectively mirror images of one another, in the head-argument rules (without changing the order of the subject rule). Here are three pairs of examples, with the first structure for English (SVO) word order, and the second structure for Japanese (SOV) word order.

(119) a. SVO: Lana ate pizza.

b. SOV: Lana pizza ate.

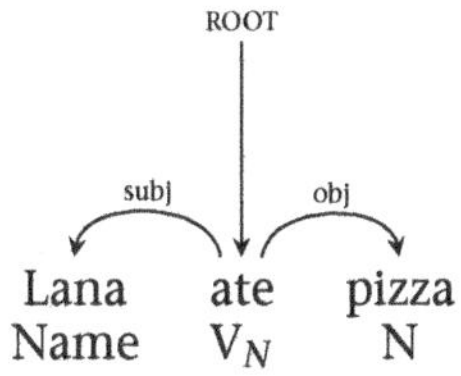

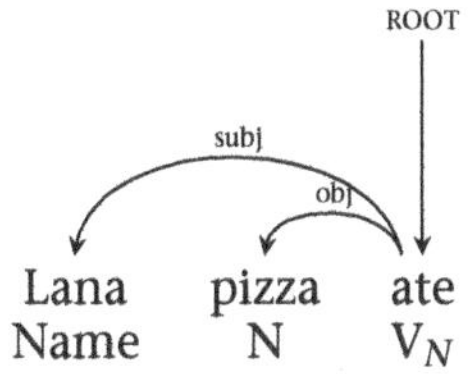

These two structures are identical except for the order of the verb "ate" and the object NP pizza: In English, the verb is first—*Lana ate pizza*—while in Japanese the NP *pizza* precedes the verb: *Lana pizza ate*. (I am not translating the words here; I am just giving the Japanese word order. It should be noted that most SOV languages have case-marking on the NPs. I am omitting these case-markers for simplicity.) The next pair of examples are for the following English sentence, and its SOV counterpart:

(120) a. SVO: Lana gave pizza to Francine.
b. SOV: Lana Francine to pizza gave.

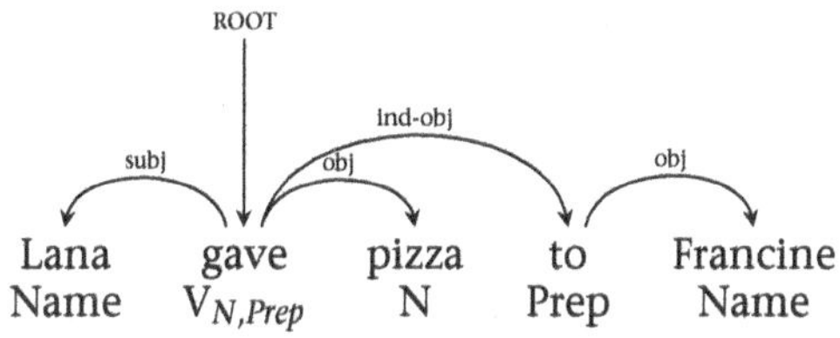

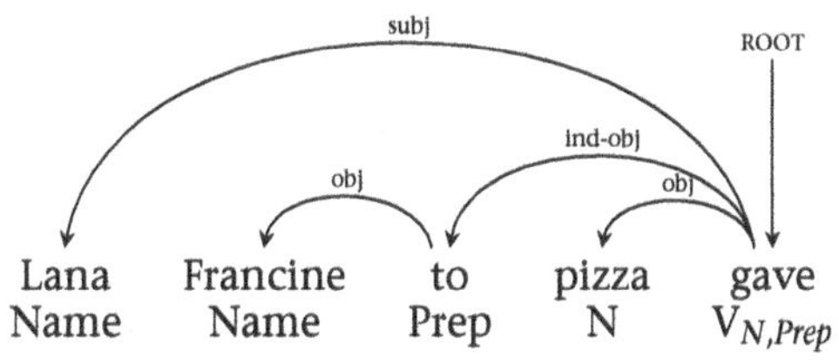

The material after the subject noun *Lana* in the English sentence *Lana gave pizza to Francine* is mirror-imaged in the SOV word order: *Francine to pizza gave*. Finally consider the word orders for the following embedded sentences:

(121) a. SVO: Alfred said that Lana gave pizza to Francine.
b. SOV: Alfred Lana Francine to pizza gave that said.

The SOV version inverts the verb *said* and its complement, headed by the subordinator *that*. Furthermore, the subordinator *that* and its complement clause are inverted from the SVO word order. Then the embedded sentence is identical to the SOV version of that sentence presented above.

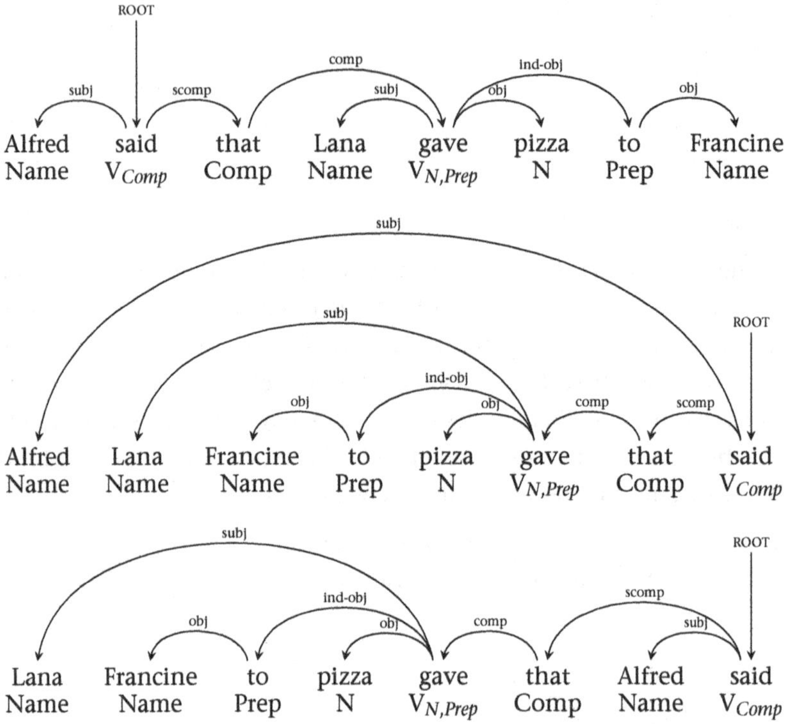

5.3 Dependency Length Minimization Explains Harmonic Cross-Linguistic Word Order Generalizations

According to Greenberg's harmomic word order generalizations, there is a bias for word orders in different kinds of constructions to align within a language in the same head direction (Greenberg, 1963; Lehmann, 1973; Vennemann, 1974; Hawkins, 1983, 1990; Dryer, 1992; Hahn et al., 2020). The generalization is that argument structures across different classes of words are mostly ordered in the same direction relative to a head, within a language. All of these harmonic alignments follow from dependency length minimization: Dependencies can be shorter when they are aligned harmonically (Futrell et al., 2015a, 2020b; Hawkins, 1990, 1994) (cf. Hahn et al. [2020] for a different but related hypothesis).[4]

In particular, languages with head-first word order in one kind of dependency relationship (such as a verb-object dependency) tend to have matching head-first word order in other dependency relationships, such as in prepositional-object word order or subordinator-verb word order. I show how dependency length minimization leads to a bias for these effects within a language.

Consider a case where each word has only one dependent. If the head-direction is uniformly head-first or head-final, the dependencies are all local (Temperley, 2007):

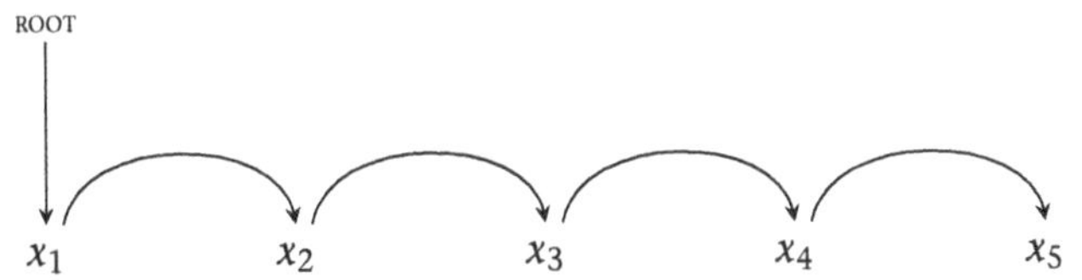

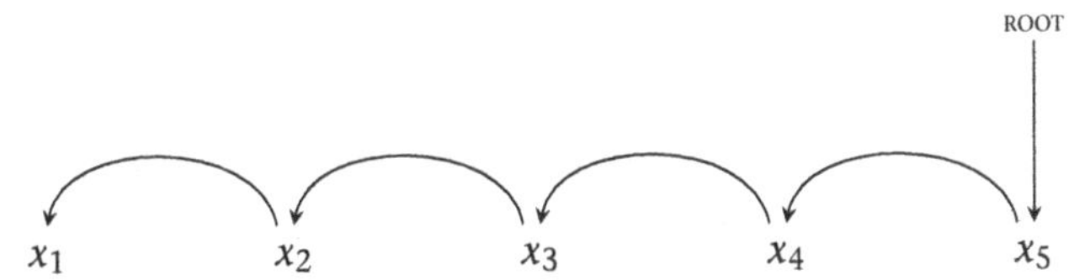

When some are head-first and some are head-final, then the dependency lengths are much longer:

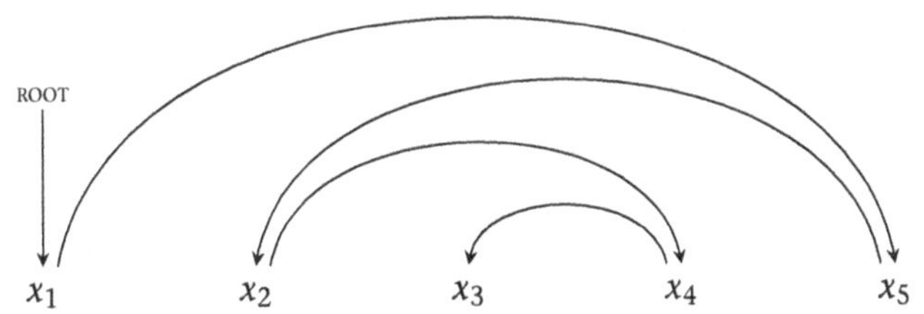

In the remainder of the sections below, I show how four cases of such harmonic orders follow dependency length minimization. First, the word order for a verb relative to its dependents is the same across verb argument types. So when a language takes an object following the verb, it will also tend to take sentence complements following the verb. English is verb-initial (except for the subject) for all verbal argument structures, from clausal complements, to double objects, to argument structures consisting

Table 5.1
The number of languages in the world as listed in WALS (Dryer, 2013) with orders of verb-object / object-verb and prepositions / postpositions. Numbers obtained in November 2023 from https://wals.info/combinations/83A_85A#2/16.4/153.0

Verb-object prepositions	Verb-object postpositions	Object-verb prepositions	Object-verb postpositions
454	41	14	472

of nouns and different kinds of prepositional phrases or clauses. And SOV languages like Japanese or Korean are verb-final for all of their verbal argument structures. For example, Dryer (1992) shows that (a) verb-object word order for transitive verbs in general tend to go with a head-initial word order for verbs like *want* that take a verbal complement (e.g., *I want to go*), and (b) verb-object word order for transitive verbs tends to go with verb-initial word order for copula verbs (forms of the verb *to be* in English) (see also Hahn et al., 2020).

Second, head-initial languages usually tend to have head-initial **adpositions** (**prepositions**), whereas head-final languages usually have head-final adpositions (**postpositions**) (Dryer, 2013). The numbers of languages with verb-object vs. object-verb and prepositions vs. postpositions are presented in table 5.1. Most verb-object languages have prepositions: 454 out of 499 languages. And most object-verb languages have postpositions: 472 out of 486 languages.

Third, head-initial languages usually have head-initial subordinators, whereas head-final languages usually have head-final subordinators (Dryer, 1991, 2013). The numbers of languages that have subordinating words from WALS 2023 are presented for verb-object/object-verb in table 5.2. Almost all verb-object languages with subordinator words have the subordinator initially, before the subordinate clause: 302 out of 304 languages. And most object-verb languages with subordinator words have the subordinator following the subordinate clause: 91 out of 152 such languages.

Fourth, head-initial languages usually have head-initial relative clauses (with the noun first), whereas head-final languages usually have head-final relative clauses, with the head noun at the end (Dryer, 1991, 2013). The numbers of languages with verb-object vs. object-verb and head-initial relative clauses vs. head-final relative clauses are presented in table 5.3. Most

Table 5.2
The number of languages in the world as listed in WALS (Dryer, 2013) with orders of verb-object / object-verb and subordinator-initial / subordinator-final subordinator words (complementizers). Numbers obtained in November 2023 from https://wals.info/combinations/94A_83A#2/17.2/152.8

Verb-object subordinator-initial	Verb-object subordinator-final	Object-verb subordinator-initial	Object-verb subordinator-final
302	2	61	91

Table 5.3
Number of languages in the world as listed in WALS (Dryer, 2013) with orders of Verb-object / object-verb and relative-clause-noun / noun-relative-clause orders. Numbers obtained in November 2023 from https://wals.info/combinations/83A_96A#2/24.3/153.0

Verb-object noun-relative-clause	Verb-object relative-clause-noun	Object-verb noun-relative-clause	Object-verb relative-clause-noun
415	5	113	132

verb-object languages have head-initial relative clauses: 415 out of 420 languages. And most object-verb languages have head-final relative clauses: 132 out of 245 languages (although this is clearly only a slight bias).[5]

5.3.1 Aligning the Direction of Verb-Object Dependencies and the Complements of Verbs Like *Want*

Consider an English example, with a main clause and an embedded clausal argument of *wanted*, along with its dependency structure:

(122) Alfred wanted to eat bananas from Hawaii.

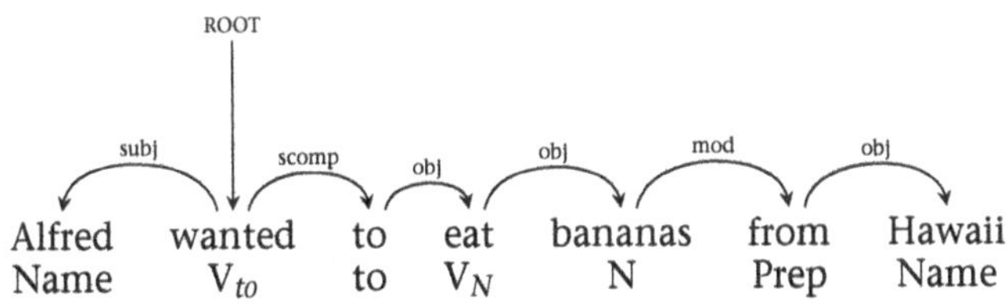

All dependencies are immediately adjacent in this structure, for a total dependency distance of only 6 word-units for a 7-word sentence: the minimum possible dependency distance.

In a head-final structure for the same words, all dependencies are reversed, except the subject-verb dependency:

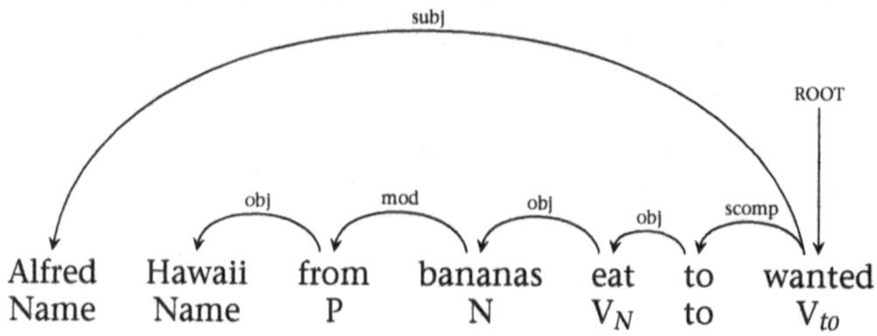

In a head-final language, the subject can occur next to the verb, as in:

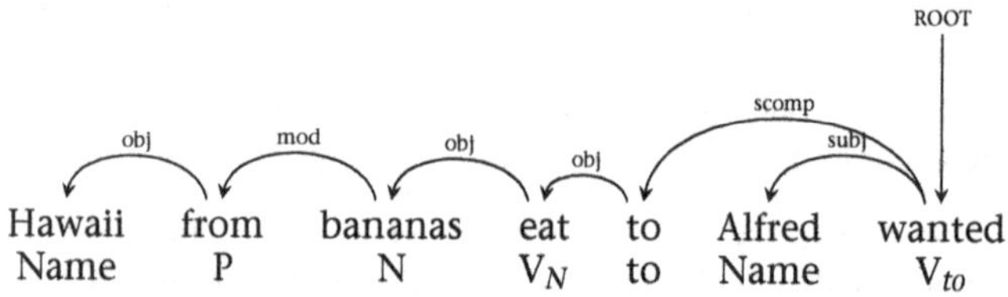

The total dependency length for this structure is only 7 word-units, one more than the minimum possible.

Let us now see what the dependency lengths look like when the headedness order for the verb *eat* (a verb-object relationship) don't match the headedness order for the verb *wanted* (a verb-scomp relationship). First, let's see what the dependency lengths look like for a verb-object order for *eat* and an scomp-verb order for *wanted*:

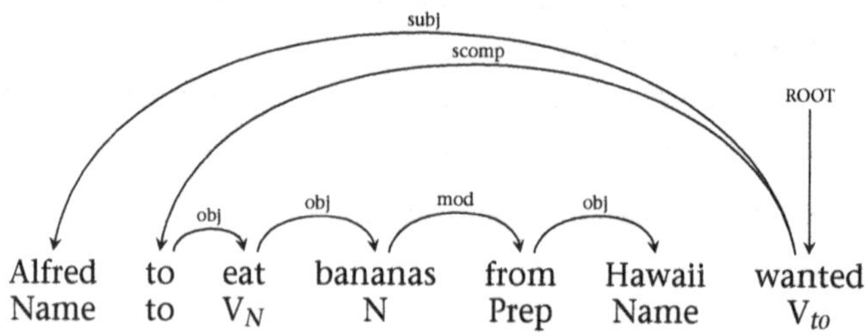

The dependency lengths are much longer, at 15 word-units vs. 6 or 7 as a baseline where the head-dependency relationships are matched. Now let's see what the dependency lengths look like for an object-verb order for *eat* and a verb-scomp order for *wanted*:

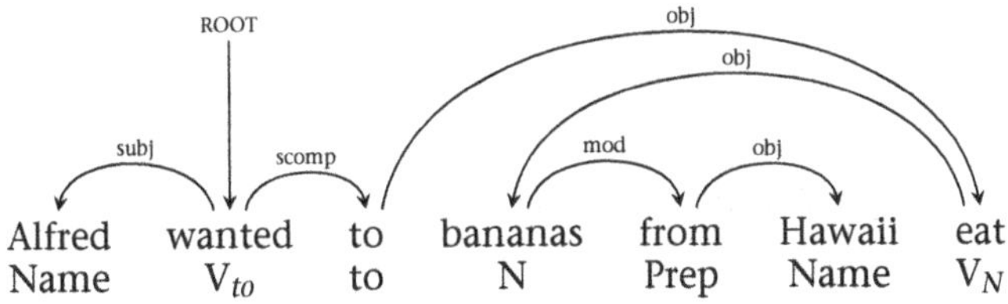

Again, the dependency lengths are much longer, at 11 word-units vs. 6 or 7 as a baseline where the head-dependency relationships are matched.

5.3.2 Aligning Verb-Object and Subordinator-Verb Dependency Directions

Consider an English example, with a main clause and an embedded clause (with a subordinator-verb relation), and a preposition followed by a somewhat long noun phrase:

(123) Alfred said that Lana gave pizza to monkeys who wanted bananas.

Here is the English dependency structure for this sentence:

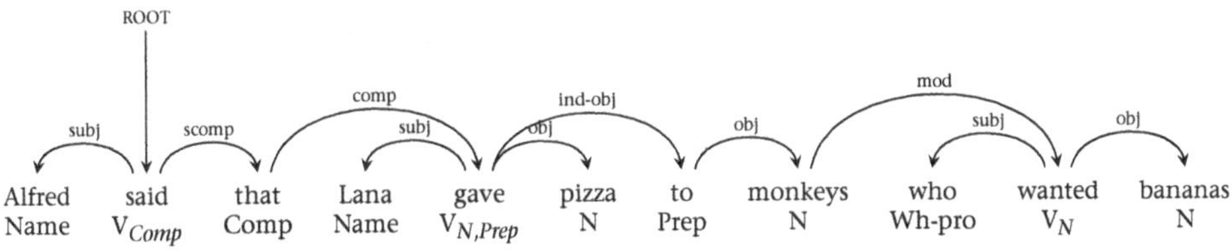

The total dependency length (in words) for this structure is 13, which is very low for 11 words total, because most of the dependencies connect to the immediately adjacent word.

Here is a head-final structure for this sentence, for a language like Japanese or Korean:

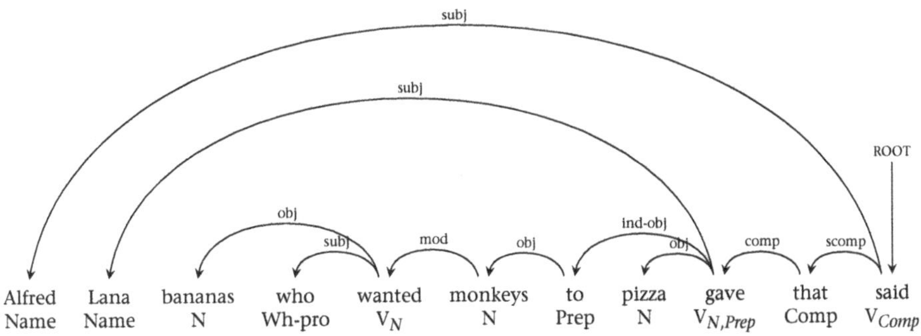

The total dependency lengths for this structure is 27, which is much higher than the English structure. This greater dependency score is driven by the long subject dependencies for clauses headed by *gave* and *said*. But this is not actually the way that a Japanese person would typically produce this material. Head-final languages like Japanese are flexible about their argument ordering, as long as they are head-final, so a more natural word order for this meaning would put both subject nouns adjacent to their verbs (rather than first, as in English):

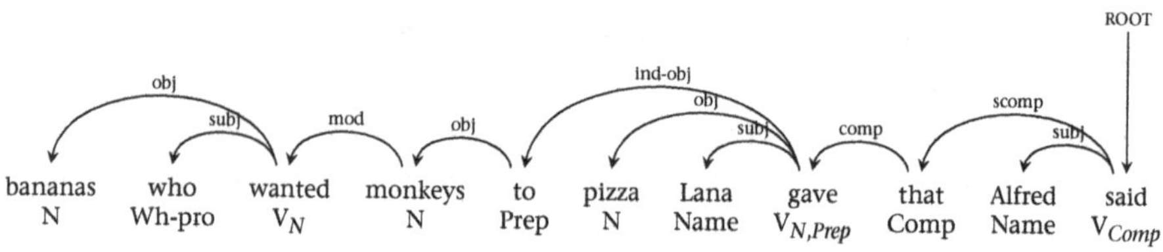

The total dependency length for this structure is now 15, similar to the low dependency score for the verb-initial structure above for English.

Now let's see what happens when we have head-initial word order for verbs but head-final order for subordinator-verb word order:

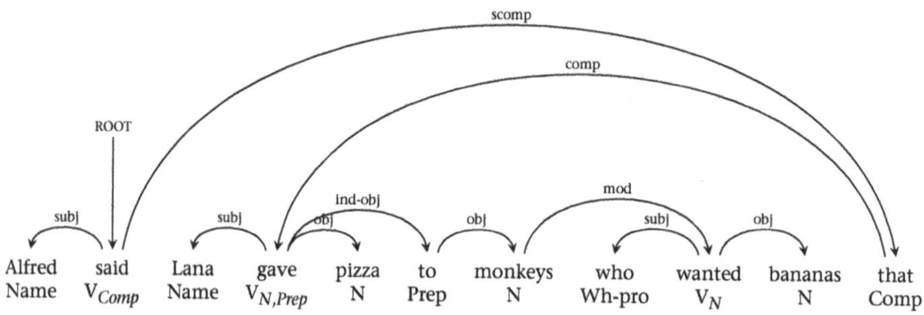

The total dependency length for this structure is now 26, much more than the baseline 13. This big difference is caused by forcing the subordinator *that* to the end of the sentence, following the clause that it heads, necessitating two long dependencies instead of two short ones. It is easy to see that verb-initial subordinator-final word orders always result in much longer dependency lengths than verb-initial subordinator-first word orders. Hence verb-initial subordinator-final word orders never occur across languages, plausibly because of a desire to minimize dependency lengths within a grammar.

Now consider when we have head-final word order for verbs but head-initial order for subordinator-verb word order:

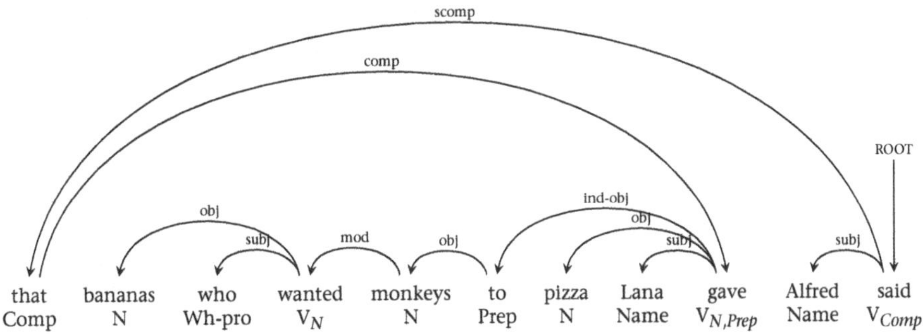

The total dependency length for this structure is now 30, much more than the baseline 15. Again, the big difference is caused by forcing the subordinator *that* to the extreme of the sentence (now the beginning), preceding the clause that it heads, which then necessitates two long dependencies instead of two short ones. It is also easy to see that verb-final subordinator-initial word orders always result in much longer dependency lengths than verb-final subordinator-final word orders. Hence verb-final subordinator-first word orders are rarer than one might expect across languages, plausibly because of a desire to minimize dependency lengths within a grammar.[6]

5.3.3 Aligning Verb-Complement and Adposition-Noun Dependency Directions

Now let's see what happens with adposition-noun word order and verb-complement word order. The same kind of generalizations follow, but because the complements of adpositions aren't so long, the differences aren't usually so extreme. I repeat the baseline structures below for the head-initial and head-final structures associated with (123)

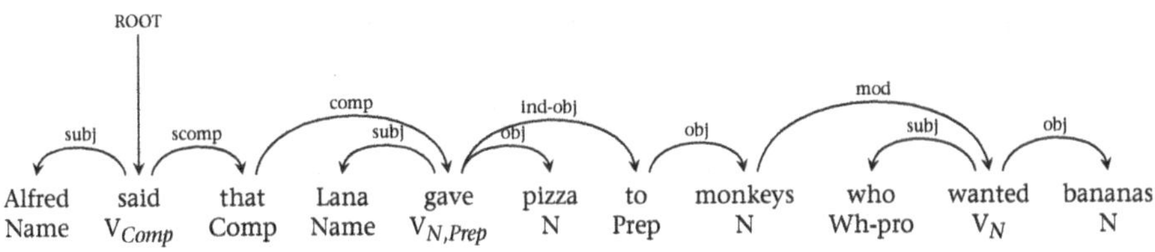

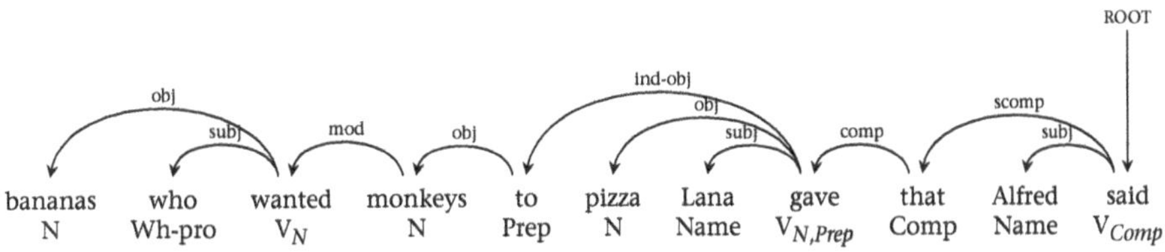

Let's first examine a case where we have head-initial word order for verbs but head-final order for adposition-noun word order (postpositions):

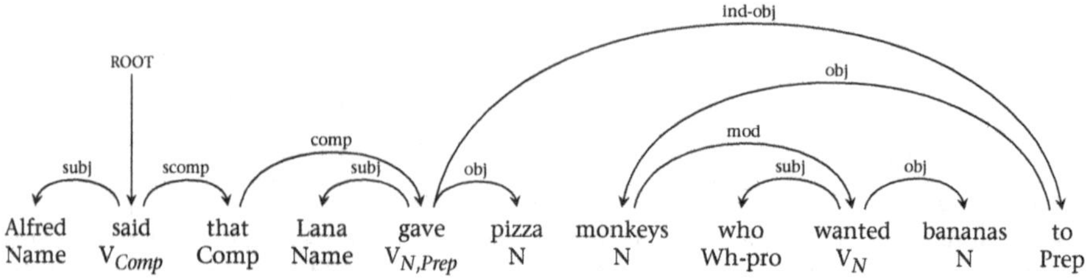

The total dependency length for this structure is 20, much more than the baseline 13. This difference is caused by forcing the preposition *to* to the end of the sentence, following the noun and clausal modifier which it heads, necessitating two long dependencies instead of two short ones. Hence verb-initial preposition-final word orders are rare across languages, plausibly because of a desire to minimize dependency lengths within a grammar.

Finally consider when we have head-final word order for verbs but head-initial order for preposition-noun word order:

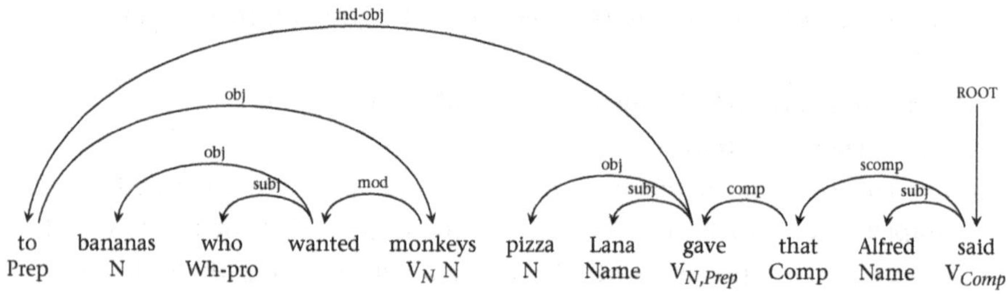

The total dependency length for this structure is now 22, much more than the baseline 15. The big difference is caused by forcing the preposition *to* to the beginning of the sentence, preceding the noun and clausal modifier which it heads, necessitating two long dependencies instead of two short ones. Hence verb-final preposition-first word orders are rare across languages, plausibly because of a desire to minimize dependency lengths within a grammar.

5.3.4 Aligning Verb-Complement and Relative Clause Noun Dependency Directions

Now let's see what happens with verb-complement and relative clause noun dependency word orders. The baseline structures are once again provided below for the head-initial and head-final structures associated with (123):

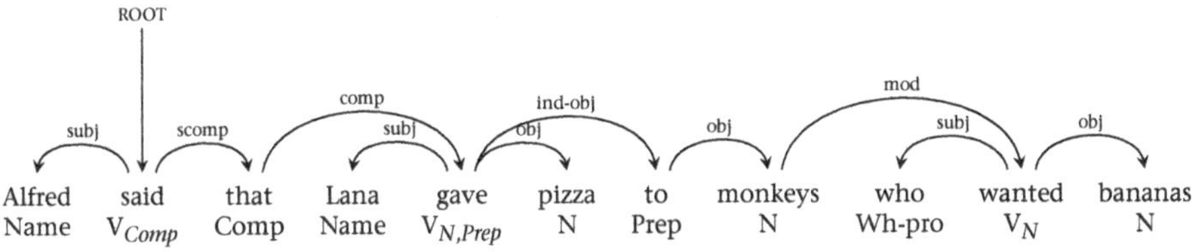

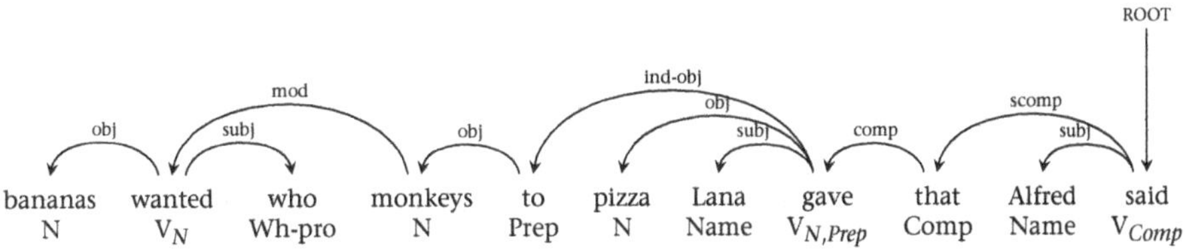

Let's first examine a case where we have head-initial word order for verbs and other categories, but head-final order for relative clauses for their head nouns:

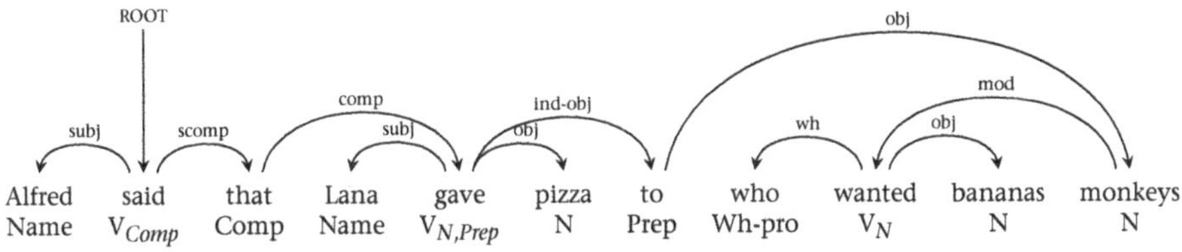

The total dependency length increases from the baseline of 12 word-units to 16 word-units. And now let's examine a case where we have head-final word order for verbs and other categories, but head-initial order for relative clauses for their head nouns:

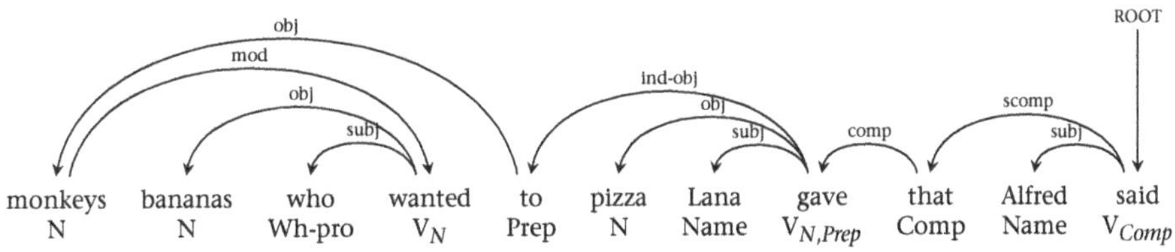

The total dependency length increases from the baseline of 15 word-units to 20 word-units.

5.3.5 Head-Directions Need Not Align when the Dependent Item of One Relationship Is Very Short

Dryer (1992) observes several cases where the order of the verb and its object don't seem to correlate with the head-dependent ordering for some categories, consisting of the set in table 5.4. These are cases like noun and

Table 5.4
Pairs of heads and dependents whose order does not correlate with the verb-object order across languages, in general.

Head	Dependent	Example
Noun	Adjective	*tall man*
Noun	Demonstrative	*that man*
Adjective	Intensifier	*very tall*
Verb	Negative particle	*not go*

adjective: The head is the noun and the dependent is the adjective. The order of the noun and the adjective within a language does not correlate with the order of the verb and its object. Although these are cases of violations of harmonic alignment, they are not problematic for the dependency length explanation of such alignments. This is because the dependent in all of these cases is a single short word, which cannot be lengthened arbitrarily, as in the case of objects, which can be arbitrarily long, including whole clauses. Because the dependents in table 5.4 are all single words, they don't contribute much to dependency lengths, and hence, these word orders need not align with the verb-object order.[7]

6 The Surprising Lack of Dependency Locality in Legalese

As we saw in section 5.1, most language that people produce has local dependencies. Interestingly there is one genre of English text that has unusually long dependencies compared to other genres: legal language or **Legalese**. For example, consider the extract from a contract in (124) from Martínez et al. (2022), along with part of its dependency structure below:

(124) Legalese contract sentence:
In the event that any payment or benefit by the Company (all such payments and benefits, including the payments and benefits under Section 3(a) hereof, being hereinafter referred to as the 'Total Payments'), would be subject to excise tax, then the cash severance payments shall be reduced.

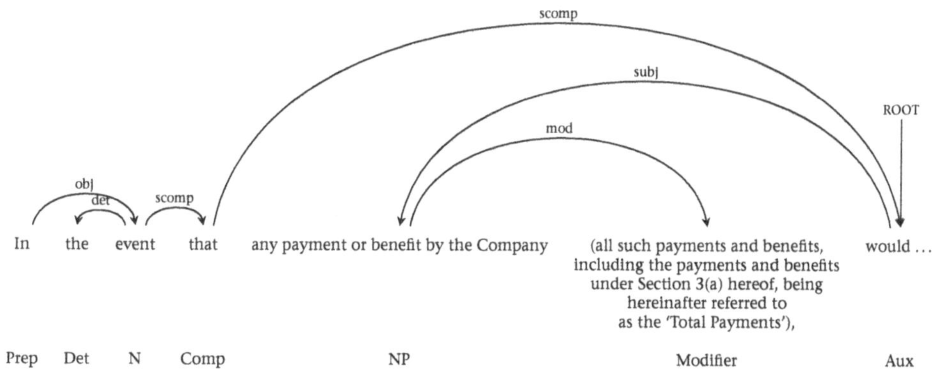

The author of this contract inserted the definition of what a payment and benefit is between the subject-verb dependency between *any payment or benefit* and the auxiliary verb *would*. This results in a very long dependency between the subject and auxiliary verb. It turns out that this kind of center-embedded clause is very common in US legal language relative to any other English genre, as documented by Martínez et al. (2022). In figure 6.1, panel

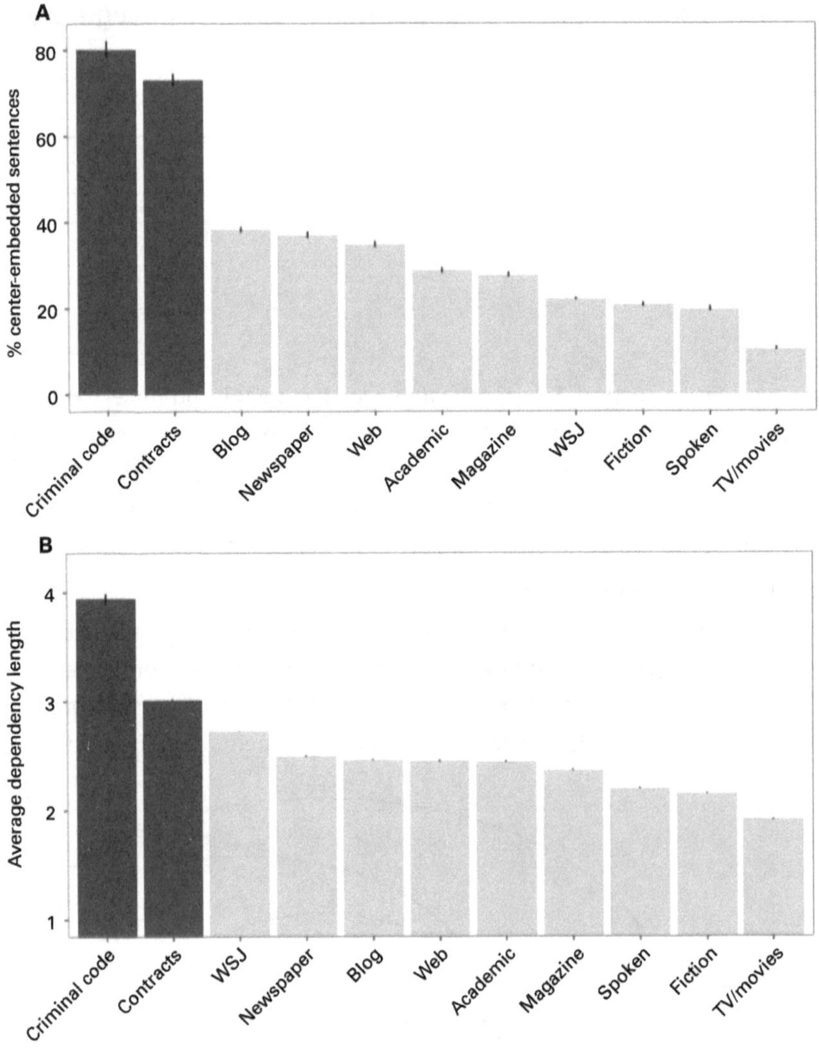

Figure 6.1
Panel A: Comparison of the number of center-embedded clauses per sentence across eleven genres: (1) legal contracts, from a corpus of 3.5 million words from two sources: the Westlaw database and Goźdź-Roszkowski (2011); (2) Title 18 of the United States Criminal Code (2021 edition), 1.1 million words; (3)–(10) from a ten million word subset of the Corpus of Contemporary American English (COCA) Davies (2009) (3) texts from blogs; (4) newspaper texts; (5) text from web pages; (6) academic texts; (7) magazine texts; (8) *The Wall Street Journal*, a five million word corpus from 1996 Paul and Baker (1992); (9) Fiction from books; (10) Spoken American English;

A, we see that the percent of center-embedded clauses per sentence is much higher in US contracts (0.72) and in the US criminal code (0.80) than in any other genre, including newspaper texts, blogs, academic texts, or *The Wall Street Journal* (one particular newspaper, which has a reputation as being meant for educated readers). In panel B, we can see that this increased rate of center-embedding—the measure of syntactic complexity that Martínez et al. (2022) used in their analysis—results in longer average dependency distances in US contracts and in the US criminal code relative to all other genres.

Some further examples of center-embedding from real US contracts are provided in (125)–(127), and from laws in (128)–(130).

(125) From Elon Musk's Twitter acquisition agreement
https://www.sec.gov/Archives/edgar/data/1418091/000119312522120474/d310843ddefa14a.htm
(c) Timing of Exchange. Upon surrender of a Certificate (or affidavit of loss in lieu thereof) or Book-Entry Share for cancellation to the Paying Agent, together with, in the case of Certificates, a letter of transmittal duly completed and validly executed in accordance with the instructions thereto, or, in the case of Book-Entry Shares, receipt of an "agent's message" by the Paying Agent (it being understood that holders of Book-Entry Shares will be deemed to have surrendered such Book-Entry Shares upon receipt of an "agent's message" with respect to such Book-Entry Shares), and such other customary evidence of surrender as the Paying Agent may reasonably require, the holder of such Certificate or Book-Entry Share shall be entitled to receive in exchange therefor (and Parent shall cause the Paying Agent to promptly deliver in exchange therefor) the Merger Consideration for each share of Company Common Stock formerly represented by such

Figure 6.1 (continued)
and (11) TV and movie scripts. (A center-embedded clause is a clause within another subject-verb relation.) The percent of center-embedded clauses per sentence is much higher in US contracts (0.72) and in US criminal code (0.80) than in any other genre (at most 0.39). Panel B: Comparison of the dependency lengths across the same eleven genres. Dependency lengths are on average longer in legal contracts and in the criminal code than in other genres. (Note that the baseline minimal length of any dependency is length 1, so that the y-axis starts at 1.) Figures generated by Eric Martinez and Frank Mollica based on analyses from Martínez et al. (2022).

Certificate or Book-Entry Share upon the later to occur of (i) the Effective Time or (ii) the Paying Agent's receipt of such Certificate (or affidavit of loss in lieu thereof) or Book-Entry Share, in accordance with Section 3.2(b), as applicable, and the Certificate (or affidavit of loss in lieu thereof) or Book-Entry Share so surrendered shall be forthwith canceled.

(126) A Loan Modification Agreement from the US SECURITIES AND EXCHANGE COMMISSION (SEC) website
https://www.sec.gov/Archives/edgar/data/1750106/000165495418012554/filename30.htm
A. Pursuant to the terms of a Construction Loan Agreement dated November 23, 2015 executed by and between the Borrower and the Lender (such Construction Loan Agreement, together with all modifications thereto, extensions or renewals thereof and substitutions therefor being hereinafter referred to as the "Loan Agreement"), the Lender extended to the Borrower a land development loan in an original principal amount not to exceed at any one time outstanding the sum of US$8,000,000 (as the same may be modified, amended, extended or renewed from time to time, the "Land Development Loan") and a letter of credit facility in the aggregate stated amount of US$800,000 (as the same may be modified, amended, extended or renewed from time to time, the "Letter of Credit Facility"; such Land Development Loan and Letter of Credit Facility, as the same may be modified, amended, extended or renewed from time to time, being hereinafter sometimes referred to both individually and collectively as the "Loan") to finance the first stage of the development by the Borrower of certain real property located in Frederick County, Maryland into a residential subdivision to be known as "Ballenger Run" containing two hundred seventy-six (276) single-family building lots (individually, a "Lot" and collectively, the "Lots") and other building parcels (individually, a "Parcel" and collectively, the "Parcels") by clearing and grading and the installation of, among other things, sediment control, electric lines, communication lines, water and sewer lines, sidewalks, curbs and paved roads.

(127) A shareholder rights agreement from the US SECURITIES AND EXCHANGE COMMISSION (SEC) website
https://www.sec.gov/Archives/edgar/data/1597659/000091957419001858/
Notwithstanding the foregoing, if the Company's Board of Directors determines in good faith that a Person who would otherwise be an

"Acquiring Person," as defined pursuant to the foregoing provisions of this paragraph, has become such inadvertently (including, without limitation, because (A) such Person was unaware that it beneficially owned a percentage of the Common Shares that would otherwise cause such Person to be an "Acquiring Person," as defined pursuant to the foregoing provisions of this paragraph, or (B) such Person was aware of the extent of the Common Shares it beneficially owned but had no actual knowledge of the consequences of such beneficial ownership under this Rights Agreement) and without any intention of changing or influencing control of the Company, and if such Person divested or divests as promptly as practicable a sufficient number of Common Shares so that such Person would no longer be an Acquiring Person, as defined pursuant to the foregoing provisions of this paragraph, then such Person shall not be deemed to be or have ever been an Acquiring Person for any purposes of this Rights Agreement.

(128) Alabama Constitution
https://alison.legislature.state.al.us/files/pdf/lsa/proposed-constitution/Proposed_Final_Statewide_Provisions.pdf
The Alabama state docks department (which term as used herein shall be construed to include any other agency of the state that may succeed to said department's functions) shall, subject to the provisions of the bond order relating to the sale of the $10,000,000 principal amount of general obligation seaport facilities bonds of the state of Alabama dated March 1, 1964, pledge and use so much of the revenues derived from its seaport facilities as may be necessary to pay at their maturities the principal of and interest on said bonds, and may pledge, agree to use, and use so much of said revenues as the said department with the approval of the governor may determine shall be necessary or desirable to build up and maintain reserves for the payment of said principal and interest for the maintenance, replacement and improvement of its seaport facilities.

(129) Kidnapping, California penal code
https://leginfo.legislature.ca.gov/faces/codes_displaySection.xhtml?sectionNum=207.&lawCode=PEN
Every person who forcibly, or by any other means of instilling fear, takes or holds, detains, or arrests any person, with a design to take the person out of this state, without having established a claim, according to the laws of the United States, or of this state, or who hires, persuades, entices, decoys, or

seduces by false promises, misrepresentations, or the like, any person to go out of this state, or to be taken or removed therefrom, for the purpose and with the intent to sell that person into slavery or involuntary servitude, or otherwise to employ that person for his or her own use, or to the use of another, without the free will and consent of that persuaded person, is guilty of kidnapping.

(130) Arson from Florida law
http://www.leg.state.fl.us/Statutes/

(1) Any person who willfully and unlawfully, or while in the commission of any felony, by fire or explosion, damages or causes to be damaged:
   (a) Any dwelling, whether occupied or not, or its contents;
   (b) Any structure, or contents thereof, where persons are normally present, such as: jails, prisons, or detention centers; hospitals, nursing homes, or other health care facilities; department stores, office buildings, business establishments, churches, or educational institutions during normal hours of occupancy; or other similar structures; or
   (c) Any other structure that he or she knew or had reasonable grounds to believe was occupied by a human being, is guilty of arson in the first degree, which constitutes a felony of the first degree, punishable as provided in s. 775.082, s. 775.083, or s. 775.084.

In order to investigate the potential complexity of comprehending Legalese, Martínez et al. (2022) had experimental participants read contract excerpts consisting of a few hundred words each, which were written in either Legalese or plain English. The participants then answered comprehension questions about these texts, and finally they were asked to recall as much as they could of the texts. Each of the twelve Legalese versions was adapted from a real contract, and the plain English texts were constructed from these. For example, the plain English version of the complex sentence in (124) is provided in (131). Note that the long center-embedded clause—a definition of "payments and benefits by the Company"—is separated into a second and third sentence in the simpler version. The resulting structure has more local syntactic dependencies.

(131) Plain English contract version of (124):
In the event that any payment or benefit by the Company would be subject to excise tax, then the cash severance payments shall be reduced. All

payments and benefits by the Company shall hereinafter be referred to as the "Total Payments." This includes the payments and benefits under Section 3(a) hereof.

Does Center-Embedded Syntax Add Critical Meaning to Legalese?

A standard reaction to our work over the years is that perhaps center-embedded syntax adds some critical meaning to a sentence, so that lawyers write it this way with that intended meaning. But this does not seem to be the case: It turns out that we can always paraphrase a center-embedded text by putting the material that is embedded in the center of a long dependency into a separate clause, and then using referring expressions—the defined terms—to refer to those items. We have never found any example of a center-embedded sentence that couldn't be paraphrased in this way. Hence, there is no particular meaning associated with this syntax.

Martínez et al. (2022) worked with two linguists to evaluate the semantics of the pairs of texts in their study, until they agreed that the Legalese and plain English were identical in propositional content. In addition to changing the center-embedded feature of Legalese to make it more readable, Martínez et al. (2022) also considered three other kinds of linguistic features that had been claimed to be common in Legalese in prior literature: (a) low-frequency Legalese terms; (b) the use of the passive voice; and (c) the prevalence of all-capitals, for sections of the contract that were deemed to be of extra importance (approximately 10–15 percent of US contracts are in all capitals).

Participants answered comprehension questions better for the plain English versions, and recalled the plain English versions much better (see figure 6.2, panels A and B). The recall data could then be analyzed to see which features led to better and worse recall across the two genres. It turned out that the center-embedding was responsible for most of the difference between recall behavior in the two genres, with word frequency also contributing a small but significant amount. Passive voice and all-caps format had no effect on recall performance. See figure 6.2, panel C.

Although many people have long noted that legal language is hard to understand, this is the first analysis of what factors cause this difficulty. Going back to Richard Nixon's presidency in the early 1970s, several US

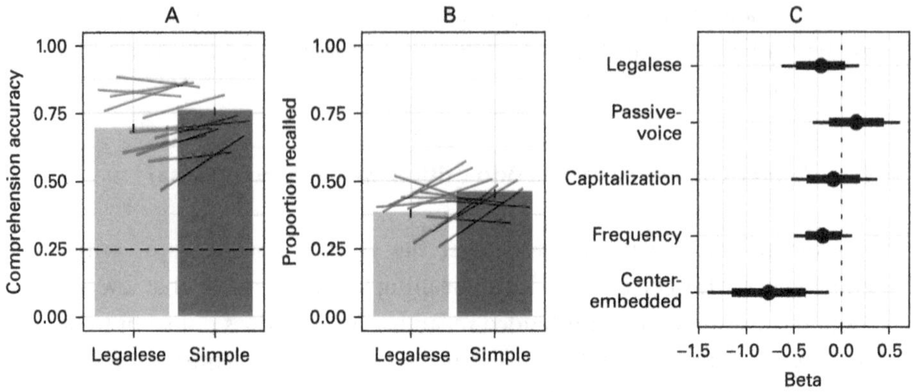

Figure 6.2
Effect of text register (Legalese vs. simple) on comprehension accuracy in the main experiment (A) and recall of legal content (B). The faint lines represent item averages over the 12 items. (C) Posterior distribution over logistic regression coefficients reflecting the influence of condition and each surface property on recall. Negative coefficient values reflect a decrease in recall performance. Points reflect the median; the outer line range reflects the 95 percent credible intervals and the inner line range reflect the 80 percent credible intervals. Figures generated by Frank Mollica based on analyses from Martínez et al. (2022).

presidents have instigated programs to help lower the complexity of legal language: the "Plain Language" movement. But without an analysis of what factors might be causing the perceived complexity in the first place, it is difficult to see how anyone might have succeeded in this movement. It is therefore not surprising that the the rate of center-embedding has not changed in laws. Martínez et al. (2024b) provide an analysis of many linguistic features in US laws and show that none have changed measurably over the period of 1950–2020. Figure 6.3 shows the rate of center-embedded sentences in laws from 1950–2010, remaining constant at about 40 percent of sentences with a center-embedded clause, much higher than other genres.

The behavioral analysis of Martínez et al. (2022) is the first to analyze the complexity of legal language by linguistic feature. This analysis showed that the center-embedded structure of such texts was one feature that leads to the complexity of such texts. Fortunately, a center-embedded text can always be rewritten as a non-center-embedded structure with the same meaning. So in the future, we may be able to make Legalese more processable.

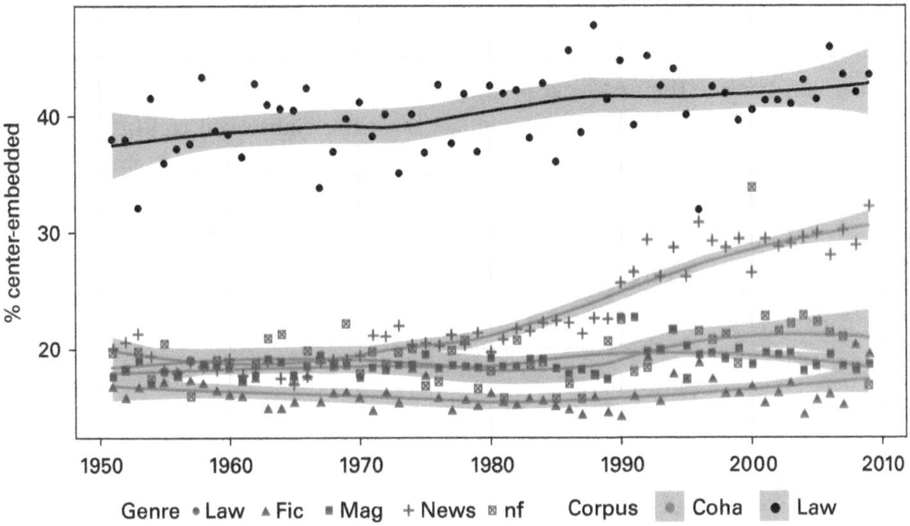

Figure 6.3
The rate of center-embedded clauses in US laws, 1950–2010. The proportion of sentences in US laws that have a center-embedded clause remains roughly constant at about 40 percent over this time frame. This is a much higher proportion than from other genres (fiction, nonfiction, news, magazine), all from an analysis of COCA from Martínez et al. (2024b). Figure generated by Eric Martínez.

It currently remains somewhat of a mystery why legal texts have so many center-embedded syntactic structures, given that center-embedded structures are so hard to comprehend and produce. Moreover, it turns out that lawyers themselves don't like legal language any more than laypeople do. Martínez et al. (2023) conducted a behavioral analysis with over one hundred US lawyers as participants, similar to the one performed on laypeople from Martínez et al. (2022), and found that although the lawyers were better than laypeople at understanding and recalling the texts overall, the lawyers showed the same bias for the plain English texts as laypeople. That is, just like laypeople, lawyers were better at answering comprehension questions and recalling Plain English compared to Legalese. Furthermore, the lawyers didn't even like the Legalese versions: The lawyers greatly preferred plain English to Legalese, even for professional reasons. So why then does Legalese persist, if no one likes this writing style? According to recent work by Eric Martínez, Frank Mollica, and me, it may be that people in general think that Legalese, in its current complex state, simply sounds more official than other styles of writing, such that this style is something of a "magic spell" for legal writing (Martínez et al., 2024a). This may go all the way back to the first legal writing that we know of, Hammurabi's legal code: 282 legal rules carved into pillars from the eighteenth century BCE in ancient Babylon. It may be that others have mimicked the style that was presented there, and that this style sounds like official legal writing. While this kind of text be easy for lawyers to produce (especially if they edit the texts from preexisting ones), it unfortunately results in overly complex text for the reader.

7 Alternative Grammar Formalisms

There are many grammar formalisms other than the dependency grammar approach presented here. The most thorough current summary of grammatical approaches that I am aware of is provided by Müller (2023), who surveys eleven different approaches, most of which are still used. That book includes an extensive introduction to dependency grammar, which I highly recommend.

In this chapter, I discuss formalisms that are closely related to the current dependency grammar approach. In the following chapter, chapter 8, I discuss perhaps the most famous class of theories within linguistics in the US, the transformation-based approaches proposed by Chomsky and his colleagues.

7.1 Other Dependency Grammar Approaches: Universal Dependencies

The grammar and approach outlined here are closely in line with other dependency grammar approaches, such as those of Hudson (1984, 1990, 2008), Mel'čuk (1988), Nivre et al. (2015), and Osborne (2019) (see also Müller, 2023). There are slight differences among these theories in what each proposes to be the head vs. dependent in particular dependency relationships. As discussed above, I assume that the noun is the head for a determiner, whereas Hudson assumes the determiner is the head of such phrases. Perhaps the biggest differences in headedness assumptions with dependency grammar theories are present in the Universal Dependencies framework (Nivre et al., 2016, 2020; De Marneffe et al., 2021), which assumes that the content word (noun, verb, adjective, adverb) is always the head, for head-dependencies between function words and content words.

This assumption is made in the UD framework in order to maximize the cross-linguistic similarity of tree structures and to make it easier to write annotator guidelines, which is clearly a very different kind of motivation than what I follow here (or what Hudson and others follow).

In any case, UD assumes that the noun is the head of a noun phrase (as I do here), but also that verbs are the heads for auxiliary verbs (contrary to what is assumed here), nouns are the heads for prepositions (contrary to what is assumed here), and verbs are the heads for complementizers (contrary to what is assumed here). For example, we can compare the structure assumed here for (132) to the structure for the same sentence under UD assumptions:

(132) Ollie might buy a picture of a puppy at the market.

Dependency Grammar approach here:

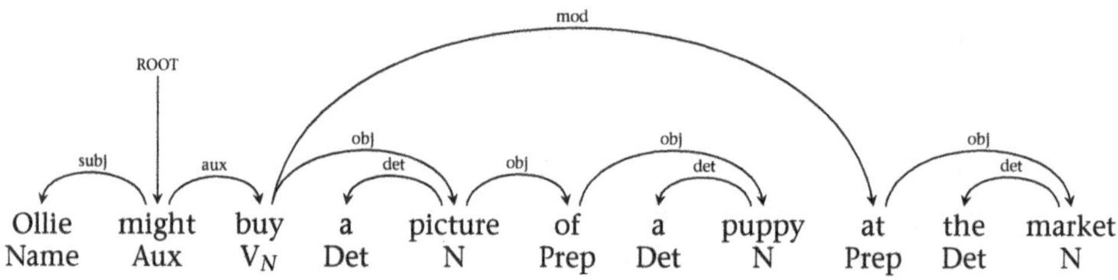

Universal Dependencies approach (note that the labels of the arcs are a little different too):

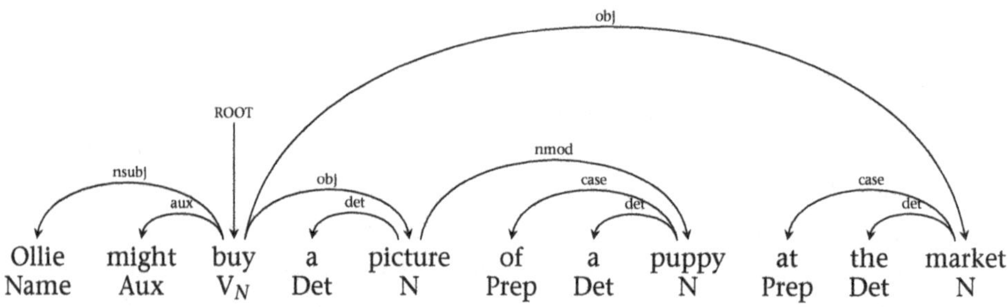

Although these are potentially interesting differences among the frameworks, they actually don't affect the main points here: that dependency distances between elements that depend on one another are associated with processing cost, which then drives certain word orders to be more prevalent than others. The details of which element of a function word and content word is the head is not particularly important for this claim because the primary processing costs occur between content words that indirectly depend on one another (nouns upon verbs, and verbs upon further verbs).

7.2 Construction Grammar

As discussed in the introduction, I see the current dependency grammar proposal as an elaboration of construction grammars (Hopper, 1987; Goldberg, 1995; Langacker, 1987, 1991; Bybee, 2006; Croft, 2001; Bybee and Hopper, 2001; Tomasello, 2003; Goldberg, 2006; Bybee, 2010; Croft, 2010; Steels, 2011, 2012; Diessel, 2017; Goldberg, 2019). In construction grammar, a *construction* has a form and a meaning. Words and morphemes are constructions in the lexicon; additional constructions can be formed from other constructions. The primary tenet of construction grammar is that language is **usage-based** (Croft and Cruse, 2004): It describes the syntactic and lexical combinations that people use. Construction grammar is consistent with either dependency rules or phrase structure rules underlying the system. The dependency grammar proposal being put forward here can be seen as the basis for a construction grammar, with its focus on the form of the grammatical rules underlying syntactic constraints within a language.

Construction grammar has a further goal of trying to understand what the *pieces* are—the constructions—that contribute to such representations in typical language use. We can see the various rules that have been proposed here as constructions. Of course, a construction can be formed from any combination of other constructions, if the constructions are used that way. This makes forming a full list of the constructions that people actually use complicated.

A second tenet of some versions of cognitive grammar is that "language is not an autonomous cognitive faculty" (Croft and Cruse, 2004; cf. Hudson, 2015 for a similar claim about word grammar). Contrary to a strong interpretation of this claim, language actually *is* autonomous to some degree. That is, it appears that (a) there is a brain network responsible for representing and processing language, and (b) this network does nothing else: It is specific to language (Fedorenko et al., 2011, 2012; Pritchett et al., 2018; Ivanova et al., 2020, 2021); see chapter 9. Alternatively, if all that Croft and colleagues meant was that similar computations take place in the language network as in other cognitive computational systems (Fedorenko and Shain, 2021), then this is indeed likely.

A third tenet of construction and cognitive grammars has to do with the meanings in their grammars. Researchers in cognitive grammar (Langacker, 1987, 1997), cognitive linguistics (Croft, 2001; Croft and Cruse, 2004), and construction grammar (Fillmore, 1988; Goldberg, 2006; Croft, 2010; Hilpert, 2014; Jackendoff, 2013; Steels, 2011, 2012; Goldberg, 2019) argue for the importance of meaning in grammar, but they explicitly argue against a formal semantics underlying meaning. One such researcher suggested to me that the meaning underlying language might best be represented by the language itself. This doesn't seem like a solution to me, but I agree that the current formal semantic views don't seem to be particularly helpful in enlightening us about most meanings that we might typically want to convey. It seems obvious that the meaning of a whole is often some complex function of the meanings of its parts: For example, the meaning of *Ollie ate some pizza* is some complex eating event, where *Ollie* is the agent of eating, and an indeterminate quantity of pizza is the patient of being eaten, but the details of such a semantics are complex. I will follow construction grammarians in being informal about meaning, but unlike construction grammarians, I will not attempt to categorize regularities in the meaning space.

7.3 Phrase Structure Grammar

A closely related formalism to dependency grammar is *phrase structure grammar* (Chomsky, 1957; Gazdar et al., 1985). In dependency grammar, relationships are headed, such that each word depends on another. In phrase structure grammar, sequences of words join together to make higher-level categories, and these categories combine further. A projective dependency grammar (where the dependencies cannot cross) is said to be weakly equivalent to a phrase-structure grammar, such that a rule set in one formalism can be shown to generate the same language—the same sets of strings—as a corresponding rule set in the other (Gaifman, 1965). The structures may be different, so they are not strongly equivalent.

In order to get a sense of how to create a phrase structure grammar that generates the same language that a projective dependency grammar does, we can create a phrase structure rule for each dependency relation, by making a category that dominates them. For example, consider the dependency structure for the noun phrase in (133):

(133) the big dog beside me

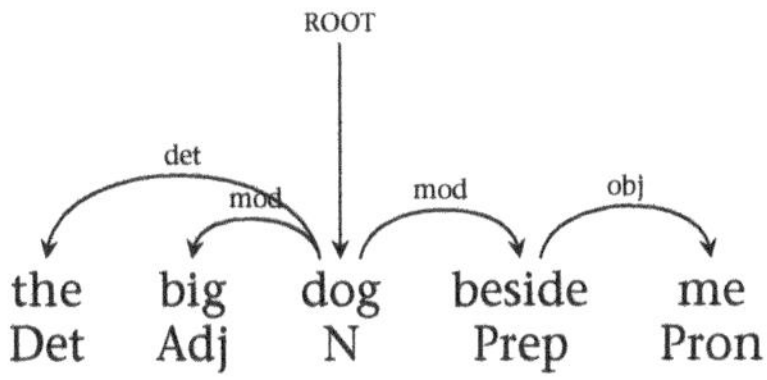

We can create a rule that combines the Adjective with the Noun to make a dominating category. Let's call this N1 (because N is the head). And we can create another that combines the Det with the resulting category. Let's call this N2:

```
N1 → Adj N
N2 → Det N1
```

This gives us a structure for the first part of the sentence:

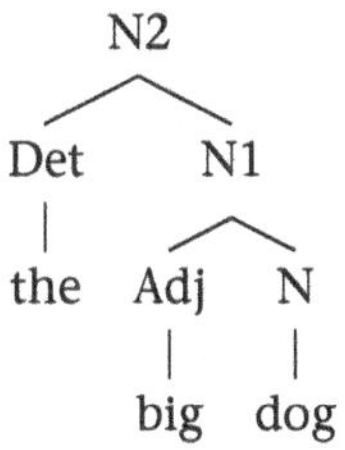

We can also combine the preposition with the Name to make a PP. And finally, we can combine the resulting PP with the N2 to create a higher noun category, which we will call N3:[1]

```
PP → Prep Pron
N3 → N2 PP
```

The resulting phrase structure is as follows:

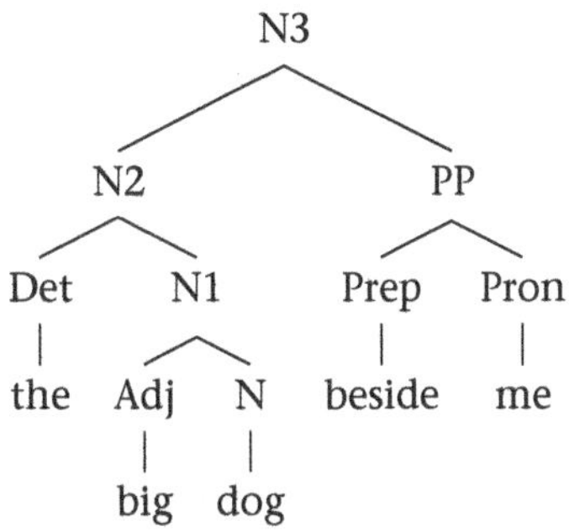

The above rules—which have one left-hand-side nonterminal category, and any number of categories on the right-hand side of the rule—are called **context-free rules**, meaning they can expand their left-hand-side category in any context in which the category occurs. Most structures in human languages adhere to this kind of rule. This ends up being equivalent to not allowing crossed dependencies in a dependency grammar framework, a property of a grammar that is called **projectivity**.

A property of phrase structure grammar that distinguishes it from dependency grammar is that many head-dependent combinations form meaningful subparts called **constituents** within phrase structure. It turns out that constituency on its own is not a good motivation for phrase structure: The various constituency tests that have been proposed in the literature can be equally explained in terms of dependency grammar notations or phrase structure notations, because such tests are usually meaning-based tests, which are represented just as well in dependency grammar, as described in detail in section 7.8 below. However, a potential true advantage of phrase structure grammars is that they easily allow semantic combination rules associated with the syntactic rules, as in categorial grammar (Steedman, 1996, 2001), but I will not elaborate semantic rules in this book. We can think of dependency grammar as an abstraction over categorial grammar, without the semantics of the phrases.

On the other hand, Nichols (1986, 1992) argues that there are some properties of the syntax of human languages that might be more simply represented using dependency grammar rather than phrase structure grammar. One property that she raises is the fact that some languages tend to be dependent-marked in their morphology (like English and Indo-European languages in general) but others tend to be head-marked in their morphology. For example (from Nichols, 1986):

(134) a. English:

the	man	-'s	house
	DEP	MORPH	HEAD

b. Hungarian:

az	ember	ház	-a
the	man	house	3sg
	DEP	HEAD	MORPH

The possessive marker goes on the dependent *man* in English and other dependent-marking languages, whereas the morphology goes on the head *house* in Hungarian and other head-marking languages. The type of morphology within a language may also depend on the feature. Nichols suggests (personal communication, February 2024) that person information is usually head-marked, while possessive information is less likely to be head-marked than core clause relations are.

Nichols (1986) argues that these differences are easier to represent using dependency grammars than phrase structure grammars. I think this is a similar argument that I am making here: Dependency grammars make certain kinds of relationships more perspicuous (head-dependent relationships), and, hence, easier for researchers to theorize about. But since phrase structure grammars actually have the same mechanisms embedded in them, phrase structure grammars may actually be used to explain the same kinds of phenomena, but perhaps less perspicuously for researchers.

7.4 Simpler Syntax

The simpler syntax approach of Culicover and Jackendoff (2005) seeks to simplify the syntactic rules, relative to the elaborate phrase structure / movement theories of Chomsky and colleagues. This approach is a usage-based approach like the one proposed here. Culicover and Jackendoff (2005) keep phrase structure as the base syntax (as opposed to dependency grammar), but they eschew complex phrase structures in favor of simpler ones, with fewer syntactic nodes.

Unlike construction grammar, Culicover and Jackendoff (2005), Jackendoff (2007), and Jackendoff and Audring (2020) reject the thrid tenet of construction grammar, in not requiring that all syntax rules have a semantics (Croft and Cruse, 2004). Like Jackendoff (2007) and Jackendoff and Audring (2020), I also do not assume that there is a semantics for every syntactic rule. Syntactic rules may have evolved for a variety of reasons in human language: Some syntactic rules may have evolved there for ease of learning—grammar compression—leading to a smaller set of rules. Other rules have evolved to ease language production: It is easier for people to keep talking about the same entities that they had been talking about before. The existence of alternative voices—active vs. passive—is a potential example of such a rule choice. Suppose we want to convey the meaning *Mary was hired by Microsoft*. If we were just talking about the company *Microsoft*, then it is easier for us to use the active voice with respect to the verb *hired*: *Microsoft hired Mary*. But if we were just talking about *Mary*, then it may be easier for us to use the passive voice: *Mary was hired by Microsoft*. The two voice rules—active vs. passive—don't add semantics. The meanings are inherited from the word meanings.

The split between syntax and semantics is what Jackendoff has labeled the "parallel architecture" of syntax and semantics. I don't use this terminology, because it suggests an independence between syntax and semantics. Rather, there is semantics with most words, and many rule combinations. And all language meanings come from some spoken/signed form. Thus semantics is heavily dependent on form (syntax).

7.5 Combinatory Categorial Grammar

Another phrase structure grammar formalism is combinatory categorial grammar (CCG) (Steedman, 1996, 2001). According to CCG, each word is associated with a syntactic category that can combine with other syntactic categories, in order to form further categories. There are three primary categories—N, NP, and S—such that other words' categories are defined relative to these. Thus a determiner in this formalism is an NP missing a N to the right. The combinations to the left are formed through a backslash operator (\), while the combinations to the right are formed using a forward slash operator (/). For example, consider the following simple lexicon:

```
the, some:     NP/N
dog, pizza:    N
Lana, Ollie:  NP
saw, ate:      (S\NP)/NP
```

In order to parse or generate the sentence *the dog saw Lana*, we could first put together *the* and *dog*: This is an NP/N category and an N. The forward slash means the first category is looking to form an NP when it finds an N to its immediate right. So together these form an NP. (The order of these operations is not determined by CCG: This is just a left-to-right parse of this sentence using some CCG syntax rules.) The verb category is complex: (S\NP)/NP. This means that this word category needs an NP to the left and an NP to the right, in CCG format. We can collapse this category with the preceding NP to form the category (S\NP). This category can then collapse with the category of the word *Lana* (NP), to form an S.

```
the + dog:              NP/N  +  N          -> NP
the dog + saw:          NP + (S\NP)/NP      -> S\NP
the dog saw + Lana:     S\NP + NP           -> S
```

Overall, CCG has several useful features. First, it allows a simple analysis of many constructions, including coordination, as discussed above in section 3.17. As discussed below in chapter 7, coordination is notoriously difficult to handle in X-bar phrase structure grammars with movement, as in the Chomskyan generative tradition mentioned above in section 8. A second important property of CCG is that there is also a semantics for each category, and rules for composing the semantics. These rules allow the composition of rules that are non-projective (connections that cross dependencies), in cases such as cross-serial dependencies in languages like Swiss-German (Shieber, 1985; Steedman, 2023). For example, the embedded clause in (135) can be phrased grammatically as in (136) in Swiss-German, in spite of the crossed-dependencies (Shieber, 1985):

(135)

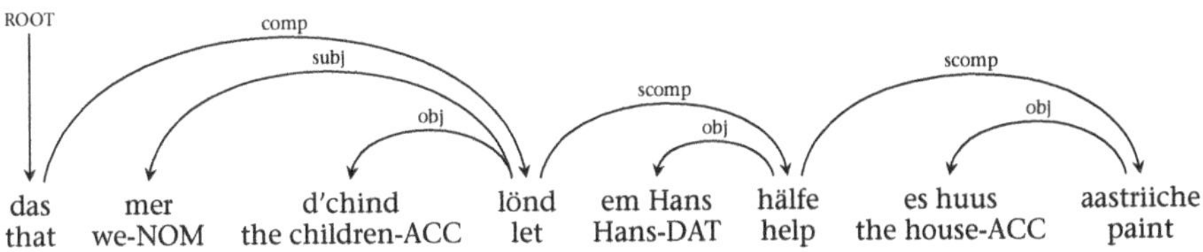

"that we let the children help Hans paint the house"

(136)

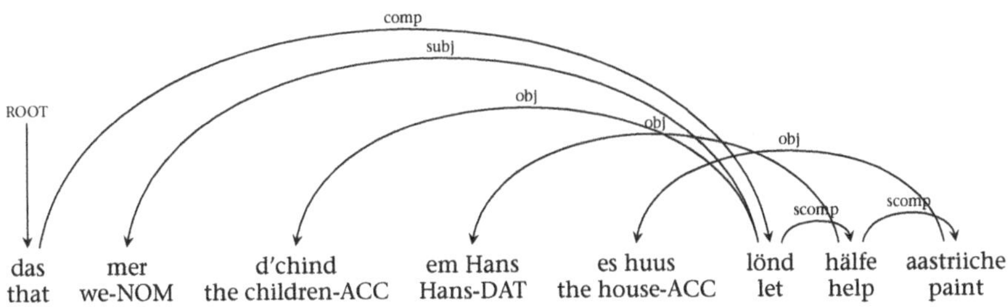

"that we let the children help Hans paint the house"

Such structures can be generated in CCG, in spite of the crossed dependencies. (The details of how this works are beyond the scope of the discussion here.) While CCG has some advantages over other approaches—notably its detailed analyses of complex structures in Swiss German—dependency grammar represents argument structure more directly than CCG (or any other phrase structure grammar), which leads to a more transparent explanation for processing phenomena and word order phenomena.

7.6 X-bar Phrase Structure

Perhaps the most popular version of phrase structure grammar in the linguistic literature is called X-bar theory (Jackendoff, 1977). X-bar theory assumes a context-free phrase structure base, with several general principles applied to how the CFG rules should look. According to most versions of X-bar theory, there are three levels of nodes for each head: a head-level (X^0), an argument level (X' or X^1, where arguments get connected), and a maximal level (XP), where constituents called **specifiers** are connected. These are template rules, which all word categories are proposed to obey.

```
XP → SpecP X'
X' → X0 ArgP
```

We can fill them in with particular word categories, such as a noun (N), perhaps a word like *manager*, which might have a specifier (a DetP, corresponding to a structure for a word like *the*) and an argument PP, corresponding to a phrase like *of the restaurant*:

```
NP → DetP N'
N' → N0 PP
```

In most current uses of X-bar theory, there is a lot of additional proposed structure in tensed clauses, corresponding to additional heads for tense (T) and "little v" (*v*), among other heads (e.g., Adger, 2003; Carnie, 2013). Here I present a simplified X-bar theory from Chomsky (1986), with only one additional head within a tensed clause, the category Infl (or I, short for inflection). Under this version of X-bar theory, the structures for (137a) and (137b) are given below, where the tensed verbs *slept* and *ate* are represented as two nodes in the syntax: a silent +tense node in I, and the verb (*slept* or *ate*):

(137) a. The girl slept.
b. Some neighbors ate a pizza.

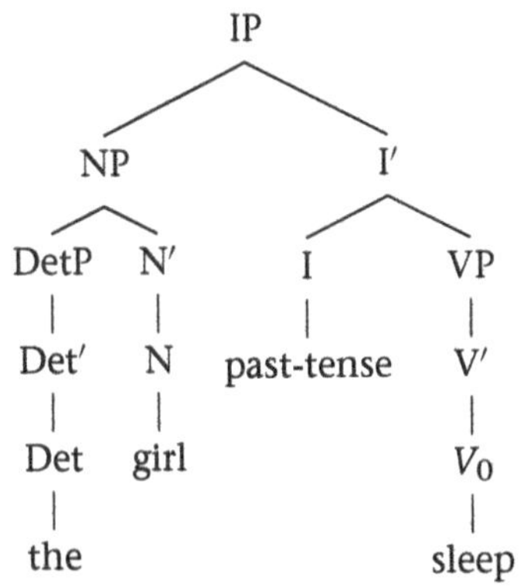

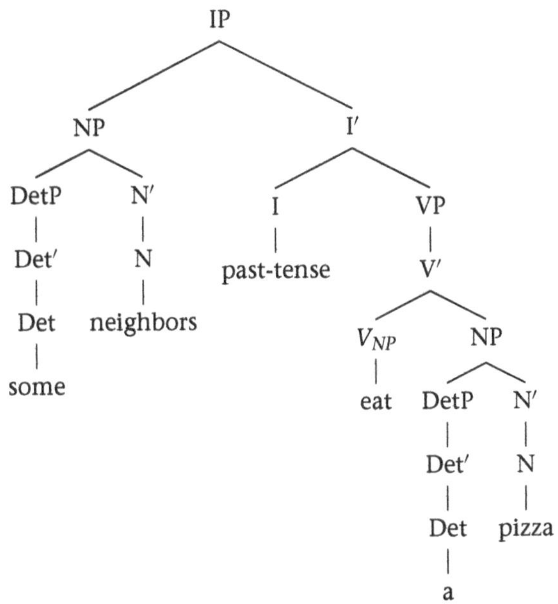

The implicit idea behind X-bar theory is that the grammar is simple if all categories are treated in the same way. The complexity of the system is much greater if heads and XPs are permitted to move to other places in the structure (as in the assumption that *slept* is at least two syntactic heads—an I and a V), but I will not delve into those proposals here.

7.6.1 Arguments vs. Modifiers in X-bar Theory

Arguments fill semantic slots in the meaning of the head. In contrast, **modifiers** provide additional information about a head (and its arguments). In all languages, modifiers are optional in the syntax. In English, the arguments are often obligatory in the syntax, but this varies across languages. In Indonesian, for example, even arguments are optional. In (138), the prepositional phrase *in the room* indicates the location where *the girl* is. This is not part of the core meaning of *girl*. Hence, this is a modifier. The prepositional phrase *in the bed* in (138) is also a modifier of the verb *slept*.

(138) The girl in the room slept in the bed.

Similarly, none of the prepositional phrases *in the hall, on Tuesday, at nine,* or *for 3 hours* are parts of the core meaning of the verb *slept*, and hence all are modifiers:

(139) Anna slept in the hall on Tuesday at nine for 3 hours.

In a dependency grammar, arguments are notated as distinct from modifiers only in the interpretations of the labels in the arcs (cf. Osborne, 2019). The dependency structures for (138) and (139) are given below:

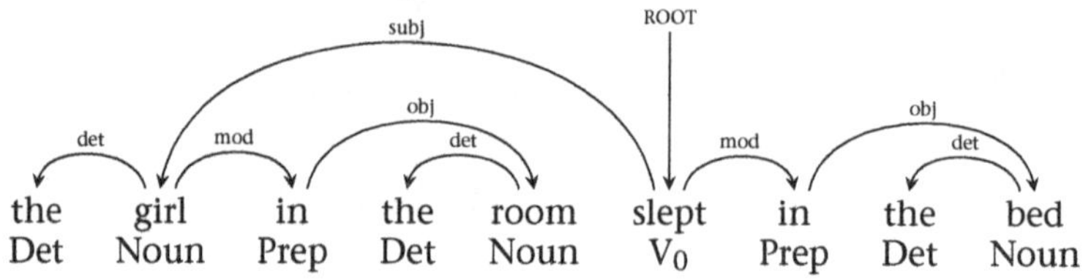

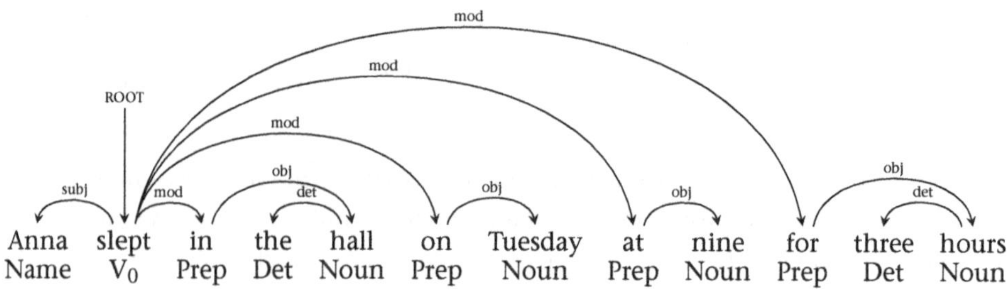

In X-bar phrase structure grammars, arguments and modifiers are sometimes associated with special phrasal locations. In such a notation, modifiers are indicated using **adjunction** rules, where the left-hand category is repeated on the right-hand of the rule, so that the modifier is said to **adjoin** to the head category. In (138), the PP *in the room* adjoins to the NP *the girl*, and the PP *in the bed* adjoins to the VP *slept*.

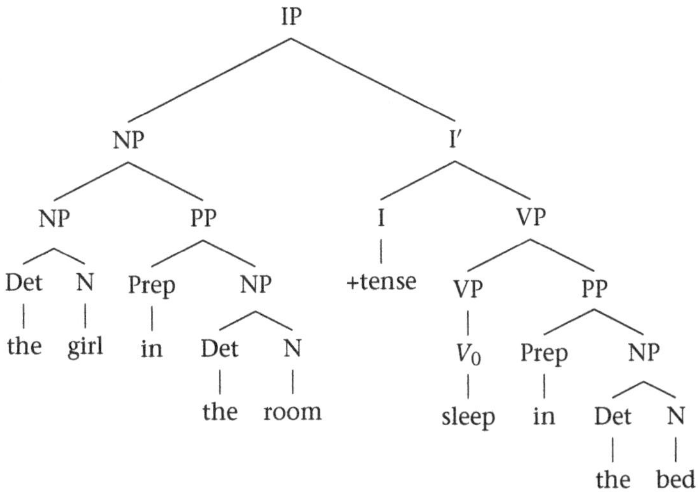

This repetition of structural nodes makes for a simple phrase structure rule for modifiers:

```
XP → XP Modifier
VP → VP Modifier
NP → NP Modifier
etc.
```

This leads to a lot of structure for materials with a few modifiers, as in (139):

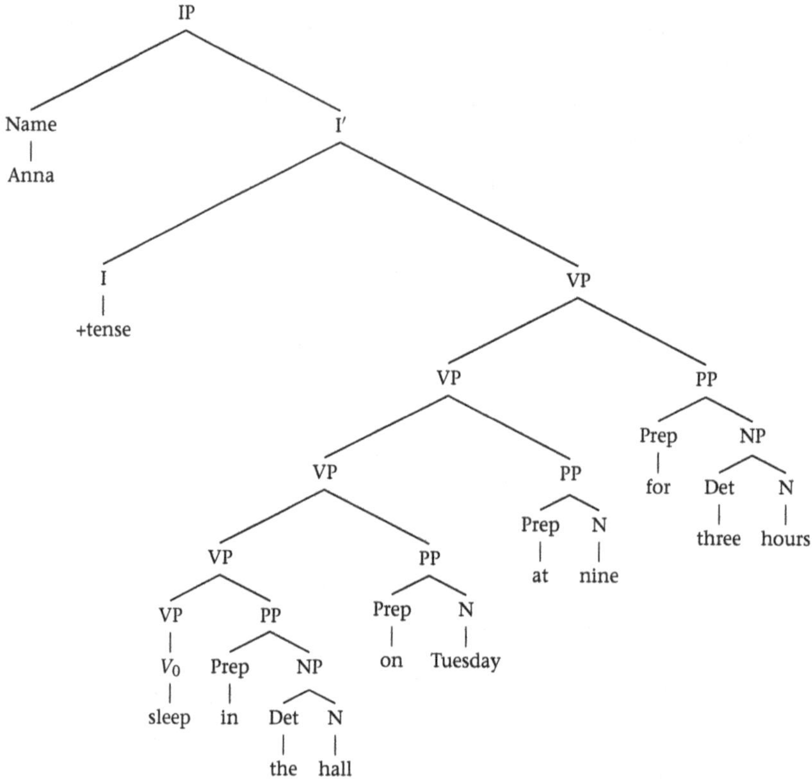

7.6.2 Binary Branching X-bar Theory

Another assumption common in current generative phrase structure grammars is that the phrase structures are *binary-branching* (Kayne, 1983; Adger, 2003; Radford, 2004). In such a framework, if there is more than one post-verbal argument, it will be adjoined to a V-bar level, where verbal modifiers are also adjoined. So a possible binary-branching structure for (140) is as follows:

(140) Some neighbors gave some nuts to a squirrel.

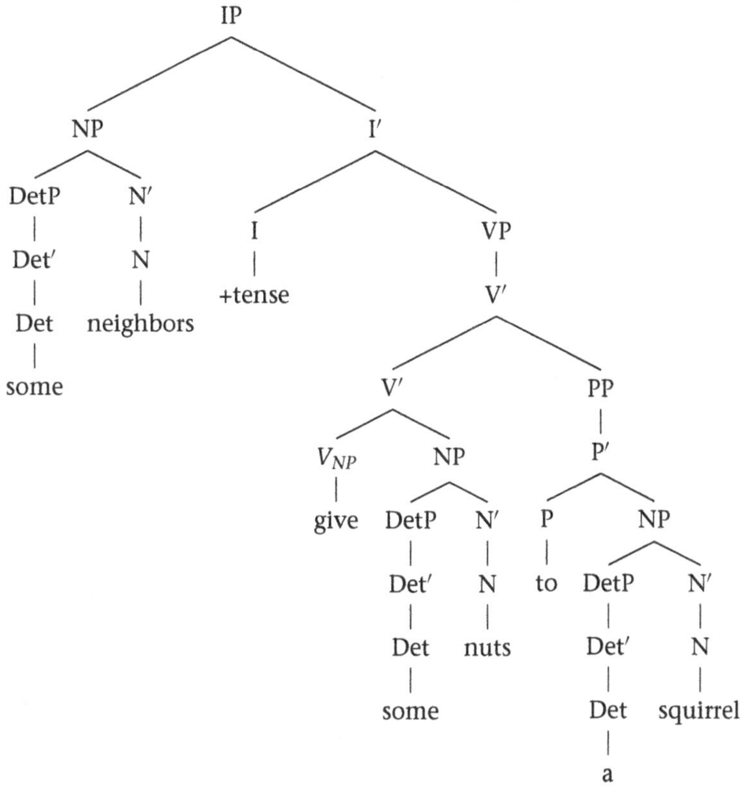

No empirical evidence is provided for the assumption of binary-branching, however. It seems that the main motivation for this assumption is some vague notion of simplicity often couched in terms of "learnability" (e.g., Kayne, 1983) but no details of why binary-branching might be more learnable are provided.

At this point, the relative simplicity of dependency grammar compared to X-bar theory seems clear. For comparison, here is the dependency grammar structure for (140):

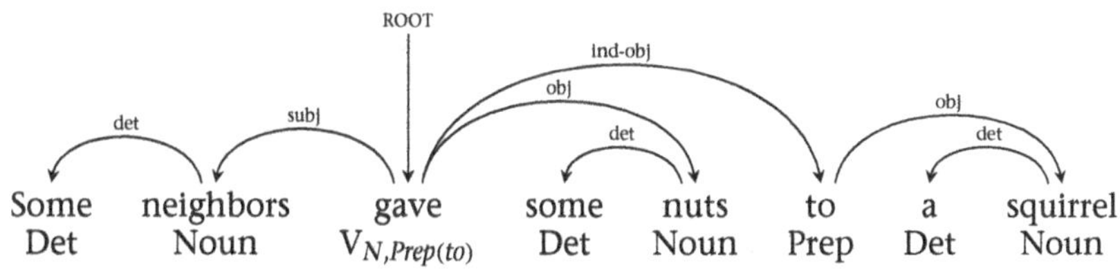

7.7 No Crossed Dependencies in Context-Free Phrase Structure

Both dependency grammars and phrase structure grammars (especially variants of X-bar theory) are widely used in linguistics and computational linguistics. One difference between the two formalisms is that phrase structure grammars are more constrained: They do not generate dependency structures with crossed dependencies. This is something of a double-edged sword with respect to human language. Mostly, human languages are context-free, dispreferring crossed dependencies. In English, modifications that cross other dependencies sound pretty bad, as in the noun phrase in (141a) and the sentence in (141b):

(141) a. ?? the man in the glasses who just entered the room which were bright pink
b. ?? Mary gave the flowers to her friend which were long-stemmed red roses.

Note that the relative clause *which were bright pink* has a plural verb *were*, so that it should connect to the plural noun *glasses*. Similarly, the relative clause *which were long-stemmed red roses* is plural and so should connect to the plural noun *flowers*. Neither of these connections is possible without crossing dependencies. The dependency structures for (141a) and (141b) are provided below. The relative pronoun *which* needs to cross a dependency arc in order to connect to its head *glasses* in (141a), and to connect to its head *flowers* in (141b).

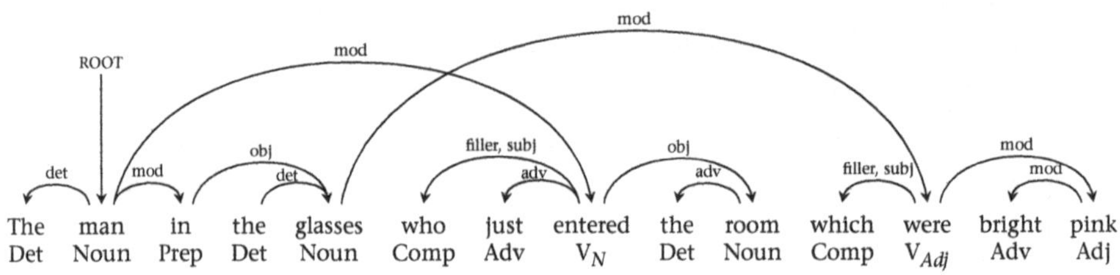

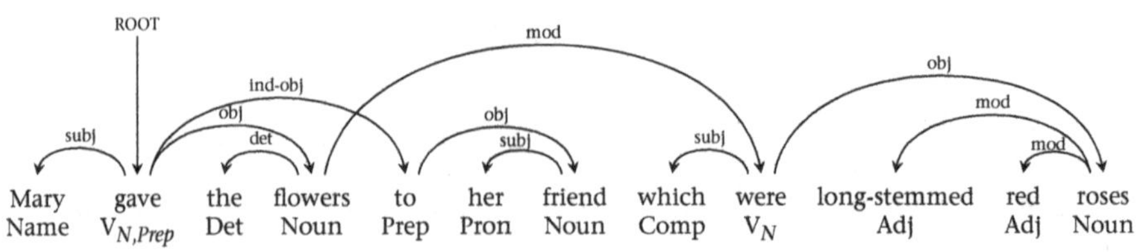

Condensed forms of X-bar phrase structures for the noun phrase *The man in the glasses who just entered the room*, and the relative clause *which were*

bright pink from (141a) are provided below. The relative clause is represented as a complementizer phrase (CP), following Chomsky (1986). Note that the relative clause needs to connect to *glasses*, but it cannot in the CFG formalism, because that would entail crossing branches. A similar issue applies for (141b).

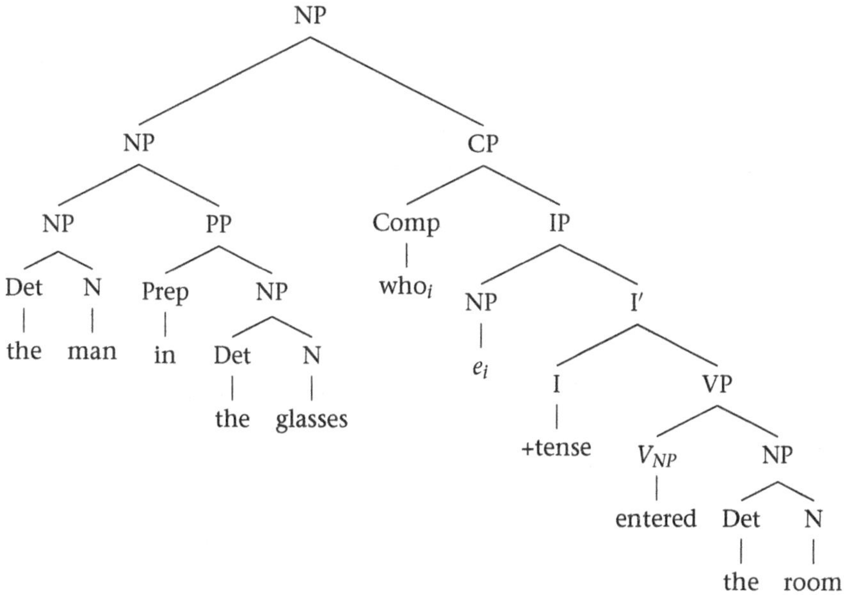

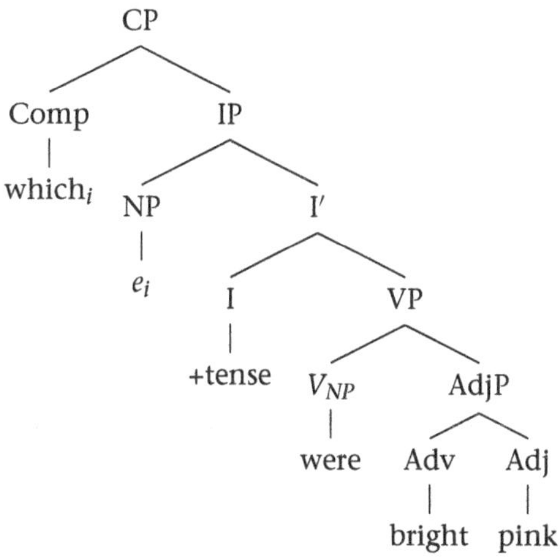

Because such materials are difficult to process in English and across languages, it might seem plausible to have a global constraint blocking any crossed branches in human languages in general. But as we saw in chapter 4, there are cases where crossed dependencies seem to be necessary, even in English. Here are two examples of acceptable "extraposition" out of the subject noun phrase (Levy and Keller, 2013):

(142) a. Yesterday a woman arrived who I knew. (Levy et al., 2012)
b. After the show, a performer came on who impressed the audience.

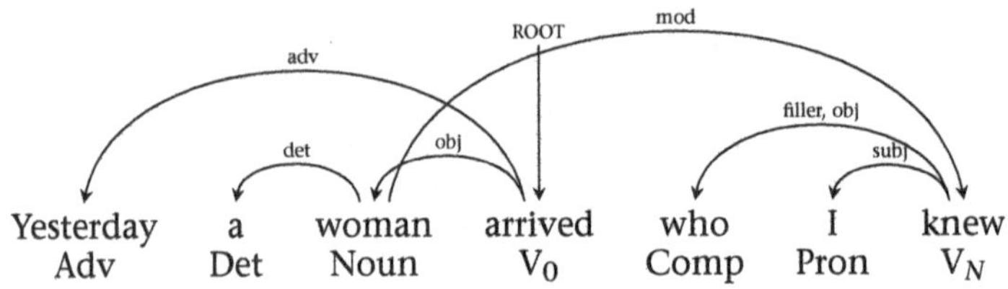

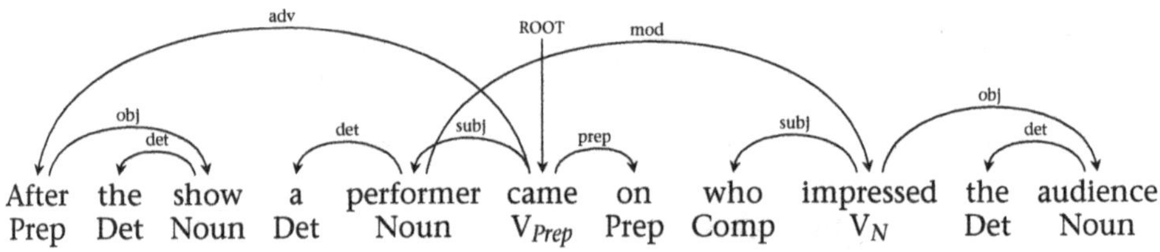

Because these sentences are possible English sentences, we need to be able to generate them in our formalism. A solution to this problem in phrase structure grammar is to allow "movement" of constituents, with empty categories mediating these movements, such as below:

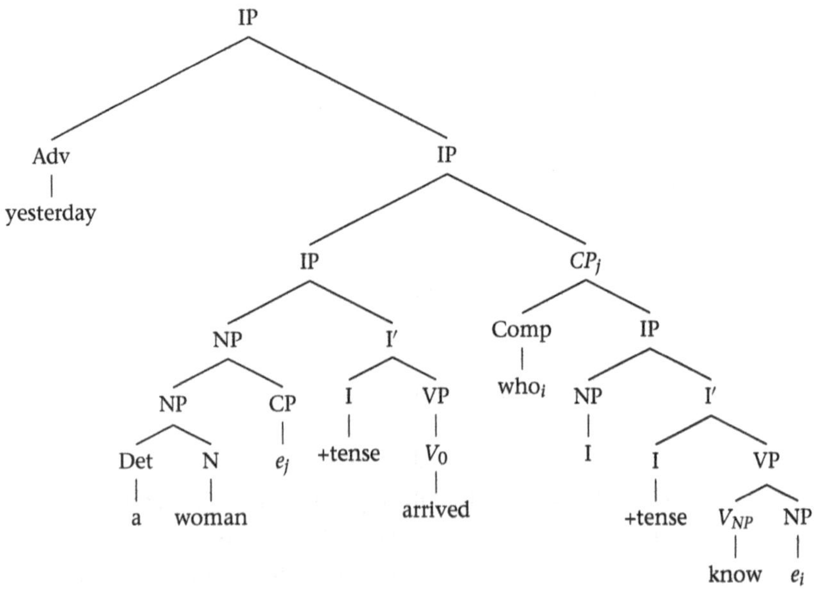

In this structure, the CP *who I know* is coindexed with an empty element e_j, which modifies *a woman*. This co-indexation solution gets around the constraint on crossed dependencies. But of course, this is only a partial solution, because it applies equally well to the bad examples of extrapositon in (141).[2]

There is nothing in principle to block crossing dependencies in the dependency grammar framework, but many DG researchers assume projectivity (no crossed dependencies) as part of their system. In order to map better with human languages, I simply assume that crossed dependencies have some cost, as discussed in section 4.3. Within phrase structure grammar, one can have a similar cost associated with extraposition. Consequently, the bias toward non-crossed dependencies in human languages doesn't really favor one formalism or the other. Indeed it has been suggested that the bias against crossed dependencies may follow from a bias toward local dependencies, because connecting to an arbitrary earlier position is more likely to cross a dependency than connecting to a more local position (Ferrer-i-Cancho, 2006; cf. Yadav et al., 2021).

7.8 Constituency Is Semantic, Not Syntactic

One of the motivations often given for phrase structure grammar over dependency grammar is *constituency*. Constituents in phrase structure grammar are motivated by meaning-based tests, such that constituents are contiguous sequences of the words that combine together to make a cohesive meaning. For example, in (143), the NPs *a squirrel* and *the neighbors* are constituents, as is the VP *kicked the neighbors*. But the sequences *squirrel kicked* and *kicked the* are not, because these are not complete meanings on their own (and, in phrase structure grammar logic, consequently there are no English grammar rules that combine only those parts of speech). For most of the remainder of the chapter, I present simplified phrase structure grammar (PSG) representations, without all the extra X-bar components. The claims apply equally to simple PSG or an X-bar PSG.

(143) A squirrel kicked the neighbors.

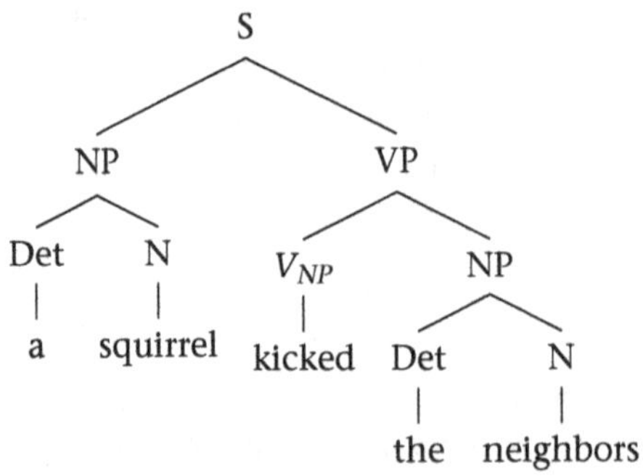

Many tests for constituency have been proposed in the literature, almost exclusively for English. Osborne (2018) provides fifteen tests in English, gathered from fifty-one syntax textbooks dating from 1976 to 2015 (e.g., Atkinson et al., 1982; Quirk et al., 1985; Mel'čuk and Pertsov, 1986; Radford, 1988; Baker, 1989; Akmajian et al., 1990; Haegeman, 1991; Cowper, 1992; Radford, 1997; Haegeman and Guéron, 1999; Sag et al., 1999; Van Valin, 2001; Adger, 2003; Hudson, 2010; Carnie, 2010, 2013; see Anderson [2018], Roberts [2023] for some more recent textbooks with the same issues). The overwhelming majority of these tests—thirteen of fifteen—identify so-called "maximal projections" in X-bar theoretic terms (Jackendoff, 1977). Each head word in X-bar theory (e.g., a noun, verb, or preposition) has a maximal projection (an XP), and intermediate levels (X′) where the arguments and modifiers can be connected. A noun has a noun phrase (NP) maximal projection; a verb has a verb phrase (VP) maximal projection; a preposition has a prepositional phrase (PP) maximal projection, and so on Most of Osborne's (2018) fifteen tests identify maximal projections, like NP, VP, and PP.

But it turns out that these tests could just as plausibly be identifying a **phrase** within dependency grammar, without the need for the extra syntactic structure in X-bar phrase structure grammars. Recall from chapter 3 that a phrase within dependency grammar is simply a word plus all the words that depend on it, directly or indirectly (e.g., Langacker, 1997). Any test that finds a maximal projection in X-bar theory also finds a phrase in dependency grammar.

Below, I show how the phrasal account can be applied to the first four of Osborne's (2018) tests, listed below; indeed, the semantic account offers a better account than the syntactic account for two of these tests: clefts and topicalization. The other maximal projection tests can be accounted for similarly.

1. Pronoun substitution using a definite pronoun like "she," "he," "it," or "they"
2. "Do-so" substitution of a verb phrase
3. Topicalization (fronting)
4. Clefting
5. Answer fragments
6. VP-ellipsis
7. Pseudo-clefting
8. Passivization
9. Intrusion
10. Omission
11. Wh-fronting
12. General substitution
13. Right-node Raising

The remaining two tests identify intermediate-level projections:

1. *one* substitution, which purportedly identifies an N′ level structure);
2. Coordination/conjunction, which purportedly identifies all levels of structure

It turns out that neither of these tests actually identifies a syntactic level. In the case of the *one*-replacement test, it can be shown that what is being referred to by *one* is not in the syntax. And in the case of coordination, it is easy to show that many sequences coordinate that are not possibly syntactic constituents, so this test is also not syntactic. These two tests are discussed in depth below also.

Overall, these analyses suggest that there is no need for the notion of syntactic constituent. Despite its popularity in current models of syntax, there does not appear to be any evidence for such a notion. Dependency grammar offers the advantages of being simpler, with better empirical coverage (see Jacobson [2023] for further potential issues with constituency tests and their uses in syntax).

7.8.1 Pronouns and *Do So*

Perhaps the most well-known constituency tests are those for pronouns and so-called verb phrase *do so*. Together, pronouns and *do so* are sometimes called *pro-forms*: Pronouns refer to noun phrases and *do so* is sometimes called a pro-verb-phrase, because it can refer to parts of a verbal complex.

Regarding pronouns, we can refer to *the squirrel* in (143) *A squirrel kicked the neighbors* with the pronoun *it*, and *the neighbors* in (143) with the pronoun *them*, as in (144a). Proponents of constituency for pronominal reference argue that we need an NP in the syntax corresponding to these pronouns. Hence there should be an NP covering *the squirrel* and *the neighbors* in the structure for (143), and there is, as shown above. Furthermore, we can refer to *kicked the neighbors* with *did so* in (144b), so there should be a verb phrase for this referent in the structure for (143).

(144) a. It kicked them.
b. A squirrel kicked the neighbors on Thursday and a rabbit did so on Friday.

In dependency grammar, the pronoun has the same referent as the noun (with its dependents): The phrase headed by the noun. Similarly for *do so*: *Do so* refers to a verb and its postverbal dependents, without needing any extra structure in the syntax. Note that we need some rule in either theory for how *do so* might refer.

7.8.2 Topicalization (Fronting)

A third test of constituency is fronting via *topicalization*. Topicalization is a rare construction in English, where we can front an element to the beginning of the sentence, typically in order to contrast it with respect to some other element of the event/state in question. Given the meaning in (145), we can topicalize all of the sequences in (146):

(145) A squirrel might steal the old dogfood from the dog dish.

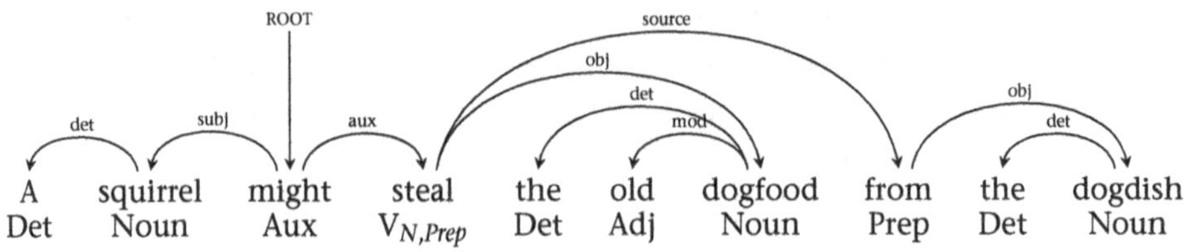

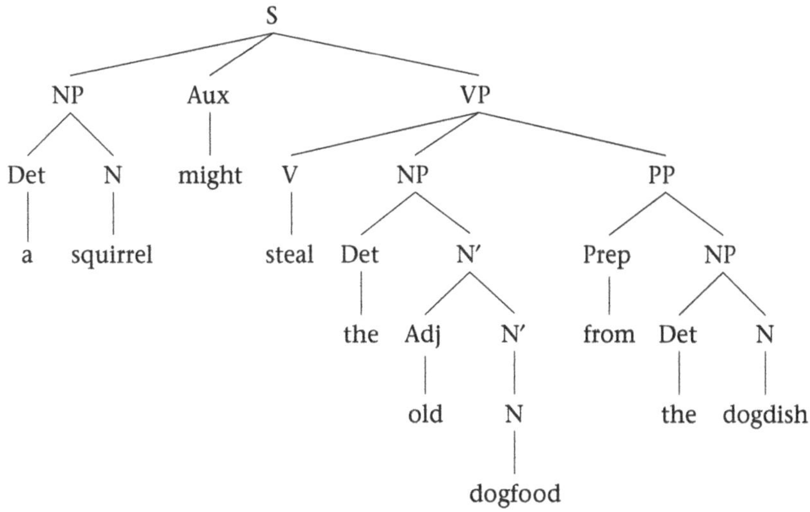

(146) a. The old dogfood, a squirrel might steal from the dog dish.
b. From the dog dish, a squirrel might steal the old dogfood.
c. Steal the old dogfood from the dog dish, a squirrel might.

The examples in (146) sound a little stilted in a null context; in order to sound natural, they would need a supportive context, where there is some contrasting element. But they sound like possible English sentences, in a supporting context.[3]

In contrast, we can't topicalize any of the sequences in (147):

(147) a. * The old, a squirrel might steal dogfood from the dog dish.
b. * Might steal, a squirrel the old dogfood from the dog dish.
c. * Dogfood from, a squirrel might steal the old dogfood from the dog dish.
d. * Old dogfood, a squirrel might steal the from the dog dish.
e. * Old, a squirrel might steal the dogfood from the dog dish.
f. * The, a squirrel might steal old dogfood from the dog dish.

The badness of examples like those in (147) has been provided as evidence against the possibility that the fronted sequences might be syntactic constituents (see many of the syntax texts cited above). The implicit claim in the constituency test for topicalization is that *maximal projection constituents (NP, PP, VP) should be able to topicalize*. Examples (147a)–(147c) are cases of clear nonconstituents. Example (147d) is a constituent (an N′), but it is not an NP, so this can't topicalize. Examples (147e) and (147f) are cases of single words that are part of NPs attempting to topicalize, which is not possible (even if these are maximal projections, in some versions of X-bar theory [Osborne, 2018]).

But this is not the right generalization about topicalization. Most critically, the fronted element must be headed by a word with some meaning. While we can usually topicalize a prepositional phrase (148), we cannot do so if the preposition has no meaning, such as the preposition *of* (149):

(148) a. We should talk to the users about their experience.
b. To the users, we should talk about their experience.
c. About their experience, we should talk to the users.

(149) a. The board approved of the new policy.
b. * Of the new policy, the board approved.
c. The new policy, the board approved of.
d. The team consists of experienced professionals.
e. * Of experienced professionals, the team consists.
f. Experienced professionals, the team consists of.
g. We should take care of the children during the trip.
h. * Of the children, we should take care during the trip.
i. The children, we should take care of during the trip.
j. The couple disliked the price of the apartment.
k. * Of the apartment, the young couple disliked the price.
l. Andrea had some anxiety over the coming election.
m. Over the coming election, Andrea had anxiety.

In (149c), the NP *the new policy* is fronted from (149a), which is acceptable. But trying to topicalize *of the new policy* from (149a) doesn't work, as in (149b). This is plausibly because the preposition *of* has no meaning, and so it cannot be topicalized. The preposition *of* is present for grammatical reasons only: In English, noun phrases need a case-marker—like a verb or a preposition—to license them. Similarly, topicalizing a PP with a contentful preposition like *over* out of an NP is possible in (149m), but not when the preposition is *of* as in (149k).

If topicalization were sensitive to syntactic categories only, then it would allow all kinds of PPs. Simplified phrase structures for (148a) and (149a) are presented below. The syntax is identical, so trying to work out a syntactic hypothesis (constituency) for the possibility of fronting cannot be right.

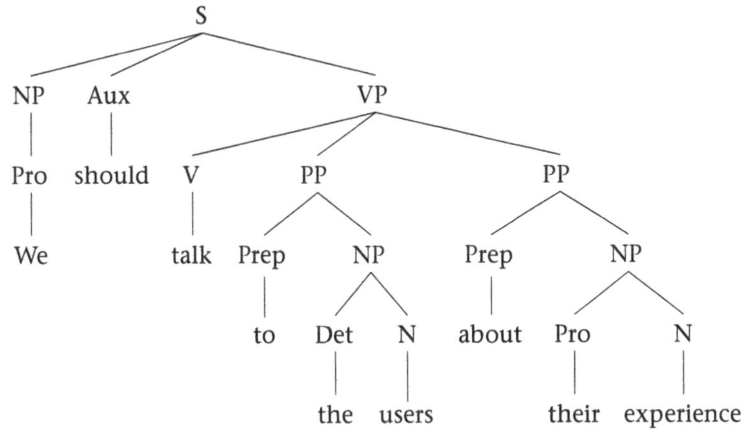

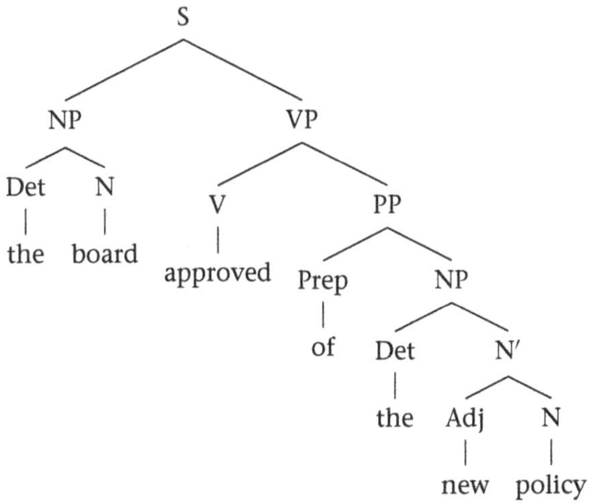

The fact that topicalization only allows PPs headed by a semantically contentful preposition shows that topicalization is a semantic construction: The topicalized element (and its dependents) must have a meaning that can be understood in the context. This is not a purely syntactic constraint, so it is irrelevant to the definition of constituent.[4]

7.8.3 Clefting

The cleft construction is similar in both form and meaning to the topicalization construction in English. From the base sentence (150a), we can cleft the same kinds of noun phrases, prepositional phrases, and verb phrases as we can topicalize from (as in (146)):

(150) a. A squirrel was stealing the old dogfood from the dog dish.
b. NP cleft: It is the old dogfood that a squirrel was stealing from the dog dish.
c. PP cleft: It is from the dog dish that a squirrel was stealing the old dogfood.
d. VP cleft: It was stealing the old dogfood from the dog dish that a squirrel was.

Again, this kind of evidence has been argued to support syntactic constituency in clefts, but the same problems with this hypothesis are present as for topicalization. Most prominently, only elements headed by semantically contentful words can cleft.

(151) a. It is the children that we should take care of during the trip.
b. * It is of the children that we should take care during the trip.
c. It is experienced professionals that the team consists of.
d. * It is of experienced professionals that the team consists.
e. It was over the coming election that Andrea had anxiety.
f. * It was of the apartment that the young couple disliked the price.

These problems for the syntactic account suggest a semantic account of clefting: The item that can be clefted is semantically contentful, is relevant to the main assertion, and includes its dependents. This is a semantic definition, which is easy to implement in dependency grammar. No additional syntactic elements are needed.

7.8.4 The *One*-Replacement Test

A fifth well-known test is the *one*-replacement test—a test specific to English—which has been used to argue for complex structure within a noun phrase. Consider the examples in (152) from Carnie (2010)'s book on constituent structure:

(152) a. I bought the big **bag of groceries** with the plastic handle, not the small **one** with the ugly logo.
b. I bought the big **bag of groceries with the plastic handle**, not the small **one**.

The claim is that the pronoun *one* needs to refer to a constituent within the syntax: an N′. Consequently, we need a constituent structure within the noun phrase for *bag of groceries* in order for (152a) to work, and we need a constituent structure within the noun phrase for *bag of groceries with the plastic handle* for (152b) to work. X-bar theory (see section 7.6 above) was proposed in part to accommodate cases like these. In X-bar theory, each head word (e.g., a noun) has a maximal projection (an XP) and intermediate levels (X′) where the arguments and modifiers can be connected. In this case, a noun (*bag*) has a maximal projection (NP) and three intermediate N′ levels, which the pronoun *one* can refer to later.

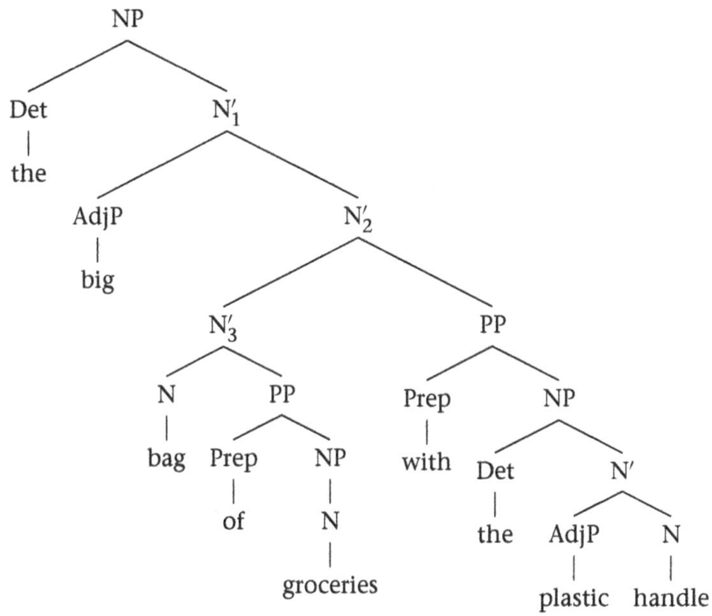

In (152a) the pronoun *one* refers to N'_3, whereas in (152b) the pronoun "one" refers to N'_2.

Let's compare the phrase structure above to the dependency structure for the same string, below:

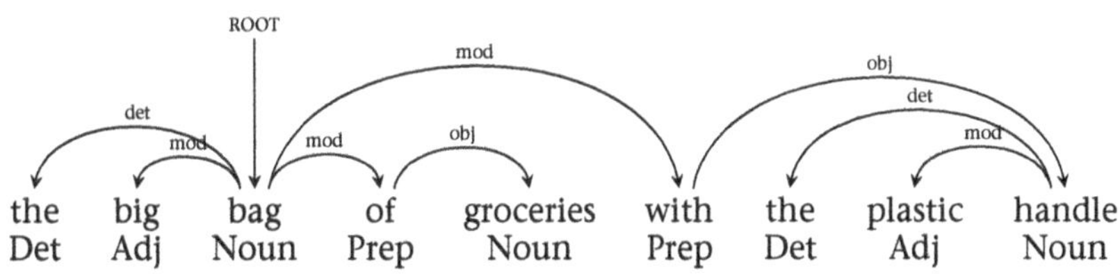

The dependency structure is much simpler. The extra nodes in the phrase structure are motivated in terms of reference, but it turns out that the pronoun *one* doesn't refer to syntactic elements at all: It picks out relevant elements in the context. We can see this by examining examples like (153) (Culicover and Jackendoff, 2005; Osborne, 2018):

(153) a. that silly picture of Robin from Mary that is on the table, and this artful one from Susan (Culicover and Jackendoff, 2005): p. 137
b. that silly picture of Robin from Mary that is on the table, and this one from Susan (Culicover and Jackendoff, 2005): p. 137

One possible phrase structure for the initial sequence *that silly picture of Robin from Mary that is on the table* is provided below:

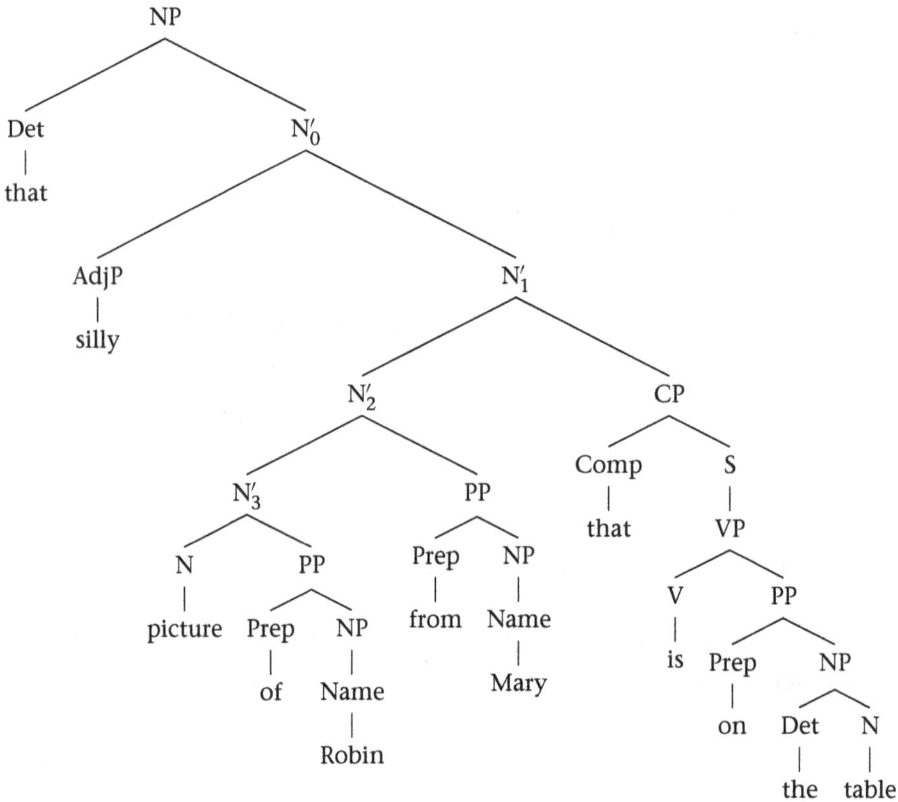

In (153a), the pronoun *one* refers to *picture of Robin . . . that is on the table*, critically skipping over the PP *from Mary*, which is filled in as *from Susan* in the referent. There is no N′ node that dominates just this sequence of words, because it references a discontinuous sequence of words, with parts on either side of *from Susan*. A similar point applies to (153a), where the pronoun *one* refers to *silly picture of Robin ... that is on the table*. Culicover and Jackendoff (2005) therefore reject the idea that the pronominal *one* identifies constituents. See also Osborne (2018) for other issues with the syntactic constituent analysis of *one*.

Goldberg and Michaelis (2017) provide further related evidence, arguing against claims made by Lidz et al. (2003) regarding the structure of English noun phrases. Lidz et al. (2003) suggested that the infant participants in their study need to have understood the existence of a constituent for *yellow bottle* in order to know how to correctly interpret *another one* in (154a) as *another yellow bottle*.

(154) a. Look! A yellow bottle. Now look do you see another one?
b. Look! A bottle! It's yellow! Now do you see another one?

But Goldberg and Michaelis (2017) observe that the referent for *one* is also *yellow bottle* in (154b) despite the lack of a syntactic constituent in the sentence for this meaning. They conclude that a referent for *one* is contextually, not syntactically, determined. In this case, the bottle was just described as yellow, and *another one* refers to a second example that is somehow similar to one of the things in the current context (Tomasello, 2004; Akhtar et al., 2004).

The one-replacement test is the only test that motivates internal structure to maximal projections in X-bar theory. And this is not a syntactic test. Hence the internal extra structure is not needed.

7.8.5 Coordination

Coordination is often provided as a test of syntactic constituency. The idea is that items that can coordinate should be represented by a syntactic constituent. So the conjuncts in (155) should have a syntactic element to coordinate, as in the tree structures below for (155b), (155c), and (155f)

(155) a. A neighbor yelled, chased the cat, and gave the dog a bone. (Sang and De Meulder, 2003)
b. Mary kicked the ball over the big bushes and trees.
c. Mary kicked the ball over the big bushes and small trees.
d. Mary kicked the ball over the big bushes and the small trees.
e. Mary kicked the ball over the big bushes and into the park.
f. Mary was kicking the ball over the big bushes and laughing.

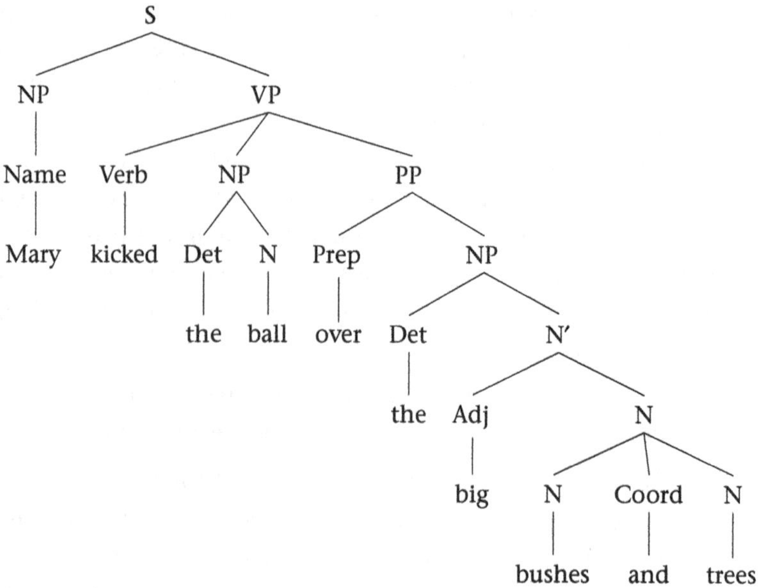
S
NP VP
Name Verb NP PP
Mary kicked Det N Prep NP
the ball over Det N′
the Adj N
big N Coord N
bushes and trees

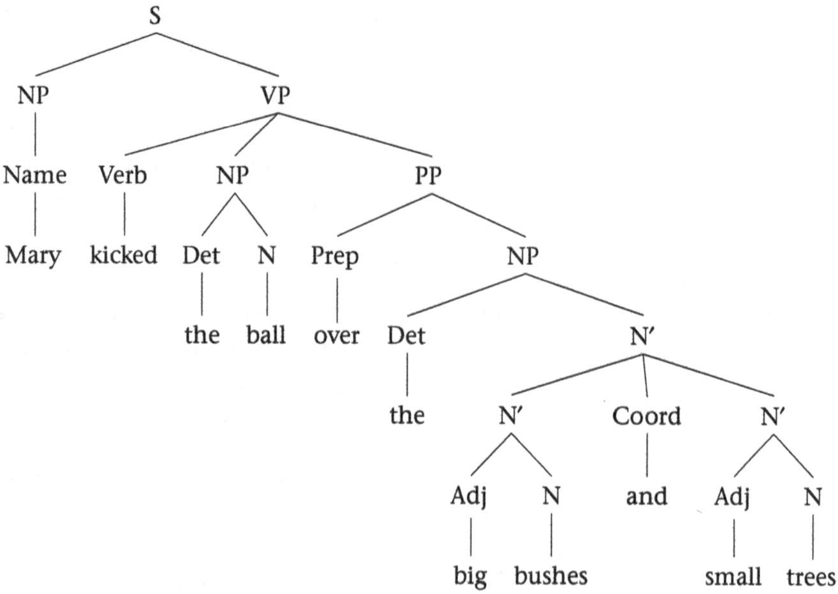
S
NP VP
Name Verb NP PP
Mary kicked Det N Prep NP
the ball over Det N′
the N′ Coord N′
Adj N and Adj N
big bushes small trees

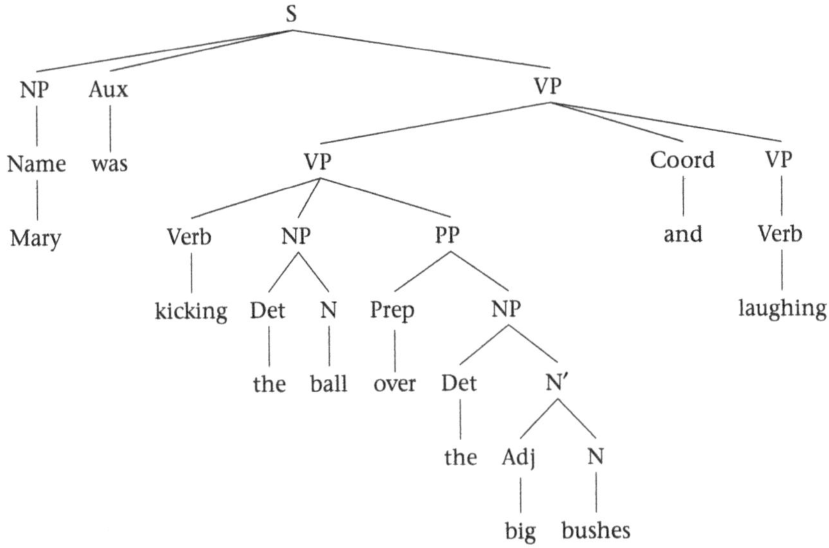

Whereas the examples in (155) are indeed acceptable, they do not actually provide evidence for the syntactic constituent hypothesis, because many other coordinations are also possible that are certainly not semantic constituents, like the examples in (156):

(156) a. Antonia ordered seven and paid for only three pizzas.
b. Mary kicked several larger and juggled a few smaller soccer balls.
c. Some louder boys might have been—and quieter girls probably were—laughing at the teacher.

Contrary to the X-bar phrase structure analysis, it seems that almost any sequence of words can be coordinated with another sequence of words, if they are parallel in some way. Thus, it is possible to conjoin a verb with a following determiner—only part of the noun phrase to come—with some other verb and determiner (quantifier). This is the case in (156a): The verb and numeral *ordered seven* is coordinated with the verb and its following argument: *paid for only three*. This coordination does not include the noun for each quantifier—*pizzas*—that follows. A similar coordination takes place in (156b). In (156c), a part of the subject noun phrase plus following auxiliary verbs *louder boys might have been* are coordinated with a parallel part of a noun phrase and auxiliary verb *quieter girls probably were*. In none of these cases is there plausibly a complete semantic constituent. Coordination appears to allow any sequence of words, so coordination is not a test of syntactic constituency in phrase structure.

8 Chomsky's Transformation-Based Theories of Grammar

A popular idea in syntactic research—going back to early work of Noam Chomsky—is that there are two critical components to syntactic structure: putting words together (what Chomsky now calls **merge**; Chomsky [1993]) and **moving** structures around (Chomsky, 1965, 1981; cf. Chomsky, 1957, 1993). According to this proposal, there is a **base structure** for each sentence, and **transformations or movement** to get to less basic kinds of things that we might like to say. The base structure (or **deep structure**) is *different* structure that is present in your mind before you form the order of the sentence that is produced.

Chomsky proposed that the transformations from a base structure to the utterances we speak will pose a problem for learning, which suggested to him that language structure is not learnable, and must be innate. This was an example of what came to be known as the "poverty of the stimulus" hypothesis. In section 8.1, I summarize Chomsky's analysis of English subject-auxiliary inversion, and how this leads to the poverty of the stimulus hypothesis. However, I also show that Chomsky's analysis of the subject-auxiliary inversion has several problems, which suggest that the movement analysis is not correct, and that the lexical rule hypothesis is more on the right track. In section 8.2, I observe that current large language models (LLMs) falsify Chomsky's claim that English syntax is not learnable: English syntax is indeed learnable based on the language input alone. In section 8.3, I discuss some English complexity phenomena from long-distance dependencies that are more easily explained in a grammar theory that lacks movement than in theory with movement of phrases. And finally in section 8.4, I discuss the second most famous learnability argument of Chomsky and colleagues: the "syntactic island" argument. Chomsky's claim here is that the acceptability of a range of constructions involving long-distance dependency relationships with fronted wh-words—such as *who, what, or which*—suggest that aspects of these structures must be innate. Chomsky's specific proposal is that there is a syntactic constraint on the movement of a phrase from a position in a declarative structure to its fronted position. This theory predicts that movement out of any construction that crosses the same number and kind of syntactic boundaries will give rise to similar unacceptability. Contrary to this prediction, it is shown that there is a wide spectrum of acceptability of the resulting structures, for transformations in different construction types, each of which would involve crossing the same kinds of phrase structure nodes. These observations argue against the syntactic approach to the unacceptability of certain long-distance dependency cases, and for a usage-based approach.

8.1 Chomsky's Movement Analysis of Subject-Auxiliary Inversion, and the Poverty of the Stimulus

Chomsky (1955, 1956, 1957) proposed a simple and clever analysis of English subject-auxiliary inversion, whereby an auxiliary verb "moves" from its position in the declarative clause to a fronted position in the interrogative. Let's look at some examples of declarative and interrogative English sentences below.

(157) a. Ollie might chase a squirrel.
b. Ollie is chasing a squirrel.
c. Some neighbors were drinking lots of beer.
d. An apple could fall from the tree.
e. The students had hoped for a good teacher.

(158) a. Might Ollie chase a squirrel?
b. Is Ollie chasing a squirrel?
c. Were some neighbors drinking lots of beer?
d. Could an apple fall from the tree?
e. Had the students hoped for a good teacher?

The sentences in (157) are declarative sentences. The function of a declarative sentence is to pass information from the producer to the comprehender. In contrast, the sentences in (158) are interrogative sentences. In an interrogative sentence, the speaker is trying to find something out from the comprehender. If the interrogative sentence is a yes-no question as in (158), then a yes or no answer is required: one bit of information.

Under the movement analysis of interrogatives, the auxiliary verb moves from its base position in the declarative to the front of the sentence. For example, in (158a), the auxiliary verb *might* moves from its base position in the declarative (157a) to the front of the sentence. Similarly, the auxiliary verb *is* moves from its base position in the declarative (157b) to the front of the sentence (158b). Below, I provide two analyses of the movement for (157a) to (158a): one using the phrase structure categories from 1970s (e.g., Chomsky, 1973, 1977) and another with the categories that Chomsky used in the 1980s Barriers framework (Chomsky, 1986):

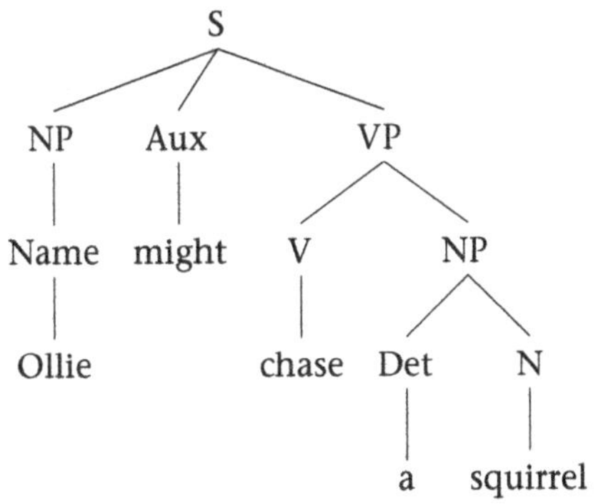

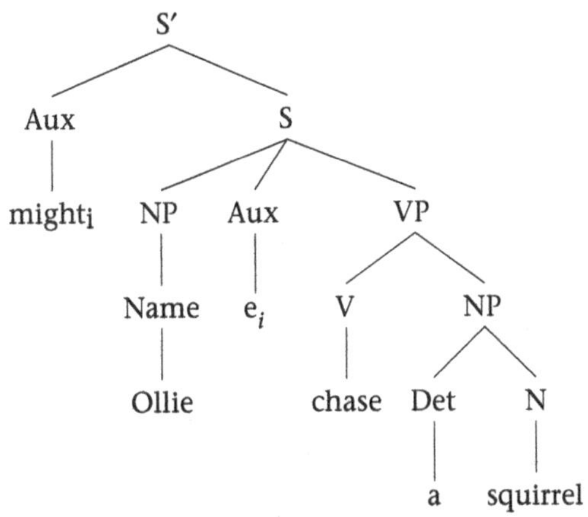

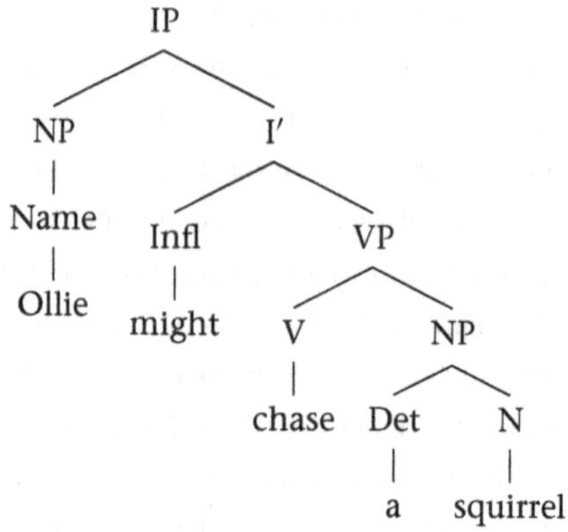

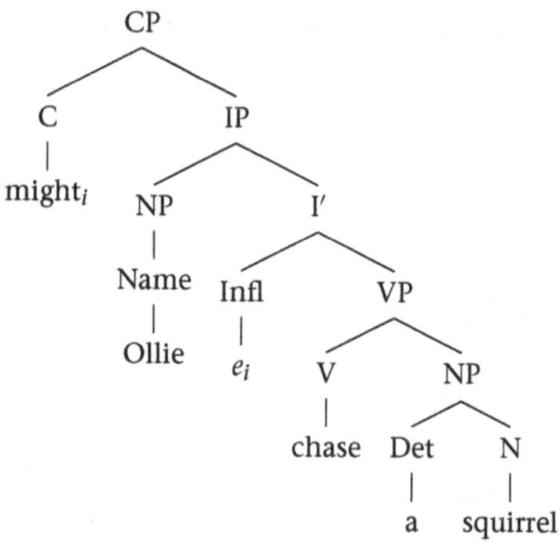

The details of the labels and structures of the categories have changed over time, but the core of the analysis remains the same. The auxiliary verb *might* starts in an **Aux** or **Infl** category, and moves to position below an S′ category at the front of the sentence, or to the head of a CP at the front of the sentence. In any of these cases, the **Aux/Infl** category moves, leaving behind a trace of the movement e_i, which is coindexed with the word that is moved to the front. The index I use here is *i*, which is a standard index for researchers using the movement framework.

The key idea here for Chomsky is that, contrary to the analysis presented in section 3.9, there is only one lexical entry for each of the auxiliary verbs. The same lexical entry is used in generating either the declarative structure or the interrogative structure. In order to produce an interrogative sentence, the speaker starts with the declarative structure, and applies the movement rule to move the auxiliary to the front of the clause. Consequently, there is just one extra rule for the interrogative meaning: All the lexical items are kept the same. This seems like a simple analysis of an interesting pattern of data.

Despite the apparent simplicity of having only one more rule—the movement rule—this rule is of a different format than the rules in the context-free base. The rule may be simple to state (in a loose way), but this kind of rule may lead to problems in identifying the appropriate structure for an input, which then might make the language system as a whole difficult to learn.

8.1.1 Chomsky's "Poverty of the Stimulus" Hypothesis

Chomsky (1971, 1980a) suggests that aspects of human language are complex, and the data that would be required for a learner aren't present in the input. These aspects of human language are argued to be unlearnable, and therefore innate. This hypothesis is called the "poverty of the stimulus": There isn't enough data of the right kind in order to learn the target behavior. This problem has been claimed to be present in a few domains of language, perhaps most famously in the English auxiliary verb system.

One critical observation that Chomsky (1971, 1980a) makes is that it is the auxiliary verb associated with the **main clause** that is fronted, which need not be the first clause. That is, the way English speakers form the interrogative from the examples in (159) is (160) not (161):

(159) a. The boy who is walking away is kicking a ball.
b. Some neighbors who were usually quiet were drinking lots of beer.
c. An apple which may be getting rotten might fall from the tree.

(160) a. Is the boy who is walking away ___ kicking a ball?
b. Were some neighbors who were usually quiet ___ drinking lots of beer?
c. Might an apple which may be getting rotten ___ fall from the tree?

(161) a. * Is the boy who ___ walking away is kicking a ball.
b. * Were some neighbors who ___ usually quiet were drinking lots of beer.
c. * May an apple which ___ be getting rotten might fall from the tree.

In (159a) there are two auxiliary verbs: one in the relative clause modifying the subject *boy* and one in the main clause. It is the auxiliary verb associated with the main clause that is in sentence-initial position to correctly forms the interrogative, as in (160a). If the auxiliary verb associated with the relative clause is fronted, this results in the ungrammatical (161a), which is not the way to form the interrogative meaning of (159a).

Chomsky (1971, 1980a) correctly points out that examples like (160) are rare in the child's input: "It is quite possible for a person to go through life without having heard any of the relevant examples that would choose between the two principles" (Chomsky, 1971).[1] Consequently, he argues that there is no way for a learner to distinguish whether the movement rule moves the *first* auxiliary in a sentence to the front of the sentence (as it would for the ungrammatical examples in (161)) vs. the auxiliary associated with the main clause. Because native English speakers overwhelmingly agree that the right rule is the one that is associated with the main clause and not the first clause, he postulates that this structure-sensitive rule must be innate.

8.1.2 Chomsky Is Right That a Grammar with Movement Is Hard to Learn

The presentation in this book thus far should make it clear that there is a fallacy in Chomsky's poverty of the stimulus hypothesis. Chomsky's argument only works *if there is a movement or derivation rule linking the declarative to the interrogative syntax rules.*[2] If there is no such derivation or movement rule that needs to be learned, then there is nothing making the learning particularly problematic.

Indeed, Chomsky is correct that learning a set of syntactic rules that includes the possibility that elements can move around is much more difficult than if movement is not possible. Let's consider (158a), repeated below, and two possible representations that one might need to learn, depending on the syntactic theory: a dependency grammar analysis, or a movement-based phrase structure analysis like the one presented above around the time of Chomsky's "barriers" framework, with slightly more movement, in the precursor to the "minimalist" program (Chomsky, 1993): where the subject NP *Ollie* starts inside the VP, and moves to the subject position of IP (Fukui and Speas, 1986; Koopman and Sportiche, 1991):

(158a) Might Ollie chase the squirrel?

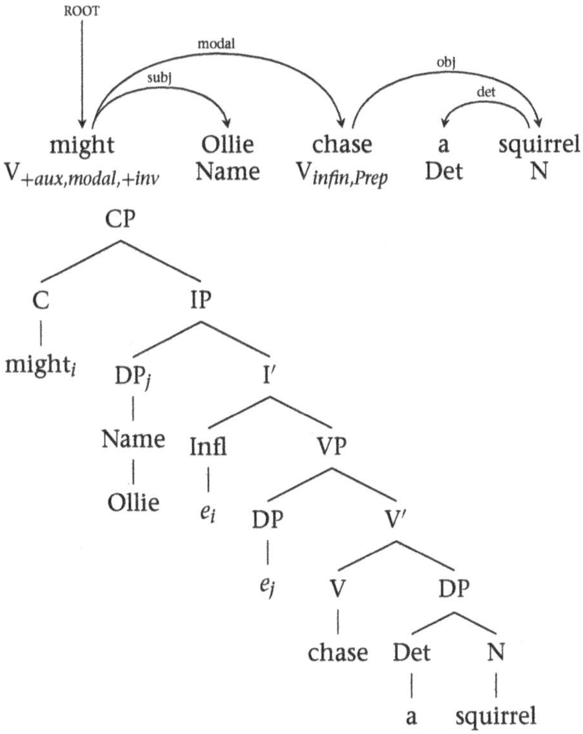

For simplicity, I also include a simplified dependency representation of the above phrase structure, without the phrase structure categories. This contains all the headedness information in the phrase structure above.

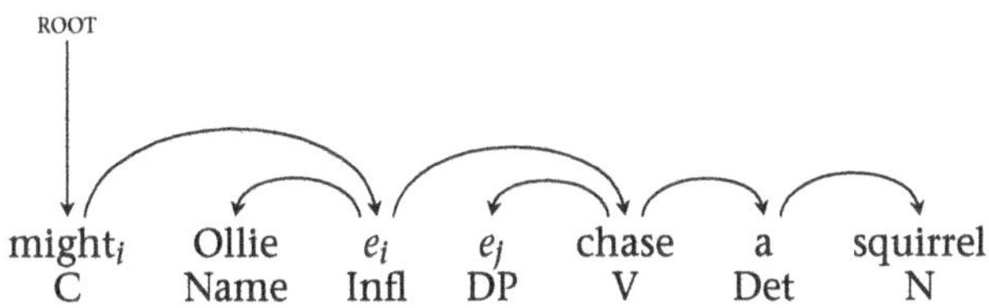

All the information in the dependency structure is included in phrase structure version, but with more information in the phrase structure. So learning structures like those in the dependency structure is strictly easier than learning the phrase structures. Let us first assume that the learner can learn the words and morphemes, such that the learning problem amounts to learning how these words connect to one another. Under the what-you-see-is-what-you-get (WYSIWYG) dependency grammar approach, a learner only needs to learn how to form a directed acyclic graph for each sequence of words. If there are only two words a and b, then there are only two possibilities: a is a dependent of b, or b is a dependent of a. For a three word sentence, the possibilities multiply quickly: Any of the three words might be the head of the whole sentence, and there are three structures for each of these:

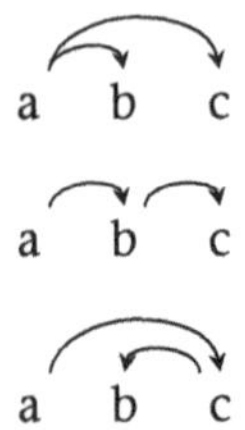

Hence there are nine possible dependency structures for a set of three words. In general, there are n^{n-1} possible structures for a sequence of n words (Prufer, 1918; Caminiti et al., 2007), see https://en.wikipedia.org/wiki/Pr%C3%BCfer_sequence. This is large number of possible structures, but presumably we can learn the structures for smaller parts of sentences first before figuring out the structure of a whole sentence. So for a four-word sequence like *Ollie might chase Lana*, we have 64 possible structures. And for a five-word sequence like *Might Ollie chase a squirrel*, we have 625 possible structures.

Let us now consider the learning problem for the movement-based grammar. Not only do we need to learn the headedness structure of a directed acyclic graph – the tree structure – but we also have to allow for the possibility that any of the words started out somewhere else and moved some number of times. Let us consider the simpler possibility that each word moved at most once. For an n-word sequence, we increase the search space from n^{n-1} possible dependency structures by another factor of n^n: Each word can either stay where it is, or move to each of n positions. (If the moved element a_0 is immediately beside its root element a, this is "vacuous" movement: movement which is not across any words. We consider this equivalent to the unmoved variant, and we consider vacuous movement only to one side.) The number of structures to be considered for base dependency structures is provided first; the number of structures to be considered for structures with transformations of only one per word is provided second

(This still underestimates the search involved for transformed structures in two ways: (1) it is not only words that can move, but whole constituents; and (2) they may move more than once in each structure):

Number of possible base structures: $S_{NoTransformations} = n^{n-1}$
Number of structures transformations of only one word: $S_{Transformations} = n^{n-1} \times n^n$

For example, in each of the nine structures for three-word sequences, each word can move to three other positions: this is 27 possibilities for each of the source structures. We provide three of these below, for the first structure connecting a, b, and c from above, where *b* and *c* are unmoved.

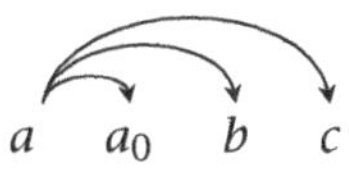

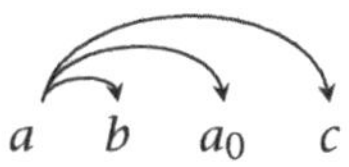

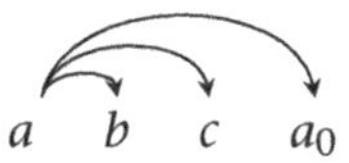

Thus for a 3-word sequence, we increase the search space from 9 possible dependency structures by a factor of 27, to 243 possible structures. And for a 4-word sequence, we increase the search space from 64 possible dependency structures by a factor of 256 to 16,384 possible structures. For a sequence of 5 words, the search goes from 625 possible structures to 1,953,125 structures. This is an astronomical search. So Chomsky is indeed right that his particular grammar is difficult to learn. In contrast, the dependency grammar structures—with no movement or empty elements—are far easier to learn.

In more recent movement-based versions of Chomsky's grammar—the minimalist framework (Chomsky, 1993)—even more empty elements are assumed than in previous versions of the movement theories. A structure for the simple sentence *John likes Mary* starts at the deep structure given below, from which each of the nouns and the verb moves to higher positions in the tree, including the additional empty heads C, Agr_S, T, and Agr_O (Laurence and Margolis, 2001). The learning problem is indeed a difficult one for such grammar assumptions.

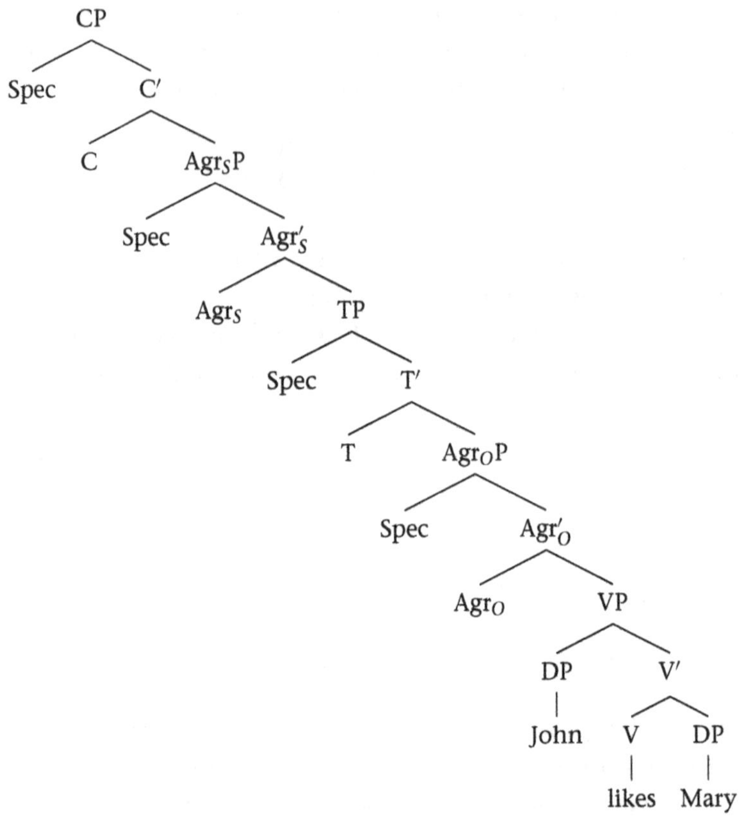

8.1.3 Problems with the Movement Analysis of English Auxiliary Verbs

Without empty elements and movement, the dependency structure for the input is much easier to learn.[3] In any case, the movement proposal and the construction-based lexical-rule proposal also make different predictions about the ways that the declarative and interrogative auxiliary verbs are represented. Each of these differences favors the construction-based approach over the movement approach.

8.1.3.1 The existence of "do-support" for simple past and present tense

The learning problem that Chomsky identifies relies critically on there being a movement rule to link declarative and interrogative meanings. A central tenet of the movement analysis is that any form of a verb that is possible in the declarative is also valid in the interrogative. Verbs in the simple past and present tense present an immediate challenge for this analysis:

(162) a. Ollie chased the squirrel.
b. Ollie chases the squirrel.

In order to form an interrogative version of a simple past (162a) or simple present tense example (162a), it is not possible to front the verb, as shown by the unacceptability of (163a) and (163b):

(163) a. * chased Ollie the squirrel?
b. * chases Ollie the squirrel?

Instead, it is necessary to use a special auxiliary verb, a form of the verb *do*, which on the surface, seems like an interrogative-only form of a verb, contrary to what should be possible according to the movement analysis:

(164) a. Did Ollie chase the squirrel?
b. Does Ollie chase the squirrel?

Indeed, these forms of the verb *do* are not valid in ordinary declaratives, as shown by the unacceptability of examples like (165a) and (165b) when *did* or *does* is unstressed, as in a typical context:

(165) a. ? Ollie did chase the squirrel. (unstressed *did*; only acceptable when *did* is stressed)
b. ? Ollie does chase the squirrel. (unstressed *does*; only acceptable when *does* is stressed)

Although there are contexts where examples like (165a) and (165b) are acceptable, such contexts are rare: Only when the speaker thinks that current state of knowledge is that the event described by the verb did not occur (e.g., the speaker believes that the listener thinks that Ollie did not chase the squirrel, for (165a)), and so the speaker seeks to contradict this belief).

Thus, contrary to the central tenet of the movement analysis, non-auxiliary verbs—the vast majority of verbs—are are all exceptions to the movement rule: Simple past, and present-tense verbs are declarative-only forms; and forms of *do* are interrogative-only forms. Of course, proponents of the movement analysis can propose special rules for the simple past- and present-tense declarative and interrogative formation rules (as Chomsky does, with the "do-support" rule), but the existence of all of these exceptions weakens the analysis.

8.1.3.2 The existence of auxiliary verbs that appear in only the interrogative or the declarative form There are additional examples of auxiliary verbs like *aren't* that appear only in interrogative contexts for particular subject types, such as (166a), and there are further examples of auxiliary verbs like *better* and *ought* that appear only in declarative contexts (167):[4]

(166) a. Aren't I invited to the party?
b. ∗ I aren't invited to the party.

(167) a. He ought to go now.
b. ∗ Ought he to go now?
c. I better go now.
d. ∗ Better I go now?

For example, the default first-person singular copula negative is *aren't* in an interrogative in (166a), but this form is not licensed in the declarative (166b). Instead, for the same meaning, we have to say *I am not invited*. There are similar asymmetries for auxiliaries that are possible in the declarative, but not the interrogative: *better* and *ought* as in (167).

The existence of these cases is not expected under the movement hypothesis, where, if they came from movement, you would really expect to see them in declaratives. What's the movement theory for why not? In contrast, the existence of each of these auxiliaries is not a problem for the lexical rule hypothesis, where we learn which words the lexical rule applies to, in their usage. The rule simply doesn't apply to *better* and *ought*; and the verb *aren't* has an argument structure like the inverted one (from other uses of *aren't*, which are valid in the non-inverted form, like second person). The argument structures for "aren't" as an interrogative auxiliary, and "better" as a declarative auxiliary are given below:

$V_{+aux,modal,1person,+inv}$: aren't

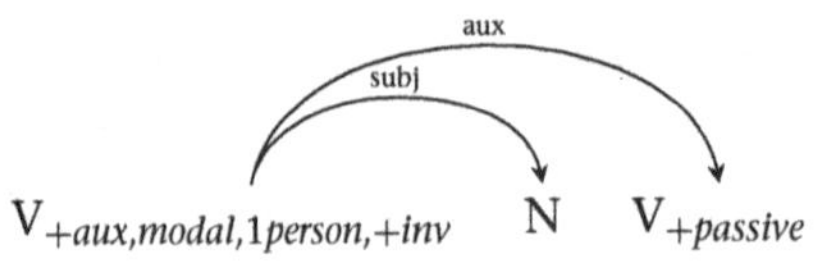

$V_{+aux,modal,-inv}$: better

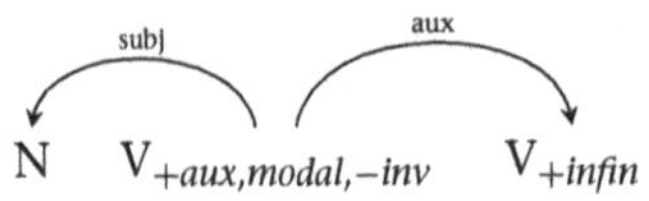

8.1.3.3 Shifts in meaning for some auxiliary verbs, depending on the declarative vs. interrogative context There are auxiliary verbs whose meaning changes between declarative and interrogative contexts (Sag et al.,

2020; Gazdar et al., 1982). For example, the meaning of *shall* in (168a) is an offer and/or permission request, whereas the meaning of *shall* in (168b) is only the future intent meaning.

(168) a. Shall I open the window? (offer and permission request)
b. I shall open the window. (not possible with permission (deontic) meaning; only possible with future (intent) meaning)
c. May he refuse? (ok with permission (deontic) meaning; odd with possibility (epistemic) meaning)
d. He may refuse. (odd with permission (deontic) meaning; preferable with possibility (epistemic) meaning)

If there were a rule such that the declarative moved to form the interrogative, then none of these asymmetries would exist. The existence of these asymmetries suggests that *shall* and *may* are just different auxiliary verbs, with different meanings and usage (where the lexical rule doesn't apply).

8.1.3.4 Summary Each of the differences between the movement proposal and the construction-based lexical-rule proposal favors the construction-based approach over the movement approach. The differences that I discussed were as follows:

1. The simple past and present tense don't work according to the movement analysis. Consequently, a complex special case is needed under the movement analysis, called "do-support." In contrast, within the construction-based analysis, the existence of construction-specific forms of the verbs for the simple past and present tense is as expected.
2. There are auxiliary verbs other than forms of *do* that appear only in either the declarative or interrogative, contrary to the prediction of the movement analysis, but as predicted by the construction-based account.
3. There are auxiliary verbs whose meaning changes in declarative vs. interrogative contexts (Gazdar et al., 1982; Sag et al., 2020) as expected under the construction-based analysis, but in contrast to the prediction of the movement analysis.

8.1.4 How Do Children Acquire English Auxiliary Inversion?

Chomsky (1980a) suggested that although complex materials like (159a) and (160a) (repeated below) are extremely rare in the child's input, the child will "nevertheless unerringly employ the structure-dependent generalization on the first relevant occasion" (p. 145). Chomsky then suggested that this meant that the structure-dependent rule must therefore be innate. A great deal of research has since investigated the acquisition of English auxiliary inversion: Do children ever make auxiliary-inversion errors? And if so, what kinds of errors do children make?

(159a) The boy who is walking away is kicking a ball.
(160a) Is the boy who is walking away kicking a ball?

In one of the most influential studies of children's production of English auxiliary-inversion, Crain and Nakayama (1987) had thirty children aged three years, two months (3;2)—five years, eleven months (5;11) form yes-no-questions from the following set of declarative materials:

(169) Pre-test sentences
  a. The girl is tall.
  b. The man is tired.
  c. The pig next to the tree is red.

(170) Test sentences
  a. The dog that is sleeping is on the blue bench.
  b. The ball that the girl is sitting on is big.
  c. The boy who is watching Mickey Mouse is happy.
  d. The boy who is unhappy is watching Mickey Mouse.
  e. The boy who is being kissed by his mother is happy.
  f. The boy who was holding the plate is crying.

In the task, each child was asked to pose each of the above declarative sentences as questions, in order, to a doll (Jabba the Hutt, a figure from *Star Wars*) about a set of pictures that Jabba was shown by an experimenter. Jabba would respond *Yes* or *No* for the corresponding picture, and if Jabba was correct, then the child would pretend to feed Jabba. Almost all children got all three of the pre-test sentences in (169) correct: There were only two errors out of ninety trials. The critical trials were those in (170). The younger children in this task produced extensive errors when trying to produce these sentences, as documented in table 8.1.[5]

There are several notable observations from this table of error patterns. First, the younger children in Group I (ages 3;2—4;7) made errors on 62 percent of the trials (50/81 trials). The most common kind of error (30/81 trials = 37 percent) was an auxiliary-doubling error, such that the inverted auxiliary verb at the front of the sentence was repeated in its declarative position, such as *Is the boy who is watching Mickey Mouse is happy?* as the

Table 8.1
Number of errors by groups of children in experiment 1 of Crain and Nakayama (1987). Child participants were asked to pose each of six complex questions to a doll (Jabba the Hutt from *Star Wars*), based on a source sentence and picture (e.g., *The boy who is watching Mickey Mouse is happy*). A correct question would be *Is the boy who is watching Mickey Mouse happy?* An example incorrect question often involved doubling the auxiliary, as in *Is the boy who is watching Mickey Mouse is happy?*

	Correct	Total errors	Auxiliary doubled	Fragment question	Other	Structural independent "move"
Group I (n = 15) age 3;2 to 4;7; mean 4;3	31	50	30	10	10	0
Group II n = 15) age 4;7 to 5;11; mean 5;3	70	17	9	5	3	0
Total 1 (n = 30) age 3;2 to 5;11; mean 4;9	101	67	39	15	13	0

question for item (170c). The older children in Group II (ages 4;7 to 5;11) made many fewer errors: only 20 percent (17/87 trials). So there seems to be a developmental pattern here.

Second, what Crain and Nakayama (1987) focus on is that no child ever makes what Chomsky calls a structural independence error "moving" the auxiliary out of the relative clause. So, while many trials are produced correctly—for example, *Is the boy who is watching Mickey Mouse happy?* as the question for item (170a)—no child ever said *Is the boy who watching Mickey Mouse is happy?* as the question for the same item. Based on this observation, Crain and Nakayama (1987) conclude that Chomsky's nativist theory of forming the interrogative by moving the auxiliary from the declarative position in the main clause to the front of the sentence is probably on the right track.

This conclusion strikes me as premature. There are several problems with the inference. First, there are potentially many theories other than Chomsky's preferred movement theory that would predict that children wouldn't attempt to form a yes-no question by "fronting" the auxiliary from inside a relative clause. Indeed, the theory that I am arguing for here—the lexical rule theory, such that there are two lexical entries for these tensed auxiliary verbs—makes this prediction, but for a different reason than Chomsky's movement theory. In the lexical-rule theory, the way to make a yes-no question is to start with a +inverted auxiliary for the main clause assertion and work your way down from there. So given item (170a) *The dog that is sleeping is on the blue bench?*, we start from the word *is* (the root of the sentence), make it +inverted, and work our way down the structure. We produce the complex subject next—*the dog that is sleeping*—and then go to the main assertion *on the blue bench*. There is no movement in this theory and no innate structure. Importantly, this theory also predicts that people will not produce materials like *Is the dog that sleeping is on the blue bench?*

Second, the movement theory that Crain and Nakayama (1987) argue for does not predict the pattern of errors children produce when they attempt to produce these materials. Crain and Nakayama (1987) refer to these errors as "performance" errors, but it is striking that there are so many of them: Sixty-two percent of the trials contain an error for the younger children, the most common of which is a repetition of the inverted verb in the non-inverted position. If movement is innate (as proposed by Chomsky's theory), then it is unclear why there is cost associated with the inverted structure, such that there might be complexity, leading to errors. Crain and colleagues could speculate that at points of high memory cost (in long-distance dependencies as in these examples), perhaps children repeat the heads for long-distance connections. But this explanation would also predict that children would repeat other heads that take part in long-distance connections, such as subject nouns before verbs. For example, when probed to produce examples like (170c) *The boy who is watching Mickey Mouse is happy*, children at a similar age should produce materials like *The boy who is watching Mickey Mouse the boy is happy*. This would be a similar repetition of a head taking part in a long-distance relationship. But children don't make such errors: This kind of "performance" error seems to be restricted to inverted auxiliary verbs.

In contrast, the lexical-rule theory is more consistent with these kinds of errors. In the lexical-rule theory, there are two lexical entries for each tensed invertable verb (like *is* in this case). The interrogative +inverted entry is less frequent and, hence, acquired later. The children in this experiment have all already acquired the –inverted entry but are working on acquiring the +inverted entry. When given a complex environment such as with a long-distance dependency, they make errors.

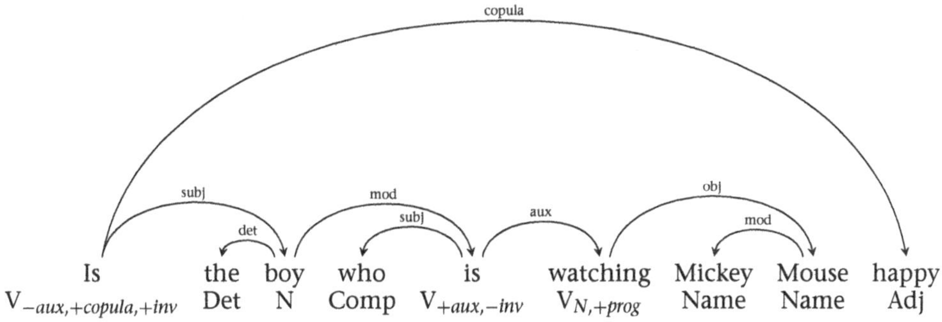

There is more to understand about why children are making this specific error: Perhaps it is because they are guessing that a fronted auxiliary requires a further auxiliary verb like it to follow, in –inverted state. That is, for a +inverted verb, the child might guess that it goes with a –inverted version of the same verb, because that fits many sequences that they will have heard, such as in sequences like *will be*, *might have*, and *is having*.

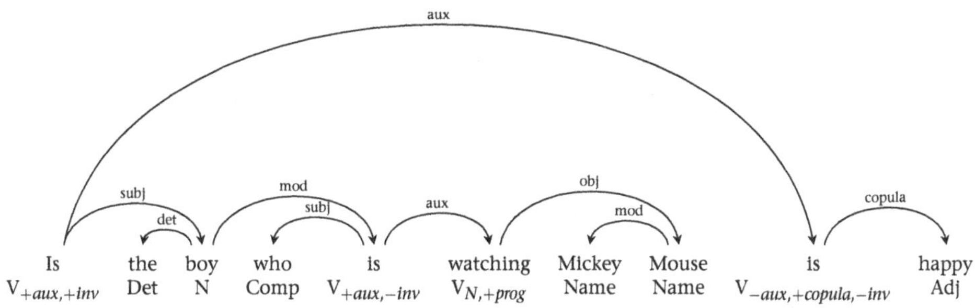

Thus, it remains an open question within the lexical-rule theory as to why children seem to double the auxiliary especially when the subject gets long, as in the above example, *the boy who is watching Mickey Mouse*. While this is an open question for the lexical-rule hypothesis, the problem seems deeper for the movement hypothesis, where movement is supposed to be innate. Under the movement hypothesis, nothing is being acquired—auxiliary-inversion is already known, just as well as the declarative structure, by hypothesis—so there is no complexity asymmetry here to drive errors.[6]

Because a movement rule is not what is being learned, the acquisition problem that Chomsky (1971, 1980a) has presented now disappears, as suggested by Perfors et al. (2013) and Yang and Piantadosi (2022). Perfors et al. (2013) shows that a simple phrase structure grammar that might be acquired in the course of language acquisition is one without movement. In the grammars that Perfors et al. (2013) investigate, the relevant rules with auxiliary verbs are as below:

```
Declarative:
S → NP VP
S → NP Aux VP
Interrogative
S → Aux NP VP
```

Like the dependency grammar rules that I discuss here, there is no movement in these rules. That is, there are declarative rules and interrogative rules, and there are no dependencies between the two. Perfors et al. (2013) shows that this grammar is "simpler" in a Bayesian sense than several other possibilities that a learner might consider.

Yang and Piantadosi (2022) provide a solution for how learning grammars like these might take place. They show that a learner with a minimal initial state can make guesses about what the simplest way to generate the sentences that it is exposed to would be, and then quickly come to the same kinds of conclusions that people arrive at, in few steps. Following Chater and Vitányi (2007), Yang and Piantadosi (2022) propose a Bayesian learner where the data are sampled from a typical distribution, such that no critical items are withheld. The learner tries to figure out the stochastically created grammar, and with more and more data, it gets closer and closer to the target. This model makes different assumptions from Gold (1967) and Angluin (1979) and Angluin (1980) who hypothesize an *antagonistic* teacher who can hold out critical data arbitrarily long. Under such antagonistic assumptions, it is indeed impossible to learn the target language, but such assumptions are nothing like normal language learning. Hence, arguments based on the proofs from Gold (1967) and Angluin (1979, 1980) do not apply to normal language learning, contrary to some recent syntax textbooks, such as Carnie (2013).

8.2 The Advent of LLMs Falsifies Chomsky's Learnability Claim

In spite of Chomsky's prediction that human language would not be learnable by exposure to the input alone, we now have many counterexamples, in the form of LLMs discussed in chapter 1. Chomsky, however, was unimpressed with the expressivity of these models. In a *New York Times* interview, Chomsky et al. (2023) say, "The predictions of machine learning systems will always be superficial and dubious. Because these programs cannot explain the rules of English syntax, for example, they may well predict, incorrectly, that "John is too stubborn to talk to" means that John is so stubborn that he will not talk to someone or other (rather than that he is too stubborn to be reasoned with)."

There is a lot to unpack here. The first implicit idea is that an English learning system needs to be able "explain the rules of English syntax" in order to be a credible learner of such a system. But surely being able to *explain something* is irrelevant to having implicit knowledge of it. Most native English speakers implicitly know the rules of English but would be hopeless at explaining them correctly. The second implicit idea is that chatGPT doesn't learn the right (subtle) generalizations of English syntax. But it's unclear what Chomsky et al. (2023)'s complaint is based on. Contra Chomsky and colleagues' claim, ChatGPT seems to use the "TOO ADJECTIVE TO VERB TO" construction perfectly in normal usage, just like a fluent English speaker, as observed by many researchers in an internet response to the *NYT* article as soon as it was published.

What, then, went wrong with Chomsky's analysis? As discussed above, one possibility is the inclusion of movement in his theory of grammar. Allowing components of base structures to move around arbitrarily creates a problem for the learner in figuring out what the appropriate structure was, as Chomsky correctly observed.

8.3 Grammars without Movement Better Explain Complexity Phenomena Than Grammars with Movement

Pickering and Barry (1991) present compelling evidence from the processing of nested English structures that suggests that there are direct links between heads and dependents, rather than having them mediated by empty elements in the canonical positions of the missing arguments. One contrast that Pickering and Barry (1991) discuss is presented below (see DaCunha and Gibson [2025] for experimental evidence in favor of the observations put forward here):

(171) a. This is the saucer on which Mary put the cup into which she poured the milk.

b. # This is the saucer which Mary put the cup which she poured the milk into on.

(171a) is much easier to understand than (171b). This contrast follows naturally from a dependency-length approach to these materials, as long as there are no empty categories mediating the dependencies. Consider the dependency structures for (171a) and (171b), where the structures include direct dependencies between the wh-elements and the verbs or prepositions that they connect to, as shown in (172) and (173) (I go back to using word-count as the dependency measure here, for simplicity):

(172)

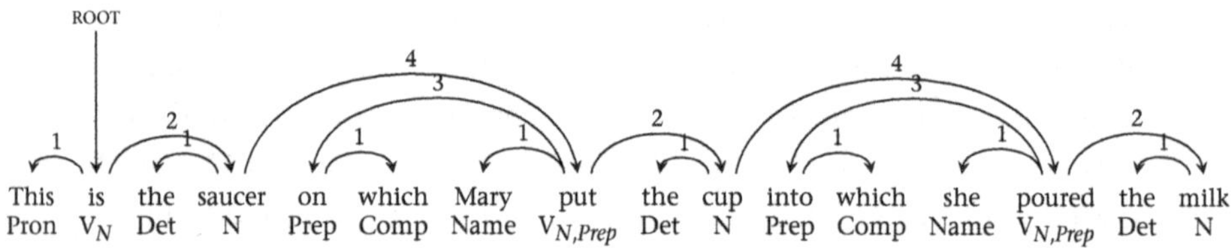

(173)

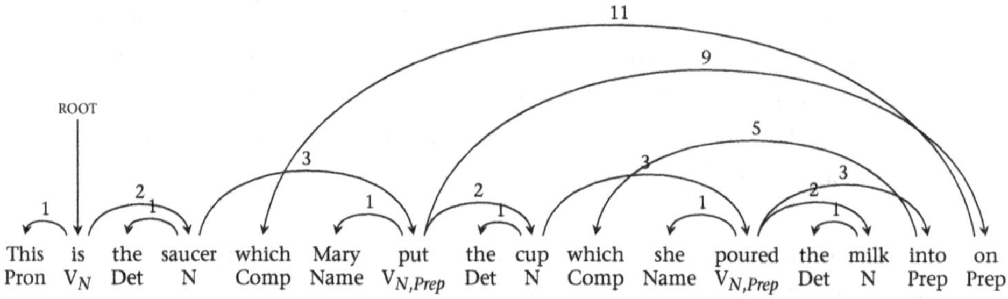

(172)—corresponding to (171a)—has only short dependencies, and this sentence is correspondingly easy to produce and understand. In contrast, (173)—corresponding to (171b)—has two long-distance dependencies—between *which* and *on*, and between *put* and *on*—and so this structure is relatively difficult to produce and comprehend.

In contrast, in a theory where empty categories mediate the relationship between wh-words like *which* and their role-assigning words, the structures for both (171a) and (171b) are similarly complex, in terms of long-distance connections. In such theories, the empty elements are proposed to be present in the same positions as the declarative counterparts of the fronted items. Consequently, the empty elements appear in the second position following the verbs *put* and *pour* in each of these structures. Consider the representation for (171a) with empty categories in (174) and the one for (171b) with empty categories in (175):

(174)

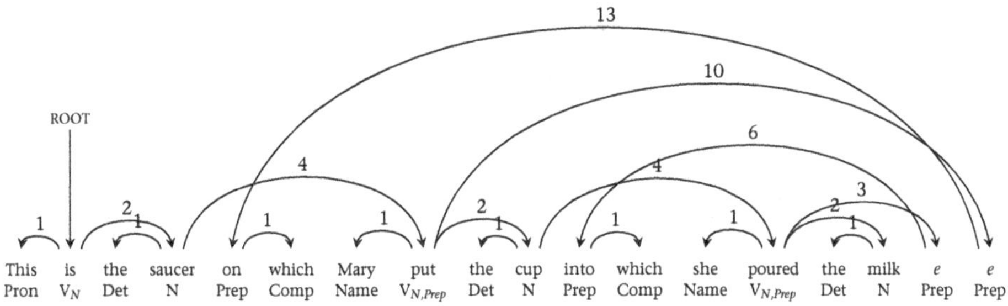

(175)

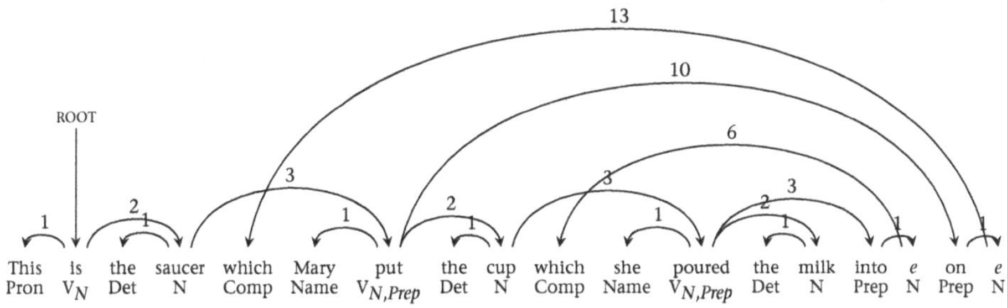

The structure for (171b) with empty elements in (175) is similar to its counterpart without empty elements in (173). In both, there are long-distance connections between *which* and *on* (or the empty position after *on*), and between *put* and *on*. So either theory is compatible with the high complexity of producing and understanding this sentence.

The weakness of the empty category theory is in its treatment of (171a). Whereas all the connections are local in the representation that lacks empty elements in (172), the representation with empty elements in (174) contains several long-distance connections: between *on* and an empty element at the end of the sentence; between *put* and the empty element at the end of the sentence; and between *into* and another empty element also at the end of the sentence. Typically, long-distance dependencies are associated with processing cost. Why aren't these long-distance dependencies associated with high processing cost? Note that it's not possible to say that connections with empty elements don't incur processing costs, because the source of the difficulty in (174) is long-distance connections between lexical items and empty elements. The problem here is the order of the categories in (174): A prepositional phrase associated with *put* or *pour* normally comes after the object noun phrase, so that's where the empty prepositional phrase elements should occur, in an empty category approach. A simple solution is to not include the empty elements in the first place, and allow direct associations, as in dependency grammar.

A similar complexity contrast is observed by Pickering and Barry (1991), for (176a) vs. (176b):

(176) a. In which box did you put the beautiful wedding cake from the expensive bakery?

b. # Which box did you put the beautiful wedding cake from the expensive bakery in?

The dependency structures without empty categories are provided in (177) and (178), respectively:

(177)

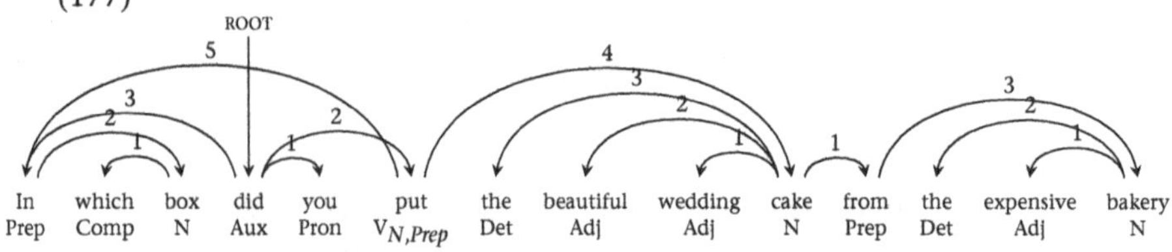

(178)

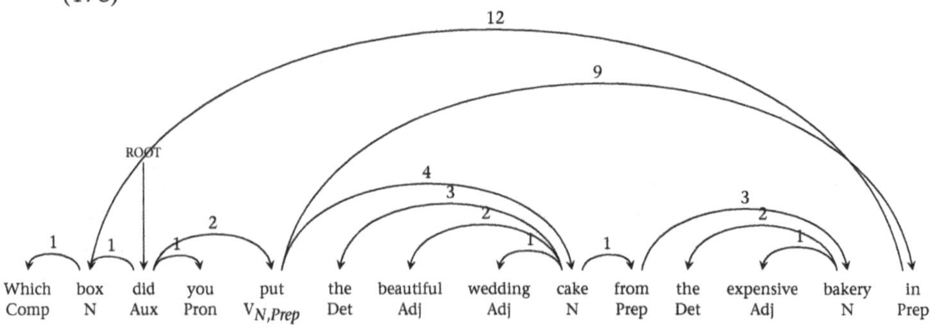

(176a) has mostly local dependencies as shown in (177), whereas (176b) has two long dependencies between *which box* and *in*, and between *put* and *in*, as shown in (178). Consequently, (176b) is harder to process.

The dependency structures with empty categories for (176a) and (176b) are shown in (179) and (180), respectively:

(179)

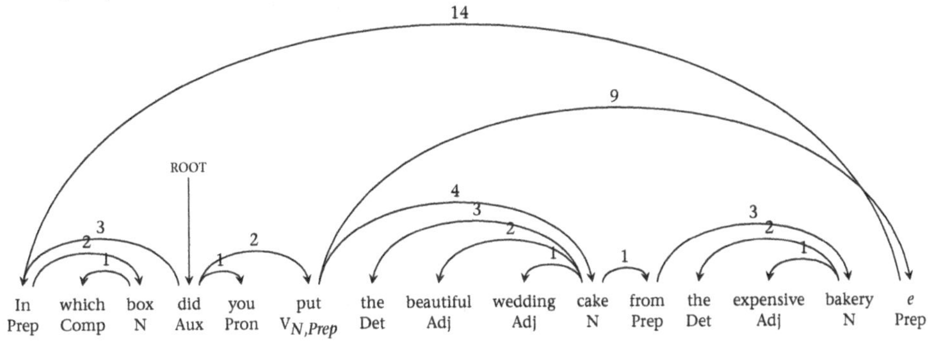

(180)

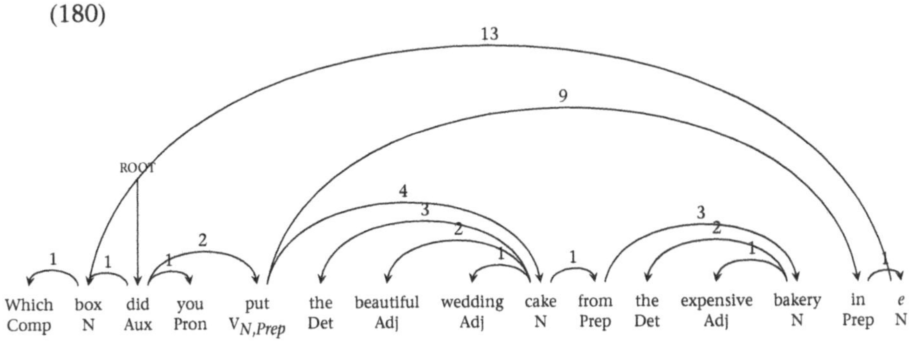

The dependency structures for (176b) are similar with or without empty categories mediating the long-distance dependencies: In each structure, there are two long dependencies. In the structure without empty elements, the two long dependencies are: between *put* and *in*, and between *box* and *in*. In the structure with empty elements, the two long dependencies are: between *put* and *in*, and between *box* and the empty element after *in*. In contrast to the dependency lengths for (176b), the dependency lengths for (176a) are quite different with empty categories mediating the long-distance dependencies. Whereas the connection is quite local between *put* and *in* for the structure without empty elements in (177), this dependency is separated into two long dependencies in the structure with empty elements: a long dependency between *in* and the empty element at the end of the sentence and another long dependency between *put* and the empty element, as shown in (179).

Hence, as Pickering and Barry (1991) argue, having empty elements mediating long-distance dependencies incorrectly predicts that sentences like (176a) should be similarly complex as sentences like (176b). Similarly, having empty elements mediating long-distance dependencies incorrectly predicts complexity for sentences like (171a) should be similarly complex as sentences like (171b).

Gibson and Hickok (1993) argued that an empty-category theory could still be maintained: The low complexity of examples like (171a) and (176a) could be explained if empty elements are added to the structure as soon as possible when parsing left to right, and then additional material could be added across these empty elements. The processing load cost-counts might thus only apply in the left-to-right construction of adding the empty elements, and would not reflect the final distances but only the distances when the empty categories are first added to the structure. So in parsing or speaking (171a), we might have the following partial structures after each verb is processed:

(181)

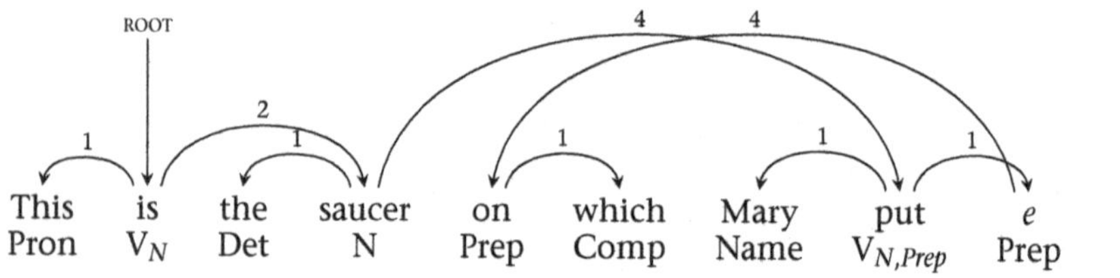

(182)

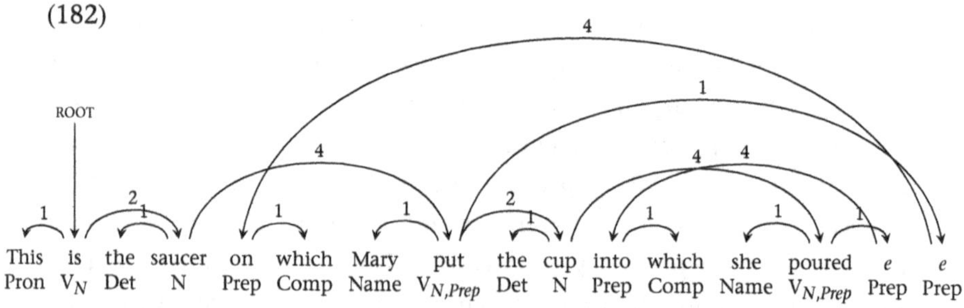

When *put* is added to the structure in (181), the empty element associated with *on* can be connected to the structure, for a dependency length of only four words at this point and a cost of only one for the arc connecting the element to the verb *put*. According to this proposal, later occurring material can be attached inside these arcs, but the costs of these dependency arcs do not increase. We see this in (182), where the verb *poured* is connected: Again the empty element associated with *into* can be connected at this point, and *into* can be connected to *poured*. Note that the costs for the outer empty element (associated with the first main verb *put*) do not get incremented, by hypothesis.

Gibson and Hickok's (1993) solution is possible in principle, but it is messy. An obvious problem is that it is not obvious why we would ever get length effects under this proposal, for two dependents following a verb. Recall from section 4.2 that as one dependent gets longer relative to another, there is a strong preference to have the longer one occur second, in a head-initial word order language like English. For example, consider examples (99a) and (99b), repeated below:

(99a) Mary threw away the important documents that she brought home yesterday.

(99b) Mary threw the important documents that she brought home yesterday away.

(99b) sounds worse than (99a), plausibly because we have ordered a long dependent before a short one in (99b). Under Gibson and Hickok's (1993) proposal, it is not clear why both post-verbal dependents can be predicted and constructed at the verb (as proposed in Gibson [1991] for example). Why then does the cost for the more distant dependent increase in this case, as words are connected to the first dependent, but not in cases like (171b)? It is possible to make this work, but it is complex, with additional theoretical stipulations needed. It seems simpler to drop the mechanism of empty elements altogether.

8.3.1 Behavioral Attempts to Test the Existence of Empty Elements in Long-Distance Dependencies

There have been many attempts to find behavioral associates of empty elements from syntactic theories, but none of these have ended up being reliable (e.g., MacDonald, 1989; Nicol and Swinney, 1989; Nicol et al., 1994; Bever and McElree, 1988; Bever and Sanz, 1997).

Several of these studies used a cross-modal paradigm, where participants listened to sentences presented to them over headphones and then had to do a lexical decision task at what seemed like an arbitrary point during the sentence (Nicol and Swinney, 1989; Nicol et al., 1994). Researchers found speeded lexical decision at the empty category site for words related to the moved element at the beginning of the clause (the *filler*, see section 3.19) relative to unrelated words. For example, participants might be asked to listen to a sentence like (183):

(183) The old man picked up the apple which the baby in the carriage threw in the gutter.

Then, at the point where they just heard *threw*, they would be asked whether FRUIT or BENCH is a word or not. Note that the pronoun *which* refers to *apple*, and is related to FRUIT but not BENCH. Nicol and Swinney (1989) found faster response times for FRUIT relative to BENCH, and concluded that an empty element at *threw* (coindexed with *apple*) led to this speed-up in reaction time.

But McKoon and Ratcliff (1994) and McKoon et al. (1996) noticed that the semantically related words that Nicol and Swinney (1989) and Nicol et al. (1994) used (like FRUIT) were also better fits at the target location—following a verb like *threw*—than the control semantically unrelated words (like BENCH). That is, we can throw a fruit more easily than we can throw a bench, independent of whether there is a filler like *which* before. So McKoon et al. (1996) reran the experiment with items where the control materials were matched for this context effect, and they found no effect of filler. It seems that all such studies purporting to have found evidence of empty elements have this contextual confound.

8.4 Syntactic "Islands"

In a 1995 language acquisition summary article, Steven Pinker described a potential learning problem associated with syntactic "islands" as follows:

> To see how linguistic research cannot be ignored in understanding language acquisition, consider the sentences below. In each of the examples a learner who heard the (a) and (b) sentences could quite sensibly extract a general rule that, when applied to the (c) sentence, yields version (d). Yet the result is an odd sentence that no one would say:
>
> (1)
>
> a. John saw Mary with her best friend's husband.
>
> b. Who did John see Mary with?
>
> c. John saw Mary and her best friend's husband.
>
> d. * Who did John see Mary and?

> The solution to the problem must be that children's learning mechanisms ultimately do not allow them to make what would otherwise be a tempting generalization. For example, in (1), constraints that prevent extraction of a single phrase out of a coordinate structure (phrases joined by a word like *and* or *or*) would block what otherwise would be a natural generalization from other examples of extraction, such as 1 (a-b). The other examples present other puzzles that the theory of universal grammar, as part of a theory of language acquisition, must solve. Because of the subtlety of these examples—and the abstractness of the principles of universal grammar that must be posited to explain them—Chomsky has claimed that the overall structure of language must be innate, based on his paper-and-pencil examination of the facts of language alone (Pinker, 1995), pp. 151–152.

In this section, I elaborate the problem that Pinker observes. As discussed briefly in chapter 3, English and other languages have many different constructions that form long-distance dependencies between words, such as wh-questions, relative clauses, exclamatives, clefts, topicalizations, among others (see section 3.19; examples repeated from (92)). Here I notate the position associated with the filler at the front of the clause with the symbol __, a gap. Of course, I assume a theory with no empty categories (see section 3.19 for details).

(184) a. Declarative: Mary bought the apple.
b. Wh-question: What did Mary buy __?
c. Relative clause: I like the apple which Mary bought __.
d. Exclamative: What an apple Mary bought __!
e. It-cleft: It was the apple that Mary bought __.
f. Topicalization: The apple, Mary bought __.

Going back to Ross (1967), it has been observed that some long-distance associations are not possible, such as in (185) (examples like Pinker's (1d)):[7]

(185) # What did Ollie state the claim that Mary bought __?

Chomsky has claimed that the unacceptability of such long-distance dependencies is due to the grammar not generating such structures. This hypothesis is based on the claim that their unacceptability is **independent of the construction in which they are used** (Schütze et al., 2015; Chomsky, 1973, 1977). Thus, a long-distance wh-question like that in (185) is purported to be equally unacceptable if it is realized in any other construction that realizes movement in the generative framework, such as relative clauses, exclamatives, clefts, and topicalizations. Because their unacceptability is claimed to be independent of the meaning (the construction), Chomsky and colleagues have claimed that the existence of such "island" constraints[8] provides evidence that such constraints in the syntax are not learnable, and hence must be innate (Schütze et al., 2015).

Many researchers have taken issue with this argumentation, at various levels. First, it is not obvious that the reasoning goes through: At most, if the constraints to be learned are purely syntactic (not due to meaning), that might make such constraints *harder* to learn than if the constraints were based on meaning. But it doesn't make the constraints *unlearnable* (Pearl and Sprouse, 2013; Hudson, 2008). That is, the constraints might still be learnable, contra Chomsky's claim. Here, I simply show that the claim that Chomsky's learnability hypothesis is predicated on—that the construction in which a long-distance dependency occurs does not affect its acceptability—is incorrect. That is, I show that the construction in which a long-distance dependency occurs *does* affect its acceptability.

In this section I first summarize Chomsky's original "subjacency" theory of syntactic movement—a phrase-structure-based theory—and show how it is intended to account for the unacceptability of certain long-distance connections (Chomsky, 1973, 1977, 1986).[9] Chomsky's theories of the badness of "island" phenomena all depend crucially on the existence of phrase structure. Hence, the success of the syntactic explanation for the unacceptability of islands has been taken to be support for the phrase structure and movement approach to syntax.

Next, I show that, contrary to the syntactic movement hypothesis, the acceptability of island structures varies widely across constructions. The badness of the examples that have been generally studied may have to do with the particular construction that has dominated the discussions in the syntactic literature: wh-questions. It turns out that wh-questions have discourse properties that are more restrictive than other long-distance dependency constructions, such as relative clauses. Thus only looking at wh-questions may give a biased view. Indeed, there may be other constructions—such as exclamatives—whose constraints on long-distance dependencies are even stricter than wh-questions. These observations suggest that a discourse-based explanation of the unacceptability of most long-distance extractions may be much better suited to explain the range of phenomena than a syntactic one. Under a discourse-based approach, each construction has its own meaning and usage (and extraction properties).

We can then learn each construction and its constraints by exposure to its usage, and the learnability puzzle that Chomsky and others had noted disappears. Hence, I conclude that island structures are plausibly explained within a construction-based dependency-grammar framework, where each construction has its own discourse meaning properties (cf. Liu et al. [2022b], Chaves and Putnam [2020] for similar ideas).

8.4.1 Chomsky's Subjacency Theory of Island Constraints

Ross (1967) observed that while some long-distance dependency connections are acceptable in English, others are much harder to make. For example, the wh-question dependencies in (186) are all acceptable to many English speakers, but the ones in (187) are much less so (examples in (187) simplified from Sprouse et al. [2016]).

(186) a. What did $[_S$ John buy ___] ?
b. What did $[_S$ Mary say $[_{S'}$ that $[_S$ John bought ___]]]?
c. What did $[_S$ you think $[_{S'}$ that $[_S$ Mary said $[_{S'}$ that $[_S$ John bought ___]]]]]?

(187) a. # Who did you read $[_{NP}$ the statement $[_{S'}$ that $[_S$ the CEO promoted ___]]]?
b. # Who did $[_S$ $[_{NP}$ the gift from ___] prompt the rumor]?
c. # What did $[_S$ John buy $[_{NP}$ $[_{NP}$ a shirt] and ___]]]?
d. # What did $[_S$ you wonder $[_{S'}$ whether $[_S$ John bought ___]]]?
e. # What did $[_S$ you worry $[_{S'}$ if $[_S$ John bought ___]]]?

Following Ross (1967), Chomsky (1973, 1977, 1986), Rizzi (1982), and Huang (1982) proposed that the unacceptability of materials like those in (187) was due to the grammar. Specifically, they proposed that the English phrase structure grammar does not generate these kinds of sentence types. Under Chomsky's (1973, 1986) view, these structures are not possible because the wh-phrase at the beginning of the sentence is too far structurally from its underlying source position before movement (notated as an empty element ___ in these items).

In particular, Chomsky (1973, 1977) proposed his theory of "subjacency" (his invented term): A phrase cannot move across more than one NP or S syntactic category in each of its movements from deep structure (the structure associated with the declarative) and the wh-question position at the front of the clause. In each of (187a)–(187c), an NP and S node (among other phrasal categories) structurally block the empty position __ from connecting with the wh-word position at the front of the sentence, so these movements would not be generated by the grammar. Similarly two S nodes separate the empty position __ from the wh-word position at the front of the sentence in (187d) and (187e), so these sentences would also not be generated by the grammar. Phrase structures for (187a)–(187d) are given below, with the nodes that block movement circled:

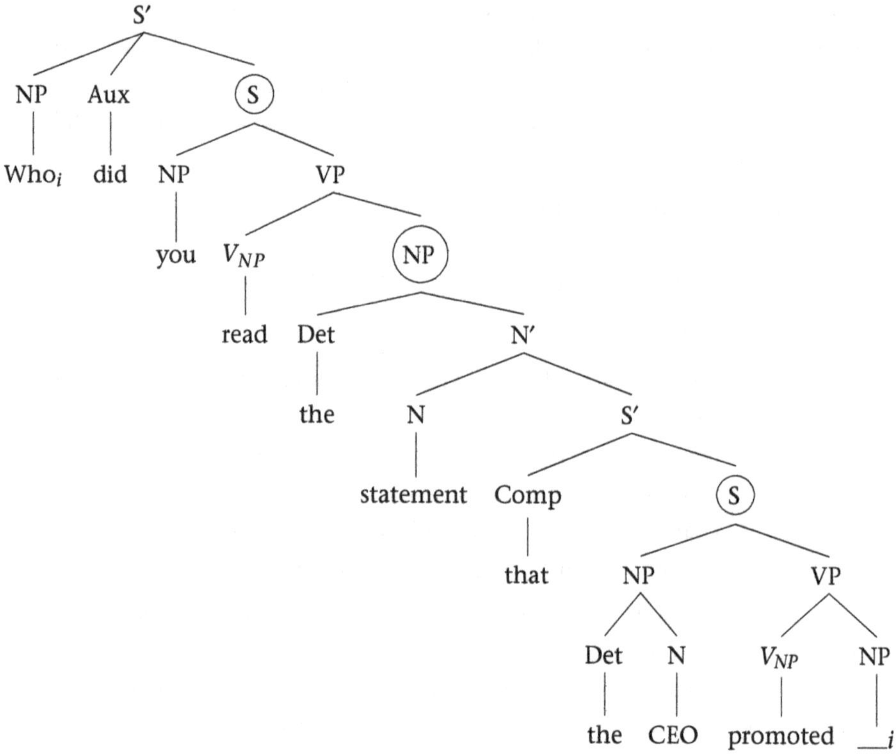

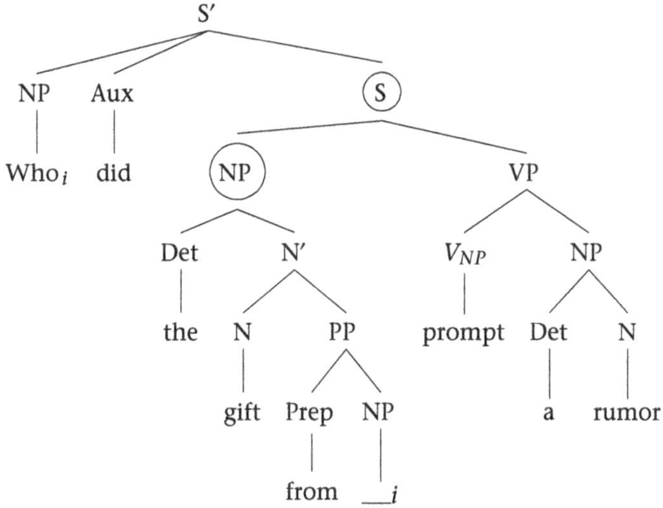
S′
NP
Aux
S
Whoᵢ
did
NP
VP
Det
N′
V_{NP}
NP
the
N
PP
prompt
Det
N
gift
Prep
NP
a
rumor
from
__ᵢ

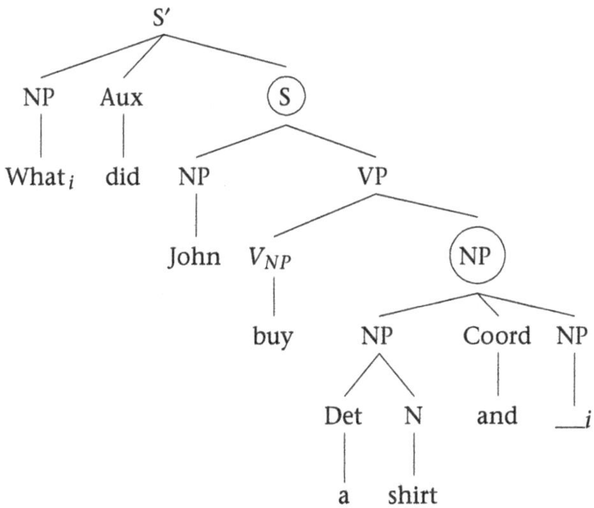
S′
NP
Aux
S
Whatᵢ
did
NP
VP
John
V_{NP}
NP
buy
NP
Coord
NP
Det
N
and
__ᵢ
a
shirt

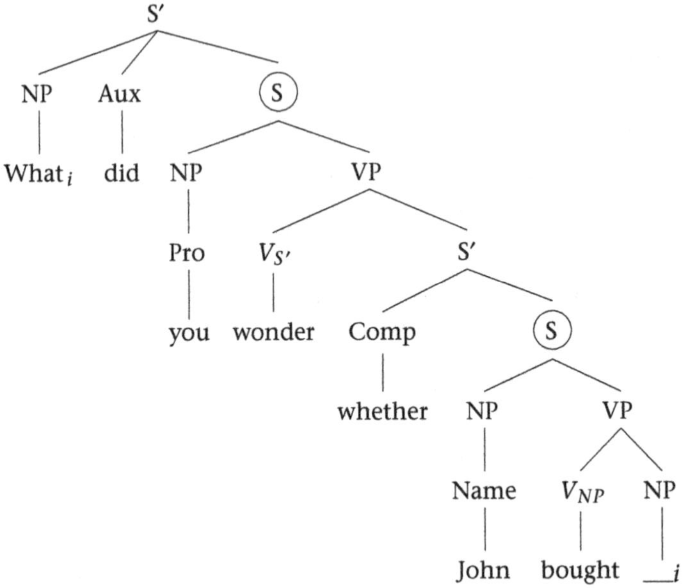

In contrast, only one such node is crossed in (186a): an S node.

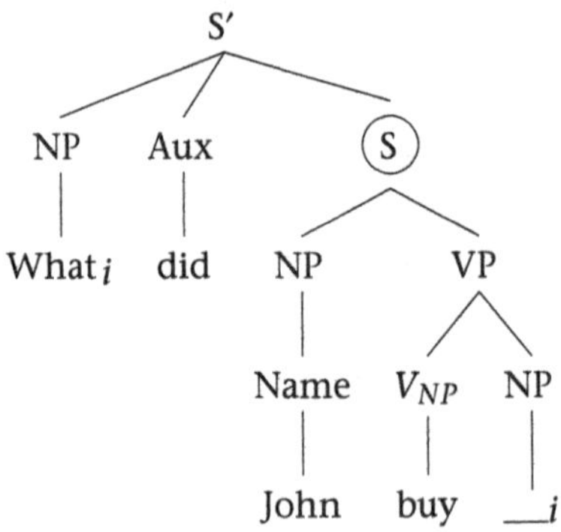

The astute reader will notice that the supposedly ungrammatical (187d) and (187e) are structurally similar to the grammatical (186b). In each of these cases, there are two S nodes separating the empty position "__" from the wh-word position at the front of the sentence. Yet (186b) is more acceptable than (187d) and (187e). In order to account for this acceptability difference, Chomsky (1977) proposed that the *S′* category intervening between the S nodes in (186b) could serve as a temporary landing site for the movement from the base position __ and the position at the front of the sentence. This way, each movement would only cross one bounding node (S in this case), and the structure could be licensed. Chomsky (1977) calls this proposed process *successive cyclic movement*. Below, I circle the temporary *S′* landing sites in red for the structures associated with (187d) and (187e):

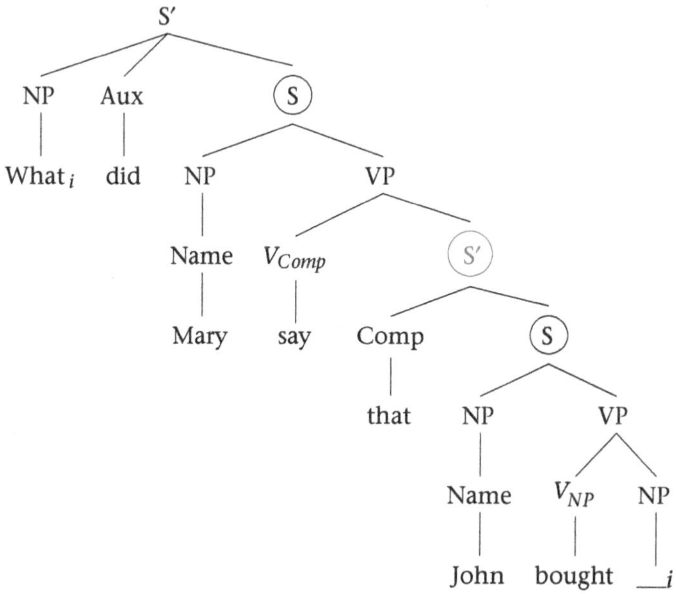

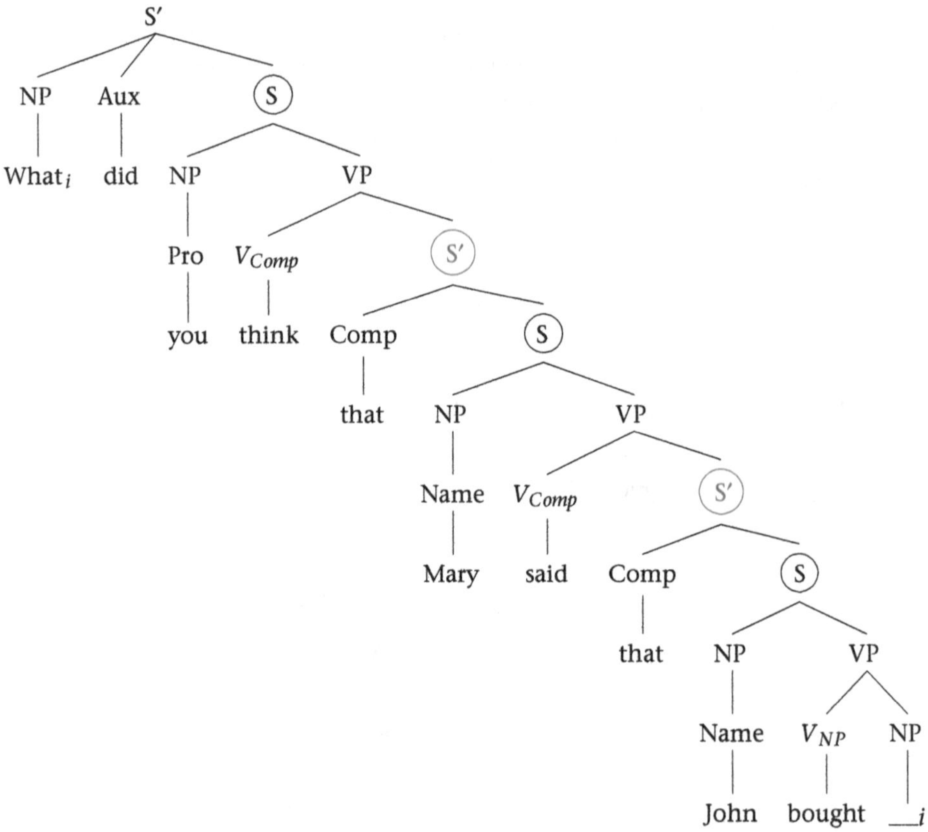

Chomsky also proposed that the intermediate landing site is blocked in cases like (187d) and (187e) because of the features on these syntactic nodes: They are question *S′* nodes, which don't allow the movement in them (because they are proposed to be already filled. This is admittedly a complex theory with lots of assumptions, but at least it can possibly account for the acceptability judgments under consideration here.

8.4.2 Hypothesis from Generative Syntacticians: The Acceptability of "Island" Structures Is Constant across Constructions

As discussed above, one of the primary reasons that Chomsky and other generative grammarians have been so interested in the unacceptability of "island" structures is that their unacceptability appeared to be independent of the construction in which the long-distance dependency takes place, which suggested that their unacceptability could not be learned. Hence, it was argued that island structures must be part of Universal Grammar (UG). This argument is made clearly in Schütze et al. (2015), who suggest that island effects hold similarly in English across wh-questions, relative clauses, topicalization, clefts, pseudo-clefts, and though-preposing, despite the different meanings associated with each construction. Following Schütze et al. (2015), let's concentrate on one island-type, the so-called wh-island, along with four constructions: wh-questions, relative clauses, topicalization, and clefts (examples of the last three from Schütze et al. [2015]). Each of these pairs compares a long-distance extraction across a clause headed by *whether* to one headed by *that*:[10]

(188) Wh-questions
- a. Intermediate "that" clause:
  What$_i$ did [$_S$ Mary say [$_{S'}$ that [$_S$ John bought ___$_i$]]]?
- b. Intermediate "whether" clause:
  ∗ What$_i$ did [$_S$ Mary wonder [$_{S'}$ whether [$_S$ John bought ___$_i$]]]?

(189) Relative clauses
- a. Intermediate "that" clause:
  I would pity a man who$_i$ [$_S$ Sue knows [$_{S'}$ that [$_S$ she should dump ___$_i$]]].
- b. Intermediate "whether" clause:
  ∗ I would pity a man who$_i$ [$_S$ Sue wonders [$_{S'}$ whether [$_S$ she should dump ___$_i$]]].

(190) Topicalization
- a. Intermediate "that" clause:
  I think that John likes most of these cars, but that car$_i$, [$_S$ I think [$_{S'}$ that [$_S$ John loves ___$_i$]]].
- b. Intermediate "whether" clause:
  ∗ I wonder whether John likes most of these cars, but that car$_i$, [$_S$ I wonder [$_{S'}$ whether [$_S$ John loves ___$_i$]]].

(191) Clefting
- a. Intermediate "that" clause:
  Please don't tell me again that it is Judy who$_i$ [$_S$ you think [$_{S'}$ that [$_S$ John should marry ___$_i$]]].

b. Intermediate "whether" clause:
   * Please don't tell me again that it is Judy who$_i$ [$_S$ you wonder [$_{S'}$ whether [$_S$ John should marry __$_i$]]].

Even if we accept that there may be a difference in each of these pairs in the claimed direction, this does not demonstrate the point that Schütze et al. (2015) want to make. There are two important issues here. First, as argued at length by Sprouse (2007) and Sprouse et al. (2012) and Sprouse et al. (2016), a simple comparison between two conditions does not demonstrate an "island" effect: We at least need a further control comparison to show that the same patterns don't also appear in comparable materials without the long-distance dependencies. There are many potential controls for any comparison; Sprouse (2007) and Sprouse et al. (2012, 2016) usually include a local-extraction control. With these additional controls, for there to be an "island" effect, there needs to be an interaction between the two conditions, such that the "island" condition is much the worst of the four, as in figure 8.1. Let's consider just the first comparison, wh-questions (188). A declarative control for this comparison, like (192) is possible:

(192) Wh-questions
   a. [$_S$ Mary said [$_{S'}$ that [$_S$ John bought something]]].
   b. [$_S$ Mary wondered [$_{S'}$ whether [$_S$ John bought something]]].

For there to be an "island" effect, (188b) should be the worst of the four, much worse than either of its controls in (188a) or (192b), and the difference between (188b) and (188a) needs to be larger than any difference that might be present between (192a) and (192b).

The 2 x 2 effect crossing (188) and (192) for wh-questions has been demonstrated before (e.g., in Sprouse et al., 2012, 2016), but the other four constructions were not evaluated experimentally by Schütze et al. (2015) or others. It may be the case that some of these comparisons result only in a main effect of extraction but not the interaction that is needed in order to consider them "island" effects.[11]

Furthermore, even if we do an experiment and we find an interaction, we cannot infer the source of the interaction, without further experimentation. If a researcher finds an "island"-like interaction, and then rules out one likely cause, they cannot conclude that the source must be syntactic. Sprouse et al. (2012) provide a published example of this fallacy

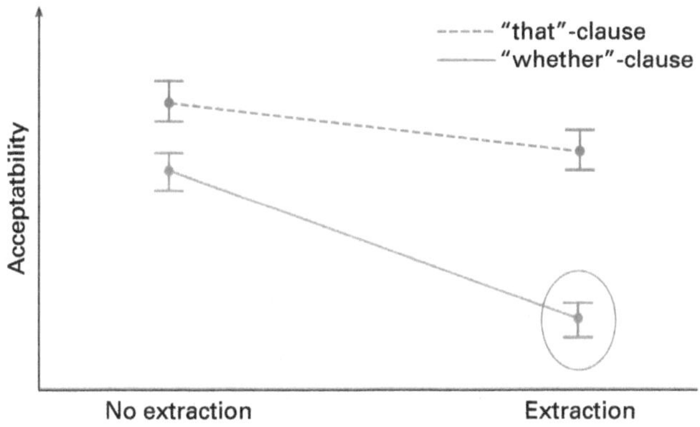

Figure 8.1
An illustration of an island effect as defined by Sprouse et al. (2016): a superadditive interaction between extraction (extraction, no-extraction) and intermediate-clause type (whether, that), such that the extraction/whether is much the worst of the four conditions: a so-called "wh-island" (red circle).

of argumentation. First, they found interactions in 2 x 2 acceptability experiments that investigate purported syntactic islands. They then proceeded to test a resource (working-memory) theory of the acceptability of these island effects and found no evidence for that theory. They then concluded:

> We believe that the results of the experiments presented in this article provide strong support for grammatical theories of island effects because we can find no evidence of a relationship between processing resource capacity and island effects. Sprouse et al. (2012), p. 118

But Sprouse et al. (2012) did not provide a grammatical theory of the island effects they observed, nor did they provide any evidence for such a theory. They just ruled out one particular resource theory for their experiments. We should be careful of making this kind of invalid inference in general.

8.4.3 The Acceptability of "Island" Structures Varies across Constructions

8.4.3.1 Extractions out of Subjects: "Subject" Islands It has long been claimed in the generative syntax literature that extractions out of subject position are impossible, blocked by a movement constraint (Chomsky, 1973, 1977, 1986; Schütze et al., 2015). Consequently, Abeillé et al. (2020a) investigated the acceptability of extractions out of parts of subject positions in English and French. Counter to the prediction of the syntactic approach, Abeillé et al. (2020a) found substantial differences in the acceptability of these extractions depending on whether they were from wh-questions or relative clauses. In wh-questions, Abeillé et al. (2020a) found the standard "island" effect, such that extractions out of parts of subjects were rated poorly, compared with extractions out of parts of objects, but there was no such difference in control non-extracted versions:

(193) a. NP Extraction from subject: Which sportscar did $[_S$ $[_{NP}$ the color of ___] delight the baseball player] because of its surprising luminance?

b. PP Extraction from subject: Of which sportscar did $[_S$ $[_{NP}$ the color ___] delight the baseball player] because of its surprising luminance?

c. Subject control, no extraction: Did the color of the sportscar delight the baseball player because of its surprising luminance?

d. NP Extraction from object: Which sportscar did $[_S$ the baseball player love $[_{NP}$ the color of ___]] because of its surprising luminance?

e. PP Extraction from object: Of which sportscar did $[_S$ the baseball player love $[_{NP}$ the color ___]] because of its surprising luminance?

f. Object control, no extraction: Did the baseball player love the color of the sportscar because of its surprising luminance?

English favors wh-questions involving NPs rather than prepositional phrases (PPs), so neither the PP-extracted wh-question out of subject (193b) nor object (193e) was rated highly. But extractions of NPs out of objects (193d) were rated reasonably highly, much better than corresponding extractions of NPs out of subjects (193a), with no such difference in the controls (193c) and (193f). We can see this in panel A of figure 8.2: The extractions from subject position were rated much the lowest. We see the same pattern in French (panel B), Abeillé et al. (2020a), and Italian (panel C), Sprouse et al. (2016).

These results contrast sharply with the results obtained when examining extractions out of subjects in relative clauses, as in (194). There, Abeillé et al. (2020a) found no difference in acceptability of extraction from subject vs. extraction from object, as we can see in panel D of figure 8.2.

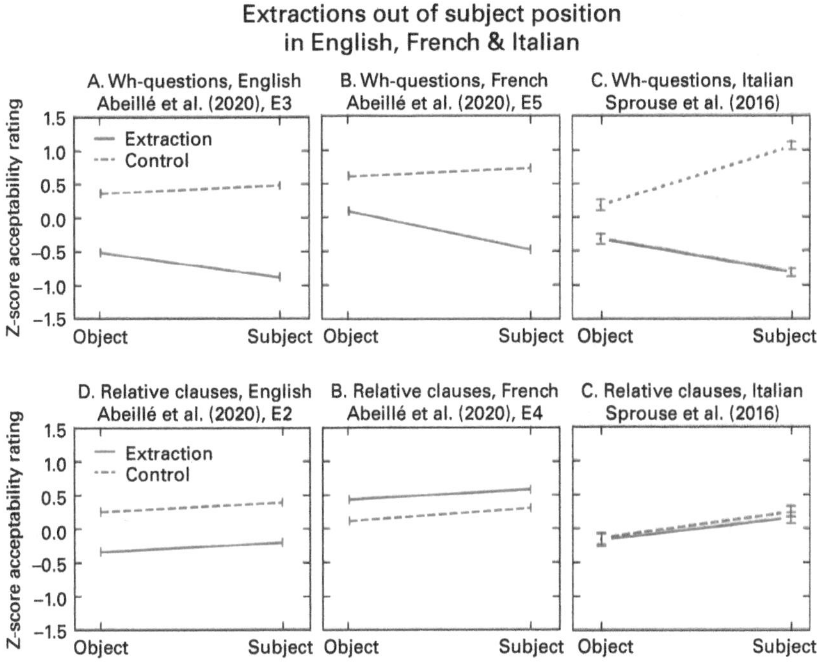

Figure 8.2

Z-scored acceptability ratings for extractions out of subjects, for wh-questions and relative clauses in English, French, and Italian. Two-by-two comparisons crossing two factors (subject, object) × (filler-gap, non-filler-gap) show a clear contrast such that the two factors interact for wh-questions (an "island") but do not interact for relative clauses (no "island").

(194) a. PP Extraction from subject: The dealer sold a sportscar, of which [$_S$ [$_{NP}$ the color __] delighted the baseball player] because of its surprising luminance.

b. Subject control, no extraction: The dealer sold a sportscar, and the color of the sportscar delighted the baseball player because of its surprising luminance.

c. PP Extraction from object: The dealer sold a sportscar, of which [$_S$ the baseball player loved [$_{NP}$ the color __]] because of its surprising luminance.

d. Object control, no extraction: The dealer sold a sportscar, and the baseball player loved the color of the sportscar because of its surprising luminance.

Furthermore (and critically), the results interact with those of the wh-questions: There is a three-way interaction between construction (relative clause, wh-question), extraction (+extraction, no extraction), and position (subject, object), such that the "island" effects (the 2 x 2 interaction) occurs only in wh-questions, not in relative clauses. The results for French were similar: no 2 x 2 interaction in relative clauses, and a three-way (2 x 2 x 2) interaction between construction, extraction, and position, suggesting that the difficulty is restricted to wh-questions in French, just like English. And fascinatingly, the results look similar to results published by Sprouse et al. (2016) for Italian: an interaction in wh-questions, but none in relative clauses (panels C and F of figure 8.2).

Moreover, Abeillé et al. (2020a) provide corpus evidence in English and French suggesting that extractions out of subjects in relative clauses are typical, as they are present in many texts, such as in (195). Thus Abeillé et al. (2020a) show convincingly that the acceptability of extractions out of subject positions differs based on construction type, contra to the purely syntactic position put forward by Chomsky (1973, 1977, 1986) and others.

(195) a. ... a letter of which [every line ___] was an insult (Jane Austen. 1981. The complete novels. New York: Gramercy. 84.)

b. that voluminous publication, of which [either the matter or manner ___] would not disgust a young person of taste (Jane Austen. 1981. The complete novels. New York: Gramercy. 828.)

c. (...) Franzenia has 44 staff working with children, of whom [sixteen ___] are kindergarten teachers. (The Guardian, September, 2016) (Chaves and Dery, 2019)

d. A coalition of US groups including USA Today surveyed 850 women in the film industry of whom [the vast majority ___] reported some form of sexual misconduct (The Guardian, 21, February 2018)

e. Doctors diagnosed a rare brain disease for which [the cure ___] was radical: the left hemisphere of his brain would have to be surgically removed. (www.thirteen.org)

8.4.3.2 Extractions in the exclamative construction A second example of the variability in acceptability across constructions for long-distance dependencies is provided by comparing the *exclamative* construction (cf. Ginzburg and Sag, 2000) to any other construction. In extracting from out of a subject, we have seen that wh-questions seem to constrain their long-distance connections to be more local than relative clauses. On the other direction, we can find constructions that are more constrained than wh-questions. One such construction is the exclamative, whose extractions are typically more local than wh-questions (or relative clauses). DaCunha and Gibson (2025) compared simple and complex exclamatives to wh-questions, and declaratives, as a baseline:

(196) a. Simple declarative: You bought a nice jacket.
b. Simple wh-question: Which nice jacket did you buy __?
c. Simple exclamative: What a nice jacket you bought __!
d. Complex declarative: I think you bought a nice jacket.
e. Complex wh-question: Which nice jacket do you think I bought __?
f. Complex exclamative: What a nice jacket I think you bought __!

DaCunha and Gibson (2025) found that there was a main effect of ratings for the simple vs. complex, and for declarative vs. wh-question, but no interaction between the two (replicating, e.g., Liu et al. [2022a]). Turning to the construction of interest, the exclamative, there were main effects of construction type and complexity for the exclamatives vs. wh-questions, but critically, there was also an interaction, such that the complex exclamative was rated much the lowest. This means that extractions in exclamatives are even more restricted than those in wh-questions. Thus, like the case of subject-islands, a purely syntactic theory of the complexity of these constructions does not seem workable. More plausibly, a discourse theory seems possible: People typically only exclaim about things that they are pretty sure of, and the embedded verbs introduced uncertainties.

8.4.4 Discourse Constraints on Long-Distance Dependencies

There appear to be several kinds of factors that constrain long-distance dependencies (Chaves and Putnam, 2020; Liu et al., 2022b). The most important ones seem to be discourse factors. Going back to Erteschik-Shir (1973), researchers have noted that it is difficult to extract an element out of a phrase that is backgrounded or presupposed as part of the discourse. Accordingly, Goldberg (2006) proposed that Backgrounded Constructions are Islands (BCI) (cf. Erteschik-Shir, 1973; Ertescik-Shir, 1979; Erteschik-Shir, 1997; Takami, 1988; Deane, 1991; Van Valin, 1993, 1995; Van Valin and LaPolla, 1997). According to this simple principle, it is difficult to extract parts of relative clauses or complements of nouns, because these are typically backgrounded positions.

(197) ?? Who$_i$ did she see the report that was about __?

In (197), the words *that was about* form a relative clause modifying the noun *report*. In a relative clause, the information modifying the head noun is given in the context. In contrast, a wh-question asks for information from the conversation partner that is not known. So according to Goldberg's BCI constraint, the reason that (197) sounds so bad is because it makes no sense. That is, it is infelicitous to ask for information about something that is backgrounded.

Although Goldberg's proposal makes a lot of intuitive sense, it cannot explain the observations in the last section, where the construction in which extraction takes place affects the possibility of extraction. According to Goldberg's BCI constraint, all that should matter for the acceptability of an extraction is the position from which one is attempting to extract, not the type of extraction that this might be (e.g., wh-question vs. relative clause vs. cleft vs. topicalization). Consequently, Abeillé et al. (2020a) proposed the focus-background-conflict constraint:[12]

(198) Focus-background-conflict (FBC) Constraint: A focused element should not be part of a backgrounded constituent. Abeillé et al. (2020a), p. 3

A focused element is one that carries the main (and usually new) information of the sentence. In a wh-question, the focus is the element being asked: the fronted element, marked with a wh-word. In contrast, the positions inside a relative clause are backgrounded. Hence wh-extraction from inside a relative clause is blocked by the focus-background conflict constraint, just as in Goldberg's background-constituents-are-islands constraint. But in contrast to wh-questions, the FBC does not apply to relative clauses as fronting constructions, because the function of fronting in a relative clause is not to focus an element: The fronted element is another backgrounded element (but perhaps not as backgrounded as the rest of the relative clause).

Consequently, a wh-question out of subject position as in (199a) is not good according to the focus-background conflict constraint because the subject position is typically a backgrounded position, and a wh-question focuses the element in question. But a relative clause out of subject position as in (199c) is okay, because the fronted position in a relative clause is not focused. Because the extraction position is not backgrounded for extractions out of objects, the focus-background conflict constraint does not apply to either (199b) or (199d), and both should be ok, as we observe.

(199) a. NP Extraction from subject: Which sportscar did $[_S$ $[_{NP}$ the color of ___] delight the baseball player] because of its surprising luminance?
b. NP Extraction from object: Which sportscar did $[_S$ the baseball player love $[_{NP}$ the color of ___]] because of its surprising luminance?
c. PP Extraction from subject: The dealer sold a sportscar, of which $[_S$ $[_{NP}$ the color ___] delighted the baseball player] because of its surprising luminance.
d. PP Extraction from object: The dealer sold a sportscar, of which $[_S$ the baseball player loved $[_{NP}$ the color ___]] because of its surprising luminance.

The focus-background conflict constraint therefore accounts for the differential acceptability of extraction out of subjects, depending on the construction. Strikingly, the focus-background conflict constraint predicts differential effects for relative clauses vs. clefts, despite the superficial similarity of these two constructions. That is, the function of a relative clause is to refer to some backgrounded information, whereas the function of a cleft is to contrastively focus on some old information. Hence, extractions in clefts should be less good out of parts of subject positions, because these are backgrounded positions. Abeillé et al. (2020b) explored this potential contrast experimentally in materials like (200), and found the predicted contrast:

(200) a. PP-extracted, subject: It is to this kind of problem that [a solution ___] astonished all the participants.
b. PP-extracted, object: It is to this kind of problem that all the participants admire [a solution ___].
c. whole NP, subject: It is a solution to this kind of problem that ___ astonished all the participants.
d. whole NP, object: It is a solution to this kind of problem that all the participants admire ___.

e. PP-extracted, subject: The mediator considered a problem, to which [the solution ___] astonished the participants.
f. PP-extracted, object: The mediator considered a problem, to which the participants admired [the solution ___].
g. whole NP, subject: The mediator considered the solution to a problem, which astonished the participants.
h. whole NP, object: The mediator considered the solution to a problem, which the participants admired ___.

In particular, Abeillé et al. (2020b) found that clefting out of part of a subject as in (200a) was not very acceptable, as compared with a lexically matched version for relative clauses, as in (200e). There were no differences among the extractions from object position, across construction. This is remarkable evidence for something like the focus-background conflict constraint: The acceptability of similar syntactic constructions varies greatly depending on the function of the construction (and again contra the pure syntax view).

Further evidence for the focus-background conflict constraint is provided by the graded nature of the felicity of extraction of noun complements, depending on the definiteness of the noun complement in (201). For example, people prefer an indefinite (201a) over a definite (201b) when questioning the complement of a noun (Erteschik-Shir, 1973; Davies and Dubinsky, 2003; Keller, 2000):

(201) a. Which actress did you buy [a picture of ___]?
b. ?? Which actress did you buy [that picture of ___]?
c. That is the actress who I bought [a/that picture of ___].

The oddness of examples like (201b) has always been a puzzle for syntax-based theories of extraction constraints: (201b) involves no syntactic islands, and yet it is not as acceptable as (201a). Furthermore, as noted by Grosu (1981), the same contrast does not appear with relative clauses as shown in (201c).

The preference for (201a) over (201b) follows from focus-background conflict constraint directly: Because indefinite NPs introduce new entities (unlike definite NPs), the questioned element is more likely to belong to the focal domain in (201a) than in (201b), which results in (201a) being more acceptable than (201b). And the fact that the contrast disappears in (201c) is as predicted by the focus-background conflict constraint: The extraction in (201c) is in a relative clause, which does not involve a focused element, so the focus-background conflict constraint does not apply.

Furthermore, the focus-background conflict constraint predicts an improvement in extractions from subject position when the extracted position is focused. That is, subject position isn't necessarily non-focused (backgrounded). We can focus the subject position by using a focus particle like *even* or *only*, as in (202).

(202) a. ?? [Which car] did the color of __ please the baseball player?
b. [Which car] did even the color of __ please the baseball player?
c. [Which car] did only the color of __ please the baseball player?

The acceptability of (202a) seems to be improved by adding the focus markers *only* or *even*, as predicted by the focus-background conflict constraint.

9 Language and Thought

Given that human language has a dependency structure component, we can ask some broader questions:

- How is language—syntax and lexicon—represented in the mind and brain? According to the **domain-general** hypothesis, language might be represented using the same brain regions as those that represent and compute information in other domains, which may include working memory, social reasoning, causal reasoning, arithmetic and other mathematical reasoning, spatial reasoning, music, and other domains. Alternatively, according to the **domain-specific** hypothesis, language may be represented in its own area or network of areas in the brain, exclusive of other functions.
- How is syntactic information—like dependency structure—represented relative to lexical structure, in the mind and brain?
- Does the structure or lexicon of the language that we speak affect the kinds of concepts that we can represent and the kinds of things we can think about? This is the **Sapir-Whorf hypothesis**: That the language that we speak may affect cognition in some deep way. There are several flavors of this claim. I elaborate two positions below.

To address the first two of these questions, the best current method is functional magnetic resonance imaging (fMRI). I first review other methods and then describe this method in section 9.1. To answer the first question above—to try to understand the relationship between language and thought—we can use fMRI to see if the brain regions that represent and process language also represent or process some other cognitive domains. As presented in section 9.2, the short answer to this question appears to be that the brain areas that support language processing—at least the core frontal and temporal ones in the left hemisphere—do not process other information, including information relevant to diverse forms of reasoning. Thus, the language system is not used for thinking.

We can then use fMRI to try to answer the second question: How is lexical and syntactic information represented in the language network? At this point, the state of the art suggests that these representations are intermingled: Each of the core language areas processes both syntactic and lexical information, as presented in 9.3.

Finally, in section 9.4, I discuss the Sapir-Whorf hypothesis. Of relevance to many studies of the effects of language on thought is the observation that languages differ in how they lexicalize some concepts. That is, a particular concept may be important in one culture but not in another, with the consequence that that concept may be labeled in one language but not in the second. A classic example of a large conceptual difference between cultures is in the realm of number knowledge: Some cultures such as Pirahã—a hunter-gather population in the Brazilian Amazon—don't label any exact number concepts in their language, not even the concept associated with the number "one." So a Pirahã speaker who learned Spanish (for example) would need to learn not only the words for numbers but also the concepts. Smaller conceptual differences between languages include how a language labels the color space: It may include distinctions not present in another language so that learning the new language will necessitate learning a new division in the color space.

9.1 Language and the Brain

Recent work in many labs has now established that the brain contains areas and networks—sets of interconnected areas—that specialize for different functions (e.g., Kanwisher et al., 1997; Kanwisher, 2010). Aside from our perceptual and motor areas with diverse kinds of specialization, there are several distinct networks that support high-level cognition, including a social reasoning network (e.g., Saxe and Kanwisher, 2003; Paunov et al., 2019), an executive control network (e.g., Duncan, 2010; Fedorenko et al., 2013), and a language processing network (e.g., Fedorenko et al., 2010, 2011). Work in Ev Fedorenko's group and other groups has established that higher-level language processing—language above the speech signal, such as words and sentences—takes place in a brain network that specializes for processing linguistic information (Fedorenko et al., 2011, 2012; Blank et al., 2014; Mineroff et al., 2018; Pritchett et al., 2018; Jouravlev et al., 2019; Ivanova et al., 2020, 2021; X. Chen et al., 2023).

9.1.1 Brain Imaging Methods and What They Tell Us about Domain-Specificity

How do we discover what kinds of computations a specific region or network in the brain performs? For any category of computation, we need a target task—which involves the target computation—and some control task or tasks—which do not. So for language, we might compare the task of reading or listening to sentences to the task of doing nothing, or reading or listening to strings of nonwords (material that is less language-like, but has similar perceptual properties). We can then look for brain areas that work harder when participants process sentences than nonwords. The core idea is that sentences engage linguistic computations like lexical access (understanding word meanings) and combinatorial meanings (understanding how words combine together into phrases and sentences to a greater extent than nonwords).

In addition to appropriate tasks, we need a way to measure brain activity. There are several available methods, each with their advantages and disadvantages. This section is about localizing brain function, so we need a method that has good spatial localization properties. Here are some currently used methods, with their advantages and disadvantages:

- Event-related potentials (ERPs). This method consists of measuring voltage changes on the scalp, corresponding to the firing of neurons in the brain. This method has excellent temporal resolution (down to millisecond and below) but poor spatial resolution: The signals are such that we can't accurately figure out where they are coming from.
- Magneto-encephalography (MEG). This method consists of measuring changes in the magnetic fields near the scalp, corresponding to the firing of neurons in the brain. Like ERP, this method has excellent temporal resolution but poor spatial resolution: The signals are such that we can't accurately figure out where they are coming from.
- Positron emission tomography (PET). In this method, a participant ingests a radioactive tracer (a radiotracer) so that blood flow can be visualized in the brain. The spatial resolution of this method is

reasonable, down to about few millimeters cubed. The temporal resolution is somewhat poor, for studying language, because it is on the order of seconds (and so much happens within a couple of seconds in language production and comprehension). This method requires the ingestion of a radiotracer, which also means that you can only collect a small amount of data from any given individual. Consequently, this method is rarely used anymore, given the availability of magnetic resonance imaging.

- Functional magnetic resonance imaging (fMRI). This is a noninvasive method that uses magnetic fields to measure blood flow in the brain: Blood-oxygen-level dependent (BOLD) imaging. The spatial resolution of this method is very good, down to about two millimeters cubed (even better in some setups). Because this method is measuring blood flow, and it takes a few seconds for blood to reach the targeted areas of the brain, the temporal resolution is on the order of seconds, so it is not appropriate to study the time course of language processing.
- Intracranial recordings (electrocorticography [ECoG] or stereo electroencephalography [SEEG]; Mukamel and Fried, 2012). In this method, neural activity is recorded directly from the brain either by placing electrodes on the cortical surface (ECoG) or by inserting depth electrodes (SEEG). This method has both high spatial resolution (recording from populations of neurons, or even single cells) and high temporal resolution. But this method is highly invasive: Its use is restricted to patients who need brain surgery (to treat drug-resistant epilepsy or to remove a tumor). Moreover, this method is highly limited in coverage: You are only sampling activity from a few locations in the brain.

The best imaging method that can tell us about the spatial localization of language is fMRI. Neither ERP nor MEG have good enough spatial resolution for this goal (despite their excellent temporal resolution). PET has good spatial localization, but it is invasive, so it is no longer in wide use. And intracranial recordings only measure activity in a small number of locations, in contrast to fMRI, which can record activity across all of the brain. I therefore focus on fMRI evidence here.

9.1.2 The Traditional Group-Averaging Analysis Method

Up until about 2010, the standard method in fMRI investigations of language processing was the *group-averaging analysis* method, which is often referred to as simply the "group analysis" method. This method relies on averaging brains together in a "common space" (a brain template such as the standardized Montreal Neurological Institute [MNI] template; Poldrack et al., 2011), and the key assumption is that in this common space there is functional correspondence at the voxel level across individuals.[1] In other words, the same voxel is doing the same thing across participants, when aligned in an average brain space. So, for example, when we align my brain and your brain into the common space, a voxel in a particular location, which performs language computations in my brain, is assumed to also perform language computations in your brain.

In the group analysis method, we perform a statistical analysis (most commonly, a t-test) in each voxel to see if the activation difference across the two conditions (e.g., language processing and some control task, or arithmetic and its control task) is reliable across the group. This gives us a set of voxels (or regions, if responsive voxels are spatially clustered) that are generally more activated in our critical (e.g., language) task than in the control task, across participants.

To ask whether, for example, language and arithmetic processing draw on the same neural structures, we can compare the voxels that we get for the language contrast (responding more during the language task than the control condition) and for the arithmetic contrast. If there is overlap in the voxels between the two tasks, then we conclude that the two tasks overlap in their neural substrates. In some cases, researchers do not even perform a direct comparison between tasks, but instead compare the activations for their task to activations reported in some earlier study, and if the activated voxels are "close enough" (e.g., fall within the same gyrus), they conclude that functional overlap exists between the two tasks in question. Researchers have often made this kind of inference over the years: It has been claimed that some set of voxels in the left inferior frontal cortex (often called "Broca's area") computes language, music, and a variety of working memory and cognitive control tasks (Tettamanti and Weniger, 2006; Fadiga et al., 2009; Fitch and Martins, 2014; Wang et al., 2015; Thompson-Schill et al., 1997; Cabeza and Nyberg, 2000; Novick et al., 2005).

Unfortunately, the assumption that underlies the group analysis fMRI method is not sound: There is some functional spatial correspondence between people when our brains are aligned in an average brain, but this correspondence is far from perfect, especially for the association cortex, including frontal and lateral temporal areas, where a lot of language machinery typically resides. A helpful analogy for inter-individual differences is human faces: If we tried to align someone's face to an average face, the eyes, nose, and mouth would be roughly in the same place, but there are important differences across people that the method would just miss. That is, we might find some overlap with the "left eye" area, for my left eye, but my left eye might be further to the left and higher than an average eye, so the method might miss a lot. Consequently, the brain averaging method is flawed: It tends to underestimate the areas that might be computing the same function across people and to overestimate overlap between nearby functionally distinct areas. Hence, this method will miss a lot of potential language-responsive areas, if those areas happen to differ slightly in spatial location across people, and will lead researchers to conclude that overlap exists between two tasks even if they occupy completely nonoverlapping areas in any given individual. Consequently, building on work in domains like vision and social cognition, Fedorenko et al. (2010) developed the *language localizer* method where language areas are identified in each individual brain.

9.1.3 The Language Localizer Method

The language localizer method builds from work in high-level vision (Kanwisher et al., 1997) and social cognition (Saxe and Kanwisher, 2003). For example, each person has a small area in the right fusiform gyrus that responds more strongly to faces than to any other visual stimulus (Kanwisher et al., 1997). This region (the fusiform face area) can be robustly identified in any given individual in just a few minutes of fMRI scanning by looking for voxels that respond more strongly to faces than to non-face objects. So, in the functional localization approach, the area of interest is first localized (in any given individual), and then its response to different new conditions is tested. Those responses to different conditions can be evaluated across individuals to draw population-level inferences, but critically, no brain averaging is taking place.

Fedorenko did the same for language. The problem is a bit more complicated because the areas subserving language are more extensive and widespread across the left hemisphere, and there are even reliable areas in the right hemisphere and other parts of the brain for many individuals. But the principle is the same. We first find the voxels *in each participant*

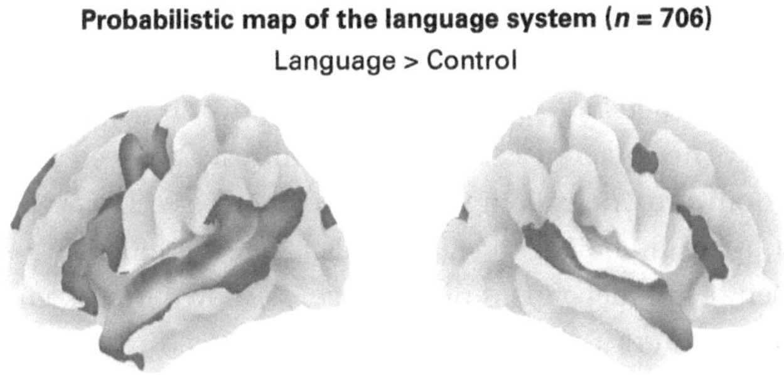

Figure 9.1
Surface projections in the FreeSurfer FSaverage space (Fischl et al., 1999) for the language > control condition contrast based on overlaid individual binarized activation maps, where in each map, the top 10 percent of voxels are selected. The grayscale reflects the proportion of participants for whom that voxel belongs to the top 10 percent of language (reading sentences) > control condition (reading nonwords) voxels (thresholded at $p = 0.2$ for visualization purposes). This figure was generated by Agata Wolna from Ev Fedorenko's lab, based on 706 participants who were run in Fedorenko's lab over the years 2013–2023. A similar map appears in Lipkin et al. (2022), where results from listening experiments are also included. See Fedorenko et al. (2010), Bedny et al. (2011), Scott et al. (2017), Lipkin et al. (2022), and Malik-Moraleda et al. (2022) for evidence that the same network is activated for reading or listening experiments. Note that the left hemisphere is presented on the left.

that respond more to language-like stimuli vs. less language-like stimuli. Fedorenko has used contrasts between sentences vs. non-words or between speech vs. backward/foreign speech. Any of these contrasts work robustly. All that matters is that the critical condition is more language-like than the control condition. This comparison will also separate out the higher-level components of language (the combinatorial syntax/compositions) from, for example, the sounds (which are in both conditions being compared). Critically, this step (the localization of language-responsive areas) is done *participant by participant*: The language areas will be broadly similar across people but will vary in their precise location, size, and shape, in much the same ways that our faces are broadly similar but also highly distinct across people.

The high-level language network (or simply the language network) is left-lateralized in most people, with predominant components in the left inferior frontal areas[2] and the left lateral temporal areas. Figure 9.1 shows the typical activations in the FreeSurfer "FSaverage" space (Fischl et al.,

1999) over 706 participants analyzed from 2013–2023 in Fedorenko's lab at MIT (Lipkin et al., 2022).

The language network as defined here responds to language regardless of modality: The same areas emerge for contrasts between reading sentences vs. nonwords, or listening to sentences vs. to speech played backward or speech in an unfamiliar foreign language. Furthermore, the same network is identified independent of language, as shown in a recent study of native speakers from forty-five languages, from twelve language families (Malik-Moraleda et al., 2022). Fascinatingly, in spite of substantial differences between where the language network is located between people the language network is remarkably constant within an individual over time. Figure 9.2 shows five people's brains performing the language localizer tasks in 2007–2012, over two sessions each, with a time gap between sessions consisting of a few weeks up to a few years, mean = 8 months (Mahowald and Fedorenko, 2016). Figure 9.3 shows fMRI scans of my brain doing the language localizer tasks (slightly different tasks in each year) in 2007, 2012, and 2022. The locations of my brain areas responding to language are remarkably stable even over these fifteen years.

9.2 Language vs. Thought

Following on Kanwisher and Saxe's methods (Kanwisher et al., 1997; Saxe and Kanwisher, 2003; Saxe et al., 2006), Fedorenko tested the responses of the brain regions identified by the language localizer to many diverse conditions. Critically, language is localized using a task vs. a control task (e.g., reading sentences vs. reading lists of nonwords; or listening to speech vs. listening to backward speech), then it is validated in independent data. Her group then tests whether other tasks elicit significant responses in the same voxels, such as tasks involving arithmetic, logic, executive function (like the Stroop task or the flankers task), problem-solving (as in IQ tasks), music, social perception and cognition, conceptual knowledge, and even computer code comprehension. Fascinatingly, there is no overlap between language and any other function. That is, the language network only does language, and doesn't do arithmetic, logic, executive function, problem-solving, music, social intelligence, conceptual knowledge, or computer programming (Fedorenko et al., 2011; Ivanova et al., 2020), not even gesture

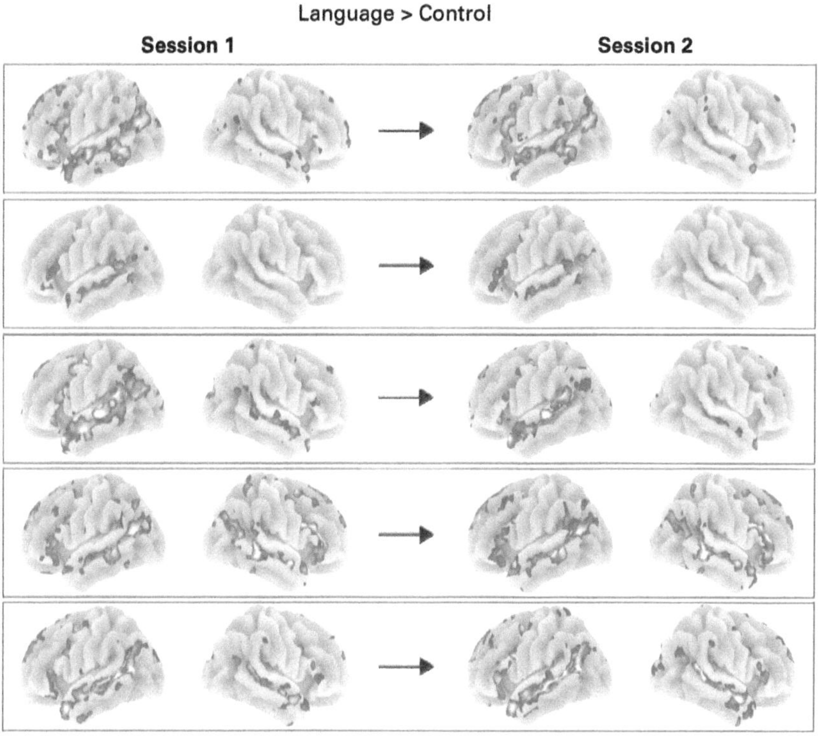

Figure 9.2
Activations for reading sentences vs. reading nonwords in five experimental participants in Ev Fedorenko's lab, 2007–2012. The right and left hemisphere scans are presented on the left for session 1, and similar scans are presented on the right for session 2. Although generally left-lateralized to a set of fronto-temporal regions, there are substantial differences between people in the precise locations in those areas where the language network shows up. For example, compare rows 1, 2, and 3 in session 1 or 2. Despite these large between-subject differences, the activations for an individual remain remarkably constant (Mahowald and Fedorenko, 2016). For example, compare the pair of images on the left for participant 1 (the first row) to the pair of images on the right for the same participant. They are remarkably similar. Thanks to Agata Wolna of Ev Fedorenko's lab for generating this image, in August 2024.

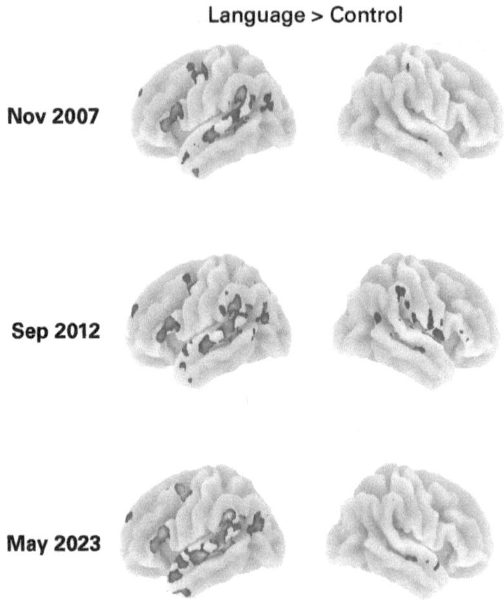

Figure 9.3
Activations for reading sentences vs. reading nonwords for both hemispheres of my brain in 2007, 2012, and 2022, scanned by Ev Fedorenko. Despite the fact that there are substantial differences between people as to where the language network shows up in its fronto-temporal regions (see figure 9.2), the activations for any one person (like me) remain remarkably constant, even over many years (Mahowald and Fedorenko, 2016). Thanks to Agata Wolna of Ev Fedorenko's lab for generating this image, in August 2024.

processing (Jouravlev et al., 2019). See figure 9.4 for some comparisons from Fedorenko et al. (2024a). So it appears that language is processed and represented separately from all other tasks. The language network is strongly domain-specific.

The fact that the language network seems to only respond to language, and respond little or not at all during diverse thinking and reasoning tasks, suggests that language and thought are distinct. We can think perfectly fine without engaging our language-processing mechanisms (Fedorenko and Varley, 2016; Mahowald et al., 2024). Other evidence suggests that language is for **communication**, not thinking (see chapter 10).

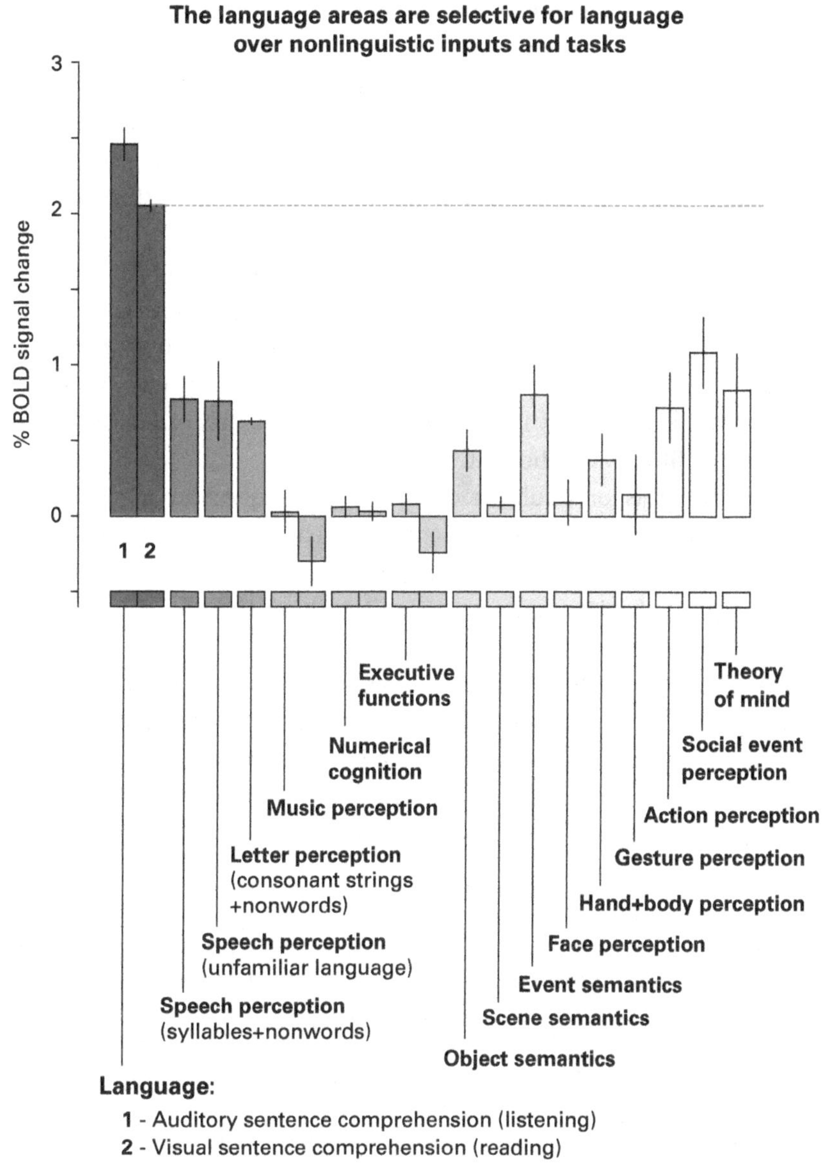

Figure 9.4

Data from Ev Fedorenko's lab; visualized by Tamar Regev, August 2024, based on analyses from Fedorenko et al. (2024b). Responses in the language network, as measured by fMRI, demonstrate selectivity for language processing compared to a wide variety of nonlinguistic tasks. The language network's response to language processing is at least twice as high as its response to any nonlinguistic input or task.

9.2.1 Evidence for Language as Communication vs. Thought from People with Global Aphasia

Further evidence for the separation of language and thought comes from investigations of patients with severe linguistic impairments (e.g., Varley et al., 2005; Siegal and Varley, 2006; Apperly et al., 2006; Benn et al., 2023). Such studies show that people with extensive brain damage to the language network—individuals with severe aphasia—can do arithmetic, logic, and many other tasks just as well as age-matched controls (Fedorenko and Varley, 2016; Fedorenko et al., 2024a). These patients can still negotiate the world in many ways: They can play complex games like chess, they can drive, they have good theory of mind, and so on. It turns out that these patients have a deficit only in their language abilities; they can do anything else that we think of as "thought."

These two sets of results resolve an age-old question in cognition and philosophy: Thought is independent of language. That is, our complex thoughts are not equal to language: Language is just the vehicle for communicating them to others. We think the thoughts without language.

These results may be surprising to people who feel like they think in language due to the strong sensation of an inner monologue or inner speech/voice; but interestingly there is a lot of variance in this feeling. A large minority of people feel like they have no "inner voice" (Nedergaard and Lupyan, 2024). For what it's worth, I am someone who lacks an inner

Figure 9.4 (continued)
These responses are averaged across five core areas in the left hemisphere. In all Fedorenko-style experiments, language functional regions of interest (fROIs) are identified in individual participants, and independent data subsets are used for defining the fROIs and estimating their responses to avoid circularity. Error bars are standard error of the mean by participants. A dashed horizontal line is drawn based on the reading-based language localizer, for which there are more data, to facilitate comparisons with nonlinguistic conditions. Note that the functional profiles of the knowledge and reasoning networks differ markedly from the language network's profile (and from each other). For example, the multiple demand network shows minimal response during sentence comprehension but robust responses during various demanding tasks. Similarly, the theory of mind network shows minimal to no response during sentence comprehension but strong responses during social reasoning tasks.

voice. I can think in language if I want to, but it's not the natural way that it feels like I think.

9.2.2 Specialization vs. Innateness

The fact that the language network specializes for language does not mean that the network is doing language processing from birth. First of all, much of language is obviously learned: We don't know the details of any language until we are exposed to them, and a baby born to speakers of one language and adopted into a family speaking a different language will learn the language of the adopted parents. Furthermore, there is strong evidence that there are specializations in our brains for relatively recently invented tasks. For example, the visual word form area responds selectively to letters/characters in a script that we can read (Baker et al., 2007). People who cannot read—children or illiterate adults—have no such selectivity; when they learn to read, they develop such selectivity. Thus, the cortex is specializing when people learn to read. The same could be true for language. This is an open question.

Furthermore, while language tends to be left-lateralized in a healthy brain, people can have a strong language system in other parts of the brain, if the left hemisphere was damaged when language would normally develop. That is, there are people who have brain damage at an early age, which may make having the language network in its normal location difficult or impossible. If the lesion occurs at a young enough age, then the language system can develop in the right hemisphere (Tuckute et al., 2022; Newport et al., 2022).

9.3 What Does the Language Network Do?

Research to date has identified a left-lateralized brain network that respond consistently and selectively to language. What exactly does this language network do? And how is it organized: Do different areas of the network perform different linguistic functions? (For example, do some areas process individual word meanings, while others—put words together into phrases and sentences?)

Currently the evidence does not support the idea of different language areas supporting different linguistic computations. To the extent that a language area or neural population shows sensitivity to combinatorics, it will also show sensitivity to word meanings. For example, Fedorenko et al. (2020) show across several tasks—tasks which had been taken previously to support different functions in different parts of the network—that all areas of the language network support both combinatorial meaning and word meaning processing, with no measurable differences across areas.

In retrospect, perhaps this shouldn't be surprising, given the kinds of brain deficits that we see. That is, if combinatorial meaning were localized in some small part of the brain (as argued by, e.g., Grodzinsky [2000]; Bemis and Pylkkänen [2011]; Pallier et al. [2011]; Pylkkänen [2019] among others), then we should occasionally see people with brain damage to that area, such that they can still store their full lexicon, but can't combine words in any way. No such patient has ever existed. There are patients with severe language loss—so-called global aphasic patients—but their deficit is typically huge, affecting much of the left hemisphere. These patients have no ability for linguistic combinatorial meaning, but they have no lexicon either. The pattern of just losing combinatorial meaning doesn't seem to occur, suggesting that combinatorial meaning is distributed across the whole language network, consistent with Fedorenko's lab's results.

9.4 Linguistic Relativism: How Does Knowledge of a Particular Language Affect Conceptual Representations?

A long-standing question in cognitive science and philosophy is whether having words for particular concepts affects how we understand those and related concepts. This is the so-called **Sapir-Whorf hypothesis** (one aspect of **linguistic relativity** or **linguistic relativism**): Does the language we speak affect the way that we think about nonlinguistic concepts (Sapir, 1921, 1929; Whorf, 1956; Kay and Kempton, 1984)?[3]

It is important to discuss what we might mean by the claim that the language we speak *affects* our thoughts. First and foremost, language obviously is fundamental for pedagogy; language helps us pass cultural information between societies, and down from generation to generation. Although this is a case where language changes thought, this is not normally what is meant by the idea that a particular language can change how we think. The typical Whorfian idea is that learning just the language causes conceptual changes, without a direct teaching of those additional concepts. Thus, learning the concepts associated with some realm of science or technology is not typically thought to be in the realm of the Whorfian claim, perhaps because these concepts are for specialists in the community, and not all speakers of the language. Even if we restrict our attention to concepts that most everyone within a language community would be aware of, there are at least two kinds of views for how to interpret the language-thought hypothesis:

- The **Strong Whorfian** view: There is a language and a set of concepts, such that only by learning the target language can the user now understand this set of concepts. This is usually discussed in terms of words and their meanings: The inclusion of some set of words enables the understanding of the concepts, which would have been impossible without the words. For example, it has occasionally been hypothesized that having words for different colors somehow enables people to distinguish these colors. And without these words, people might not be able to perceive the colors.
- The **Weak Whorfian** view: As we will see below, different languages encode different concepts in their words, plausibly because having labels for culturally relevant concepts will be useful to the speakers of the language. Language is an efficient, compressed representation that makes encoding, storing, and retrieving the culturally relevant concepts easier (Levinson, 2003b; Cantlon and Piantadosi, 2024). This can make it easier for the user to access these concepts in various tasks, as compared to if the user didn't know the language.

In the following section, I first examine some ways in which languages differ. Then I discuss each of the above views in turn, along with potential evidence for each in sections 9.4.2 and 9.4.3.

Of course, it is also possible that a particular language—with its particular set of labels—doesn't make any concepts easier to access than any other: This would be the strongest anti-Whorfian view. But because languages do encode different concepts, this hypothesis seems less likely overall. But some attempts to show experimentally measurable differences between languages in particular semantic domains are sometimes not successful. In section 9.4.4, I outline some experiments that purported to show differences but didn't really find compelling evidence in that direction. Unfortunately, such failures don't tell us very much: The existence of novel word-concept associations within a language might have behavioral consequences that are not measured by a particular experiment.

9.4.1 The Cultural Sensitivity of the Lexicon

There are currently approximately seven thousand languages in the world, across over three hundred distinct language families, such that one language family has no obvious connections with any other language family (Dryer, 2013; Campbell, 2013). In a growing fraction of these languages, we have a pretty good idea of what the lexicon looks like. Lexicography is the painstaking tabulation of all the different morphemes and words that people use within a language community, along with all the different senses in different contexts for each. There are many senses for common words in every language (e.g., Piantadosi et al., 2012b). For example, there are more than forty senses for each of the words *take*, *make*, and *run* in English, according to either Merriam Webster (an American Dictionary) or the Oxford English dictionary (from the United Kingdom).

While this may seem like a reasonable way of tabulating lexical entries, it actually underestimates the complexity of figuring out the meanings of words. First of all, it is notoriously difficult to define the meaning of almost any word (Wittgenstein, 1953; Yudkowsky, 2017; Haspelmath, 2017). Contrary to popular belief, words don't get their meanings from a dictionary. It's the other way around: Dictionaries are constructed to mirror what words already mean. Furthermore, words are not defined by some language authority. In contrast, words come into a language out of a **communication use**. But that communication use is not well understood. Consider the case of *bachelor*: A standard definition is "an unmarried adult male." While this works in general, this definition would classify the pope as a bachelor, even though this doesn't seem right (Lakoff, 1987). Another classic example of the difficulty of defining a word is provided by Fodor (1983) who tries to define the verb *paint*. Fodor's first attempt at a definition is "x covers the surface of y with paint," but he notes that this fails to capture the right meaning because the painter could miss a spot of the target object, and yet they would still be said to have painted it. So complete coverage doesn't seem to be necessary. In addition, Fodor notes that accidental coverage wouldn't count either; so intention is important. But even intention isn't enough: "For consider that when Michelangelo dipped his brush into Cerulean Blue, he thereby covered the surface of his brush with paint and did so with the primary intention that his brush should be covered with paint in consequence of his having so dipped it. But MICHELANGELO WAS NOT, . . . , PAINTING HIS PAINTBRUSH. (He was just putting paint on his paintbrush.)" (Fodor, 1983; all caps in the original—I am not so dramatic).

Perhaps as a consequence of the way words are invented and used, word meanings are almost always context-dependent to some degree. This is obviously true for relational words like scalar adjectives such as *big* or *small*: These words need head nouns in order to be interpreted. A *big ant* is very different in size from a *big baby*, a *big man*, a *big building*, or a *big galaxy*. Furthermore, the context-dependence of meaning holds even for many words that seem to have a meaning independent of context.[4] For example, the word *red* might seem to have an obvious meaning—the color red—which will be listed as one of its senses in any dictionary. But the meaning of the color word depends on the noun that it describes. A *red pen* is a different shade of red from the red in *red hair*, which is a different shade of red from the red in *red wine*, which is a different shade of red from the red in *red sand*, and so on. This context sensitivity isn't even listed in the Oxford or Merriam-Webster dictionary entries.

A further complication in figuring out a dictionary for a language is that the language is necessarily culturally dependent, with the consequence that knowing the words for one language does not give us much leverage in figuring out the dictionary for another. This may seem counterintuitive for people who speak languages in similar cultures because, in such cases, it seems pretty easy to translate words from one language to another. Consider English, French, Italian, and German. Most of the words in these languages do have pretty good translations in the other languages. So we can translate (203) into French, Italian, and German, word by word:

(203)

English:	Two	girls	ate	a	big	pizza.
French:	Deux	filles	ont mangé	une	grosse	pizza.
Italian:	Due	ragazze	hanno mangiato	una	grande	pizza.
German:	Zwei	Mädchen	aßen	eine	große	Pizza.

So *two* can be translated to *deux* in French, *due* in Italian, and *zwei* in German. And *girls* can be translated to *filles* in French, *ragazze* in Italian, and *Mädchen* in German, and so on.[5] Interestingly, the word *pizza* is expressed using the same morpheme in each of the four languages in (203): This is because the word and concept are borrowed from one into the others.

This overlap in lexical meanings across these four languages might suggest that perhaps *all* languages might be similar in their lexicons: what people want to talk about. But this is of course not right: There is huge cultural variability across the world, and hence, there is a lot of variability in what people want to talk about. For example, many cultures have never come into contact with pizza; the concept would have to be introduced, and labeled. A more interesting problem arises in translating the word *two* into some languages. Whereas all industrialized languages have words for counting (in base 10), some hunter-gatherer cultures lack such lexical items. For example, it would be impossible to accurately translate the word *two* into Pirahã, an isolate language of a hunter-gatherer population in the Brazilian Amazon (Everett, 1986, 2005; Gordon, 2004; Frank et al., 2008a; O'Shaughnessy et al., 2021), because Pirahã has no words for any exact counting concepts, not even *one, two,* or *three.* Although this is hard for people from industrialized cultures to believe, the concept "two" is not representable in Pirahã. See figure 9.5 for discussion of some relevant evidence.

Every meaning domain is a potential source for cross-cultural differences in what features may matter to a culture, and hence cross-linguistic differences in how the domain is codified in words. Number words are a fascinating test-case of how different cultures express concepts in a particular domain. Industrialized cultures all rely heavily on exact number for many reasons, including having monetary systems and trade. Some cultures have invented counting systems that are incomplete (only up to a certain number) or are based on a different base system than ten (O'Shaughnessy et al., 2021). In the extreme case, some remote hunter-gatherer cultures like the Pirahã have no need for counting, and hence have no words for such concepts at all (Frank et al., 2008a; O'Shaughnessy et al., 2021).

Another interesting meaning domain is color. People with normal trichromatic vision can differentiate millions of colors (Pointer and Attridge, 1998; Linhares et al., 2008; Masaoka et al., 2013). But our language system categorizes these into a small set of words. In an industrialized culture, maybe you know only eleven color terms (e.g., *black, white, red, green, blue, yellow, orange, brown, pink, purple, gray* in English), or maybe if you are an interior designer, you know as many as a hundred. (This difference among speakers within a language is what I had talked about in the introduction with respect to communal lexicons: Different subsets of speakers know a set of words for their trade that most other speakers of the language don't know.) This is still a tiny fraction of the millions of colors that you can distinguish. Interestingly, the ways that languages categorize color varies widely, such that nonindustrialized cultures have many fewer words for colors than industrialized cultures (Kay and Maffi, 1999). Some languages have only two color words—corresponding roughly to English *black* and *white*, for example, the Dani from Papua New Guinea Rosch-Heider and Olivier (1972)—while others have three, four, or five terms (e.g., Berinmo, from Papua New Guinea; Davidoff et al. [1999]; Roberson et al. [2000]) which the community agrees on (Berlin and Kay, 1969; Kay and Maffi, 1999). Industrialized cultures have at least eleven terms that everyone agrees on, and often such cultures have many color terms that are not as well agreed upon (such as *tan, teal, crimson, gold, chartreuse, burgundy, magenta, navy, and aquamarine* in English).

A plausible explanation for the cross-cultural difference is that people in different cultures have different needs for discussing color: People in more industrialized cultures may invent more words for distinct colors because color may selectively differentiate more objects in these cultures (e.g., Gibson et al., 2017a; cf. Wnuk et al. [2022] who suggest that it is not only industrialization that creates the need for more color terms. Why might we invent color words in the first place? The usage-based claim is that we invent words that help us to differentiate identical objects that differ only in color. In nonindustrialized cultures, such objects are rare. There are objects that are similar and differ in color, but these objects typically have many other dimensions of differences. For example, bananas can be green, yellow, or brown. One might use color words to distinguish among bananas. But there are other salient features of such bananas: Green bananas aren't ripe, yellow bananas are ripe, and brown bananas are overripe. So we might label the differences along the ripeness dimension instead. It is when humans have manufacturing, with dyes, where so many objects are arbitrarily colored. If I want you to hand me a particular sweater on the rack at a store, I may need to use a color word to tell you which one of several sweaters that I would like you to hand to me: the red one, not the blue one.

Other meaning spaces are likely to be similar to color and number, such that human cultures may have more or less of a need to use the relevant space in their daily lives, and hence, the people may have more or less need to talk about that space, and invent words there. A language may not encode an entire semantic domain at all (e.g., hunting in a forest, working with computers, smells, tactile information), or a language may do so very

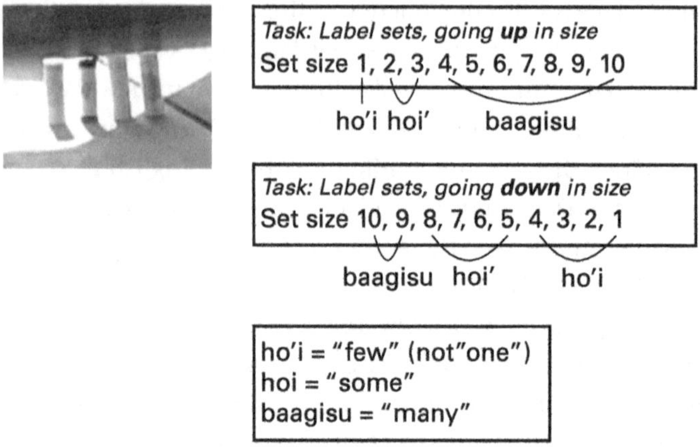

Figure 9.5
Frank et al. (2008a) devised a task where participants simply labeled sets of identical objects, which were spools of thread, as on the left above. Pirahã participants described the sets, which either increased in size from one spool of thread to ten or started with ten spools, down to one. When the sets were increasing in size, Pirahã speakers used the word *ho'i* to refer to one spool, and the word *hoi'* to refer to two or three spools, consistent with what Gordon (2004) had found. At about three or four spools of thread, Pirahã speakers usually used a third word (*baagisu* = "many"), and then they continued to use that word for sets of size four to ten. But when Frank et al. (2008b) asked participants to do the same task starting with ten spools, going down to one, they started with the word *baagisu* (= English *many*) to describe the set, and quickly shifted to what we thought was *two* at around eight spools on and then *one* starting at six objects, with most everyone using this word for four or fewer. So the first word *hoi'* actually probably means English *few*, relative to the context (a general context, or the specific context); the third word *baagisu* is like English *many*; and the middle word *hoi'* means something like *some*.

sparsely, because of low use in the community. Such cultural differences make translation difficult.

Finally, we can use the tools of information theory to work out the tradeoff between complexity of the lexicon (e.g., the number of terms within a particular semantic domain) and the informativeness of the system (Regier et al., 2015; Kemp et al., 2018; Gibson et al., 2019; Zaslavsky et al., 2019). See Kemp and Regier (2012) for discussion of kinship; see Majid and Burenhult (2014) and Majid and Kruspe (2018) for discussion of smell; Mollica et al. (2021) for discussion of number, tense, and evidentiality; see S. Chen et al. (2023b) for a discussion of spatial demonstratives.

9.4.1.1 A working hypothesis: Whorfian between-language effects are at the word level, not the syntax A working hypothesis for the ways in which languages may differ based on their conceptual structure is that such differences are at the structure of the lexicon. Whenever we talk about a semantic domain that we haven't yet talked about, we need to invent terms for the concepts that we want to describe. Critically, we can use the same syntax as we use in any other domain. For example, when explaining to you the principles of mathematics, or computer science, or linguistics, I use the same English syntax as I use to talk about the world to my five-year-old child. Indeed, it seems to me to be generally easier to understand the new concepts if we use the most basic syntax. This is a strategy followed in good textbooks of complex domains: simple syntax. Thus, all of the language that is created for a new semantic domain is in the words, not the syntax or sounds.[6] And hence differences between languages in what concepts they have labels for are similar to differences between speakers in what concepts they know labels for. My knowledge of math or linguistics or cognitive science (or any domain) requires concepts and terminology to make the discussion of the domain compressed (efficient). This is the same as for learning the relevant meaning domains in a language (culture) that I don't know. All of the meaning differences between languages are in the words, not the syntax.

9.4.2 The Strong Whorfian View: Changes in Language Cause Changes in How We Perceive and Think about the World

According to the strong Whorfian view, there are concepts that are only learned through acquisition of the target language. Although I can't find any researcher who has made this strong claim, it does show up in popular culture every now and then. For example, this is the topic of a BBC documentary, which was discussed at length in Mark Liberman's Language Log on two occasions.[7] The BBC documentary in question was based loosely on work by Roberson et al. (2005) and claimed that the Himba—a population people from a culture/language in Namibia—cannot see the difference between shades of blue and green because they don't have words for such distinctions. Whereas it was true at the time that the Himba didn't have such words, it was never claimed by any researcher that the Himba couldn't see differences between blues and greens. In the documentary, a young Himba woman says she can't see the difference between two colors that are obviously very different on the screen she is looking at: One is a bright lime green and the other is shade of light blue, which are far apart in any color space, so anyone with normal color vision would be able to see the difference.

It turns out however that the colors shown on the screen are not ones in any experiment that had been run by Roberson et al. (2005) or their collaborators: In the experiments, the sets of colors were more subtly different. And the tasks in the published experiments were also more subtle, not a simple categorization task as in the documentary. So it seems that the documentary maker must have directed the woman to say what she said, in a misunderstanding of the original tasks and results. Presumably that's why the video is now hard to find: The BBC were probably informed that the documentary maker had misunderstood the research, and had reported an effect that isn't true. My collaborator Bevil Conway was the one who brought this documentary to my attention back in about 2013. He wanted to know if there was any truth to it. This led to our collaboration. (And no, there is no truth to this idea at all.)

Indeed, this idea had been evaluated in the early 1970s by Eleanor Rosch, in the Dani. The Dani are an indigenous population of Papua New Guinea with only two color terms that most speakers agreed on (corresponding to light [white-ish] and dark [black-ish]). Rosch-Heider and Olivier (1972) and Rosch (1973) evaluated whether Dani speakers could categorize color chips by their color. If it were the case that the words themselves were important in the chip categorization task, then it might be difficult for Dani speakers to categorize chips that they had no words for. Alternatively, perhaps the words are not so important for the categorization task: Maybe chips can be categorized based on how they look, using color perception, whether or not there are words for these concepts. The Dani did as well as English speakers. This result shows that the difference in sets of labels used by the groups didn't change how the groups categorized color. This is consistent with the proposal here that language comes after perception and thought: People invent labels and syntactic constructions (language) for what they want to talk about, among all of the things that they perceive and are thinking about. The language does not restructure color perception.

The reason that Bevil was so shocked by the video was in part because he works on the neural basis of color vision, and he works with monkeys, whose color vision is very similar to that of humans. Naturally he found it shocking that the advent of words might take away a perceptual ability (which is the strong view that the documentary was implicitly suggesting). But words do no such thing: They can make concepts easier to represent, access, and manipulate (given that symbolic linguistic representations are more compact than nonsymbolic ones—see the next section for more discussion), but they don't erase underlying perceptual abilities.

9.4.3 The Weak Whorfian View: Different Conceptual Divisions across Languages Have Behavioral Consequences

Although learning words does not change our perceptual system, learning words may cause other significant conceptual changes. Language draws attention to some conceptual differences and makes the user aware of them so that it is easier (faster) to use these concepts later. These are cases of **recoding**, the mental compression of information during task execution (an external task or even just for thinking; Cantlon and Piantadosi, 2024). Humans excel at this process, employing techniques such as chunking, rules, heuristics, or verbalization to condense information, creating room for additional data. Language is one of the tools that people use to compress the information that make it easier to perform complex tasks. Words offer a way to keep track of intricate meanings (Levinson, 2003a; Isbilen and Christiansen, 2020). For instance, the terms *hundred* and *thousand* don't need to be broken down into their meanings—*ten tens* and *ten hundreds*—every time they are used, nor do terms in any complex domain, such as *aunt, grandmother*, and *cousin* within familial relationships, or *power play, icing*, and *offside* within hockey.

This connection between symbols and information capacity extends beyond humans, and is evident in symbol-trained chimpanzees experiencing advantages with symbols (Gillan et al., 1981; Oden et al., 2001; Thompson et al., 1997; Livingstone et al., 2014). The cognitive transformations are plausibly significant; grammar facilitates an "endless compacting of information limited only by human memory" (Premack, 2007) comparable to hierarchical organization for memory for concepts (e.g., Collins and Quillian, 1969).

So we should be able to see measurable effects on behavior between pairs of languages whose concepts are labeled in different ways, or between speakers who know the labels vs. don't yet know the labels. Let's explore the domains of number and color with this in mind.

9.4.3.1 Exact number: Matching tasks in the pirahã As observed above, one way that languages and cultures can differ is how they do or do not represent exact number information. It is useful in the industrialized world to represent such information in the language. It is less useful in a hunter-gatherer culture like Pirahã, and hence, there are no such words in Pirahã.

How does the lack of number words affect a Pirahã speaker in other tasks? Frank et al. (2008b) had Pirahã speakers do a series of matching tasks. In all of these tasks, the experimenter (me, in this case) put out a set of identical small objects—spools of thread—in a row. Participants were given a handful of uninflated red balloons. In the first pair of these tasks, participants simply had to put one of their balloons against each of the spools of thread. They were shown what to do with a practice participant (Mike Frank in this case), and they were asked to copy him. He correctly put one balloon near each of two and three spools of thread. Participants mostly understood on the first trial, but were corrected if they made an error on the trials with two or three spools of thread. Then they were tested on sets going up to as high as ten spools of thread. They performed nearly perfectly on these matching tasks.[8]

When the tasks involved some memory as to how many spools of thread I had put out, then the Pirahã speakers would make many mistakes. For example, in one task, I would put out an evenly spaced row of spools of thread, and then hide them behind an opaque sheet. The participant's goal was to put a balloon near the location where each of the spools of thread lay, on the other side of the opaque sheet. An easy way to do this if you have number words in your language is to count the number of spools that are put out, and put the same number of balloons, evenly spaced. Without exact count words, this task is harder. One strategy is to put out approximately the same number of balloons.[9] This is what the Pirahã speakers did: They didn't have the words for the count abstractions, so they could not reliably choose the exact number. Consequently, they put out approximately the same number. As sets get larger, it is harder to estimate set sizes exactly. This meant that as the number of spools of thread increased, the Pirahã participants made more errors, so that for ten spools of thread hardly anyone would get the right answer. But as a group, they got about the right number: Some people put down too many and some people put down too few.

Thus, the lack of number words and their associated concepts has a major behavioral impact on Pirahã speakers in tasks that require exact counting to succeed in.

9.4.3.2 Exact number: Matching tasks in the Tsimane' One possible objection to the evidence that Frank et al. (2008b) provided for weak Whorfian effects of number concepts is that the behavioral task that the Pirahã performed doesn't make sense in Pirahã culture. That is, it is possible that the answers that they gave—approximate matching values—were correct in their culture. That is, they might have been able to understand an exact match task, but this isn't how they understood the task: In their culture, approximate matching may be more plausible (Casasanto, 2005).[10]

In order to address this possible concern, Pitt et al. (2022) investigated how the Tsimane' people did a similar task. The Tsimane' are an indigenous nonindustrialized Amazonian group consisting of about ten thousand people from lowland Bolivia who live by farming, hunting, and foraging for sustenance (Leonard et al., 2015). They have a similar culture to the Pirahã but with more contact with other cultures, including substantial trade. Furthermore, there are count words in Tsimane', up to the number 100. After that, they use Spanish words. But number word knowledge is not ubiquitous within the Tsimane': All speakers know some count words, but some people only know the first few number words, up to six or ten or fifteen. Pitt et al. (2022) relied on this variability within the Tsimane' culture to investigate whether knowledge of the count list was necessary in order to successfully complete matching tasks that involve memory to complete. Consequently, Pitt et al. (2022) recruited participants with knowledge of relatively few number words (only up to around fifteen) and they recruited participants who could count arbitrarily high, as controls. Critically, Pitt et al. (2022) found that participants with limited counting knowledge could only match about as high as they could count, and never higher. This was as predicted if exact number word knowledge is needed to perform the matching task. And in this case, it is clear that all participants knew what exact counting was, and they knew that that was the goal of their matching task.

9.4.3.3 Do we need words in order to learn exact number concepts? A further question that we might ask is whether we need words to **learn** exact counting. The best current proposal for how counting is acquired was made by Piantadosi et al. (2013) (building on Carey [2009]), who speculate that a learner is trying to find the counting function using simple Bayesian optimization. The details of the algorithm aren't particularly important here: What is important is that the algorithm relies on knowledge of a **counting list**, which doesn't have meaning yet, consisting of a list of the first few counting words. In English, these would be "one," "two," "three," "four," "five," . . . "'ten." This algorithm relies on these symbols in order to infer the existence of the recursive count list. Does this mean that a spoken list of initially meaningless words is needed to learn exact counting? No. This is just one way, through this list of symbols. But it is plausibly a way that many children do learn exact counting: relying on sequences of initially meaningless words. That is, it is well known that children learn the labels for the small number words ("one, two, three, four, five, six, seven, eight, nine, ten") without knowing their meaning, initially. It is possible that knowing this sequence of labels helps in the initial learning of their meaning.

9.4.3.4 Color words Let's return again to the case of color labeling across languages. While having labels for colors doesn't change how people perceive color, knowing one set of color labels may affect how we conceptualize color categories in a second language in an interesting way. Malik-Moraleda et al. (2023) compared how monolingual speakers of Tsimane' label colors to how bilingual speakers of Tsimane' and Bolivian Spanish label colors (c.f. Athanasopoulos [2009] Athanasopoulos et al. [2010, 2011], and He et al. [2019] for weaker kinds of effects in other pairs of languages). Importantly, the color labeling systems of Tsimane' and Bolivian Spanish are very different. Monolingual Tsimane' speakers use between three and six words consistently. The three words that everyone uses are *tsincus* (roughly English *black*), *jaibes* (roughly *white*), and *jäinäs* (roughly *red*). The other common labels correspond to *cafedyesi* (roughly *brown*), *itsidyeisi* (roughly *purple*), and *chames* (roughly *yellow*). In contrast, Bolivian Spanish has twelve labels that everyone uses consistently: *negro* (*black*), *blanca* (*white*), *rojo* (*red*), *anaranjado* (*orange*), *rosada* (*pink*), *amarillo* (*yellow*), *verde* (*green*), *celeste* (roughly *light blue*), *azul* (roughly *dark blue*), *violeta* (*violet*), *cafe* (*brown*), and *gris* (*grey*).

Interestingly, bilingual Tsimane' / Bolivian Spanish speakers label colors quite differently from their monolingual counterparts, when doing the labeling task in Tsimane': They use nine labels consistently, adopting Tsimane' words that are used inconsistently by Tsimane' monolinguals in a more consistent and narrow way. For example, monolingual Tsimane' speakers use two different words to cover all of the green-blue space: *shandyes* and *yushñus*. Bilinguals co-opt one of these words to be approximately green (*shandyes*) and the other to be approximately blue (*yushñus*). The color labels used by the bilinguals aren't borrowed from Spanish: They are reused Tsimane' color terms. Furthermore, bilinguals speaking in Tsimane' don't divide the color space exactly as the Bolivian Spanish do: For example, they do not split the blue space into light and dark blues, as Bolivian Spanish speakers do. They take some of the concepts from the Spanish labeling, and relabel those in Tsimane'.

There are other robust changes in color labeling between bilingual and monolingual Tsimane' speakers: Overall, the bilinguals use their color terms more precisely, covering a narrower range of the color palate, for all the terms, relative to their monolingual compatriots. They also can then use more terms to cover the color space. This adaptation is plausibly due to the bilinguals realizing that the Bolivian Spanish way of labeling the space is more useful, as they all deal with more objects of arbitrary color from the industrialized world.[11] Here, the culture is shifting, as Tsimane' contact with Bolivian Spanish speakers is increasing. This is a weak effect of language on thought: People learn a potentially more useful way of labeling the color space in a foreign language and co-opt aspects of the foreign language categories into their native language color space. The categories that they learn are from a foreign language—a language spoken by people living in a different culture. These are foreign cultural concepts.

9.4.4 Some Experiments That Didn't Find Convincing Whorfian Effects

Given that languages differ in how they divide conceptual spaces (or even whether to include some, like exact number concepts), it seems that there have to be behavioral consequences of these different ways to categorize the world around us. I have discussed some evidence just now, but in general, there have been many instances of unsuccessful attempts to find evidence of such effects. Indeed, there are several published papers where the behavioral effects don't seem to be replicable. Such failures don't falsify the weak Whorfian hypothesis: They simply fail to find evidence for it. In each of these cases, if there is a real conceptual difference between languages, then there must be a behavioral consequence, according to the weak Whorfian hypothesis. It just may be that the behavior that was measured isn't sensitive enough, or the task isn't right to require the use of the different concepts.

One example of a purported Whorfian effect of language on thought is that Russian speakers appear to be faster than English speakers in matching a target color to one of a pair of alternatives, where the choices are across a light-blue/dark-blue color boundary (Winawer et al., 2007), a paper cited over 1,300 times as of March 2025 on Google Scholar. Critically, Russian has a word for light blue ("goluboy") and a different word for dark blue ("siniy"), whereas English does not have specific color labels across this boundary for most speakers. The claim is that having this word boundary makes the decision faster for the Russian speakers. Winawer et al. (2007) provided evidence consistent with this claim in the form of faster decision times for Russians when matching a pair that consisted of a light blue and dark blue color chip versus a pair where both color chips were either light blue or dark blue. The hypothesis is that reaction time for crossing a color boundary should be faster than for staying within the same basic color term. English speakers showed no such difference (arguably because they do not have labels within light and dark blue), resulting in a statistical interaction in the decision times, as predicted by the Whorfian hypothesis.

While this is a potential good example of a weak Whorfian effect, there are unfortunately reasons to be concerned that this might not be the best way to measure color category effects in a language. First of all, there have not yet been any successful direct replications of the effect, in spite of at least two attempts—for example, by Martinovic et al. (2020); S. Chen et al. (2023a). Second, it turns out that the critical interaction was present only relative to the lighter colors (S. Chen et al., 2023a). That is, if we analyze the decision times for the colors that cross from light- to dark-blue and compare those for the colors that were within the darker blues, there was no difference for either group. This is not predicted by Winawer et al.'s (2007) hypothesis: There should have been a difference for the Russians, but this isn't significant in their own data (generously made public by Jon Winawer). So it is possible that this method may not be the best way to tap color categories within a language.

A second domain in which there have been experiments that purport to show an effect of language on concepts was in the domain of time perception. Boroditsky (2001) examined English and Mandarin corpora and concluded that English and Mandarin speakers have different metaphors for time: English uses a front-back metaphor, while Mandarin tends to use an up-down metaphor. She then provided experimental evidence that her English participants conceived of time differently than her Mandarin participants (forward-backward vs. up-down). An issue with this study, however, is that the observed differences are potentially independent of the words that people use to describe the conceptual space. It is simply assumed in these studies that the observed differences must be due to language. A salient alternative is that the differences might be due to the culture, and people in the relevant culture invent metaphors in language for how they think about time. There is no need to appeal to language at all in this causal story.[12]

A third highly cited study from the early 2000s suggests that gender marking in a language drives how we conceive of objects. While English does not mark its nouns for gender, many languages categorize each noun into two or more gender categories, labeled masculine and feminine, if there are two such categories (and neuter for the third). Typical male things like *boy* and *man* will be labeled with masculine gender, and typical female things like *girl* and *woman* will be labeled with feminine gender. Other nouns, which don't have any inherent gender to them (such as table or book), are arbitrarily added to each category. The claim is that a noun with masculine gender will tend to be thought of in traditionally male features, and a noun with feminine gender will tend to be thought of in traditionally female features (Boroditsky et al., 2003). That is, a bridge is masculine in Spanish but feminine in German, so native speakers of each language might conceptualize a bridge as more or less male/female, depending on the language that they speak. While this would be suggestive evidence of a weak effect of language on thought, unfortunately this result has been difficult to replicate (Mickan et al., 2014; cf. Samuel et al., 2019).

9.5 Summary and Conclusion

In this chapter, I have first presented evidence that tasks that require thinking—such as solving a math problem or social reasoning—don't recruit the language network, and that some individuals with severe linguistic impairments can continue to perform such tasks. This suggests that cognition and language are somewhat independent: A lot of what we would categorize as thinking is done without activation in the language network.

Furthermore, it appears that word and syntactic information are represented together throughout the language network: It doesn't appear that we have separate brain areas for representing word meanings and combining words syntactically. Finally, I have shown that languages can differ a lot in the kinds of concepts that they label. This makes the problem of translation difficult for many concepts, especially when translating between languages that are spoken in different cultures. It also means that when we learn a new language well, we learn a new way of dividing up the world: A language can help us think about certain concepts, relative to using another language.

10 Language as Communication

As discussed in chapter 9, the primary function of the language system in the human mind/brain appears to be for communication, not for reasoning about conceptual knowledge. A natural question is then to ask how this language communication system works. The dependency grammar framework is a proposal for how syntactic information is represented, but communication is often noisy. People sometimes make errors when they speak for many kinds of reasons: because they are in a hurry; or they are trying to do many things at once; or they are impaired after drinking alcohol (or ingesting something else); or they are feeling anxious for some reason. Furthermore, comprehension is noisy because the comprehender may have any of the difficulties listed above, and the environment itself is often noisy. In addition, people's representations of the language can be imperfect, if they are just learning the language as children or if they are second-language learners. People use language in all kinds of environments, so communication needs to be robust. As a result, a full approach to language structure and processing must model how people deal with the kinds of errors that they might encounter in their environment. This chapter introduces the noisy-channel approach to language processing and language structure (Shannon, 1948, 1949; Levy, 2008b; Levy et al., 2009; Gibson et al., 2013b). Under this approach, people weigh the language input they perceive against close possible alternatives, under a noise model. They choose the interpretation that is best explained by Bayesian principles, which take into account what people are likely to say, together with a noise model, where edits of the string might be deleted, inserted, altered somehow, or exchanged. This way of thinking of language and language processing has important ramifications for the way that language is structured. In this chapter, I examine the case of word order as an example.

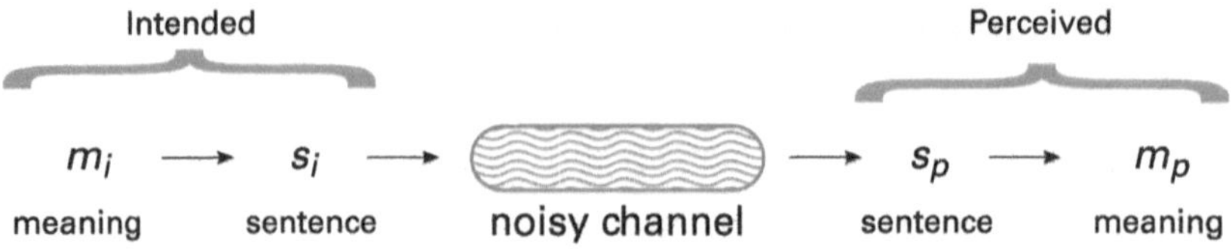

Figure 10.1
Communication across a noisy channel, from Gibson et al. (2013a), following Shannon (1948). Here, the intended sentence s_i and the perceived sentence s_p, need not be identical. As a comprehender, I am trying to guess s_i given what perceive s_p. I may perceive something that is unlikely, and hence I may guess that there was an error on the production side (or in my perception).

10.1 Noisy-Channel Language Processing

Language production and comprehension are inherently noisy processes (Shannon, 1948). People produce sentences in noisy environments under all kinds of conditions, including many circumstances under duress or doing multiple tasks, and they have different knowledge of the language, from beginners (children and second-language learners) to experts. As a consequence, comprehenders must be able to infer what the producer meant (the intended sentence S_i in the formula in (204)), given what the comprehender heard (the perceived sentence S_p). The optimal interpretation process trades off two information sources: what we generally know (called the prior) and what is true in this specific situation. This is what is called a **Bayesian** process, trading off what was literally heard against the **prior probability** of what is likely to be said, as depicted in figure 10.1 (Gibson et al., 2013a; Levy, 2008b; Levy et al., 2009).

(204) $P(S_i|S_p) \propto P(S_i) * P(S_i \rightarrow S_p)$

According to the formula, the probability that a listener will infer sentence S_i given that they perceived sentence S_p is proportional to two things:

1. The **prior** of the intended sentence S_i (in both language and meaning): People are more likely to infer things that people typically say and that typically happen in the world; and
2. The **likelihood** that a producer would accidentally produce S_p given that they wanted to say S_i. This is the noise likelihood. People are more

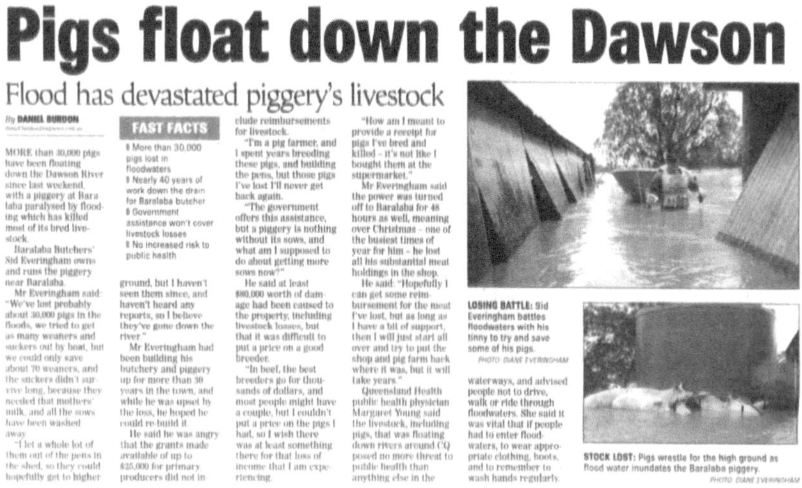

Pigs float down the Dawson

Flood has devastated piggery's livestock

By DANIEL BURDON

FAST FACTS

- More than 30,000 pigs lost in floodwaters
- Nearly 40 years of work down the drain for Baralaba butcher
- Government assistance won't cover livestock losses
- No increased risk to public health

MORE than 30,000 pigs have been floating down the Dawson River since last weekend, with a piggery at Baralaba paralysed by flooding which has killed most of its bred livestock.

Baralaba Butchers' Sid Everingham owns and runs the piggery near Baralaba.

Mr Everingham said: "We've lost probably about 30,000 pigs in the floods, we tried to get as many weaners and suckers out by boat, but we could only save about 70 weaners, and the suckers didn't survive long, because they needed that mothers' milk, and all the sows have been washed away.

"I let a whole lot of them out of the pens in the shed, so they could hopefully get to higher ground, but I haven't seen them since, and haven't heard any reports, so I believe they've gone down the river."

Mr Everingham had been building his butchery and piggery up for more than 30 years in the town, and while he was upset by the loss, he hoped he could re-build it.

He said he was angry that the grants made available of up to $25,000 for primary producers did not include reimbursements for livestock.

"I'm a pig farmer, and I spent years breeding these pigs, and building the pens, but those pigs I've lost I'll never get back again.

"The government offers this assistance, but a piggery is nothing without its sows, and what am I supposed to do about getting more sows now?"

He said at least $80,000 worth of damage had been caused to the property, including livestock losses, but that it was difficult to put a price on a good breeder.

"In beef, the best breeders go for thousands of dollars, and most people might have a couple, but I couldn't put a price on the pigs I had, so I wish there was at least something there for that loss of income that I am experiencing.

"How am I meant to provide a receipt for pigs I've bred and killed – it's not like I bought them at the supermarket."

Mr Everingham said the power was turned off to Baralaba for 48 hours as well, meaning over Christmas – one of the busiest times of year for him – he lost all his substantial meat holdings in the shop.

He said: "Hopefully I can get some reimbursement for the meat I've lost, but as long as I have a bit of support, then I will just start all over and try to put the shop and pig farm back where it was, but it will take years."

Queensland Health public health physician Margaret Young said the livestock, including pigs, that was floating down rivers around CQ posed no more threat to public health than anything else in the waterways, and advised people not to drive, walk or ride through floodwaters. She said it was vital that if people had to enter floodwaters, to wear appropriate clothing, boots, and to remember to wash hands regularly.

LOSING BATTLE: Sid Everingham battles floodwaters with his tinny to try and save some of his pigs. PHOTO: DIANE EVERINGHAM

STOCK LOST: Pigs wrestle for the high ground as flood water inundates the Baralaba piggery. PHOTO: DIANE EVERINGHAM

Figure 10.2

A story from January 6, 2011, about a flood in Australia from *The Morning Bulletin*, an Australian periodical.

likely to produce errors that are in some sense very close to what they intend.

Thus, according to the noisy-channel proposal, people are likely to infer an alternative to the literal interpretation of the string if (a) the literal interpretation is implausible (a low probability over meanings) or if the way that it is phrased is unusual (a low-probability syntactic event) and (b) there is some close alternative that is better in terms of meaning and/or language.[1] My favorite example of a noisy-channel error started with the news story from the Australian newspaper "The Bulletin," where a journalist reported that "More than 30,000 pigs have been floating down the Dawson river," as shown in figure 10.2.

The next day, the same newspaper ran a correction: What the farmer ("piggery owner") Sid Everingham actually said was "thirty sows and pigs," not "thirty-thousand pigs" (see figure 10.3).

This error is a noisy-channel misinterpretation: The sequences "thirty sows and pigs," not "thirty-thousand pigs" are very close, just "s" vs. "th" initially. The sequence "thirty-thousand" is much more common in the language: First, the word "thousand" is much more frequent than the sequence "sows and" (partly because the word "sow" [female pig] is such a

Correction

THERE was an error printed in a story titled "Pigs float down the Dawson" on Page 11 of yesterday's *Bully*.

The story, by reporter Daniel Burdon, said "more than 30,000 pigs were floating down the Dawson River".

What Baralaba piggery owner Sid Everingham actually said was "30 sows and pigs", not "30,000 pigs".

The Morning Bulletin would like to apologise for this error, which was also reprinted in today's *Rural Weekly CQ* before the mistake was known.

Figure 10.3
An error correction on January 7, 2011, from *The Morning Bulletin*, an Australian periodical.

low-frequency word); and this is especially true following the word "thirty": After the word "thirty," the word "thousand" is highly expected, but the word "sows" is not. As a consequence of this large difference in English language usage, the journalist probably mis-heard what was said as something much more expected in English.

There is a second kind of background probability—often called a *prior*, in Bayesian terms—on what we say and how it is interpreted: This is the *meaning* or *semantic* prior. We favor more plausible events over less plausible events, in our experience (see section 2.2.2). Note that the semantic prior favors what the piggery owner intended over the misinterpreted version, because thirty pigs in a river is much more plausible than thirty thousand pigs in a river. Hence, the bias for the implausible meaning shows the strength of the language prior in this case.

10.2 Using Syntactic Alternations to Investigate Noisy-Channel Processing

Gibson et al. (2013a) took advantage of the existence of syntactic alternations within a language in order to figure out some of the details for a possible noise model in language interpretation, within English initially. Syntactic alternations are different syntactic ways to provide the same meaning, such as the active-passive alternation (205a) and (205b), the double-object alternation (205c) and (205d), and different subject-object alternations such as the causative-inchoative alternation for change of state verbs (205e) and (205f) within English (Levin, 1993):[2]

(205) a. Active: The girl kicked the ball.
b. Passive: The ball was kicked by the girl.
c. Prepositional phrase object (PO): The mother gave the candle to the daughter.
d. Double object (DO): The mother gave the daughter the candle.
e. Causative: The dryer shrank the t-shirt.
f. Inchoative: The t-shirt shrank in the dryer.

Language systems provide multiple ways to say the same thing. This way we can start with any of the elements in the target event, and proceed from there. We tend to start with whatever we have been talking or thinking about—old information (the topic of conversation)—and proceed to the new information that we want to convey (Chafe, 1970; Givón, 1984, 1987; Lambrecht, 1994; Birner and Ward, 1998; Clifton and Frazier, 2004). In the case of the active-passive alternation, if we were previously talking about *the girl*, then we might say (205a) for the event *the girl kicked the ball* (or perhaps "she kicked the ball"). But if we had been talking about *the ball*, then we might use the passive structure in (205b). Similarly we might choose either of the two alternatives in the double-object alternation in (205c)/(205d) and one of the two alternatives in the causative-inchoative alternation in (205e)/(205f). Levin (1993) documents hundreds of such alternations in English.

Because there are many such alternations within a language, and because the ways of conveying the same idea involve using different morphology (along with different word order), we can see how different kinds of edits might be associated with noise processes in language production, by using alternations to probe how people might interpret materials that are implausible as presented (Gibson et al., 2013a). To see how this logic works, let's consider implausible versions of the materials in (205):

(206) Implausible active-passive materials:

a. Active: The ball kicked the girl.
b. Passive: The girl was kicked by the ball.
c. Active-passive question: Did the girl kick someone / something?
Literal answer: no

(207) Implausible DO-PO materials:

a. Prepositional phrase object (PO): The mother gave the daughter to the candle.
b. Double object (DO): The mother gave the candle the daughter.
c. DO-PO question: Did the daughter receive something / someone?
Literal answer: no

(208) Implausible Causative-inchoative materials:

a. Causative: The t-shirt shrank the dryer.
b. Inchoative: The dryer shrank in the t-shirt.
c. Causative-inchoative question: Was the dryer shrunken by anything?
Literal answer yes

Each of these examples was generated by simply exchanging two of the noun phrases in the original examples in (205). Each of these examples is literally implausible, according to the word order and morphology as given. For example, it doesn't make any sense for a ball to kick a girl, as in (206a) and (206b). And it doesn't make sense for a mother to give a person (a daughter) to an inanimate object (a candle) as in (207a) and (207b). And finally, it makes no sense for a t-shirt to cause a dryer to shrink as in (208a) and (208b).

Gibson et al. (2013a) presented materials like these to experimental participants and probed the participants' interpretations by asking simple yes-no questions about each, such as the questions presented above. If people interpreted the implausible versions in (206) and (207) literally

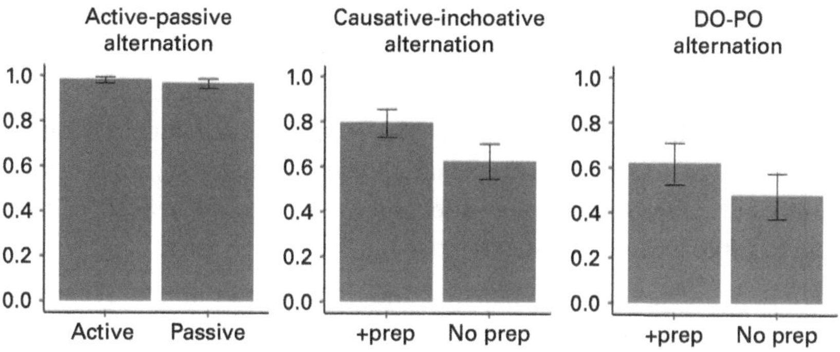

Figure 10.4
Average literal interpretation rates for implausible active-passive alternations; implausible double-object/prepositional-phrase-object alternations; and implausible causative-inchoative alternations, from Gibson et al. (2013a). The y-axis indicates the percent of trials that participants (n = 60 in each) answered the comprehension question according to the syntax (which was an implausible meaning), as opposed to inferring the more plausible alternation. These figures were generated from the data from Gibson et al. (2013a) by Moshe Poliak.

(according to the syntax) then they would have answered "no" to the materials in (206a), (206b), (207a), and (207b), and "yes" to the materials in (208a) and (208b). (These "yes" and "no" answers were counterbalanced across the items for a particular alternation.)

Interestingly, there were substantial differences in how the questions were answered, across the different kinds of materials. People almost always answered the implausible active-passive materials according to the literal (implausible) meaning, so they usually answered "no" to the question "Did the girl kick someone / something?" for the items in (206). But participants were roughly split in how they answered the rest: Sometimes they went with the literal interpretation, and sometimes they inferred the more plausible meaning. See figure 10.4 for the means of these interpretations, across participants and items (sixty participants in each experiment; twenty items in each).

Gibson et al. (2013a) interpreted these differences in interpretations across materials as evidence for a noise model that is sensitive to insertions and deletions of single-function words. In particular, they guessed that implausible materials that were only one deletion or insertion of a function word away from a more plausible interpretation might often be interpreted according to the more plausible interpretation, whereas implausible materials that required two or more deletions or insertions of function words might generally be interpreted literally (implausibly). This idea explains the observed data well: The active/passive materials require two edits to get to a more plausible interpretation (see (209)), whereas the DO-PO and causative-inchoative alternations only require a single edit in order to get to a plausible interpretation.

(209) Implausible materials; potential insertions marked in red; potential deletions are ~~crossed out~~:

a. Active: The ball **was** kicked **by** the girl.
b. Passive: The girl ~~was~~ kicked ~~by~~ the ball.
c. Prepositional phrase object (PO): The mother gave the daughter**to** the candle.
d. Double object (DO): The mother gave the candle ~~to~~ the daughter.
e. Causative: The t-shirt shrank ~~in~~ the dryer.
f. Inchoative: The dryer shrank **in** the t-shirt.

In addition, within the alternations that required only a single edit to get to a plausible interpretation, Gibson et al. (2013a) observed that materials that required a deletion were more often interpreted nonliterally than those that required an insertion of a function word. This effect is highly robust and replicable across this and many other constructions across languages. In figure 10.4, we see that the rate of literal interpretation is higher for each of the +preposition alternatives on the right than the no-preposition alternatives. Gibson et al. (2013a) hypothesize that this effect may be because there are so many ways that one can miss something. In contrast, if a word is present in the input, usually it is there for some purpose. It is impossible to know when something has been missed.

The deletion-insertion noise model works well across the five alternations that Gibson et al. (2013a) examined, which includes ten sets of implausible materials. Gibson et al. (2017b) shows similar results in auditory versions of the materials, and Zhan et al. (2023) shows similar results to Gibson et al. (2013a) for related constructions in Mandarin. Gibson et al. (2013a) also observed that when the background (distractor, or "filler") items had syntactic errors in them, participants' inference rate increased. This provides evidence for the noise component of the rational inference formula proposed in (204): When the noise rate is higher, people make more inferences. Gibson et al. (2013a) also provided some evidence for the semantic prior component of the proposal: When the five alternations were included in one experiment, there was lower inference in each of the implausible sets of materials. That is, when there is some evidence that the producer is producing descriptions of implausible events, people make less inference toward the semantic prior. Similarly, when a supportive context is provided, participants are more likely to make inferences toward the semantic prior (Chen et al., 2022).

Recent research has provided evidence that word exchanges—swaps of words of the same category (Garrett, 1975)—also play an important role in the noise model (Poppels and Levy, 2016; Ryskin et al., 2018), in addition to deletions and insertions. It appears that not all exchanges are equally likely, however: Exchanges across verbs seem less likely than exchanges that do not cross a verb (Poppels and Levy, 2016). This may explain why the exchanges in the active-passive alternation in (206) (which cross a verb) are less likely than the exchange in the DO-PO alternation (207) (which do not cross an intervening verb).

Other recent research has investigated the language prior, in addition to the meaning prior that was investigated by Gibson et al. (2013a). Liu et al. (2021) showed that English and Mandarin speakers make more inferences for rare structures than in common structures, as predicted by the noisy-channel framework. In particular, Liu et al. (2021) showed that people make more inferences in object-subject-verb topicalization structures in both English and Chinese, as in (210):

(210) a. Subject-verb-object, plausible: The boy threw the trash.
b. Object-subject-verb, plausible: The trash, the boy threw.
c. Subject-verb-object, implausible: The trash threw the boy.
d. Object-subject-verb, implausible: The boy, the trash threw.

The topicalized OVS sentence *the boy the trash threw* is similarly implausible as the SVO sentence *the trash threw the boy*, yet people make many more inferences in the rare OVS word order, suggesting a large role for structural prior in language interpretation. Similar results were obtained in Chinese (Mandarin). In addition, Poliak et al. (2024) showed a strong role for the structural prior in Russian OVS vs. SVO word orders, all in plausible materials, thus showing that these inferences obtain with or without the presence of implausible materials.

10.3 Noisy-Channel Processing and Word Order

The typical word orders for simple clauses consisting of a subject (an agent of an action, roughly), a verb, and an object (the patient of the action, roughly) are shown for around 1,200 of the world's languages in figure 10.5, from the World Atlas of Linguistic Structures (WALS) (Dryer, 2013). The languages in the Americas in this map are the native American languages; English is found on England. Red circles are subject-verb-object (SVO) languages, like English. Blue circles are subject-object-verb (SOV) languages, like Japanese. The yellow circles are verb-subject-object (VSO) languages, like Tagalog (Philipino). Notably, there are few diamonds of any color, which represent the remaining three possible orders: object-verb-subject (OVS), verb-object-subject (VOS) and object-subject-verb (OSV).

10.3.1 Generalization 1: Most Languages Have Subjects before Objects

Representing human languages with these six categories is obviously a huge simplification, because the strength of any word order bias varies within the categories. But there are still some obvious generalizations. First, most languages have subjects before objects: SVO, SOV, and VSO languages dominate among the languages with a dominant word order (Greenberg, 1963; MacWhinney, 1977). It is possible that subjects generally occur before objects because people want to talk about themselves and the other humans: These are most salient to us, and we want to start with them (MacWhinney, 1977).

10.3.2 Generalization 2: Most Languages Are SOV or SVO

Secondly, the two most dominant word orders by far are SOV and SVO word orders, accounting for 47.1 percent (SOV) and 41.2 percent (SVO) of languages with a dominant word order. (These are obviously rough percentages, because these statistics don't even account for language relatedness, in the same family. But even if we compare language families, we obtain similar results.)

10.3.3 SOV May Be the Most Natural Word Order

Why might SOV and SVO word orders be the most common among the world's languages? One idea is that SOV word order may be the most "natural" word order for humans, and then SVO word order may be derived from

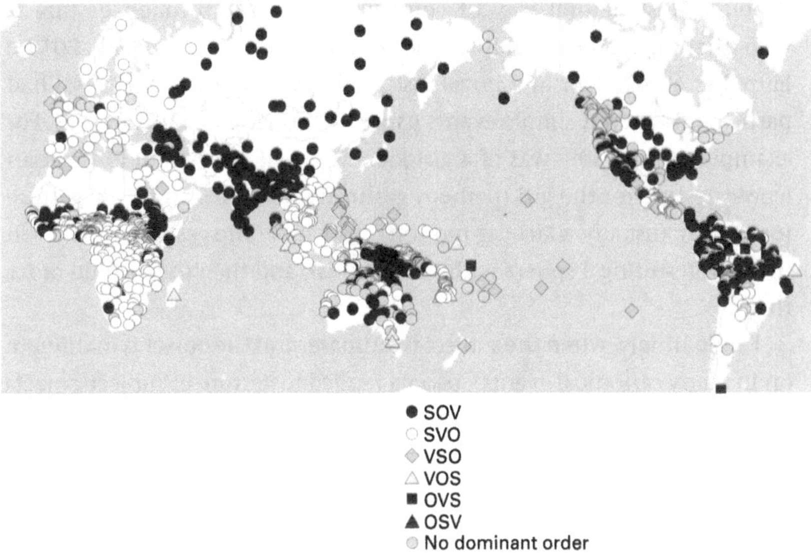

Figure 10.5
Order of subject, object, and verb across the world's languages from the World Atlas of Linguistic Structures (WALS) Map 81 (Dryer, 2013).

SOV word order in some way. Evidence that SOV word order is "natural" in some sense comes from two sources:

- The creation of new sign languages, from a sign language created to communicate at home: a home-sign system (Senghas et al., 2004; Sandler et al., 2005; Meir et al., 2010b). Although there are few such instances, it appears that when a sign language develops from a home-sign system, such languages have tended to be verb-final, as in Nicaraguan Sign Language (Senghas et al., 2004) and Al-Sayyid Bedouin Sign Language (Sandler et al., 2005). The creation of Nicaraguan Sign Language came about as an indirect consequence to a long civil war in Nicaragua, such that people could not go to schools for sign language during the civil war. There are always a small percentage of deaf babies born to hearing parents; these children created an individualizd home-sign system with their parents during the civil was in Nicaragua. When the war was over, the children were able to join together in schools for the deaf for the first time, where their new sign language then developed rapidly among the children.

- People's most natural way of conveying meaning through gesture is verb-final word order (Goldin-Meadow et al., 2008; Gibson et al., 2013b; Futrell et al., 2015a). In a novel task, Goldin-Meadow et al. (2008) had participants act out simple events using their own made-up gestures. For example, if the scene was of a girl kicking a ball, they would invent an iconic gesture for the girl (perhaps gesturing her hair), an iconic gesture for kicking (usually a kicking motion), and an iconic gesture for the ball (usually gesturing a sphere with both hands), and then they would order them.

  Fascinatingly, when the subject is animate, and the object is inanimate (as in many canonical events), people tended to gesture in subject-object-verb word order, independent of the language that the participant spoke. This result is unsurprising for speakers of Turkish (Goldin-Meadow et al., 2008) or Japanese or Korean (Gibson et al., 2013b), whose word order is SOV. But the result is surprising for participants who speak an SVO word order, such as English (Goldin-Meadow et al., 2008; Gibson et al., 2013b), Mandarin or Spanish (Goldin-Meadow et al., 2008), or Russian (Futrell et al., 2015a), and participants who speak a VSO word order, such as Modern Irish or Tagalog (Futrell et al., 2015a).

  Gibson et al. (2013b) and Schouwstra and de Swart (2014) suggest that perhaps the SOV bias is driven by preference to communicate ontologically required elements earlier than elements that build on them. Thus, people would tend to gesture the nouns representing event participants first, followed by the event label (like "kick"). Hence, verbs might come at the end. An interesting prediction of this account is that the type of verb will affect the order of gesture: For verbs that indicate building or construction such as "build" (where the patient nouns don't exist until the event is finished), SVO word order is predicted. This is exactly what Schouwstra and de Swart (2014) found.[3]

10.3.4 Noisy Channel as a Possible Explanation for Why Many Languages Have SVO Word Order

Gibson et al. (2013b) suggest that a possible reason for languages to shift from SOV word order—the word order proposed to be most natural—to SVO word order is to minimize potential confusion surrounding interpreting sentences when some elements are lost through deletion (as they often are). It is proposed that the shift to SVO may occur because SVO word order is more robust to communicating meaning than SOV word order. To see this, suppose we want to convey "girl-agent boy-patient kiss" (the girl kissed the boy) in an SOV vs. SVO language, and suppose that one of the nouns is lost somehow:

(211) Target sentence: "girl-agent boy-patient kiss" (SOV); then a noun is lost

a. SOV word order; girl kiss: girl-agent? or girl-patient?

b. SOV word order; boy kiss: boy-agent? or boy-patient?

(212) Target sentence "girl-agent kiss boy-patient" (SVO); then a noun is lost

a. SVO word order; girl kiss: girl is agent

b. SVO word order; kiss boy: boy is patient

This loss might be because the speaker did not say the word, or because the comprehender could not hear it. Or it could be because the language licenses null arguments, as many languages do.

Critically, verbs are different from nouns: They generally indicate the events and states in a language. The critical difference between SOV and SVO word order is that the location of the verb between the arguments in an SVO language provides more information for who is doing what to whom than SOV word order: In an SVO language, the noun phrase preceding the verb is the agent (subject), and other arguments follow the verb. In contrast, all noun phrases precede the verb in an SOV language, so that the verb placement doesn't provide much information as to who is doing what to whom. Consequently, their location relative to the noun phrases provides a strong cue to meaning. As a result, the noisy-channel framework predicts that languages will shift to SVO word order in order to convey meaning more robustly, all else being equal.

Of course, there are many languages that have SOV word order, so how can this hypothesis be on the right track? According to this framework, there must be some other way to convey the role of a noun relative to a verb in an SOV language: Case-marking provides this information. In most SOV languages, nouns are marked morphologically with their roles relative to a verb: This is case-marking. For example, in Japanese, the nominative marker (subject) is "ga," the accusative marker (object) is "o," and the dative marker (indirect object) is "ni":

(213)

On'na	ga	otoko	ni	ringo	o	ageta
woman	nominative	man	dative	apple	accusative	gave

"The woman gave the apple to the man."

Under the noisy-channel hypothesis, a language can convey meaning about who is doing what to whom in two different ways: via morphology (case-markings) or word order. If a language has SVO word order, it need not have the case-markings; but if a language has SOV word order, it will tend to have case-markings to convey the relevant meanings. This prediction is borne out. For example, Dryer (2002) (responding to Hawkins [2002]) found that 181 of 253 SOV languages (72 percent) have case-marking systems, whereas only 26 of 190 SVO languages (14 percent) have case-marking, a big difference.

Other ramifications of the noisy-channel approach to word order are as follows:

- Languages that shift from SOV to SVO may also lose their grammatical case systems. Old English to modern English is one such example. Old English was a case-marked SOV language, whereas modern English is an SVO language with little case-marking (except on some pronouns).
- Case-marking can be animacy-dependent. This is "differential object," as in, for example, Farsi (Aissen, 2003). In a differential-object marking language, only the animate patient gets marked with a case, presumbably to differentiate it from the subject of the action (as would be useful, under the noisy-channel hypothesis).
- Word order can be animacy-dependent, so called "word order freezing," when case does not disambiguate semantic roles. This happens in Russian, for example, for SVO materials in which the noun cases don't disambiguate thematic role (Bouma, 2011; Jakobson, 1936) and in Kata Kolok, a sign language in northern Bali, Indonesia (Marsaja, 2008; Meir et al., 2010a).

10.4 Rational Inference and Sentence Acceptability

As discussed in section 2.1, a standard assumption in the syntax literature is that the rules of the grammar must generate a string for the string to be fully *grammatical*, or else the string is *ungrammatical*. An interesting question remains regarding strings that are *not* generated by the grammar: Are all of these equally ungrammatical? Under a categorical view of grammaticality, any string that is not generated by the grammar is simply ungrammatical, and there are no distinctions to be made among them. This is clearly a naive view and not a view that researchers pursue seriously. Indeed, grammarians from many theoretical frameworks notate different levels of grammaticality among their materials, from judgments of "?," "??," "?*," "*," and "**" (e.g., Chomsky, 1981, 1986). Hence, I won't consider the categorical possibility further. So one simple model of acceptability (214a) counts the number of errors in order to predict acceptability.

A further observation is that longer sentences tend to get rated as less acceptable, possibly because they are less probable (Lau et al., 2017). Hence, a second simple model of acceptability counts the number of errors and the length of the sentence (214b).

Under a communicative account, we might also consider what sentence was intended and count the number of errors to get to that target sentence. Thus, a third model of acceptability (214c) would count the acceptability of the intended sentence, and the number of errors to get to that, weighted by how much information there is in the target sentence (because longer sentences say much more). A rough proxy of the information in a sentence is its length. So this model of acceptability counts the acceptability of the intended sentence, and the number of errors, weighted by the length of the sentence. I will call this model the rational inference model of acceptability, because it takes into account what sentence was intended and how much information there was in that sentence.

(214) a. Model 1: Acceptability varies with number of errors only:
Rating ~ Errors
b. Model 2: Acceptability varies with number of errors and sentence length:
Rating ~ Errors + Length
c. Model 3: Rational inference model of acceptability: Acceptability varies with number of errors and sentence length:
Rating ~ Errors/Length + Length

A critical prediction of the rational inference proposal (214c) is that as sentences get longer, a single error matters less. For a short sentence, a single error is very damning: People will rate it as bad. But for a long sentence, a single error is much less damaging. The rational inference proposal predicts that for a constant number of errors, sentences should get rated better as they increase in length. None of the other models make this prediction.

Poliak et al. (2025) tested these proposals by having participants rate sentences that they found from the universal dependency corpus (Nivre et al., 2016, 2020; De Marneffe et al., 2021), having three lengths, short (approximately ten words in English), medium (approximately fifteen words), and long (approximately twenty words or more in English), across eight languages. For each sentence, they had people rate four different versions:

1. The original string
2. A version with one pair of adjacent words exchanged
3. A version with three pairs of adjacent words exchanged
4. A version with a random order of the words

Examples of the four versions for short and medium English sentences are provided in (215):

(215) a. Short, original: Currently, we're in talks with people.
b. Short, one exchange: Currently, we're talks in with people.
c. Short, three exchanges: Currently, we're people in talks with.
d. Short, random order: In with currently talks we're people.
e. Medium, original: And then she had to scan and go get the shoes and then she said they didn't have the size.
f. Medium, one exchange: And then she had to scan and go get the shoes and then she said they didn't the have size.
g. Medium, three exchanges: And then she had scan to and go get the shoes and then she said they didn't size have the.
h. Medium, random order: And didn't and size shoes go had get then she scan they to then and have she said the the.

The results from the eight tested languages are presented in figure 10.6. The pattern of results strongly supports the rational inference approach to acceptability. As we can see in each language—Danish, English, French, German, Hindi, Korean, Mandarin and Russian—the intact sentences were rated highest across each of short, medium, and long lengths, with a falling slope in general, across all languages replicating an observation from

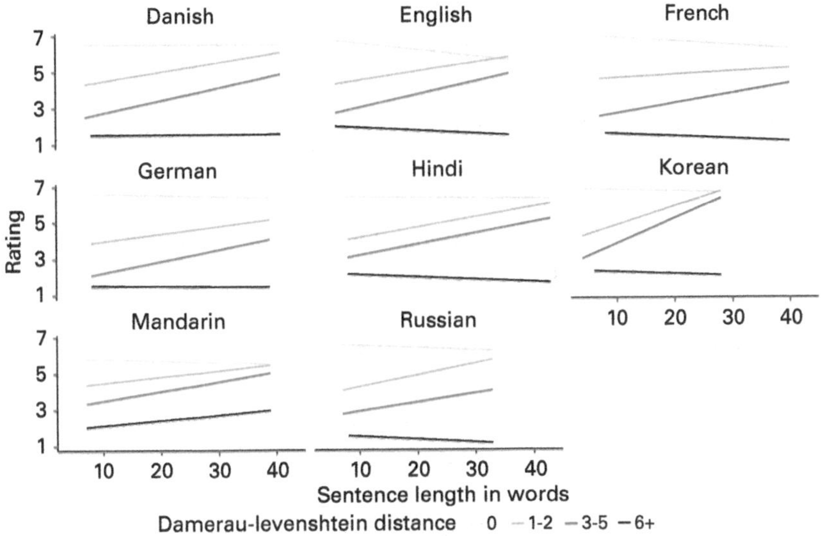

Figure 10.6
The line of best fit for acceptability rating as predicted by sentence length and the Damerau-Levenstein distance, split by language from Poliak et al. (2025), for Danish, English, French, German, Hindi, Korean, Mandarin, and Russian. The distance is the minimal number of words that need to be deleted, inserted, substituted, or transposed with the neighboring word to arrive from the presented sentence to the original sentence that was collected from the UD Treebank. The intact sentences were rated highest across all lengths, with a falling slope in general, across all languages replicating an observation from Lau et al. (2017) for English. The items with only one or two edits were rated next highest, but now with a rising slope according to length across all languages. The materials with three to five edits were rated next highest, again with a rising slope according to length across all languages. Finally, materials with six or more edits—created by scrambling the words in the sentences—were rated lowest, with no slope according to length. These results are as predicted by the rational inference approach to acceptability, but not by any of the other models. Figure generated by Moshe Poliak.

Lau et al. (2017) for English. The items with only one or two edits were rated next highest, but now with a rising slope according to length across all languages. The materials with three to five edits were rated next highest, again with a rising slope according to length across all languages. Finally, materials with six or more edits—created by scrambling the words in the sentences—were rated lowest, with no slope according to length. These results are as predicted by the rational inference approach to acceptability, but not by any of the other models.

10.5 Language Processing: Resource-Rational Lossy-Context Surprisal

The view of language processing that I have provided thus far, starting in chapter 4, is a bit simplistic. I alluded to a potentially deeper explanation of dependency locality in terms of information locality, as suggested by Futrell et al. (2020a). Under this proposal, a dependency between words is a pair of words with relatively high mutual information.

Relatedly, I have presented results consistent with the dependency locality theory in language production and comprehension, but the predictions of the DLT are actually not well supported in reading times on most texts, even in English. In contrast, reading times are roughly as predicted by surprisal theory (Hale, 2001; Levy, 2008a; Smith and Levy, 2013) (see section 2.1.2), except possibly when the materials are highly complex (Grodner and Gibson, 2005). Building on Futrell et al.'s (2020a) lossy-context surprisal proposal, Hahn et al. (2022) present a recent theory—resource-rational lossy-context surprisal—that attempts to unify the best ideas of the two theories to some degree, together with the noisy-channel approach to language.

According to this theory, people's memory for language input is always imperfect for strings longer than a few words. We are unable to remember the exact string correctly, and so we are trying to rationally reconstruct what was probably there, given the statistics of the language. As sentences get longer, we rationally reconstruct what was likely there. For a complex sentence like (216a), we might rationally reconstruct it after encountering *annoyed the patient* to be (216b), or (216c), or (216d):

(216) a. The report that the doctor who the lawyer distrusted annoyed the patient was surprising.

b. The report about the doctor who the lawyer distrusted annoyed the patient . . .
c. The report for the doctor who the lawyer distrusted annoyed the patient . . .
d. The report stated that the doctor who the lawyer distrusted annoyed the patient . . .

This leads to uncertainty as to how the sentence might finish, such that people might not expect any more verbs following *annoyed the patient*. In contrast, if I can remember the context perfectly, then there should be three verb phrases as in (216a). But if I misremember the context as in (216b) or (216c) or (216d), then I may not expect any more verbs to come.

Hahn et al.'s (2022) model calculates the likelihood of retaining each word from the previous context based on the identity of the word, and how recently it appeared in the context. The resulting memory representation—denoted as c′—includes the retained words and a placeholder symbol for the omitted ones. By applying Bayes's rule and leveraging a priori language statistics (from GPT-2; Radford et al., 2019), Hahn et al. (2022) compute a predictive distribution $P(w|c')$ for the next word w. The processing difficulty of w is then determined by its level of unpredictability from c′, quantified as surprisal. The proposal is similar to that of Futrell et al. (2020a), but with a better model of what words are forgotten. Under Futrell et al.'s (2020a) proposal, words are forgotten at random; here, the words that are forgotten are the ones that are most easily reconstructed through the GPT-2 language statistics. Hence, many nonrecent function words are forgotten, and then processing proceeds with a placeholder.

Hahn et al.'s (2022) proposal predicts that the complementizer *that* will often be forgotten in early locations of long complex sentences like (216a). The model may then incorrectly guess that the placeholder associated with *that* might be reconstructed as a preposition like *for* or *about* (as in (216b) or (216c)), which will lead to (a) increased reading times at the verb region, because there is a lot of uncertainty in what words might occur there, and (b) uncertain completions, in a sentence completion task.

This model makes many predictions that surprisal and the DLT do not make, as outlined by Hahn et al. (2022). Let's first look at the predictions regarding language production, as tested by Hahn et al. (2022) in sentence completion studies. Gibson et al. (2011) had shown that English speakers often complete materials like (217a) and (217b) with only two verb phrases, in spite of the fact that such sentence preambles require three verb phrases in order to follow the rules of English:

(217) a. The fact that the doctor who the lawyer ...
b. The report that the doctor who the lawyer ...

In spite of the fact that three verb phrases are technically required to make these materials complete, participants would often complete only two verb phrases, on over half the trials, across people. Hahn et al. (2022) extended Gibson et al.'s (2011) findings by varying the **embedding bias** of the first noun (*fact* in (217a); *report* in (217b)): a noun like *fact* strongly expects a complementizer *that* immediately after it, whereas a noun like *report* does not expect a complementizer following it as strongly. According to the lossy-context surprisal theory, people should forget the early function words (like the early occurrence of *that*), and then they will try to rationally reconstruct them based on corpus statistics. This should enable them to complete sentences starting with an s-complement biased noun like *fact* with three verb phrases more often than with a low-biased noun like *report*. This is exactly what was observed, as shown in figure 10.7, in all three languages. No other theory makes such a prediction. Furthermore, the lossy-context surprisal theory is the only theory that predicts such failures in sentence completions. Neither surprisal nor dependency locality theory makes such a prediction without other assumptions (cf. Gibson and Thomas [1999] for other theories of failures to complete and understand, but none of these theories are viable here).

Let's next compare resource-rational lossy-context surprisal theory to other theories in sentence comprehension. First, consider surprisal theory alone. Surprisal alone is very good at predicting reading times in many simple sentences, such as those in (218):

(218) a. The report was surprising.
b. The fact was surprising.

Following *report* in (218a), a verb is highly expected, and so reading times are predicted to be fast on *was*. In contrast, the complementizer *that* is highly predicted after the noun *fact* in (218b) (because of the particular usage of this word), so that the word *was* is unexpected following *fact*, leading to higher expected reading times on the verb *was*. This is

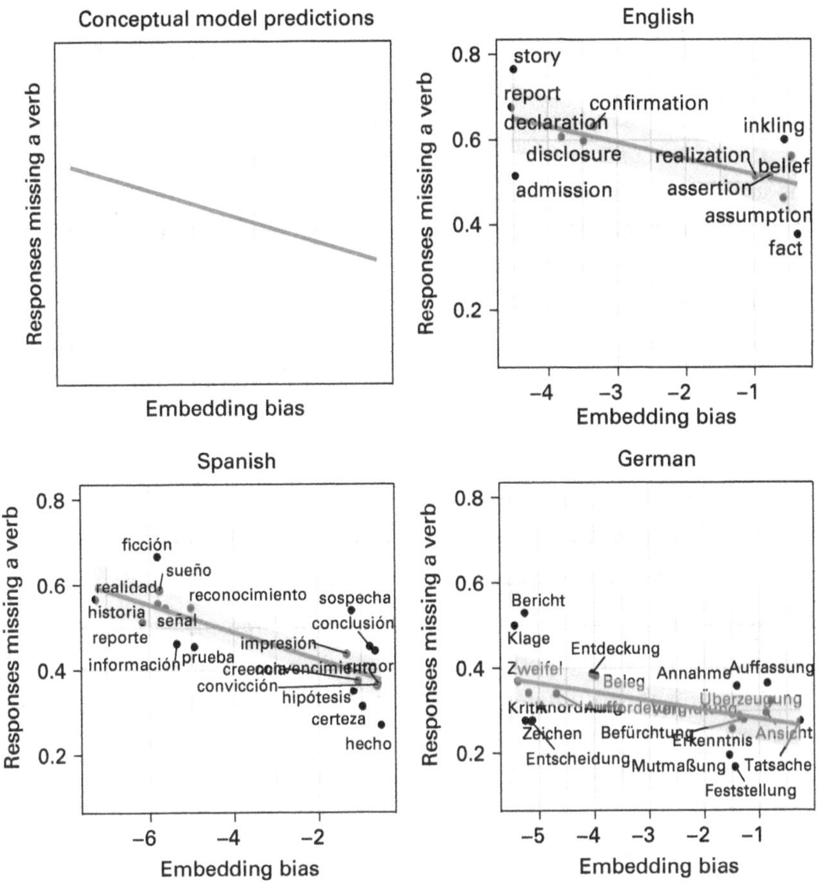

Figure 10.7

The predictions of the resource-rational lossy-context surprisal theory (Hahn et al., 2022) on the number of verb phrases that people will likely complete, given a prompt consisting of three noun phrases connected by complementizers and relative pronouns, such as *The report that the doctor who the lawyer . . .*, followed by results from completion experiments in English, Spanish, and German. The dots in the English, Spanish, and German figures correspond to the first noun in each prompt (e.g., *fact* and *report*). The x-axis is a log-transformed probability of the noun in an item being followed by *that* in English (or similar complementizer in Spanish or German) in the language statistics. The lossy-context surprisal theory predicts that people will forget the complementizers and rationally reconstruct the initial sequence when completing, so that people complete three verb phrases more often for sequences in which the first noun is biased to take a complementizer (like *fact*). This prediction was borne out in three languages: English, Spanish, and German. Only the resource-rational lossy-context surprisal theory makes this prediction. Furthermore, the lossy-context surprisal theory is the only theory that predicts such failures in sentence completions. Figure generated by Michael Hahn.

exactly the pattern that occurs (Levy, 2008a; Smith and Levy, 2013; Hahn et al., 2022). Lossy context-surprisal correctly makes the same predictions as surprisal on these simple cases, because no words are forgotten. In contrast, the dependency locality theory incorrectly predicts no difference between (218a) and (218b) at *was*, because the connection in both is equally local.

Now let's return to the complex case in (216a), repeated here as (219a), and compare how it is processed relative to (219b), where the initial noun *report* is replaced with the noun *fact*:

(219) a. The report that the doctor who the lawyer distrusted annoyed the patient was surprising.
b. The fact that the doctor who the lawyer distrusted annoyed the patient was surprising.

In these cases, people process the words *was surprising* very slowly. First, the simple surprisal theory incorrectly predicts fast reading times in both sentences, with no difference between the two, because a verb is highly expected in the veridical sentence in each. In contrast, the slow reading times are as expected by the dependency locality theory, because there is a long-distance connection between *was* and *report* (or *fact*) in each. But, contrary to the DLT, *was surprising* is processed more slowly in (219a) than in (219b): This is not predicted by the DLT because the distance back is the same in each.

Here, the lossy-context surprisal theory of Hahn et al. (2022) makes the right prediction: The verb was is processed more quickly in (219b) because when the word that is forgotten, it can be more easily reconstructed by language statistics than in (219a). Hence, a verb like was is more expected in (219b) than in (219a), and the reading times are correctly predicted. These predictions of the three theories and data from an on-line reading experiment are presented in figure 10.8.

10.6 Conclusion

In this final chapter I have suggested that although dependency locality makes the right broad kinds of predictions for reading times for long-distance connections, it does so for somewhat the wrong reasons: What

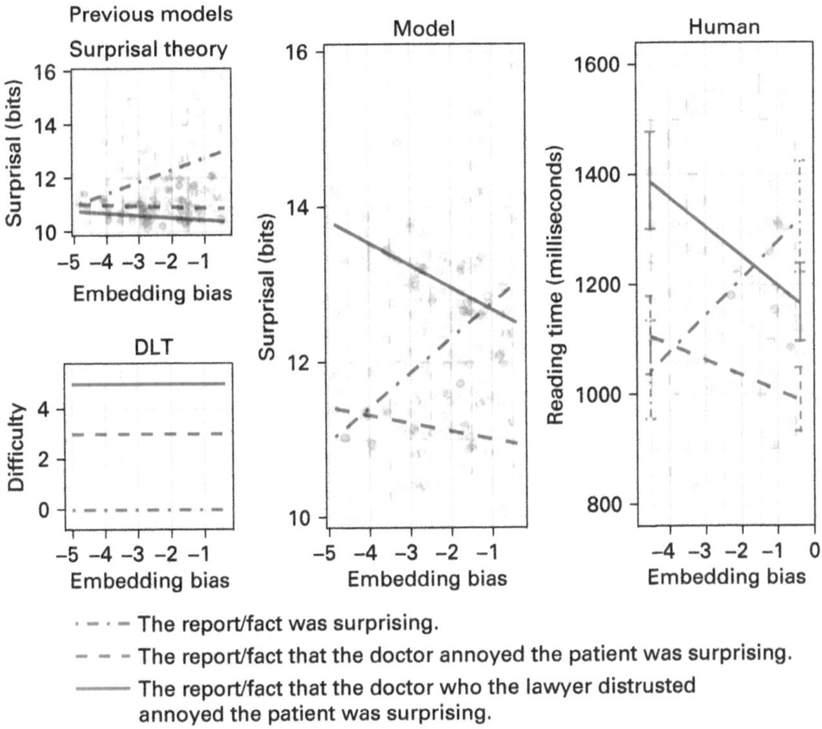

Figure 10.8

Predictions of three theories on three kinds of materials at the verb *was* (the second last word of each sentence): (a) simple sentences, (b) sentences with one embedded clause, and (c) sentences with doubly center-embedded clauses. The x-axis is a log-transformed probability of the first noun in an item being followed by *that* in English (such as *fact* vs. *report*). The dots in the figures correspond to the first noun in an item (e.g., *fact* and *report*). The predictions of surprisal theory (Hale, 2001; Levy, 2008a) are as shown on the top left: flat, fast reading times (low surprisal) for all versions except for the simple sentences with nouns that expect an embedded clause, like *fact* (nouns with *low embedding bias*). The predictions of the dependency locality theory (Gibson, 2000)) are as shown on the bottom left: fast reading times for the simple sentences, slower for the single embedded sentences, and slowest for the doubly embedded sentences, for all embedding bias nouns. The predictions of the resource-rational lossy-context surprisal theory (Hahn et al., 2022) are in the center above. RTs are predicted to pattern like simple surprisal for the simple sentences and singly-embedded versions, because none of the material will be forgotten. RTs are predicted to be very different from surprisal theory's predictions for the doubly embedded clauses, because the function words (such as *that*) are likely to be forgotten and mistakenly reconstructed as more likely connectives (like a preposition *for*). Furthermore, the complementizer *that* will be more likely to be reconstructed for high-embedding bias nouns like *fact*, leading to lower surprisals (and lower RTs) for the verb *was* in these cases compared to complex sentences initiated by nouns with low-embedding biases like *report*. The predictions of the lossy-context surprisal theory better match the observed human reading time data on the right than any of the other theories. Figure generated by Michael Hahn.

really appears to be going on is that the details of early words are forgotten, and long reading times result from people's mismatched expectations at the locations where long-distance connections would need to be made if people could remember the input veridically. Although dependency locality is therefore in some sense probably wrong, it is very similar to the forgetting component of resource-rational lossy-context surprisal theory: people are forgetting key components of earlier syntax, which essentially amount to long-distance connections that need to be made. So although dependency locality is probably the wrong mechanism underlying sentence comprehension, it serves as a rough approximation to the lossy-context forgetting component of what is probably a more correct theory of language processing.

11 Final Thoughts

Depending on when you read this, large language models may have become the norm, and so you may take them as background information, and not terribly exciting. But as someone who has been working on human language for several decades (starting in 1985, when I went to Cambridge University to learn computational linguistics),[1] I find their ability to produce essentially perfect English highly impressive. How do LLMs perform so well? I suggest here that part of the reason that they are so successful is that the underlying structure of a human language is **deceptively simple**: We know lots of words (something like fifty thousand for an educated English speaker; Brysbaert et al., 2016) and we know lots of simple rules for combining them: simple dependency structure combinations. That's pretty much it. Yes, human language is complex, but that is mostly due to the volume of the words and combinations. Any particular sentence is easy to structure.

The view of grammar that I have advocated for is a simple theory based on dependencies between words: **dependency grammar** (Tesnière, 1959; Hays, 1964; Mel'čuk, 1988; Hudson, 1984, 2015; Tesnière, 2015; Osborne, 2019; De Marneffe and Nivre, 2019; De Marneffe et al., 2021; Nefdt and Baggio, 2023). This grammar framework has its roots in the way that humans represent and process language: A dependency between words is a pair of words x and y with high mutual information, such that x occurs immediately next to y more than as predicted by simply sampling the two words' probabilities (independent of where they occur) (Futrell et al., 2020a). Current large language models represent dependency structure (Manning et al., 2020). So maybe a reason large language models do so well is that this is the right structure for a human language.

This simple framework predicts a cognitive cost when words that need to be connected get further apart. I have talked about this in terms of **dependency locality** (Gibson, 1998, 2000), which might more generally be thought of as **information locality** (Futrell et al., 2020a). The cognitive costs associated with connecting widely separated words are measurable in how people tend to order words in a language (Temperley, 2007), and in how they process words in complex structures, and in the activation in the high-level language areas of the brain (Shain et al., 2022). Furthermore, dependency locality cost is a plausible explanation for so-called "harmonic" word orders across languages (Greenberg, 1963; Dryer, 1992), such that word orders in different kinds of constructions align within a language in the same head direction (also called the head-direction generalization). For example, languages with head-first word order in one kind of dependency relationship (such as a verb-object dependency) tend to have matching head-first word order in other dependency relationships, such as in prepositional-object word order or subordinator-verb word order. It turns out that minimizing dependency lengths within a language leads to a bias for these effects. So for example, in English we have *Gretzky scored the goal* and *Gretzky passed the puck to Lemieux*. The verbs come before the objects: *The goal* comes after the verb *scored*, and *the puck* and *to Lemieux* come after the verb *passed*. And we have prepositions in English: We say ***to** Lemieux, **near** the goal, **about** the topic*, and so on. In a verb-final language like Japanese or Hindi (or any of the other 2,500+ languages like that), they tend to have postpositions. This correlation works for 95 percent of the observed languages: about 940 of 980 languages for which we have data (of the seven thousand in existence).

If the structure of language is so simple, why has it taken so long to figure this out? The first large-ish scale grammars for a language started with Chomsky (1957). My suspicion is that Chomsky has been overly influential in making guesses about the structure of language. While his initial contributions are undeniable—in being one of the first to work out the mathematics underlying formal language theory, and proposing the first **phrase structure grammar**—I think he was incorrect in his claim that human language involves hidden **movement** of words and phrases, from a deeper structure to a surface structure (and beyond). His intuition was that movement is the obvious way to treat auxiliary verbs in English, for example: The interrogative sentence *Will Gretzky pass the puck?* is derived from the declarative sentence *Gretzky will pass the puck*, in Chomsky's view. While this sounds like a simple assumption, Chomsky himself observed that this assumption leads to a learning problem, such that it's hard to figure out what the underlying rules are, and which elements have been moved (Chomsky, 1971). Instead of abandoning movement—which is causing the learning problem—Chomsky proposed that aspects of movement and the rules are innate: the **universal grammar** (UG) hypothesis.

An alternative, which Chomsky didn't adequately consider, is that there just might be two different lexical entries for an auxiliary verb like *will*: one for declarative use, for which the subject comes first, then the following main verb; and one for interrogative, which itself comes first, followed by the subject noun then the main verb. It is possible that there is a **lexical copying rule**, such that the interrogative is copied from the declarative when the interrogative is used (Sag et al., 1999; Kim and Sag, 2002; Müller et al., 2021). This analysis of auxiliary verbs doesn't have the underlying learning problem that Chomsky noted, because what we see (or hear) is what we get: The analysis is just the words, in a connected tree, with no hidden elements. This analysis has the added advantage of correctly predicting that the lexical copying rule might not apply to all auxiliary verbs: People have to use it for the rule to apply. If people don't say that, then it's not ok. So some auxiliary verbs only work in the declarative, like *ought* for most American and Canadian English speakers: *Gretzky ought to pass to Lemieux* is fine; But *Ought Gretzky to pass to Lemieux?* is not possible for most American and Canadian English speakers (including me; it sounds totally wrong to me). This contrast is difficult to explain in the movement account: Why does the movement apply sometimes but not always?

Large language models effectively model dependencies between words, together with the typical usage of each construction. English is well covered by these models. Are these models good theories of the grammar? They are arguably the most thorough, because they can adequately predict what an English speaker can say. But such a theory is probably overly complex. Dependency grammar offers a much simpler theory of many aspects of grammar.

Furthermore, although Large language models effectively represent the **form** of English, we should keep in mind that the form of a language and its meaning are distinct. Large language models do not represent meaning, only form (Mahowald et al., 2024). There is a growing literature that shows that human language is a communication system that translates thought into a mode that others can understand: language. But language is entirely distinct from thought (Fedorenko et al., 2024b). Ev Fedorenko's lab has now shown convincingly that the cortical brain areas that support human language don't engage in any other tasks (Fedorenko et al., 2011; Ivanova et al., 2020; Fedorenko et al., 2024a). These are domain-specific regions that seem to specialize for high-level language production and comprehension. Thus while large language models might adequately represent the English language, they don't represent the meanings that people might want to say. And because languages lexicalize concepts in different ways, the problem of translation cannot easily be solved by large language models, without massive training in each language. A case of extreme difficulty in translation is for concepts without corresponding forms in a language. For example, the language Pirahã has no exact count words whatsoever. Consequently, translating a concept like "five," "eleven," or even "one" into Pirahã is next to impossible.

Finally, we should keep in mind that dependency locality is a rough approximation for what is probably really going on in language production and comprehension: Dependency locality is probably explained by **information locality** (Futrell et al., 2020a). And as suggested by Hahn et al. (2022), we humans have imperfect memory of the forms that we are both producing and comprehending. We only have a perfect memory for a few words back in what we have said and what we are hearing or reading. Of course, the meaning gets incorporated into our conceptual knowledge, when possible. But the specific forms are not retained long at all. Consequently, we are always rationally reconstructing what we just heard or said. We remember the most salient words—the content words—and we are making our best guess about the words that can usually be rationally reconstructed from the context: the function words. Because our memory is imperfect, this process sometimes results in errors of production and comprehension: We can see hints of the mechanisms of language production and comprehension when the language material is complex.

Acknowledgments

I started writing this book because Ev Fedorenko asked me to write an introductory article on syntax for her collaborating researchers, who often had a computer science or psychology background but no linguistics background. I had been teaching syntax in my cognitive science and psycholinguistics lab classes for many years, but I never used a reading, because I didn't think that the available readings were quite right. I wanted to use dependency grammar, because it is so simple, but the dominant theories with prominent connections in cognitive science were all phrase structure based. So I would teach mostly phrase structure grammar. As I started to write what I thought would be a review article, the project grew and grew, as I added more context to make it interpretable in the broader field. In the end, it is kind of a textbook, kind of a general introduction to my field of psycholinguistics-focused syntax.

Thanks **first** to Ev: She motivated this book. Ev is of course a major figure in the field of language and brain/mind: She was the lead on many findings that help dissociate language—a communication system—from thought (some of which is surveyed in chapter 9). **Second**, I want to thank Steve Piantadosi, who helped structure much of the first and third chapters, and the book overall. Steve gave lots of important advice about how to make this work understandable to a broad audience. **Third**, I want to thank Dick Hudson, the inventor of Word Grammar, one of the primary dependency grammar formalisms in the field. Dick was incredibly generous with his time and energy, offering detailed feedback on everything I wrote, always with a positive welcoming spirit. I wish all syntacticians were like Dick.

There are many others who were immensely helpful in this project. Richard Futrell helped me early on in this project in details of dependency grammar and grammar in general. Ray Jackendoff read an early draft and pointed out several limitations and weaknesses, which I tried to address. I hope he likes the result. Yanis de Cunha provided me comments on an early draft, which gave me insights from the features in head-driven phrase structure grammmar that I was able to incorporate into my dependency grammar analyses. Thank you, Yanis. My student Moshe Poliak read two full drafts and commented on every detail. I greatly appreciate his careful attention.

Jack Hawkins, Martin Haspelmath, Frank Mollica, Doug Jones, Sihan Chen, and Joakim Nivre each read late complete drafts and offered many helpful suggestions. Michael Hahn gave valuable feedback on all the dependency length minimization work, and how best to present his and Richard Futrell's communication-based theory (in section 10.5). Tim Osborne gave useful feedback on the dependency grammar chapter. Rui Chaves provided me help in understanding a phrase-structure account of English auxiliary verbs, whose insights I have adapted here. Mike Frank and Rachel Ryskin helped me to reorganize parts of the language and thought chapter. Adam Przepiórkowski gave me detailed feedback on chapters 1–3, helping me to fix some "chaotic" structure (I hope). Cory Shain gave helpful comments on phrase structure grammars. Kyle Mahowald and Roger Levy gave feedback on the early chapters, giving much to think about. Michael Ramscar, Giuseppi Ricciardi, Johanna Nichols, Greta Tuckute, and Hope Kean provided me useful comments on the early chapters. And my psycholinguistics lab class from 2023—especially Catherine Mei, Quinn Langford, Kristy Lin, Emma Chabane, Shaunticlair Ruiz, Amanda Tong, Jimmy Chen, Curtis Chen, Diego Ureña, Ruihua Mao, and Pip Engeriser—found lots of errors, which I hope I got rid of.

Notes

1 Introduction

1. Pāṇini proposed a structure for Sanskrit, a now-extinct Indo-European language, the sacred language of Hinduism.

2. There is actually some small amount of information in the sounds associated with meaning, sometimes called *onomatopoeia* or *iconic* meaning (Blasi et al., 2016).

3. Although it makes my naive initial categorization a bit more complicated, there is a actually lot of structure (grammar) in the words themselves (e.g., Langacker 1987; Jackendoff 1997; Jackendoff and Audring 2020). For example, idiomatic expressions (like *beat around the bush*, or *go down in flames*, or *jump on the bandwagon*) have a lot of structure in them. The memorized sequences (along with their meanings) are defined as the lexicon.

4. Glottolog (as of 2023) lists eleven thousand dictionaries (https://glottolog.org/langdoc/complexquery?languoids=&doctypes=dictionary). While many of these dictionaries are small, there are also many large dictionaries, even of smaller languages.

5. I restrict this observation to languages from industrialized cultures, only because we know much more about such languages. This may also be true for languages from nonindustrialized cultures.

6. Some researchers use the term *utterance* to mean a complete communicative unit, and they restrict the use of the word *sentence* to utterances that also have a verb in them. Thus, complete conversational turns like *Yes*, *No*, *Hello*, or *Good morning* would not count as sentences, but would count as utterances. I will use the less formal usage *sentence* here for all of these, just to avoid excessive terminology.

7. A more general way to think about these combinatorial messages is that the connections may signal **more informative** messages, without necessarily being compositional of the meanings of the parts. I sidestep meaning here, so either way to think of meaning will work here; cf. Ramscar (2021).

8. It is actually difficult to work out the meaning of an individual word or morpheme. Words and morphemes are created through a need to communicate some idea in the world. Because the ideas that people want to talk about are complex and vary from situation to situation, the meanings of words are not formally defined (contrary to a popular belief). See section 9.4.1 for more on this issue.

9. Some nouns can refer to more abstract concepts like *fact*, *wealth*, *junk*, or *justice*.

10. For non–North American readers, *NBA* refers to the *National Basketball Association*, the men's professional league in the US and Canada.

11. There is actually a third interpretation in English "headlinese," such that *protect* is the main verb in a main clause corresponding roughly to *Toronto law will protect squirrels*. The meaning of this interpretation is close to the meaning in the second dependency structure above.

12. These are the names of the LLM products as of 2024; the names will keep changing over time.

13. https://en.wiktionary.org/wiki/theory

14. There was one small difference between the BERT-annotated structure and the hand-annotated version: In the hand-annotated version, there was a dependency between the word *by* and the three-letter short form *RTC*; whereas in the BERT-annotated version, the dependency from the word *by* connected to the immediately following word *the*.

15. See Evans and Levinson (2009) for arguments that individual languages are just "engineering solutions" to competing functional pressures.

2 Preliminaries: Components of Language Structure

1. There is another sense of "generative," which is to be associated with a proposal from Chomsky and colleagues. The reason for this conflation is probably that the first generative framework was provided by Chomsky (1957). Other non-Chomskyan frameworks are certainly generative in the original definition, as is the current framework.

2. Researchers are sometimes bothered by the use of intuitions as data. For example, (Chomsky, 1962, p. 22) (from Schütze, 1996) said the following: "I dislike reliance on intuition as much as anyone. ... We should substitute rigorous criteria just as soon as possible, instead of clinging to intuition." But I disagree: There is nothing wrong with intuitions, as data. Although acceptability judgments capture the influences of many factors (to be discussed in this section) and therefore require careful construction of the materials to isolate the factor of interest, these measurements are extremely robust, much less noisy than reaction times (for example).

3. In practice, it does not matter much what kind of scale we use when measuring acceptability: Binary scales (acceptable versus unacceptable), fixed scales from 1 to 5, from 1 to 7, or from 1–10, sliding bar scales, with more possible values in between two endpoints, and even unbounded scales are all commonly used in the literature (Weskott and Fanselow, 2011; Schütze and Sprouse, 2013; Sprouse et al., 2013). Ratings on these scales are highly correlated across materials and experiments.

It might seem that one might get more precision with a wider scale (even an unbounded one), but in practice this is not true. The limitation for a participant is not the specific rating for an item; it is comparing the item to all the other items in the experiment. If there are eighty items in the experiment, it's difficult to remember which item received which rating, even if there are only seven or five or two choices. The easiest way to do this task is to simply do each rating independently on one's own language model and not worry about consistency.

As a result of the difficulty of remembering all the sentences and performing all the relevant comparisons, any scale works equally well, across many participants (e.g., more than about twenty), even the simplest binary scale (good vs. bad).

4. There is a second sense of the distinction between competence and performance, which I think everyone agrees on. This is the distinction between knowledge (another form of competence) and use. It is possible to know something, but not be able to access the information: We would then have competence with the knowledge, without being able to use the information in a particular task or situation. The tip-of-the-tongue phenomenon is evidence of such a distinction: We can know that a word exists, and even know a lot about the form of the word, and not be able to access it. People can have implicit knowledge of different aspects of language, and might not be able to use such knowledge in some situations.

5. This is perhaps a special case of Hick's Law in decision-making, where people take logarithmically more time as the number of choices increases (Hick, 1952).

6. The N400 is a negative going EEG waveform, peaking at about 400 msec after the onset of the surprising stimulus. It is measured on the scalp, in microvolts, as people process language (Kutas and Hillyard, 1980; Kutas and Federmeier, 2011).

7. Briefly, the main differences between the more complex (27) and less complex examples in (33) are as follows:

a. The main clause subject is animate (the boy) in (27), while the main clause subject is inanimate in (33) (the book, the cake). Having these nouns as inanimate makes them easier to process as patients of the embedded relative clause verb in (33) (met and baked).
b. The most embedded relative clause has a full noun phrase agent in (27) (the cat), whereas the same position is a pronoun in (33a) and the relative pronoun serves as the subject in (33b) and (33c). Having a full noun phrase may make these structures difficult to process (Gibson, 1998).

Each of these factors makes the examples in (33) easier to understand than (27). We discuss these factors in more depth in chapter 4.

8. The metaphor relies on the existence of the idiom "to lead someone up the garden path," which means to fool someone somehow. Thanks to Dick Hudson for explaining this to me, only thirty-five years after I first heard the expression "garden-path effect."

9. Another related example is the "Moses Illusion," where an experimental participant is asked *How many of each type of animal did Moses take on the ark?* (Erickson and Mattson, 1981; Barton and Sanford, 1993; Wang et al., 2009). The trick or illusion is that it wasn't Moses who took animals on the ark at all; it was Noah. But because the question is worded in this way—with the animals mentioned first—people often don't notice the oddness is asking about Moses, another biblical old man.

3 Dependency Grammar

1. Some exceptions are certain prepositions like *of*, which are called "case-marking" prepositions, in phrases like *the destruction of Rome* and *the capital of Canada*. Other prepositions can also have no meaning, such as *in* or *on* in cases like *Lana believed in something* and *Lana relied on something*. Another kind of exception might be the word *it*, in a sentence like *it's raining*; this word is called a "dummy" or "expletive" and doesn't really have meaning.

2. In general, the meanings of prepositions sometimes end up as endings on nouns called **case-markers** in other languages. English doesn't have case-markers except on its pronouns: Other nouns are pronounced in the same way whether they are in subject (nominative) position or object (accusative) positive in English. But in a case-marking language like Japanese, the nouns have an ending that indicates its position relative to the verb. So in English, when we say *Mary sees John* or *John sees Mary*, the nouns *John* and *Mary* are pronounced the same way whether they precede or follow the verb. In Japanese, the verb comes at the end of the clause, and the nouns are marked with cases to indicate their roles relative to the verb: The subject is marked with nominative case (*-ga* in Japanese), and the object is marked with accusative case (*-o* in Japanese).

3. Many languages don't even have a word corresponding to *the*, so second-language speakers of English may sometimes use this word incorrectly, or they may express frustration at why English even bothers lexicalizing this idea, when it's clear from the context. For example, Russian does not mark definiteness of nouns, so a Russian speaker may sometimes use the English definite determiner in contexts where a native English speaker would not.

4. Like all natural languages, English is always changing. The pronouns *they* and *them* can also be singular for many speakers nowadays.

5. The notation I use here is compressed and, hence, sometimes a little confusing. Here, the category N is compatible with either count or mass features (a disjunction), whereas in most cases above, the elements are conjunctions of features that are associated with a word. I leave it to the context to resolve this ambiguity of presentation.

6. This is not to be confused with the high-definition multimedia interface (other HDMI) hypothesis, which says that it's hard to find the right cable to connect your computer to the big screen.

7. Traditionally, languages have been divided into types according to aspects of their morphology. One division that has been proposed is the division between **synthetic** and **analytic** languages with respect to the amount and type of morphology in words in them. Analytic languages like English are proposed to convey meaning using word order and auxiliary words, whereas synthetic languages convey grammatical meaning using morphological marking. But one eminent typologist—Martin Haspelmath (personal communication, 2024)—suggests that these divisions don't seem to account for real differences among languages, so I will not discuss them further here.

8. There are syntactic approaches that have tried to unify syntactic components and aspects of reference, e.g., Chomsky's government and binding theory (Chomsky, 1981), but there have never been behavioral measures linking syntactic processes with referential processes, as far as I am aware.

9. Another way that nouns, verbs, and adjectives distinguish themselves from other categories in a language is that they can all be the main point of a sentence, whereas the function words and affixes generally cannot (Boye, 2023). Thanks to Martin Haspelmath for pointing this out to me.

10. In British English, the inversion rule also applies to main verb *have*:

(i) a. Ollie has a squirrel.
b. Has Ollie a squirrel?

As a speaker of Canadian and American English, the inverted form of *have* isn't something I would say, but I recognize that speakers of British English might say this.

11. (62b) is fine in the dialect of older British speakers. Usage allows this.

12. Or anything that expresses a location.

13. Dick Hudson, who has read many drafts of this book, really dislikes the word "complementizer." I can't say that I blame him, because it is such an obscure term. But

it is more standard in much North American terminology, so I stick with it here. Moreover, Martin Haspelmath notes that in his dialect, a complementizer is a particular kind of subordinator. An adverbial subordinator such as "although" is a subordinator, but not a complementizer. In any case, I will use the two terms interchangeably here.

14. Note that a phrase in dependency grammar is the head plus all its dependents. So a verb phrase in dependency grammar would include dependents that precede the verb. These are not traditionally part of a verb phrase in phrase structure terms: The subject noun phrase is treated differently there. See section 7.3 for more on phrase structure grammar.

4 Dependency Locality in Language Processing

1. In sign languages, some words can be produced together, using different hands or positions on the face and body. But still, some connections must be made over time.

2. We haven't seen particles yet: They are like prepositions that don't take noun phrases after them.

3. Older versions of Hawkins's proposals seem to not make such predictions, and are perhaps more in line with dependency locality (Hawkins, 1990, 1994). I encourage the interested reader to delve into Hawkins's work.

4. An alternative possibility that remains to be evaluated is that there may be a pressure on language production to produce the easiest material first MacDonald (2013). This alternative would predict that all languages will show a short-before-long bias in language production.

5. See http://www.anvari.org/fortune/Quotations_-_Stupid/272.

6. The materials from Levy et al. (2012) were slightly longer versions of these sentences, for use in self-paced reading, so that the critical region at the main verb phrase was not at the end of the sentence (where we often get long reading times, for independent reasons).

7. In addition, Grodner and Gibson (2005) did not include the dependencies between the head noun (*reporter* here) and the head of the relative clause (the verb *sent* in this case), which lowers the difference between subject- and object-extracted relative clauses. That is, if we include those dependencies, then the difference between the two is predicted to be even larger at the verb *sent*. It is conservative to leave these out (as Grodner and Gibson [2005] did), so I will leave them out here from the computation too. Furthermore, as discussed in section 4.7, Shain et al. (2022) proposes that the expectations from the head noun *reporter* and the relative pronoun *who* might be collapsed into a single expectation for a verb (the verb *sent* in this case), so there might be only a single cost for matching this expectation.

8. And an extra ten units for the relative clause modifier connection between executive and worried, if we are counting these (cf. footnote 7).

9. Partial theories of on-line processing were not evaluated, such as Frazier's minimal attachment and late closure ambiguity resolution strategies (Frazier, 1979; Frazier and Rayner, 1987), or Gordon and colleagues' theories of interference-based retrieval difficulty (Gordon et al., 2001, 2004, 2006).

10. It also includes a relative pronoun *which*.

11. Shain et al. (2022) were also investigating where in the brain complex language might be processed: in the language cortex or in the multiple demands cortex. Briefly, the language cortex responds more strongly to more language-like stimuli, and the multiple demands cortex responds more strongly when tasks are more difficult, across a range of tasks. These brain areas are discussed in more detail in chapter 9.2.

5 Dependency Length Minimization as a Constraint on Grammars

1. Well before the development of tagged and parsed electronic corpora of diverse languages in the modern era, Hawkins (1994) developed manual corpora for a diverse set of ten languages—English, Finnish, German, Greek, Hungarian, Japanese, Korean, Polish, Romanian, Turkish—and documented minimal lengths for head and modifier combinations, and a gradient preference for short phrasal combination domains in all of them, which he discussed in terms of "Early Immediate Constituents" and later the "Minimize Domains principle," which relabels EIC and subsumes it under a more general efficiency claim holding for all structural domains.

2. The fact that Korean, Kurmanji, and Uyghur score poorly on DLM may have to do with the fact that they score very well on information locality, which isn't exactly the same as DLM, as Hahn and Xu (2022) suggest.

3. With the exception of the interrogative version of the rule.

4. A different hypothesis for the source of the harmonic orders comes from Culbertson and Kirby (2016), who suggest that it is easier for **learners** to consistently order dependents relative to heads. This is an interesting possibility that I don't explore further here. Clearly there are learning constraints as well as processing constraints on what languages might be learnable.

A very different hypothesis comes from Chomsky's Universal Grammar (UG) research group, such that the grammar is innately specified, and children set parameters when they are exposed to their native language (Chomsky, 1980b; Gibson and Wexler, 1994; Roberts, 1997, 2023). The proposal is that there is a parameter for argument-head relationships (head-first vs. head-final) and another for subject-verb word order. It is proposed that languages tend to be head-first or head-final because of the setting of the argument-head parameter.

Although this proposal can account for the particular tendencies that we see in this chapter, it is not really an explanation: It is simply descriptive of the observation that argument-head orders tend to go together (the harmonic generalization). Furthermore, this approach predicts no violations, which is clearly not the case: There are many cases of violations within particular languages, as would be expected if many distinct continuous pressures caused word order, under the current approach. Moreover, the parameter setting approach doesn't generalize to other properties of language. I worked extensively on the parameter-setting research program starting with Gibson and Wexler (1994), and my collaborators (Stefano Bertolo and Ken Wexler) and I built a parameter space based on many linguistic hypotheses from the Chomskyan ("generative") literature. But the resulting parameter space had billions of potential languages, almost none of which actually exist (there are only seven thousand existing languages). I have since abandoned this approach.

5. Clearly, the biases differ in their strength when measured by raw WALS counts, with some much more obvious (like "472 out of 486") than some others (like "91 out of 152" and "132 out of 245"). Two factors play a role: One is that Dryer (1992) uses genetic and areal criteria that control for concerns that effects might be driven as artifacts of overrepresented language families. Even more important is that some of the universals have a strong asymmetry where the head-initial order is generally favored and appears quite often even in OV languages (as in tables 5.2 and 5.3). Dryer (2011b) refers to these principles (e.g., preference for subordinator-initial ordering) as "Dominance Principles," orthogonal to the harmonic correlations. These principles don't have a clear explanation the way the harmony principles have, and have no obvious relationship to DLM.

6. As noted in footnote 5, there is some other unknown factor across languages that pressures languages to subordinator-first word order Dryer (1992, 2011b).

7. I would like to thank Jack Hawkins for bringing these cases of non-correlation from Dryer's work to my attention. It is worth noting that his early immediate constituents hypothesis works very similarly to dependency length minimization, and hence makes the same predictions here.

7 Alternative Grammar Formalisms

1. We could have combined the PP before we combined the adjective and determiner. That would have resulted in a different grammar with similar properties.

2. Researchers in the movement-based framework attempt to solve this problem by finding general constraints on the types of syntactic nodes that can be moved

across licitly vs. illicitly. This strategy runs into problems because what makes a long-distance association possible or not seems to greatly depend on discourse function, not syntactic structure. See chapter 8.4 for discussion of this kind of problem for related phenomena.

3. Topicalization of the verb phrase in (146c) sounds like something Yoda would say in the *Star Wars* movies.

4. It is also the case that topicalized elements must be part of the main assertion of the clause out of which they topicalize (Erteschik-Shir, 1973; Goldberg, 2006).

(220) a. A squirrel might steal the old dogfood from the dog dish that was on the porch.
b. * The porch, a squirrel might steal the old dog food from the dog dish that was on.
c. * On the porch, a squirrel might steal the old dog food from the dog dish that was.

In (220b), a noun phrase is topicalized, but this sounds terrible. Similarly for the attempted topicalization of the PP *on the porch* in (220c). In general, the acceptability of long-distance movement of a phrase depends heavily on the discourse structure: It is not possible to extract out of a relative clause, as in these examples, because of the meaning of the topicalization construction and the meaning of the position from which extraction is attempted, a relative clause (Erteschik-Shir, 1973; Goldberg, 2006). A relative clause like this one refers to something that the speaker and hearer know in the discourse, as described. It doesn't make sense to contrast any part of it because it is all supposed to be background information.

These kinds of constraints have been labeled "island" theories in phrase structure movement theories (for esoteric reasons). I discuss these kinds of constraints on long-distance dependencies in section 8.4.

8 Chomsky's Transformation-Based Theories of Grammar

1. Chomsky actually goes on to claim that such examples are nonexistent, but they do occur with some low frequency (Pullum and Scholz, 2002).

2. Indeed, others have observed that versions of the proposed movement rule linking declarative to interrogative versions of auxiliary verbs may be learnable too (e.g., Estigarribia, 2010; Pearl and Sprouse, 2013. This is possible. The approach that I pursue here makes a stronger claim: that, following Sag et al. (1999), Kim and Sag (2002), Müller et al. (2021), and Sag et al. (2020), we may not need movement rules to explain auxiliary verb usage in English.

3. It is somewhat striking that Chomsky used a clear weakness of his proposal—that it was hard to learn such a grammar—to argue *for* his theory. Perhaps this is because he did not seriously consider simpler alternatives.

4. The auxiliary verb *ought* is apparently acceptable for older British speakers in the interrogative form. It is not acceptable for Canadians and Americans that I have asked. But as I produce these examples over and over again in presentations, I am finding them more acceptable. This is as the usage-based proposal would predict, but contrary to the movement-based proposal, which predicts that they are universally acceptable.

5. Note that several of the items involve inversion of the copula main verb *is*, such as *is happy* or *is on the blue bench*. As discussed in chapter 3, copula verbs are auxiliary verbs: +aux.

6. Moreover, there is actually some question in the literature as to whether children might indeed sometimes make structure-independent errors. Ambridge and colleagues have observed that the conditions that might lead children to produce an interrogative that looks like a structure-independent error were biased against such a possibility in Crain and Nakayama's (1987) study. Ambridge et al. (2008) conducted two more elicited production studies, which had two main conclusions: (1) Children actually sometimes make structure-independent errors; and (2) the pattern of children's auxiliary-doubling errors suggests a sensitivity to surface co-occurrence patterns in the input. Ambridge et al. (2008) conclude that there is no reason to think that structure dependence is an innate constraint. Rather, the grammar is learnable from exposure (see also Ambridge and Rowland, 2009; McCauley et al., 2021).

7. I mark unacceptable long-distance dependency structures in this chapter with the prefix #, which is intended to indicate that the materials are unacceptable, but without providing a theoretical interpretation. By marking them with an asterisk (*), I would be implicitly stating that they are not generated by the grammar. I don't think that the evidence supports this inference: The badness of such materials is rarely due to the grammar, and is more often due to some other factor.

8. The name "island" comes from a movement metaphor for long-distance dependencies between the filler and the "gap" position. The idea of an "island" is a location from which we cannot move easily.

9. Notably, there is no more recent complete generative (Chomskyan) theory of these kinds of examples, hence I discuss the older theory. This is perhaps surprising, because many current generative scholars appeal to a syntactic theory of islands without giving such a theory (Sprouse and Almeida, 2012; Sprouse et al., 2016).

10. These are the intuitive judgments from Schütze et al. (2015), with no experimental work demonstrating these particular effects. I have had several readers say

that they don't get the judgments that Schütze et al. (2015) provide here for (190) and (191). This of course further undermines their claims.

11. For example, this was the case in an example of "islands" that Liu et al. (2022a) investigated, as in (221). It had been hypothesized that so-called "bridge" verbs allow long-distance connections across them as in (221a), but factive verbs as in (221c) do not:

(221) a. Bridge verb, wh-question: What did John say/think that Mary bought?
b. Bridge verb, declarative: John said/thought that Mary bought something.
c. Factive verb, wh-question: ?? What did John know/notice that Mary bought?
d. Factive verb, declarative: John knew/noticed that Mary bought something.

But when Liu et al. (2022a) compared these conditions to declarative controls as in (221b) and (221d), there was no evidence of an interaction in any of four experiments, just main effects of construction (declarative vs. wh-question) and verb-frame frequency: the frequency of the instances of the verb with a sentence complement. Thus any difficulty that people have with the factive extraction materials in (221c) was also present in the non-extracted versions in (221d).

12. The focus-background-conflict constraint includes reference to the notion of constituent. Here a constituent means a head plus all of its dependent structure.

9 Language and Thought

1. A voxel is just a volumetric pixel: a three-dimensional analogy to the two-dimensional pixel in an image.

2. The left inferior frontal areas that are active in language processing are sometimes called "Broca's area," but see Fedorenko et al. (2012) for discussion of why this is not a useful label anymore. There are several problems. One is that what is called Broca's area is different across research groups (Tremblay and Dick, 2016). A related problem is that giving the area a label implies that the area is uniform in what it does. But it turns out that there are multiple distinct networks running through these brain areas, doing different things. So naming it doesn't make sense any more.

3. It is also possible that other components of language—the syntax, the sounds—might shape other aspects of cognition, but most work has focused on words, so that's what I do here.

4. Mathematical terms like quantifiers are often the exception: It is hard to find a context-dependent meaning for a number word like *five*, for example.

5. Actually, each of these words has its own different usages in each language. *Fille* also means *daughter* in French; *ragazza* also means *girlfriend* in Italian; and so on. Thus, there are big differences even in these closely related languages.

6. Of course this is not to say that language users don't innovate syntactically: New constructions appear all the time, albeit not as often as new words—for example, "Because internet" (McCulloch, 2020).

7. https://languagelog.ldc.upenn.edu/nll/?p=17970; https://languagelog.ldc.upenn.edu/nll/?p=18237.

8. There were a few errors, but no more than when MIT students did a similar task (Frank et al., 2012). It's a low-stakes task, so people sometimes make a few errors.

9. Another strategy is put one of your objects down for each element in the set on the table and keep track of which item you are at by moving your finger through the set on the table. I have not seen anyone discover this strategy, however, in my work with indigenous people.

10. Having run the Pirahã participants myself, I actually think that several of them were sensitive to when they got the answers wrong. In many of the tasks, it was hard to know what the right answer was, but in the task described above, where an opaque sheet blocked the participant's view of the target spools of thread, the correct answer was available by looking behind the sheet. Although we did not encourage them to look at the end of a trial, several of the participants seemed to want to see if they got the "right" answer, and were sometimes disappointed when they didn't get that answer. This only makes sense if they understood the task as needing to provide an exact match. On the other hand, I have no hard data that this happened, only my faulty memory, which could be sensitive to a confirmation bias of what I think is likely.

11. It is possible that this is an effect of culture on the language, and not an effect of the Spanish language on the Tsimane' language. But the monolinguals and bilinguals live together in the same villages, so most of the object-interaction is probably overlapping between these groups. Hence, a language effect seems plausible here.

12. Furthermore, it turns out that the effect isn't robust: Other researchers have investigated English and Mandarin metaphors and have found no differences in how vertical vs. front-back metaphors are used (Chen, 2007). Possibly because of this lack of difference in the corpora, others have failed to replicate Boroditsky's (2001) behavioral results (Chen, 2007; January and Kako, 2007; Tse and Altarriba, 2008). But even if researchers had replicated Boroditsky's (2001) behavioral results, it would say nothing about the causal relationship between language and thought.

10 Language as Communication

1. A related proposal is the "good-enough" language processing framework (Ferreira et al., 2002; Ferreira and Patson, 2007). According to the good-enough language processing proposal, there are two ways to arrive at an interpretation for a linguistic string: the algorithmic way, through the meanings of the words and the syntax, and a heuristic way, whereby the processor adopts some strategies that are somehow specific to the input. The intuitions underlying this framework are similar to those that drove the development of the noisy-channel approach. I see the noisy-channel approach as a formalized version of the intuitions underlying the good-enough approach.

2. The word *inchoative*, for example (205f), is a fancy word that means to express the beginning of an action, typically one occurring of its own accord. Inchoative verbs typically alternate with causative readings, such as for the verb *shrink* here.

3. Gibson et al. (2013b) and Futrell et al. (2015a) observe that the animacy of the patient noun also affects the order of gesturing, such that people tend to prefer SVO word orders when the patient is human (e.g., an event consisting of a girl lifting a ball is gestured SOV, whereas an event consisting of a girl lifting a woman is gestured SVO). They suggested that this switch to SVO word order might be explained by noisy-channel considerations: have the verb in the middle better disambiguates who is doing what to whom. But counter to this hypothesis, Hall et al. (2013) suggested that the reason that participants gesture SVO for events where the patient is animate is simply because there is a bias to think that the noun phrase that immediately precedes the verb is the agent. Struhl et al. (2016) shows that the account of Hall et al. (2013) is preferable to the noisy-channel account in several experiments.

11 Final Thoughts

1. And to break Oxford's string of ten wins 1976–1985 in the Oxford-Cambridge Boat Race https://en.wikipedia.org/wiki/The_Boat_Race_1986.

References

Abeillé, A., Hemforth, B., Winckel, E., and Gibson, E. (2020a). Extraction from subjects: Differences in acceptability depend on the discourse function of the construction. *Cognition*, 204:104293.

Abeillé, A., Hemforth, B., Winckel, E., and Gibson, E. (2020b). The subject island as a case of focus-background conflict. *Linguistic Evidence*.

Abeillé, A. and Rambow, O. (2000). *Tree Adjoining Grammars: Formalisms, Linguistic Analysis and Processing*. CSLI Publications.

Abney, S. P. (1987). *The English noun phrase in its sentential aspect.* PhD thesis, Massachusetts Institute of Technology.

Abney, S. P. and Johnson, M. (1991). Memory requirements and local ambiguities of parsing strategies. *Journal of Psycholinguistic Research*, 20(3):233–250.

Adger, D. (2003). *Core Syntax: A Minimalist Approach.* Oxford University Press.

Ahmed, N., Wahed, M., and Thompson, N. C. (2023). The growing influence of industry in AI research. *Science*, 379(6635):884–886.

Aissen, J. (2003). Differential object marking: Iconicity vs. economy. *Natural Language & Linguistic Theory*, 21(3):435–483.

Ajdukiewicz, K. (1935). Die syntaktische konnexitat. *Studia philosophica*, pages 1–27.

Akhtar, N., Callanan, M., Pullum, G. K., and Scholz, B. C. (2004). Learning antecedents for anaphoric one. *Cognition*, 93(2):141–145.

Akmajian, A., Farmer, A. K., Bickmore, L., Demers, R. A., and Harnish, R. M. (1990). *Linguistics: An introduction to language and communication.* Cambridge University Press.

Ambridge, B. and Rowland, C. F. (2009). Predicting children's errors with negative questions: Testing a schema-combination account. *Cognitive Linguistics*, 20, 225–266. https://doi.org/10.1515/COGL.2009.014.

Ambridge, B., Rowland, C. F., and Pine, J. M. (2008). Is structure dependence an innate constraint? New experimental evidence from children's complex-question production. *Cognitive Science*, 32(1):222–255.

An, A., Poliak, M., Levy, R., and Gibson, E. (2024). Sentence acceptability is determined not only by the sentence but also the intended sentence. *in preparation*.

Anderson, C. (2018). *Essentials of Linguistics*. McMaster University.

Angluin, D. (1979). Finding patterns common to a set of strings. In *Proceedings of the Eleventh Annual ACM Symposium on Theory of Computing*, 130–141.

Angluin, D. (1980). Inductive inference of formal languages from positive data. *Information and Control*, 45(2):117–135.

Apperly, I. A., Samson, D., Carroll, N., Hussain, S., and Humphreys, G. (2006). Intact first-and second-order false belief reasoning in a patient with severely impaired grammar. *Social Neuroscience*, 1(3-4):334–348.

Arnold, J. E., Losongco, A., Wasow, T., and Ginstrom, R. (2000). Heaviness vs. newness: The effects of structural complexity and discourse status on constituent ordering. *Language*, 76(1):28–55.

Arnold, K. and Zuberbühler, K. (2006). Semantic combinations in primate calls. *Nature*, 441(7091):303–303.

Arnon, I., McCauley, S. M., and Christiansen, M. H. (2017). Digging up the building blocks of language: Age-of-acquisition effects for multiword phrases. *Journal of Memory and Language*, 92:265–280.

Arnon, I. and Snider, N. (2010). More than words: Frequency effects for multi-word phrases. *Journal of Memory and Language*, 62(1):67–82.

Athanasopoulos, P. (2009). Cognitive representation of colour in bilinguals: The case of Greek blues. *Bilingualism: Language and Cognition*, 12(1):83–95.

Athanasopoulos, P., Damjanovic, L., Krajciova, A., and Sasaki, M. (2011). Representation of colour concepts in bilingual cognition: The case of Japanese blues. *Bilingualism: Language and Cognition*, 14(1):9–17.

Athanasopoulos, P., Dering, B., Wiggett, A., Kuipers, J.-R., and Thierry, G. (2010). Perceptual shift in bilingualism: Brain potentials reveal plasticity in pre-attentive colour perception. *Cognition*, 116(3):437–443.

Atkinson, M., Roca, I., and Kilby, D. (1982). *Foundations of General Linguistics*. London: Unwin Hyman.

Baker, C. I., Liu, J., Wald, L. L., Kwong, K. K., Benner, T., and Kanwisher, N. (2007). Visual word processing and experiential origins of functional selectivity in human extrastriate cortex. *Proceedings of the National Academy of Sciences*, 104(21):9087–9092.

Baker, C. L. (1989). *English Syntax*. MIT Press.

Bartek, B., Lewis, R. L., Vasishth, S., and Smith, M. R. (2011). In search of on-line locality effects in sentence comprehension. *Journal of Experimental Psychology: Learning, Memory, and Cognition*, 37(5):1178–1198.

Barton, S. B. and Sanford, A. J. (1993). A case study of anomaly detection: Shallow semantic processing and cohesion establishment. *Memory & Cognition*, 21(4):477–487.

Beckman, M. E. (2012). Stress and non-stress accent. In *Stress and Non-Stress Accent*. De Gruyter Mouton.

Bedny, M., Pascual-Leone, A., Dodell-Feder, D., Fedorenko, E., and Saxe, R. (2011). Language processing in the occipital cortex of congenitally blind adults. *Proceedings of the National Academy of Sciences*, 108(11):4429–4434.

Behaghel, O. (1930). Von deutscher Wortstellung. *Zeitschrift für Deutschkunde*, 44:81–89.

Bemis, D. K. and Pylkkänen, L. (2011). Simple composition: A magnetoencephalography investigation into the comprehension of minimal linguistic phrases. *Journal of Neuroscience*, 31(8):2801–2814.

Benn, Y., Ivanova, A. A., Clark, O., Mineroff, Z., Seikus, C., Silva, J. S., Varley, R., and Fedorenko, E. (2023). No evidence for a special role of language in feature-based categorization. *Cerebral Cortex*, page 10380–10400.

Berlin, B. and Kay, P. (1969). *Basic Color Terms: Their Universality and Evolution*. University of California Press.

Bever, T. G. (1970). The cognitive basis for linguistic structures. In Hayes, J. R., editor, *Cognition and the Development of Language*. Wiley, New York.

Bever, T. G. (1974). The ascent of the specious, or there's a lot we don't know about mirrors. *Explaining Linguistic Phenomena*, 173–200.

Bever, T. G. and McElree, B. (1988). Empty categories access their antecedents during comprehension. *Linguistic Inquiry*, 19(1):35–43.

Bever, T. G. and Sanz, M. (1997). Empty categories access their antecedents during comprehension: Unaccusatives in Spanish. *Linguistic Inquiry*, 28(1):69–91.

Binnick, R. I. (1991). *Time and the Verb: A Guide to Tense and Aspect*. Oxford University Press.

Birner, B. J. and Ward, G. L. (1998). *Information Status and Noncanonical Word Order in English*, volume 40. John Benjamins Publishing.

Blank, I., Kanwisher, N., and Fedorenko, E. (2014). A functional dissociation between language and multiple-demand systems revealed in patterns of bold signal fluctuations. *Journal of Neurophysiology*, 112(5):1105–1118.

Blasi, D. E., Henrich, J., Adamou, E., Kemmerer, D., and Majid, A. (2022). Over-reliance on English hinders cognitive science. *Trends in Cognitive Sciences*, 26(12): 1153–1170.

Blasi, D. E., Wichmann, S., Hammarström, H., Stadler, P. F., and Christiansen, M. H. (2016). Sound–meaning association biases evidenced across thousands of languages. *Proceedings of the National Academy of Sciences*, 113(39):10818–10823.

Bloomfield, L. (1933). *Language*. Henry Holt.

Bock, K. (1986). Syntactic persistence in language production. *Cognitive Psychology*, 18(3):355–387.

Bolinger, D. (1986). *Intonation and Its Parts: Melody in Spoken English*. Stanford University Press.

Bommasani, R., Hudson, D. A., Adeli, E., Altman, R., Arora, S., von Arx, S., Bernstein, M. S., Bohg, J., Bosselut, A., Brunskill, E., et al. (2021). On the opportunities and risks of foundation models. *arXiv preprint arXiv:2108.07258*.

Boroditsky, L. (2001). Does language shape thought? Mandarin and English speakers' conceptions of time. *Cognitive Psychology*, 43(1):1–22.

Boroditsky, L., Schmidt, L. A., and Phillips, W. (2003). Sex, syntax, and semantics. *Language in Mind: Advances in the Study of Language and Thought*, 22:61–79.

Boston, M. F., Hale, J. T., Kliegl, R., Patil, U., and Vasishth, S. (2008). Parsing costs as predictors of reading difficulty: An evaluation using the Potsdam Sentence Corpus. *Journal of Eye Movement Research*, 2(1):1, 1–12.

Bouma, G. (2011). Production and comprehension in context: The case of word order freezing. In Benz, A. and Mattausch, J., editors, *Bidirectional Optimality Theory*. John Benjamins.

Boyce, V., Futrell, R., and Levy, R. P. (2020). Maze made easy: Better and easier measurement of incremental processing difficulty. *Journal of Memory and Language*, 111:104082.

Boyce, V., Levy, R., Boyce, V., and Levy, R. P. (2023). A-maze of natural stories: Comprehension and surprisal in the maze task. *Glossa Psycholinguistics*, 2(1).

Boye, K. (2023). Grammaticalization as conventionalization of discursively secondary status: Deconstructing the lexical–grammatical continuum. *Transactions of the Philological Society*, 121(2):270–292.

Braginsky, M., Yurovsky, D., Marchman, V. A., and Frank, M. (2016). From uh-oh to tomorrow: Predicting age of acquisition for early words across languages. *Proceedings of the annual meeting of the Cognitive Science Society*, volume 38, https://escholarship.org/uc/item/9sn4p5f9.

Braginsky, M., Yurovsky, D., Marchman, V. A., and Frank, M. C. (2019). Consistency and variability in children's word learning across languages. *Open Mind*, 3:52–67.

Breen, M., Fedorenko, E., Wagner, M., and Gibson, E. (2010). Acoustic correlates of information structure. *Language and Cognitive Processes*, 25(7-9):1044–1098.

Brennan, S. E. and Clark, H. H. (1996). Conceptual pacts and lexical choice in conversation. *Journal of Experimental Psychology: Learning, Memory, and Cognition*, 22(6):1482.

Bresnan, J. (1982). *The Mental Representation of Grammatical Relations*. MIT Press.

Bresnan, J., Asudeh, A., Toivonen, I., and Wechsler, S. (2015). *Lexical-Functional Syntax*. John Wiley & Sons.

Briscoe, E. (1983). Determinism and its implementation in Parsifal. *Automatic Natural Language Processing*, Ellis Horwood.

Brown, T., Mann, B., Ryder, N., Subbiah, M., Kaplan, J. D., Dhariwal, P., Neelakantan, A., Shyam, P., Sastry, G., Askell, A., et al. (2020). Language models are few-shot learners. *Advances in Neural Information Processing Systems*, 33:1877–1901.

Brysbaert, M., Buchmeier, M., Conrad, M., Jacobs, A. M., Bölte, J., and Böhl, A. (2011). The word frequency effect. *Experimental Psychology*.

Brysbaert, M. and Ghyselinck, M. (2006). The effect of age of acquisition: Partly frequency related, partly frequency independent. *Visual Cognition*, 13(7-8):992–1011.

Brysbaert, M., Mandera, P., and Keuleers, E. (2018). The word frequency effect in word processing: An updated review. *Current Directions in Psychological Science*, 27(1):45–50.

Brysbaert, M., Stevens, M., Mandera, P., and Keuleers, E. (2016). How many words do we know? Practical estimates of vocabulary size dependent on word definition, the degree of language input and the participant's age. *Frontiers in Psychology*, 7:1116.

Brysbaert, M., Van Wijnendaele, I., and De Deyne, S. (2000). Age-of-acquisition effects in semantic processing tasks. *Acta Psychologica*, 104(2):215–226.

Bybee, J. (2006). From usage to grammar: The mind's response to repetition. *Language*, 711–733.

Bybee, J. (2010). *Language, Usage and Cognition*. Cambridge University Press.

Bybee, J. and Hopper, P. (2001). Introduction to frequency and the emergence of linguistic structure. *Typological Studies in Language*, 45:1–26.

Cabeza, R. and Nyberg, L. (2000). Imaging cognition II: An empirical review of 275 pet and fMRI studies. *Journal of Cognitive Neuroscience*, 12(1):1–47.

Caminiti, S., Finocchi, I., and Petreschi, R. (2007). On coding labeled trees. *Theoretical Computer Science*, 382(2):97–108.

Campbell, L. (2013). *Historical Linguistics*. Edinburgh University Press.

Cantlon, J. F. and Piantadosi, S. T. (2024). Information capacity sparked human intelligence. *Nature Reviews Psychology*, pages 1–19.

Carey, S. (2009). *The Origin of Concepts*. Oxford University Press.

Carnap, R. (1937). *Logical Syntax of Language*. Harcourt Brace.

Carnap, R. (1947 / 1956). *Meaning and Necessity: A Study in Semantics and Modal Logic*. University of Chicago Press.

Carnie, A. (2010). *Constituent Structure*. Oxford University Press.

Carnie, A. (2013). *Syntax: A Generative Introduction*. John Wiley & Sons.

Casasanto, D. (2005). Crying "Whorf." *Science*, 307(5716):1721–1722.

Chafe, W. L. (1970). *Meaning and the structure of language*. University of Chicago Press.

Chater, N. and Vitányi, P. (2003). Simplicity: A unifying principle in cognitive science? *Trends in Cognitive Sciences*, 7(1):19–22.

Chater, N. and Vitányi, P. (2007). Ideal learning of natural language: Positive results about learning from positive evidence. *Journal of Mathematical Psychology*, 51(3):135–163.

Chaves, R. P. (2014). On the disunity of right-node raising phenomena: Extraposition, ellipsis, and deletion. *Language*, 834–886.

Chaves, R. P. and Dery, J. E. (2019). Frequency effects in subject islands. *Journal of Linguistics*, 55(3):475–521.

Chaves, R. P. and Putnam, M. T. (2020). *Unbounded Dependency Constructions: Theoretical and Experimental Perspectives*. Oxford University Press.

Chen, E., Gibson, E., and Wolf, F. (2005). Online syntactic storage costs in sentence comprehension. *Journal of Memory and Language*, 52(1):144–169.

Chen, J.-Y. (2007). Do Chinese and English speakers think about time differently? Failure of replicating Boroditsky (2001). *Cognition*, 104(2):427–436.

Chen, S., Conway, B., and Gibson, E. (2023a). Russian blues do not reveal an effect of language on perception. Poster presented at the Human Sentence Processing Conference, University of Pittsburgh, March 2023.

Chen, S., Futrell, R., and Mahowald, K. (2023b). An information-theoretic approach to the typology of spatial demonstratives. 240:105505.

Chen, S., Nathaniel, S., Ryskin, R., and Gibson, E. (2022). The effect of context on noisy-channel sentence comprehension. *Cognition*, 238:105503.

Chen, X., Affourtit, J., Ryskin, R., Regev, T. I., Norman-Haignere, S., Jouravlev, O., Malik-Moraleda, S., Kean, H., Varley, R., and Fedorenko, E. (2023). The human language system, including its inferior frontal component in "Broca's Area," does not support music perception. *Cerebral Cortex*, 33(12):7904–7929.

Chomsky, N. (1955). *The Logical Structure of Linguistic Theory*. Plenum / University of Chicago Press.

Chomsky, N. (1956). Three models for the description of language. *IRE Transactions on Information Theory*, 2(3):113–124.

Chomsky, N. (1957). *Syntactic Structures*. Mouton.

Chomsky, N. (1962). Various discussion sessions. In Hill, A. A., editor, *Third Texas Conference on Problems of Linguistic Analysis in English*, 22–33. University of Texas.

Chomsky, N. (1965). *Aspects of the Theory of Syntax*. MIT Press.

Chomsky, N. (1971). *Problems of Knowledge and Freedom: The Russell Lectures*. Fontana.

Chomsky, N. (1973). Conditions on transformations. In *A Festschrift for Morris Halle*, 232–285. Winston.

Chomsky, N. (1977). On wh-movement. In *Formal Syntax*, 71–132. Academic.

Chomsky, N. (1980a). Initial states and steady states. In Piattelli-Palmarini, M., editor, *Language and Learning: The Debate between Jean Piaget and Noam Chomsky*.

Chomsky, N. (1980b). Principles and parameters in syntactic theory. In Hornstein, N. and Lightfoot, D., editors, *Explanation in Linguistics: The Logical Problem of Language Acquisition*, pages 32–75. Longman.

Chomsky, N. (1981). *Lectures on Government and Binding*. Foris Publications.

Chomsky, N. (1986). *Barriers*. MIT Press.

Chomsky, N. (1993). A minimalist program for linguistic theory. In Hale, K. and Keyser, S. J., editors, *The View from Building 20*, pages 1–52. MIT Press.

Chomsky, N. and Miller, G. (1963). Introduction to the formal analysis of natural languages. *Handbook of Mathematical Psychology*, 2:269–321.

Chomsky, N., Roberts, I., and Watumull, J. (2023). The false promise of ChatGPT. *New York Times*.

Clark, H. H. (1998). *Communal Lexicons*, pages 63–87. Cambridge University Press.

Clark, H. H. and Brennan, S. E. (1991). Grounding in communication. In *Perspectives on Socially-Shared Cognition*, 127–149. American Psychological Association.

Clifton, C. and Frazier, L. (2004). Should given information come before new? Yes and no. *Memory & Cognition*, 32(6):886–895.

Cole, J. (2015). Prosody in context: A review. *Language, Cognition and Neuroscience*, 30(1–2):1–31.

Collins, A. M. and Quillian, M. R. (1969). Retrieval time from semantic memory. *Journal of Verbal Learning and Verbal Behavior*, 8(2):240–247.

Cooper, R. M. (1974). The control of eye fixation by the meaning of spoken language: A new methodology for the real-time investigation of speech perception, memory, and language processing. *Cognitive Psychology*, 6(1):84–107. https://doi.org/10.1016/0010-0285(74)90005-X.

Corbett, G. G., Fraser, N. M., and McGlashan, S., editors (1993). *Heads in Grammatical Theory*. Cambridge University Press.

Cowper, E. A. (1976). *Constraints on Sentence Complexity: A Model for Syntactic Processing*. Brown University.

Cowper, E. A. (1992). *A Concise Introduction to Syntactic Theory: The Government-Binding Approach*. University of Chicago Press.

Crain, S. and Nakayama, M. (1987). Structure dependence in grammar formation. *Language*, 63(3):522–543.

Croft, W. (2001). *Radical Construction Grammar: Syntactic Theory in Typological Perspective*. Oxford University Press.

Croft, W. (2010). Construction grammar. In Geeraerts, D. and Cuyckens, H., editors, *The Oxford Handbook of Cognitive Linguistics*, 463–508.

Croft, W. and Cruse, D. A. (2004). *Cognitive Linguistics*. Cambridge University Press.

Crystal, D. (1969). *Prosodic Systems and Intonation in English*. Number 1. CUP Archive.

Culbertson, J. and Kirby, S. (2016). Simplicity and specificity in language: Domain-general biases have domain-specific effects. *Frontiers in Psychology*, 6:166814.

Culicover, P. W. and Jackendoff, R. (2005). *Simpler Syntax*. OUP Oxford.

Cuneo, N. and Goldberg, A. E. (2023). The discourse functions of grammatical constructions explain an enduring syntactic puzzle. *Cognition*, 240:105563.

DaCunha, Y. and Gibson, E. (2025). Syntactic complexity phenomena are better explained without empty elements mediating long-distance dependencies. Manuscript, U. Paris & MIT.

DaCunha, Y. and Gibson, E. (2025). Nonsyntactic constraints on wh-extraction: Evidence from exclamative clauses. Manuscript, U. Paris & MIT.

Davidoff, J., Davies, I., and Roberson, D. (1999). Colour categories in a stone-age tribe. *Nature*, 398(6724):203–204.

Davies, M. (2009). The 385+ million word corpus of contemporary American English (1990–2008+): Design, architecture, and linguistic insights. *International Journal of Corpus Linguistics*, 14(2):159–190.

Davies, W. D. and Dubinsky, S. (2003). On extraction from NPs. *Natural Language & Linguistic Theory*, 21(1):1–37.

De Marneffe, M.-C., Manning, C. D., Nivre, J., and Zeman, D. (2021). Universal dependencies. *Computational Linguistics*, 47(2):255–308.

De Marneffe, M.-C. and Nivre, J. (2019). Dependency grammar. *Annual Review of Linguistics*, 5:197–218.

De Roeck, A., Johnson, R., King, M., Rosner, M., Sampson, G., and Varile, N. (1982). A myth about centre-embedding. *Lingua*, 58(3-4):327–340.

De Saussure, F. (1959 [1916]). *Course in General Linguistics*. Philosophy Library. ISBN 9780231157278.

De Saussure, F. (2006). *Writings in General Linguistics*. Oxford University Press.

Deane, P. (1991). *Limits to attention: A cognitive theory of island phenomena*. Walter de Gruyter.

Demberg, V. and Keller, F. (2008). Data from eye-tracking corpora as evidence for theories of syntactic processing complexity. *Cognition*, 109(2):193–210.

Devlin, J., Chang, M.-W., Lee, K., and Toutanova, K. (2018). BERT: Pre-training of deep bidirectional transformers for language understanding. *arXiv preprint arXiv:1810.04805*.

Diessel, H. (2017). Usage-based linguistics. Mark Aronoff (ed.), *Oxford Research Encyclopedia of Linguistics*. Oxford University Press, 1–26.

Dotlačil, J. (2021). Parsing as a cue-based retrieval model. *Cognitive Science*, 45(8):e13020.

Dowty, D. (1991). Thematic proto-roles and argument selection. *Language*, 67(3):547–619.

Dryer, M. (1991). SVO languages and the OV: VO typology. *Journal of Linguistics*, 27(2):443–482.

Dryer, M. (1992). The Greenbergian word order correlations. *Language*, 68(1):81–138.

Dryer, M. S. (2002). Case distinctions, rich verb agreement, and word order type (comments on Hawkins' paper). *Theoretical Linguistics*, 28:151–157.

Dryer, M. S. (2011a). The branching direction theory of word order correlations revisited. In Scalise, S., Magni, E., and Bisetto, A., editors, *Universals of Language Today*. Springer.

Dryer, M. S. (2011b). The evidence for word order correlations. *Linguistic Typology*, 15:335–380.

Dryer, M. S. (2013). Order of subject, object and verb. In Haspelmath, M. editor, *The World Atlas of Language Structures*. Leipzig: Max Planck Institute for Evolutionary Anthropology.

Duncan, J. (2010). The multiple-demand (md) system of the primate brain: Mental programs for intelligent behaviour. *Trends in Cognitive Sciences*, 14(4):172–179.

Ellis, A. W. and Morrison, C. M. (1998). Real age-of-acquisition effects in lexical retrieval. *Journal of Experimental Psychology: Learning, Memory, and Cognition*, 24(2):515.

Engesser, S., Ridley, A. R., and Townsend, S. W. (2016). Meaningful call combinations and compositional processing in the southern pied babbler. *Proceedings of the National Academy of Sciences*, 113(21):5976–5981.

Erickson, T. D. and Mattson, M. E. (1981). From words to meaning: A semantic illusion. *Journal of Verbal Learning and Verbal Behavior*, 20(5):540–551.

Erteschik-Shir, N. (1973). *On the Nature of Island Constraints*. PhD thesis, Massachusetts Institute of Technology.

Erteschik-Shir, N. (1997). *The Dynamics of Focus Structure*. Cambridge University Press.

Ertescik-Shir, N. (1979). Discourse constraints on dative movement. In *Discourse and Syntax*, 441–467. Brill.

Estigarribia, B. (2010). Facilitation by variation: Right-to-left learning of English yes/no questions. *Cognitive Science*, 34(1):68–93.

Evans, N. and Levinson, S. (2009). The myth of language universals: Language diversity and its importance for cognitive science. *Behavioral and Brain Sciences*, 32(05):429–448.

Everett, D. L. (1986). Pirahã. *Handbook of Amazonian Languages*, 1:200–325.

Everett, D. L. (2005). Cultural constraints on grammar and cognition in Pirahã. *Current Anthropology*, 46(4):621–646.

Fadiga, L., Craighero, L., and D'Ausilio, A. (2009). Broca's area in language, action, and music. *Annals of the New York Academy of Sciences*, 1169(1):448–458.

Fedorenko, E., Behr, M. K., and Kanwisher, N. (2011). Functional specificity for high-level linguistic processing in the human brain. *Proceedings of the National Academy of Sciences*, 108(39):16428–16433.

Fedorenko, E., Blank, I. A., Siegelman, M., and Mineroff, Z. (2020). Lack of selectivity for syntax relative to word meanings throughout the language network. *Cognition*, 203:104348.

Fedorenko, E., Duncan, J., and Kanwisher, N. (2012). Language-selective and domain-general regions lie side by side within Broca's area. *Current Biology*, 22(21): 2059–2062.

Fedorenko, E., Duncan, J., and Kanwisher, N. (2013). Broad domain generality in focal regions of frontal and parietal cortex. *Proceedings of the National Academy of Sciences*, 110(41):16616–16621.

Fedorenko, E., Hsieh, P.-J., Nieto-Castañón, A., Whitfield-Gabrieli, S., and Kanwisher, N. (2010). New method for fMRI investigations of language: Defining ROIs functionally in individual subjects. *Journal of Neurophysiology*, 104(2): 1177–1194.

Fedorenko, E., Ivanova, A. A., and Regev, T. I. (2024a). The language network as a natural kind within the broader landscape of the human brain. *Nature Reviews Neuroscience*, 25(5):289–312.

Fedorenko, E., Piantadosi, S. T., and Gibson, E. (2024b). Language is a tool for communication, not for thought. *Nature*, 630 (8017):575–586.

Fedorenko, E. and Shain, C. (2021). Similarity of computations across domains does not imply shared implementation: The case of language comprehension. *Current Directions in Psychological Science*, 30(6):526–534.

Fedorenko, E. and Varley, R. (2016). Language and thought are not the same thing: Evidence from neuroimaging and neurological patients. *Annals of the New York Academy of Sciences*, 1369(1):132.

Ferreira, F. (2003). The misinterpretation of noncanonical sentences. *Cognitive Psychology*, 47(2):164–203.

Ferreira, F., Bailey, K. G., and Ferraro, V. (2002). Good-enough representations in language comprehension. *Current Directions in Psychological Science*, 11(1):11–15.

Ferreira, F. and Clifton, C. (1986). The independence of syntactic processing. *Journal of Memory and Language*, 25(3):348–368.

Ferreira, F. and Patson, N. D. (2007). The "good enough" approach to language comprehension. *Language and Linguistics Compass*, 1(1–2):71–83.

Ferrer-i-Cancho, R. (2004). Euclidean distance between syntactically linked words. *Physical Review E*, 70:056135.

Ferrer-i-Cancho, R. (2006). Why do syntactic links not cross? *Europhysics Letters*, 76(6):1228–1235.

Ferrer-i-Cancho, R. (2015). The placement of the head that minimizes online memory: A complex systems approach. *Language Dynamics and Change*, 5(1):114–137.

Ferrer-i-Cancho, R. (2016). Non-crossing dependencies: Least effort, not grammar. In *Towards a Theoretical Framework for Analyzing Complex Linguistic Networks*, 203–234. Springer.

Fillmore, C. J. (1982). Towards a descriptive framework for spatial deixis. *Speech, Place and Action: Studies in Deixis and Related Topics*, 31–59.

Fillmore, C. J. (1988). The mechanisms of "construction grammar." In *Annual Meeting of the Berkeley Linguistics Society*, volume 14, 35–55.

Fischl, B., Sereno, M. I., Tootell, R. B., and Dale, A. M. (1999). High-resolution intersubject averaging and a coordinate system for the cortical surface. *Human Brain Mapping*, 8(4):272–284.

Fitch, W. T. and Martins, M. D. (2014). Hierarchical processing in music, language, and action: Lashley revisited. *Annals of the New York Academy of Sciences*, 1316(1):87–104.

Flickinger, D. P. (1987). *Lexical Rules in the Hierarchical Lexicon*. PhD thesis, Stanford University unpublished doctoral dissertation.

Fodor, J. A. (1983). *Representations: Philosophical Essays on the Foundations of Cognitive Science*. MIT Press.

Fodor, J. D. and Inoue, A. (1994). The diagnosis and cure of garden paths. *Journal of Psycholinguistic Research*, 23(5):407–434.

Forster, K. I., Guerrera, C., and Elliot, L. (2009). The maze task: Measuring forced incremental sentence processing time. *Behavioral Research Methods*, 41(1):163–171.

Francis, E. J. (2010). Grammatical weight and relative clause extraposition in English. *Cognitive Linguistics*, 21(1):35–74.

Francis, E. J. and Michaelis, L. A. (2014). Why move? How weight and discourse factors combine to predict relative clause extraposition in English. In *Competing Motivations in Grammar and Usage*, ed. by Edith Moravcsik and Andrej Malchukov, Oxford University Press, 70–87.

Francis, E. J. and Michaelis, L. A. (2017). When relative clause extraposition is the right choice, it's easier. *Language and Cognition*, 9(2):332–370.

Frank, M., Everett, D., Fedorenko, E., and Gibson, E. (2008a). Number as a cognitive technology: Evidence from Pirahã language and cognition. *Cognition*, 108(3):819–824.

Frank, M. C., Braginsky, M., Yurovsky, D., and Marchman, V. A. (2017). Wordbank: An open repository for developmental vocabulary data. *Journal of Child Language*, 44(3):677–694.

Frank, M. C., Braginsky, M., Yurovsky, D., and Marchman, V. A. (2021). *Variability and Consistency in Early Language Learning: The Wordbank Project.* MIT Press.

Frank, M. C., Everett, D. L., Fedorenko, E., and Gibson, E. (2008b). Language as a cognitive technology: English-speakers match like Pirahã when you don't let them count. In *Proceedings of the 30th Annual Meeting of the Cognitive Science Society.*

Frank, M. C., Fedorenko, E., Lai, P., Saxe, R., and Gibson, E. (2012). Verbal interference suppresses exact numerical representation. *Cognitive Psychology*, 64(1–2):74–92.

Frank, R. E. (1992). *Syntactic Locality and Tree Adjoining Grammar: Grammatical, Acquisition and Processing Perspectives.* University of Pennsylvania.

Frazier, L. (1979). On comprehending sentences: Syntactic parsing strategies. Doctoral Dissertation. ETD Collection for University of Connecticut.

Frazier, L. and Fodor, J. D. (1978). The sausage machine: A new two-stage parsing model. *Cognition*, 6(4):291–325.

Frazier, L. and Rayner, K. (1982). Making and correcting errors during sentence comprehension: Eye movements in the analysis of structurally ambiguous sentences. *Cognitive Psychology*, 14(2):178–210.

Frazier, L. and Rayner, K. (1987). Resolution of syntactic category ambiguities: Eye movements in parsing lexically ambiguous sentences. *Journal of Memory and Language*, 26(5):505–526.

Frege, G. et al. (1892). Über sinn und bedeutung. *Zeitschrift für Philosophie und philosophische Kritik*, 100(1):25–50.

Fry, D. B. (1955). Duration and intensity as physical correlates of linguistic stress. *Journal of the Acoustical Society of America*, 27(4):765–768.

Fukui, N. and Speas, M. (1986). Specifiers and projection. *MIT Working Papers in Linguistics*, 8(128):72.

Futrell, R. (2019). Information-theoretic locality properties of natural language. In *Proceedings of the First Workshop on Quantitative Syntax (Quasy, SyntaxFest 2019)*, 2–15, Paris, France. Association for Computational Linguistics.

Futrell, R., Gibson, E., and Levy, R. P. (2020a). Lossy-context surprisal: An information-theoretic model of memory effects in sentence processing. *Cognitive Science*, 44:e12814.

Futrell, R., Gibson, E., Tily, H. J., Blank, I., Vishnevetsky, A., Piantadosi, S. T., and Fedorenko, E. (2018). The natural stories corpus. In *Proceedings of LREC 2018, Eleventh International Conference on Language Resources and Evaluation*, 76–82, Miyazaki, Japan. European Language Resources Association.

Futrell, R., Hickey, T., Lee, A., Lim, E., Luchkina, E., and Gibson, E. (2015a). Cross-linguistic gestures reflect typological universals: A subject-initial, verb-final bias in speakers of diverse languages. *Cognition*, 136:215–221.

Futrell, R., Levy, R. P., and Gibson, E. (2020b). Dependency locality as an explanatory principle for word order. *Language*, 96(2):371–413.

Futrell, R., Mahowald, K., and Gibson, E. (2015b). Large-scale evidence of dependency length minimization in 37 languages. *Proceedings of the National Academy of Sciences*, 112(33):10336–10341.

Futrell, R., Wilcox, E., Morita, T., Qian, P., Ballesteros, M., and Levy, R. (2019). Neural language models as psycholinguistic subjects: Representations of syntactic state. *arXiv preprint arXiv:1903.03260*.

Gaifman, H. (1965). Dependency systems and phrase-structure systems. *Information and Control*, 8:304–337.

Garnsey, S. M., Pearlmutter, N. J., Myers, E., and Lotocky, M. A. (1997). The contributions of verb bias and plausibility to the comprehension of temporarily ambiguous sentences. *Journal of Memory and Language*, 37(1):58–93.

Garrett, M. F. (1975). The analysis of sentence production. In Bower, G. H., editor, *The Psychology of Learning and Motivation*, volume 9. Academic Press.

Gauthier, J., Hu, J., Wilcox, E., Qian, P., and Levy, R. (2020). SyntaxGym: An online platform for targeted evaluation of language models. In *Proceedings of the 58th Annual Meeting of the Association for Computational Linguistics: System Demonstrations*, 70–76.

Gazdar, G., Klein, E., Pullum, G. K., and Sag, I. A. (1985). *Generalized Phrase Structure Grammar*. Harvard University Press.

Gazdar, G., Pullum, G. K., and Sag, I. A. (1982). Auxiliaries and related phenomena in a restrictive theory of grammar. *Language*, 58(3):591–638.

Gibson, E. (1991). *A Computational Theory of Human Linguistic Processing: Memory Limitations and Processing Breakdown*. PhD thesis, Carnegie Mellon University.

Gibson, E. (1998). Linguistic complexity: Locality of syntactic dependencies. *Cognition*, 68(1):1–76.

Gibson, E. (2000). The dependency locality theory: A distance-based theory of linguistic complexity. In Marantz, A., Miyashita, Y., O'Neil, W., & O'Neil, W. A. (Eds.). *Language, Brain: Papers from the First Mind Articulation Project Symposium*. MIT Press, 95–126.

Gibson, E., Bergen, L., and Piantadosi, S. T. (2013a). Rational integration of noisy evidence and prior semantic expectations in sentence interpretation. *Proceedings of the National Academy of Sciences*, 110(20):8051–8056.

Gibson, E. and Fedorenko, E. (2010). Weak quantitative standards in linguistics research. *Trends in Cognitive Sciences*, 14(6):233–234.

Gibson, E. and Fedorenko, E. (2013). The need for quantitative methods in syntax and semantics research. *Language and Cognitive Processes*, 28(1-2):88–124.

Gibson, E., Fedorenko, E., and Mahowald, K. (2011). The domain-generality of working memory resources for language. Poster presented at the 17th Architectures and Mechanisms in Language Processing (Amlap), Diderot University (Paris VII), Paris.

Gibson, E., Futrell, R., Jara-Ettinger, J., Mahowald, K., Bergen, L., Ratnasingam, S., Gibson, M., Piantadosi, S. T., and Conway, B. R. (2017a). Color naming across languages reflects color use. *Proceedings of the National Academy of Sciences*, 114(40): 10785–10790.

Gibson, E., Futrell, R., Piantadosi, S. P., Dautriche, I., Mahowald, K., Bergen, L., and Levy, R. (2019). How efficiency shapes human language. *Trends in Cognitive Sciences*, 23(5):389–407.

Gibson, E. and Hickok, G. (1993). Sentence processing with empty categories. *Language and Cognitive Processes*, 8(2):147–161.

Gibson, E., Piantadosi, S. T., Brink, K., Bergen, L., Lim, E., and Saxe, R. (2013b). A noisy-channel account of crosslinguistic word-order variation. *Psychological Science*, 24(7):1079–1088.

Gibson, E., Piantadosi, S. T., and Fedorenko, E. (2013c). Quantitative methods in syntax/semantics research: A response to Sprouse and Almeida (2013). *Language and Cognitive Processes*, 28(3):229–240.

Gibson, E., Tan, C., Futrell, R., Mahowald, K., Konieczny, L., Hemforth, B., and Fedorenko, E. (2017b). Don't underestimate the benefits of being misunderstood. *Psychological Science*, 28(6):703–712.

Gibson, E. and Thomas, J. (1997). The complexity of nested structures in english: Evidence for the syntactic prediction locality theory of linguistic complexity. Unpublished manuscript, MIT Brain and Cognitive Sciences.

Gibson, E. and Thomas, J. (1999). Memory limitations and structural forgetting: The perception of complex ungrammatical sentences as grammatical. *Language and Cognitive Processes*, 14(3):225–248.

Gibson, E. and Wexler, K. (1994). Triggers. *Linguistic Inquiry*, 25(3):407–454.

Gildea, D. and Temperley, D. (2010). Do grammars minimize dependency length? *Cognitive Science*, 34(2):286–310.

Gillan, D. J., Premack, D., and Woodruff, G. (1981). Reasoning in the chimpanzee: I. analogical reasoning. *Journal of Experimental Psychology: Animal Behavior Processes*, 7(1):1.

Ginzburg, J. and Sag, I. (2000). *Interrogative Investigations*. CSLI publications.

Givón, T. (1984). *Syntax: A Functional-Typological Introduction*. John Benjamins.

Givón, T. (1987). Beyond foreground and background. In Tomlin, R.S. (ed.) *Coherence and Grounding in Discourse*, 175–188.

Gold, E. (1967). Language identification in the limit. *Information and Control*, 10(5):447–474.

Goldberg, A. E. (1995). *Construction Grammar: A Construction Grammar Approach to Argument Structure*. University of Chicago Press.

Goldberg, A. E. (2006). *Constructions at Work*. Oxford University Press, Oxford.

Goldberg, A. E. (2019). *Explain Me This: Creativity, Competition, and the Partial Productivity of Constructions*. Princeton University Press.

Goldberg, A. E. and Michaelis, L. A. (2017). One among many: Anaphoric one and its relationship with numeral one. *Cognitive Science*, 41:233–258.

Goldin-Meadow, S., So, W., Özyürek, A., and Mylander, C. (2008). The natural order of events: How speakers of different languages represent events nonverbally. *Proceedings of the National Academy of Sciences*, 105(27):9163–9168.

Gordon, P. (2004). Numerical cognition without words: Evidence from Amazonia. *Science*, 306(5695):496.

Gordon, P., Hendrick, R., and Johnson, M. (2004). Effects of noun phrase type on sentence complexity. *Journal of Memory and Language*, 51(1):97–114.

Gordon, P. C., Hendrick, R., and Johnson, M. (2001). Memory interference during language processing. *Journal of Experimental Psychology: Learning, Memory, and Cognition*, 27(6):1411.

Gordon, P. C., Hendrick, R., Johnson, M., and Lee, Y. (2006). Similarity-based interference during language comprehension: Evidence from eye tracking during reading. *Journal of Experimental Psychology: Learning, Memory, and Cognition*, 32(6):1304–1321.

Goźdź-Roszkowski, S. (2011). *Patterns of Linguistic Variation in American Legal English: A Corpus-Based Study*. Peter Lang Frankfurt am Main.

Greenberg, J. H. (1963). Some universals of grammar with particular reference to the order of meaningful elements. In Greenberg, J. H., editor, *Universals of Language*, 73–113. MIT Press.

Grodner, D. and Gibson, E. (2005). Consequences of the serial nature of linguistic input for sentential complexity. *Cognitive Science*, 29(2):261–290.

Grodzinsky, Y. (2000). The neurology of syntax: Language use without Broca's area. *Behavioral and Brain Sciences*, 23(1):1–21.

Grosu, A. (1981). *Approaches to Island Phenomena*, volume 45. North Holland.

Haegeman, L. (1991). *Introduction to Government and Binding Theory*. Wiley-Blackwell.

Haegeman, L. and Guéron, J. (1999). *English Grammar: A Generative Perspective*. Blackwell Publishing.

Hahn, M., Futrell, R., Levy, R., and Gibson, E. (2022). A resource-rational model of human processing of recursive linguistic structure. *Proceedings of the National Academy of Sciences*, 119(43):e2122602119.

Hahn, M., Jurafsky, D., and Futrell, R. (2020). Universals of word order reflect optimization of grammars for efficient communication. *Proceedings of the National Academy of Sciences*, 117(5):2347–2353.

Hahn, M. and Xu, Y. (2022). Crosslinguistic word order variation reflects evolutionary pressures of dependency and information locality. *Proceedings of the National Academy of Sciences*, 119(24):e2122604119.

Hale, J. (2001). A probabilistic Earley parser as a psycholinguistic model. In *Proceedings of the Second Meeting of the North American Chapter of the Association for Computational Linguistics on Language Technologies*, 1–8. Association for Computational Linguistics.

Hall, M. L., Mayberry, R. I., and Ferreira, V. S. (2013). Cognitive constraints on constituent order: Evidence from elicited pantomime. *Cognition*, 129(1):1–17.

Halliday, M. A. K. (2015). Intonation and grammar in british english. In *Intonation and Grammar in British English*. De Gruyter Mouton.

Hartshorne, J. K., Tenenbaum, J. B., and Pinker, S. (2018). A critical period for second language acquisition: Evidence from 2/3 million English speakers. *Cognition*, 177:263–277.

Haskell, T. R. and MacDonald, M. C. (2003). Conflicting cues and competition in subject–verb agreement. *Journal of Memory and Language*, 48(4):760–778.

Haspelmath, M. (2001). *Word Classes and Parts of Speech*, 16538–16545. https://doi.org/10.1016/B0-08-043076-7/02959-4.

Haspelmath, M. (2017). The indeterminacy of word segmentation and the nature of morphology and syntax. *Folia Linguistica*, 51(s1000):31–80.

Haspelmath, M. (2023). Defining the word. *WORD*, 69(3):283–297.

Hawkins, J. A. (1983). *Word Order Universals: Quantitative Analyses of Linguistic Structure*. New York: Academic Press.

Hawkins, J. A. (1990). A parsing theory of word order universals. *Linguistic Inquiry*, 21(2):223–261.

Hawkins, J. A. (1994). *A Performance Theory of Order and Constituency*. Cambridge University Press, Cambridge.

Hawkins, J. A. (2001). Why are categories adjacent? *Journal of Linguistics*, 37:1–34.

Hawkins, J. A. (2002). Symmetries and asymmetries: Their grammar, typology and parsing. *Theoretical Linguistics*, 28:95–149.

Hawkins, J. A. (2004). *Efficiency and Complexity in Grammars*. Oxford University Press.

Hays, D. G. (1964). Dependency theory: A formalism and some observations. *Language*, 40:511–525.

He, H., Li, J., Xiao, Q., Jiang, S., Yang, Y., and Zhi, S. (2019). Language and color perception: Evidence from Mongolian and Chinese speakers. *Frontiers in Psychology*, 10:551.

Heim, I. and Kratzer, A. (1998). *Semantics in Generative Grammar*. Wiley-Blackwell.

Henrich, J., Heine, S. J., and Norenzayan, A. (2010). Most people are not weird. *Nature*, 466(7302):29–29.

Hewitt, J. and Manning, C. D. (2019). A structural probe for finding syntax in word representations. In *Proceedings of the 2019 Conference of the North American Chapter of the Association for Computational Linguistics: Human Language Technologies, Volume 1 (Long and Short Papers)*, 4129–4138.

Hick, W. E. (1952). On the rate of gain of information. *Quarterly Journal of Experimental Psychology*, 4(1):11–26.

Hicks, G. (2009). Tough-constructions and their derivation. *Linguistic Inquiry*, 40(4):535–566.

Hilpert, M. (2014). *Construction Grammar and Its Application to English*. Edinburgh University Press.

Hirst, D. and Di Cristo, A. (1998). Intonation systems. *A Survey of Twenty Languages*.

Hopper, P. (1987). Emergent grammar. In *Annual Meeting of the Berkeley Linguistics Society*, volume 13, 139–157.

Howes, D. H. and Solomon, R. L. (1951). Visual duration threshold as a function of word-probability. *Journal of Experimental Psychology*, 41(6):401.

Hsu, A., Chater, N., and Vitányi, P. (2011). The probabilistic analysis of language acquisition: Theoretical, computational, and experimental analysis. *Cognition*, 120(3):380–390.

Hu, J., Gauthier, J., Qian, P., Wilcox, E., and Levy, R. P. (2020). A systematic assessment of syntactic generalization in neural language models. In *Proceedings of the 58th Annual*

Meeting of the Association for Computational Linguistics, 1725–1744, online. Association for Computational Linguistics.

Huang, C.-T. J. (1982). *Logical Relations in Chinese and the Theory of Grammar*. PhD thesis, MIT.

Hudson, R. (2008). Word grammar and construction grammar. In Traugott, E. C., Kortmann, B., Trousdale, G., and Gisborne, N., editors, *Constructional Approaches to English Grammar*, 257–302. Mouton de Gruyter.

Hudson, R. (2010). *An Introduction to Word Grammar*. Cambridge University Press.

Hudson, R. (2015). Word grammar. In B. Heine & Narrog, H., *The Oxford Handbook of Linguistic Analysis*, Oxford University Press, 981–1008.

Hudson, R. A. (1984). *Word Grammar*. Blackwell.

Hudson, R. A. (1990). *English Word Grammar*. Blackwell.

Hudson, R. A. (1995). Measuring syntactic difficulty. Unpublished manuscript, University College, London.

Hudson, R. A. (2004). Are determiners heads? *Functions of Language*, 11(1):7–42.

Hudson, R. A. (2006). *Language Networks: The New Word Grammar*. Oxford University Press.

Huettig, F., Rommers, J., and Meyer, A. S. (2011). Using the visual world paradigm to study language processing: A review and critical evaluation. *Acta Psychologica*, 137(2):151–171.

Isbilen, E. S. and Christiansen, M. H. (2020). Chunk-based memory constraints on the cultural evolution of language. *Topics in Cognitive Science*, 12(2):713–726.

Ivanova, A. A., Mineroff, Z., Zimmerer, V., Kanwisher, N., Varley, R., and Fedorenko, E. (2021). The language network is recruited but not required for nonverbal event semantics. *Neurobiology of Language*, 2(2):176–201.

Ivanova, A. A., Srikant, S., Sueoka, Y., Kean, H. H., Dhamala, R., O'reilly, U.-M., Bers, M. U., and Fedorenko, E. (2020). Comprehension of computer code relies primarily on domain-general executive brain regions. *Elife*, 9:e58906.

Jackendoff, R. (1977). X syntax: A study of phrase structure. *Linguistic Inquiry Monographs* (2):1–249.

Jackendoff, R. (1997). *The Architecture of the Language Faculty*. Number 28. MIT Press.

Jackendoff, R. (2007). A parallel architecture perspective on language processing. *Brain Research*, 1146:2–22.

Jackendoff, R. (2013). Constructions in the parallel architecture. In Hoffmann, T. and Trousdale, G., editors, *Oxford Handbook of Construction Grammar*.

Jackendoff, R. and Audring, J. (2020). *The Texture of the Lexicon: Relational Morphology and the Parallel Architecture*. Oxford University Press.

Jacobson, P. (2023). *Losing Sight of the Forest through the Trees: Remarks on Constituent Structure and Constituent Structure Tests*. Ordinary Working Grammarian [Blog]: http://ordinaryworkinggrammarian.blogspot.com/2023/06/guest-blog-post-by-pauline-jacobson-on.html.

Jaeger, T. (2010). Redundancy and reduction: Speakers manage syntactic information density. *Cognitive Psychology*, 61(1):23–62.

Jakobson, R. (1936). *Contribution to the General Theory of Case: General Meanings of the Russian Cases [Translation of Beitrag zur allgemeinen Kasuslehre: Gesamtbedeutung der russischen Kasus.]*. Number 6.

January, D. and Kako, E. (2007). Re-evaluating evidence for linguistic relativity: Reply to Boroditsky (2001). *Cognition*, 104(2):417–426.

Johnson-Laird, P. N. (1983). *Mental Models: Towards a Cognitive Science of Language, Inference, and Consciousness*. Number 6. Harvard University Press.

Joshi, A. and Rambow, O. (2003). A formalism for dependency grammar based on tree adjoining grammar. In *Proceedings of the Conference on Meaning-text Theory*, pages 207–216. MTT Paris, France.

Jouravlev, O., Zheng, D., Balewski, Z., Pongos, A. L. A., Levan, Z., Goldin-Meadow, S., and Fedorenko, E. (2019). Speech-accompanying gestures are not processed by the language-processing mechanisms. *Neuropsychologia*, 132:107132.

Juhasz, B. J. (2005). Age-of-acquisition effects in word and picture identification. *Psychological Bulletin*, 131(5):684.

Jun, S.-A. (2005). *Prosodic Typology: The Phonology of Intonation and Phrasing*. Oxford University Press.

Jun, S.-A. (2014). Prosodic typology: By prominence type, word prosody, and macro-rhythm. *Prosodic Typology II: The Phonology of Intonation and Phrasing*, 520539.

Just, M. A., Carpenter, P. A., and Woolley, J. D. (1982). Paradigms and processes in reading comprehension. *Journal of Experimental Psychology: General*, 111(2):228.

Kac, M. B. (1981). Center-embedding revisited. In *Proceedings of the Third Annual Conference of the Cognitive Science Society*, pages 123–124. Lawrence Erlbaum Hillsdale.

Kanwisher, N. (2010). Functional specificity in the human brain: A window into the functional architecture of the mind. *Proceedings of the National Academy of Sciences*, 107(25):11163–11170.

Kanwisher, N., McDermott, J., and Chun, M. (1997). The fusiform face area: A module in human extrastriate cortex specialized for face perception. *Journal of Neuroscience*, 17(11):4302.

Karlsson, F. (2007). Constraints on multiple center-embedding of clauses. *Journal of Linguistics*, 43(2):365–392.

Kauf, C., Kim, H. S., Lee, E. J., Jhingan, N., She, J. S., Taliaferro, M., Gibson, E., and Fedorenko, E. (2024). Linguistic inputs must be syntactically parsable to fully engage the language network. *bioRxiv*.

Kay, P. and Kempton, W. (1984). What is the Sapir-Whorf hypothesis? *American Anthropologist*, 86(1):65–79.

Kay, P. and Maffi, L. (1999). Color appearance and the emergence and evolution of basic color lexicons. *American Anthropologist*, 101(4):743–760.

Kayne, R. S. (1983). *Connectedness and Binary Branching*. Foris publications.

Keller, F. (2000). *Gradience in Grammar: Experimental and Computational Aspects of Degrees of Grammaticality*. PhD thesis.

Kemp, C. and Regier, T. (2012). Kinship categories across languages reflect general communicative principles. *Science*, 336(6084):1049–1054.

Kemp, C., Xu, Y., and Regier, T. (2018). Semantic typology and efficient communication. *Annual Review of Linguistics*, 4:109–128.

Kim, J.-B. and Sag, I. A. (2002). Negation without head-movement. *Natural Language & Linguistic Theory*, 20(2):339–412.

Kimball, J. (1973). Seven principles of surface structure parsing in natural language. *Cognition*, 2:15–47.

Kiparsky, P. (1995). Pāinian linguistics. In *Concise History of the Language Sciences*, 59–65. Elsevier.

Kolmogorov, A. N. (1963). On tables of random numbers. *Sankhyā: The Indian Journal of Statistics, Series A*, 369–376.

Koopman, H. and Sportiche, D. (1991). The position of subjects. *Lingua*, 85(2-3):211–258.

Kruijff, G. and Vasishth, S. (2003). Quantifying word order freedom in natural language: Implications for sentence processing. In *Proceedings of the Architectures and Mechanisms for Language Processing Conference*, San Sebastián, Spain.

Kulmizev, A. and Nivre, J. (2022). Schrödinger's tree–on syntax and neural language models. *Frontiers in Artificial Intelligence*, 5:796788.

Kuno, S. (1987). *Functional Syntax: Anaphora, Discourse and Empathy.* University of Chicago Press.

Kuperman, V., Stadthagen-Gonzalez, H., and Brysbaert, M. (2012). Age-of-acquisition ratings for 30,000 english words. *Behavior Research Methods*, 44(4):978–990.

Kutas, M. and Federmeier, K. D. (2011). Thirty years and counting: Finding meaning in the N400 component of the event-related brain potential (ERP). *Annual Review of Psychology*, 62:621–647.

Kutas, M. and Hillyard, S. A. (1980). Reading senseless sentences: Brain potentials reflect semantic incongruity. *Science*, 207(4427):203–205.

Kutas, M. and Hillyard, S. A. (1984). Brain potentials during reading reflect word expectancy and semantic association. *Nature*, 307:161–163.

Ladd, D. R. (2008). *Intonational Phonology.* Cambridge University Press.

Lakoff, G. (1987). *Women, Fire, and Dangerous Things: What Categories Reveal about the Mind.* University of Chicago Press.

Lakretz, Y., Kruszewski, G., Desbordes, T., Hupkes, D., Dehaene, S., and Baroni, M. (2019). The emergence of number and syntax units in LSTM language models. In *Proceedings of the 2019 Conference of the North American Chapter of the Association for Computational Linguistics: Human Language Technologies, Volume 1 (Long and Short Papers)*, 11–20, Minneapolis, Minnesota. Association for Computational Linguistics.

Lambrecht, K. (1994). *Information Structure and Sentence Form.* Cambridge University Press.

Langacker, R. (1987). *Foundations of Cognitive Grammar*, volume 1. Stanford University Press.

Langacker, R. (1991). *Foundations of Cognitive Grammar*, volume 2. Stanford University Press.

Langacker, R. W. (1997). Constituency, dependency, and conceptual grouping. *Cognitive Linguistics*, 8(1):1–32.

Larson, R. K. and Marušič, F. (2004). On indefinite pronoun structures with APS: Reply to Kishimoto. *Linguistic Inquiry*, 35(2):268–287.

Lau, J. H., Clark, A., and Lappin, S. (2017). Grammaticality, acceptability, and probability: A probabilistic view of linguistic knowledge. *Cognitive Science*, 41(5):1202–1241.

Laurence, S. and Margolis, E. (2001). The poverty of the stimulus argument. *British Journal for the Philosophy of Science*, 52(2):217–276.

LeCun, Y., Bengio, Y., and Hinton, G. (2015). Deep learning. *Nature*, 521(7553):436–444.

Lehmann, W. P. (1973). A structural principle of language and its implications. *Language*, 49:47–66.

Leivada, E. (2020). Language processing at its trickiest: Grammatical illusions and heuristics of judgment. *Languages*, 5(3):29.

Leonard, W. R., Reyes-García, V., Tanner, S., Rosinger, A., Schultz, A., Vadez, V., Zhang, R., and Godoy, R. (2015). Tsimane' Amazonian panel study (TAPS): Nine years (2002–2010) of annual data available to the public. *Economics & Human Biology*, 19:51–61.

Levin, B. (1993). *English Verb Classes and Alternations: A Preliminary Investigation.* University of Chicago Press.

Levinson, S. C. (2003a). Language and mind: Let's get the issues straight. In Blum, S. D., editor, *Making Sense of Language*, 68–80. Oxford University Press.

Levinson, S. C. (2003b). *Space in Language and Cognition: Explorations in Cognitive Diversity*, volume 5. Cambridge University Press.

Levy, R. (2008a). Expectation-based syntactic comprehension. *Cognition*, 106(3): 1126–1177.

Levy, R. (2008b). A noisy-channel model of rational human sentence comprehension under uncertain input. In *Proceedings of the Conference on Empirical Methods in Natural Language Processing*, pages 234–243. Association for Computational Linguistics.

Levy, R., Bicknell, K., Slattery, T., and Rayner, K. (2009). Eye movement evidence that readers maintain and act on uncertainty about past linguistic input. *Proceedings of the National Academy of Sciences*, 106(50):21086–21090.

Levy, R., Fedorenko, E., Breen, M., and Gibson, T. (2012). The processing of extraposed structures in English. *Cognition*, 122(1):12–36.

Levy, R. and Keller, F. (2013). Expectation and locality effects in German verb-final structures. *Journal of Memory and Language*, 68(2):199–222.

Levy, R. and Manning, C. D. (2004). Deep dependencies from context-free statistical parsers: Correcting the surface dependency approximation. In *Proceedings of the 42nd Annual Meeting of the Association for Computational Linguistics (ACL-04)*, 327–334.

Lewis, R. and Vasishth, S. (2005a). An activation-based model of sentence processing as skilled memory retrieval. *Cognitive Science*, 29(3):375–419.

Lewis, R. L. (1996). Interference in short-term memory: The magical number two (or three) in sentence processing. *Journal of Psycholinguistic Research*, 25(1):93–115.

Lewis, R. L. and Vasishth, S. (2005b). An activation-based model of sentence processing as skilled memory retrieval. *Cognitive Science*, 29(3):375–419.

Lewis, R. L., Vasishth, S., and van Dyke, J. A. (2006). Computational principles of working memory in sentence comprehension. *Trends in Cognitive Science*, 10(10):447–454.

Lidz, J., Waxman, S., and Freedman, J. (2003). What infants know about syntax but couldn't have learned: Experimental evidence for syntactic structure at 18 months. *Cognition*, 89(3):295–303.

Linhares, J. M. M., Pinto, P. D., and Nascimento, S. M. C. (2008). The number of discernible colors in natural scenes. *Journal of the Optical Society of America A*, 25(12):2918–2924.

Linzen, T. and Baroni, M. (2021). Syntactic structure from deep learning. *Annual Review of Linguistics*, 7:195–212.

Linzen, T. and Oseki, Y. (2018). The reliability of acceptability judgments across languages. *Glossa: A Journal of General Linguistics*, 3(1).

Lipkin, B., Tuckute, G., Affourtit, J., Small, H., Mineroff, Z., Kean, H., Jouravlev, O., Rakocevic, L., Pritchett, B., Siegelman, M., et al. (2022). Probabilistic atlas for the language network based on precision fMRI data from >800 individuals. *Scientific Data*, 9(1):1–10.

Liu, H. (2008). Dependency distance as a metric of language comprehension difficulty. *Journal of Cognitive Science*, 9(2):159–191.

Liu, Y., Ryskin, R., Futrell, R., and Gibson, E. (2021). Structural frequency effects in noisy-channel comprehension. 46th Annual Penn Linguistics Conference, University of Pennsylvania, Philadelphia, PA.

Liu, Y., Ryskin, R., Futrell, R., and Gibson, E. (2022a). A verb-frame frequency account of constraints on long-distance dependencies in English. *Cognition*, 222:104902.

Liu, Y., Winckel, E., Abeillé, A., Hemforth, B., and Gibson, E. (2022b). Structural, functional, and processing perspectives on linguistic island effects. *Annual Review of Linguistics*, 8:495–525.

Liu, Z. (2020). Mixed evidence for crosslinguistic dependency length minimization. *STUF-Language Typology and Universals*, 73(4):605–633.

Livingstone, M. S., Pettine, W. W., Srihasam, K., Moore, B., Morocz, I. A., and Lee, D. (2014). Symbol addition by monkeys provides evidence for normalized quantity coding. *Proceedings of the National Academy of Sciences*, 111(18):6822–6827.

Lowe, J. J. (2019). The syntax and semantics of nonfinite forms. *Annual Review of Linguistics*, 5:309–328.

MacDonald, M. C. (1989). Priming effects from gaps to antecedents. *Language and Cognitive Processes*, 4(1):35–56.

MacDonald, M. C. (2013). How language production shapes language form and comprehension. *Frontiers in Psychology*, 4:40296.

MacDonald, M. C., Pearlmutter, N. J., and Seidenberg, M. S. (1994). The lexical nature of syntactic ambiguity resolution. *Psychological Review*, 101(4):676.

MacWhinney, B. (1977). Starting points. *Language*, 53(1):152–168.

Madabushi, H. T., Romain, L., Divjak, D., and Milin, P. (2020). CxG-BERT: BERT meets construction grammar. *arXiv preprint arXiv:2011.04134*. https://arxiv.org/abs/2011.04134.

Mahowald, K. and Fedorenko, E. (2016). Reliable individual-level neural markers of high-level language processing: A necessary precursor for relating neural variability to behavioral and genetic variability. *Neuroimage*, 139:74–93.

Mahowald, K., Hartman, J., Graff, P., and Gibson, E. (2016). Snap judgments: A small N acceptability paradigm (SNAP) for linguistic acceptability judgments. *Language*, 619–635.

Mahowald, K., Ivanova, A. A., Blank, I. A., Kanwisher, N., Tenenbaum, J. B., and Fedorenko, E. (2024). Dissociating language and thought in large language models. *Trends in Cognitive Science*, 28(6):517–540.

Majid, A. and Burenhult, N. (2014). Odors are expressible in language, as long as you speak the right language. *Cognition*, 130(2):266–270.

Majid, A. and Kruspe, N. (2018). Hunter-gatherer olfaction is special. *Current Biology*, 28(3):409–413.

Malik-Moraleda, S., Ayyash, D., Gallée, J., Affourtit, J., Hoffmann, M., Mineroff, Z., Jouravlev, O., and Fedorenko, E. (2022). An investigation across 45 languages and 12 language families reveals a universal language network. *Nature Neuroscience*, 25(8):1014–1019.

Malik-Moraleda, S., Mahowald, K., Conway, B. R., and Gibson, E. (2023). Concepts are restructured during language contact: The birth of blue and other color concepts in Tsimane'-Spanish bilinguals. *Psychological Science*, 34(12):1350–1362.

Manning, C. D., Clark, K., Hewitt, J., Khandelwal, U., and Levy, O. (2020). Emergent linguistic structure in artificial neural networks trained by self-supervision. *Proceedings of the National Academy of Sciences*.

Marantz, A. (2005). Generative linguistics within the cognitive neuroscience of language. *Linguistic Review*, 22(2–4):429–445.

Marcus, M. P. (1978). *A Theory of Syntactic Recognition for Natural Language*. PhD thesis, Massachusetts Institute of Technology.

Marr, D. (1982). *Vision: A Computational Investigation into the Human Representation and Processing of Visual Information.* W.H. Freeman & Company.

Marsaja, I. G. (2008). *Desa Kolok - A Deaf Village and Its Sign Language in Bali, Indonesia.* Ishara Press.

Martínez, E., Mollica, F., and Gibson, E. (2022). Poor writing, not specialized concepts, drives processing difficulty in legal language. *Cognition,* 224:105070.

Martínez, E., Mollica, F., and Gibson, E. (2023). Even lawyers do not like legalese. *Proceedings of the National Academy of Sciences,* 120(23):e2302672120.

Martínez, E., Mollica, F., and Gibson, E. (2024a). Even laypeople use legalese. *Proceedings of the National Academy of Sciences,* 121(35):e2405564121.

Martínez, E., Mollica, F., and Gibson, E. (2024b). So much for plain language: An analysis of the accessibility of US federal laws over time. *Journal of Experimental Psychology: General,* 153(5):1153.

Martinovic, J., Paramei, G. V., and MacInnes, W. J. (2020). Russian blues reveal the limits of language influencing colour discrimination. *Cognition,* 201:104281.

Marvin, R. and Linzen, T. (2018). Targeted syntactic evaluation of language models. *arXiv preprint arXiv:1808.09031.* https://arxiv.org/abs/1808.09031

Masaoka, K., Berns, R. S., Fairchild, M. D., and Abed, F. M. (2013). Number of discernible object colors is a conundrum. *Journal of the Optical Society of America A,* 30(2):264–277.

McCauley, S. M., Bannard, C., Theakston, A., Davis, M., Cameron-Faulkner, T., and Ambridge, B. (2021). Multiword units lead to errors of commission in children's spontaneous production:"What corpus data can tell us?*" *Developmental Science,* 24(6):e13125.

McCulloch, G. (2020). *Because internet: Understanding the new rules of language.* Penguin.

McElree, B., Foraker, S., and Dyer, L. (2003). Memory structures that subserve sentence comprehension. *Journal of Memory and Language,* 48:67–91.

McKoon, G., Allbritton, D., and Ratcliff, R. (1996). Sentential context effects on lexical decisions with a cross-modal instead of an all-visual procedure. *Journal of Experimental Psychology: Learning, Memory, and Cognition,* 22(6):1494.

McKoon, G. and Ratcliff, R. (1994). Sentential context and on-line lexical decision. *Journal of Experimental Psychology: Learning, Memory, and Cognition,* 20(5):1239–1243.

Meir, I., Sandler, W., Padden, C., and Aronoff, M. (2010a). Emerging sign languages. In Marschark, M. and Spencer, P., editors, *Oxford Handbook of Deaf Studies, Language, and Education,* volume 2. Oxford University Press.

Meir, I., Sandler, W., Padden, C., Aronoff, M., et al. (2010b). Emerging sign languages. *Oxford handbook of deaf studies, language, and education*, 2:267–280.

Mel'čuk, I. A. (1988). *Dependency syntax: Theory and practice*. SUNY Press.

Mel'čuk, I. A. and Pertsov, N. V. (1986). *Surface syntax of English: A formal model within the meaning-text framework*. John Benjamins.

Meurers, W. D. (2001). On expressing lexical generalizations in HPSG. *Nordic Journal of Linguistics*, 24(2):161–217.

Mickan, A., Schiefke, M., and Stefanowitsch, A. (2014). Key is a llave is a Schlüssel: A failure to replicate an experiment from Boroditsky et al. 2003. *Yearbook of the German Cognitive Linguistics Association*, 2(1):39–50.

Milne, R. W. (1982). Predicting garden path sentences. *Cognitive Science*, 6(4):349–373.

Mineroff, Z., Blank, I. A., Mahowald, K., and Fedorenko, E. (2018). A robust dissociation among the language, multiple demand, and default mode networks: Evidence from inter-region correlations in effect size. *Neuropsychologia*, 119:501–511.

Mollica, F., Bacon, G., Zaslavsky, N., Xu, Y., Regier, T., and Kemp, C. (2021). The forms and meanings of grammatical markers support efficient communication. *Proceedings of the National Academy of Sciences*, 118(49):e2025993118.

Monsell, S. (1991). The nature and locus of word frequency effects in reading. In *Basic Processes in Reading, Visual Word Recognition*, 156–205. Routledge.

Montague, R. (1970). English as a formal language. *Linguaggi Nella Societae Nella Tecnica*, 189–224.

Morton, J. (1969). Interaction of information in word recognition. *Psychological Review*, 76(2):165–178.

Mukamel, R. and Fried, I. (2012). Human intracranial recordings and cognitive neuroscience. *Annual Review of Psychology*, 63:511–537.

Müller, S. (2003). Object-to-subject-raising and lexical rule: An analysis of the German passive. In *Proceedings of the HPSG-2003 Conference, Michigan State University, East Lansing*, 278–297. Citeseer.

Müller, S. (2023). *Grammatical Theory: From Transformational Grammar to Constraint-Based Approaches*. Language Science Press.

Müller, S., Abeillé, A., Borsley, R. D., and Koenig, J.-P. (2021). *Head-Driven Phrase Structure Grammar: The Handbook (Volume 9)*. Language Science Press.

Nakajima, H. (2006). Adverbial cognate objects. *Linguistic Inquiry*, 37(4):674–684.

Nakatani, K. and Gibson, E. (2010). An on-line study of Japanese nesting complexity. *Cognitive Science*, 34(1):94–112.

Nedergaard, J. S. and Lupyan, G. (2024). Not everybody has an inner voice: Behavioral consequences of anendophasia. *Psychological Science*, page 09567976241243004.

Nefdt, R. M. and Baggio, G. (2023). Notational variants and cognition: The case of dependency grammar. *Erkenntnis*, pages 1–31.

Newell, A. (1990). *Unified Theories of Cognition*. Harvard University Press.

Newport, E. L., Seydell-Greenwald, A., Landau, B., Turkeltaub, P. E., Chambers, C. E., Martin, K. C., Rennert, R., Giannetti, M., Dromerick, A. W., Ichord, R. N., et al. (2022). Language and developmental plasticity after perinatal stroke. *Proceedings of the National Academy of Sciences*, 119(42):e2207293119.

Nichols, J. (1986). Head-marking and dependent-marking grammar. *Language*, 62(1):56–119.

Nichols, J. (1992). *Linguistic Diversity in Space and Time*. University of Chicago Press.

Nicol, J. and Swinney, D. (1989). The role of structure in coreference assignment during sentence comprehension. *Journal of Psycholinguistic Research*, 18(1): 5–19.

Nicol, J. L., Fodor, J. D., and Swinney, D. (1994). Using cross-modal lexical decision tasks to investigate sentence processing. *Journal of Experimental Psychology: Learning, Memory, and Cognition*, 20(5):1229–1238.

Nieuwland, M. S. and Van Berkum, J. J. (2006). When peanuts fall in love: N400 evidence for the power of discourse. *Journal of Cognitive Neuroscience*, 18(7):1098–1111.

Nivre, J. (2005). *Dependency Grammar and Dependency Parsing*. Technical report, Växjö University.

Nivre, J., Bosco, C., Choi, J., et al. (2015). *Universal Dependencies 1.0*. Universal Dependencies Consortium.

Nivre, J., De Marneffe, M.-C., Ginter, F., et al. (2016). Universal dependencies v1: A multilingual treebank collection. In *Proceedings of the Tenth International Conference on Language Resources and Evaluation (LREC'16)*, 1659–1666.

Nivre, J., De Marneffe, M.-C., Ginter, F., Hajič, J., Manning, C. D., Pyysalo, S., Schuster, S., Tyers, F., and Zeman, D. (2020). Universal dependencies v2: An evergrowing multilingual treebank collection. *arXiv preprint arXiv:2004.10643*.

Novick, J. M., Trueswell, J. C., and Thompson-Schill, S. L. (2005). Cognitive control and parsing: Reexamining the role of Broca's area in sentence comprehension. *Cognitive, Affective, & Behavioral Neuroscience*, 5(3):263–281.

O'Connor, E. (2015). *Comparative Illusions at the Syntax-Semantics Interface*. PhD thesis, University of Southern California.

Oden, D. L., Thompson, R. K., and Premack, D. (2001). Can an ape reason analogically? Comprehension and production of analogical problems by Sarah, a chimpanzee (pan troglodytes). *The Analogical Mind*, ed. D. Gentner, KJ Holyoak & BN Kokinov, 471–498.

Ogden, C. K. and Richards, I. A. (1927). *The Meaning of Meaning: A Study of the Influence of Language upon Thought and of the Science of Symbolism*, volume 29. K. Paul, Trench, Trubner & Company.

Osborne, T. (2019). *A Dependency Grammar of English: An Introduction and Beyond*. John Benjamins Publishing Company.

Osborne, T. J. (2018). Tests for constituents: What they really reveal about the nature of syntactic structure. *Language under Discussion*, 5(1):1–41.

O'Shaughnessy, D. M., Gibson, E., and Piantadosi, S. T. (2021). The cultural origins of symbolic number. *Psychological Review*, 129(6):1442–1456. https://doi.org/10.1037/rev0000289.

Osterhout, L. and Holcomb, P. J. (1992). Event-related brain potentials elicited by syntactic anomaly. *Journal of Memory and Language*, 31(6):785–806.

Ouattara, K., Lemasson, A., and Zuberbühler, K. (2009). Campbell's monkeys concatenate vocalizations into context-specific call sequences. *Proceedings of the National Academy of Sciences*, 106(51):22026–22031.

Paape, D., Vasishth, S., and von der Malsburg, T. (2020). Quadruplex negatio invertit? The on-line processing of depth charge sentences. *Journal of Semantics*, 37(4): 509–555.

Pallier, C., Devauchelle, A.-D., and Dehaene, S. (2011). Cortical representation of the constituent structure of sentences. *Proceedings of the National Academy of Sciences*, 108(6):2522–2527.

Papadimitriou, I. and Jurafsky, D. (2023). Injecting structural hints: Using language models to study inductive biases in language learning. In *Findings of the Association for Computational Linguistics: EMNLP 2023*, 8402–8413.

Paul, D. B. and Baker, J. (1992). The design for the wall street journal-based CSR corpus. In Speech and Natural Language: Proceedings of a Workshop Held at Harriman, New York, February 23-26, 1992.

Paunov, A. M., Blank, I. A., and Fedorenko, E. (2019). Functionally distinct language and theory of mind networks are synchronized at rest and during language comprehension. *Journal of Neurophysiology*, 121(4):1244–1265.

Pearl, L. and Sprouse, J. (2013). Syntactic islands and learning biases: Combining experimental syntax and computational modeling to investigate the language acquisition problem. *Language Acquisition*, 20(1):23–68.

Perfors, A., Tenenbaum, J. B., and Regier, T. (2013). The learnability of abstract syntactic principles. *Cognition*, 118(3):306–338.

Phillips, C. (2009). Should we impeach armchair linguists. *Japanese/Korean Linguistics*, 17:49–64.

Piantadosi, S., Tenenbaum, J. B., and Goodman, N. D. (2013). Bootstrapping in a language of thought: A formal model of numerical concept learning. *Cognition*, 123(2):199–217.

Piantadosi, S., Tily, H., and Gibson, E. (2012a). The communicative function of ambiguity in language. *Cognition*, 122(3):280–291.

Piantadosi, S. T. (2024). Modern language models refute Chomsky's approach to language. In Gibson, E. and Polliak, M., editors, *From Fieldwork to Linguistic Theory: A Tribute to Dan Everett*. Language Science Press.

Piantadosi, S. T., Tily, H., and Gibson, E. (2012b). The communicative function of ambiguity in language. *Cognition*, 122(3):280–291.

Pickering, M. and Barry, G. (1991). Sentence processing without empty categories. *Language and Cognitive Processes*, 6(3):229–259.

Pinker, S. (1995). *Language Acquisition*, In Osherson, D.N. & Gleitman, L.R. An invitation to cognitive science. 135–181.

Pitt, B., Gibson, E., and Piantadosi, S. T. (2022). Exact number concepts are limited to the verbal count range. *Psychological Science*, 33(3):371–381.

Pointer, M. and Attridge, G. (1998). The number of discernible colours. *Color Research & Application: Endorsed by Inter-Society Color Council, The Colour Group (Great Britain), Canadian Society for Color, Color Science Association of Japan, Dutch Society for the Study of Color, The Swedish Colour Centre Foundation, Colour Society of Australia, Centre Français de la Couleur*, 23(1):52–54.

Poldrack, R. A., Mumford, J. A., and Nichols, T. E. (2011). *Handbook of Functional MRI Data Analysis*. Cambridge University Press.

Poliak, M., Ryskin, R., Braginsky, M., and Gibson, E. (2022). It's not what you say but how you say it: Evidence from russian shows robust effects of the structural prior on noisy channel inferences. *submitted*.

Poliak, M., Ryskin, R., Braginsky, M., and Gibson, E. (2024). It is not what you say but how you say it: Evidence from Russian shows robust effects of the structural prior on noisy channel inferences. *Journal of Experimental Psychology: Learning, Memory, and Cognition*, 50(4):637.

Poliak, M., An, A., Levy, R., and Gibson, E. (2025). Rational inference underlies judgments of grammatical well-formedness. submitted.

Pollard, C. and Sag, I. A. (1987). *Information-Based Syntax and Semantics*. Center for the Study of Language and Information.

Pollard, C. and Sag, I. A. (1994). *Head-Driven Phrase Structure Grammar*. Center for the Study of Language and Information.

Poppels, T. and Levy, R. (2016). Structure-sensitive noise inference: Comprehenders expect exchange errors. In *Proceedings of the 38th Annual Meeting of the Cognitive Science Society*, 378–383, Philadelphia, PA.

Potts, C. G. (2023). Characterizing English preposing in PP constructions. *URL lingbuzz.net/lingbuzz/007495*.

Premack, D. (2007). Human and animal cognition: Continuity and discontinuity. *Proceedings of the National Academy of Sciences*, 104(35):13861–13867.

Pritchett, B. L. (1988). Garden path phenomena and the grammatical basis of language processing. *Language*, 64(3):539–576.

Pritchett, B. L., Hoeflin, C., Koldewyn, K., Dechter, E., and Fedorenko, E. (2018). High-level language processing regions are not engaged in action observation or imitation. *Journal of Neurophysiology*, 120(5):2555–2570.

Prufer, H. (1918). Neuer beweis eines satzes uber per mutationen. *Archiv derMathematik und Physik*, 27:742–744.

Pullum, G. K. and Scholz, B. C. (2002). Empirical assessment of stimulus poverty arguments. *The Linguistic Review*, 19(1-2):9–50.

Pylkkänen, L. (2019). The neural basis of combinatory syntax and semantics. *Science*, 366(6461):62–66.

Quirk, R., Greenbaum, S., Leech, G., and Svartvik, J. (1985). *A Comprehensive Grammar of the English Language*. Longman.

Radford, A. (1988). *Transformational Grammar: A First Course*. Cambridge University Press.

Radford, A. (1997). *Syntactic Theory and the Structure of English: A Minimalist Approach*. Cambridge University Press.

Radford, A. (2004). *Minimalist Syntax: Exploring the Structure of English*. Cambridge University Press.

Radford, A., Wu, J., Child, R., Luan, D., Amodei, D., and Sutskever, I. (2019). Language models are unsupervised multitask learners. *OpenAI Blog*, 1(8):9.

Ramscar, M. (2021). How children learn to communicate discriminatively. *Journal of Child Language*, 48(5):984–1022.

Ramscar, M., Hendrix, P., Shaoul, C., Milin, P., and Baayen, H. (2014). The myth of cognitive decline: Non-linear dynamics of lifelong learning. *Topics in Cognitive Science*, 6(1):5–42.

Rasmussen, N. E. and Schuler, W. (2018). Left-corner parsing with distributed associative memory produces surprisal and locality effects. *Cognitive Science*, 42:1009–1042.

Regier, T., Kemp, C., and Kay, P. (2015). Word meanings across languages support efficient communication. In *The Handbook of Language Emergence*, 237–263. Wiley-Blackwell.

Resnik, P. (1992). Left-corner parsing and psychological plausibility. In *COLING 1992 Volume 1: The 14th International Conference on Computational Linguistics*.

Rijkhoff, J. N. (1986). Word order universals revisited. *Belgian Journal of Linguistics*, 1(95):125.

Ritchie, G. and Thompson, H. (1984). Natural language processing. *O'Shea, Tim; and Eisenstadt, Marc*.

Ritter, F. E., Tehranchi, F., and Oury, J. D. (2019). ACT-R: A cognitive architecture for modeling cognition. *Wiley Interdisciplinary Reviews: Cognitive Science*, 10(3):e1488.

Rizzi, L. (1982). Issues in italian syntax. In *Issues in Italian Syntax*. De Gruyter Mouton.

Roberson, D., Davidoff, J., Davies, I. R., and Shapiro, L. R. (2005). Color categories: Evidence for the cultural relativity hypothesis. *Cognitive Psychology*, 50(4):378–411.

Roberson, D., Davies, I., and Davidoff, J. (2000). Color categories are not universal: Replications and new evidence from a stone-age culture. *Journal of Experimental Psychology: General*, 129(3):369.

Roberts, I. (1997). *Comparative Syntax*. Arnold.

Roberts, I. (2023). *Beginning Syntax*. Cambridge University Press.

Robins, R. (1967). *A Short History of Linguistics*. Longman.

Rosch, E. H. (1973). Natural categories. *Cognitive Psychology*, 4(3):328–350.

Rosch-Heider, E. and Olivier, D. C. (1972). The structure of the color space in naming and memory for two languages. *Cognitive Psychology*, 3(2):337–354.

Rosenkrantz, D. J. and Lewis, P. M. (1970). Deterministic left corner parsing. In *11th Annual Symposium on Switching and Automata Theory (swat 1970)*, 139–152. IEEE.

Ross, J. R. (1967). Constraints on variables in syntax. Unpublished MIT PhD dissertation.

Ryskin, R., Futrell, R., Kiran, S., and Gibson, E. (2018). Comprehenders model the nature of noise in the environment. *Cognition*, 181:141–150.

Sag, I. A., Chaves, R. P., Abeillé, A., Estigarribia, B., Flickinger, D., Kay, P., Michaelis, L. A., Müller, S., Pullum, G. K., Van Eynde, F., et al. (2020). Lessons from the English auxiliary system. *Journal of Linguistics*, 56(1):87–155.

Sag, I. A. and Fodor, J. D. (1994). Extraction without traces. In *West Coast Conference on Formal Linguistics*, volume 13, 365–384. Citeseer.

Sag, I. A., Gazdar, G., Wasow, T., and Weisler, S. (1985). Coordination and how to distinguish categories. *Natural Language & Linguistic Theory*, 3:117–171.

Sag, I. A., Wasow, T., and Bender, E. M. (1999). *Syntactic theory: A formal introduction*. Center for the Study of Language and Information.

Salmelin, R. (2007). Clinical neurophysiology of language: The MEG approach. *Clinical Neurophysiology*, 118(2):237–254.

Samuel, S., Cole, G., and Eacott, M. J. (2019). Grammatical gender and linguistic relativity: A systematic review. *Psychonomic Bulletin & Review*, 26(6):1767–1786.

Sandler, W., Meir, I., Padden, C., and Aronoff, M. (2005). The emergence of grammar: Systematic structure in a new language. *Proceedings of the National Academy of Sciences*, 102(7):2661–2665.

Sanford, A. J. and Emmott, C. (2012). *Mind, Brain and Narrative*. Cambridge University Press.

Sang, E. F. and De Meulder, F. (2003). Introduction to the CoNLL-2003 shared task: Language-independent named entity recognition. *arXiv preprint cs/0306050*.

Sapir, E. (1921). *Language, an Introduction to the Study of Speech*. Harcourt, Brace.

Sapir, E. (1929). A study in phonetic symbolism. *Journal of Experimental Psychology*, 12(3):225.

Saxe, R., Brett, M., and Kanwisher, N. (2006). Divide and conquer: A defense of functional localizers. *Neuroimage*, 30(4):1088–1096.

Saxe, R. and Kanwisher, N. (2003). People thinking about thinking people: The role of the temporo-parietal junction in "theory of mind." *NeuroImage*, 19:1835–1842.

Schlenker, P., Chemla, E., and Zuberbühler, K. (2016). What do monkey calls mean? *Trends in Cognitive Sciences*, 20(12):894–904.

Schmidt, L. (2009). *Meaning and Compositionality as Statistical Induction of Categories and Constraints*. PhD thesis, Citeseer.

Schouwstra, M. and de Swart, H. (2014). The semantic origins of word order. *Cognition*, 131(3):431–436.

Schütze, C. T. (1996). *The Empirical Base of Linguistics: Grammaticality Judgments and Linguistic Methodology*. University of Chicago Press.

Schütze, C. T. and Sprouse, J. (2013). Judgment data. *Research Methods in Linguistics*, pages 27–50.

Schütze, C. T., Sprouse, J., and Caponigro, I. (2015). Challenges for a theory of islands: A broader perspective on Ambridge, Pine, and Lieven. *Language*, 91(2):e31–e39.

Scott, T. L., Gallée, J., and Fedorenko, E. (2017). A new fun and robust version of an fMRI localizer for the frontotemporal language system. *Cognitive Neuroscience*, 8(3):167–176.

Senghas, A., Kita, S., and Ozyurek, A. (2004). Children creating core properties of language: Evidence from an emerging sign language in Nicaragua. *Science*, 305(5691):1779–1782.

Shain, C. (2019). A large-scale study of the effects of word frequency and predictability in naturalistic reading. In *Proceedings of the 2019 Conference of the North American Chapter of the Association for Computational Linguistics: Human Language Technologies, Volume 1 (Long and Short Papers)*, 4086–4094, Minneapolis, Minnesota. Association for Computational Linguistics.

Shain, C., Blank, I. A., Fedorenko, E., Gibson, E., and Schuler, W. (2022). Robust effects of working memory demand during naturalistic language comprehension in language-selective cortex. *Journal of Neuroscience*, 42(39):7412–7430.

Shain, C., Blank, I. A., van Schijndel, M., Schuler, W., and Fedorenko, E. (2020). fMRI reveals language-specific predictive coding during naturalistic sentence comprehension. *Neuropsychologia*, 138:107307.

Shain, C., Meister, C., Pimentel, T., Cotterell, R., and Levy, R. (2024). Large-scale evidence for logarithmic effects of word predictability on reading time. *Proceedings of the National Academy of Sciences*, 121(10):e2307876121.

Shain, C. and Schuler, W. (2021). Continuous-time deconvolutional regression for psycholinguistic modeling. *Cognition*, 215:104735.

Shain, C., van Schijndel, M., Gibson, E., and Schuler, W. (2016). Exploring memory and processing through a gold standard annotation of dundee. *Proceedings of CUNY*.

Shannon, C. E. (1948). A mathematical theory of communication. *Bell System Technical Journal*, 27(3):379–423.

Shannon, C. E. (1949). Communication in the presence of noise. *Proceedings of the IRE*, 37(1):10–21.

Shieber, S. M. (1985). Evidence against the context-freeness of natural language. In *The Formal Complexity of Natural Language*, 320–334. Springer.

Shieber, S. M. (1986). *An Introduction to Unification-Based Approaches to Grammar*. CSLI.

Shiraïshi, A., Abeillé, A., Hemforth, B., and Miller, P. (2019). Verbal mismatch in right-node raising. *Glossa: A Journal of General Linguistics*, 4(1).

Siegal, M. and Varley, R. (2006). Aphasia, language, and theory of mind. *Social Neuroscience*, 1(3-4):167–174.

Smith, N. J. and Levy, R. (2013). The effect of word predictability on reading time is logarithmic. *Cognition*, 128(3):302–319.

Sprouse, J. (2007). *A Program for Experimental Syntax: Finding the Relationship between Acceptability and Grammatical Knowledge*. University of Maryland.

Sprouse, J. and Almeida, D. (2012). Assessing the reliability of textbook data in syntax: Adger's core syntax. *Journal of Linguistics*, 48(3):609–652.

Sprouse, J. and Almeida, D. (2013). The empirical status of data in syntax: A reply to Gibson and Fedorenko. *Language and Cognitive Processes*, 28(3):222–228.

Sprouse, J., Caponigro, I., Greco, C., and Cecchetto, C. (2016). Experimental syntax and the variation of island effects in English and Italian. *Natural Language & Linguistic Theory*, 34(1):307–344.

Sprouse, J., Schütze, C. T., and Almeida, D. (2013). A comparison of informal and formal acceptability judgments using a random sample from Linguistic Inquiry 2001–2010. *Lingua*, 134:219–248.

Sprouse, J., Wagers, M., and Phillips, C. (2012). A test of the relation between working-memory capacity and syntactic island effects. *Language*, pages 82–123.

Steedman, M. (1996). *Surface Structure and Interpretation*. MIT Press.

Steedman, M. (2001). *The Syntactic Process*. MIT Press.

Steedman, M. (2023). On internal merge. *Linguistic Inquiry*, 1–83.

Steels, L. (2011). *Design Patterns in Fluid Construction Grammar*, volume 11. John Benjamins Publishing.

Steels, L. (2012). *Computational Issues in Fluid Construction Grammar*. Springer.

Struhl, M. K., Salinas, M. A., Lim, E., Fedorenko, E., and Gibson, E. (2016). Word order patterns in gesture are sensitive to modality-specific production constraints. Manuscript, MIT Department of Brain and Cognitive Sciences.

Suzuki, T. N., Wheatcroft, D., and Griesser, M. (2016). Experimental evidence for compositional syntax in bird calls. *Nature Communications*, 7(1):1–7.

Takami, K.-i. (1988). Preposition stranding: Arguments against syntactic analyses and an alternative functional explanation. *Lingua*, 76(4):299–335.

Tanenhaus, M., Spivey-Knowlton, M., Eberhard, K., and Sedivy, J. (1995). Integration of visual and linguistic information in spoken language comprehension. *Science*, 268(5217):1632.

Temperley, D. (2007). Minimization of dependency length in written English. *Cognition*, 105(2):300–333.

Temperley, D. (2008). Dependency-length minimization in natural and artificial languages. *Journal of Quantitative Linguistics*, 15(3):256–282.

Tesnière, L. (1959). *Eléments de syntaxe structurale*. Librairie C. Klincksieck.

Tesnière, L. (2015). *Elements of Structural Syntax*. John Benjamins Publishing Company.

Tettamanti, M. and Weniger, D. (2006). Broca's area: A supramodal hierarchical processor? *Cortex*, 42(4):491–494.

Thompson, R. K., Oden, D. L., and Boysen, S. T. (1997). Language-naive chimpanzees (pan troglodytes) judge relations between relations in a conceptual matching-to-sample task. *Journal of Experimental Psychology: Animal Behavior Processes*, 23(1):31.

Thompson-Schill, S. L., D'Esposito, M., Aguirre, G. K., and Farah, M. J. (1997). Role of left inferior prefrontal cortex in retrieval of semantic knowledge: A reevaluation. *Proceedings of the National Academy of Sciences*, 94(26):14792–14797.

Tomasello, M. (2003). *Constructing a Language: A Usage-Based Theory of Language Acquisition*. Harvard University Press.

Tomasello, M. (2004). Syntax or semantics? Response to Lidz et al.-linguistics. *Cognition*, 93:139–140.

Townsend, S. W., Engesser, S., Stoll, S., Zuberbühler, K., and Bickel, B. (2018). Compositionality in animals and humans. *PLoS Biology*, 16(8):e2006425.

Tremblay, P. and Dick, A. S. (2016). Broca and Wernicke are dead, or moving past the classic model of language neurobiology. *Brain and Language*, 162:60–71.

Trueswell, J., Tanenhaus, M., and Garnsey, S. (1994a). Semantic influences on parsing: Use of thematic role information in syntactic ambiguity resolution. *Memory and Language*, 33:285–318.

Trueswell, J. C., Tanenhaus, M. K., and Garnsey, S. (1994b). Semantic influences on parsing: Use of thematic role information in syntactic ambiguity resolution. *Journal of Memory and Language*, 33:285–318.

Tse, C.-S. and Altarriba, J. (2008). Evidence against linguistic relativity in chinese and english: A case study of spatial and temporal metaphors. *Journal of Cognition and Culture*, 8(3-4):335–357.

Tseng, Y.-H., Shih, C.-F., Chen, P.-E., Chou, H.-Y., Ku, M.-C., and Hsieh, S.-K. (2022). CxLM: A construction and context-aware language model. In *Proceedings of the Thirteenth Language Resources and Evaluation Conference*, 6361–6369.

Tuckute, G., Paunov, A., Kean, H., Small, H., Mineroff, Z., Blank, I., and Fedorenko, E. (2022). Frontal language areas do not emerge in the absence of temporal language areas: A case study of an individual born without a left temporal lobe. *Neuropsychologia*, 169:108184.

Uszkoreit, H., Brants, T., Duchier, D., Krenn, B., Konieczny, L., Oepen, S., and Skut, W. (1998). Studien zur performanzorientierten linguistik. *Kognitionswissenschaft*, 7(3):129–133.

van Dyke, J. A. and Lewis, R. L. (2003). Distinguishing effects of structure and decay on attachment and repair: A cue-based parsing account of recovery from misanalyzed ambiguities. *Journal of Memory and Language*, 49(3):285–316.

van Dyke, J. A. and McElree, B. (2006). Retrieval interference in sentence comprehension. *Journal of Memory and Language*, 55:157–166.

van Schijndel, M., Exley, A., and Schuler, W. (2013). A model of language processing as hierarchic sequential prediction. *Topics in Cognitive Science*, 5(3):522–540.

Van Schijndel, M. and Schuler, W. (2013). An analysis of frequency-and memory-based processing costs. In *Proceedings of the 2013 Conference of the North American Chapter of the Association for Computational Linguistics: Human Language Technologies*, 95–105.

Van Valin, R. D. (1993). *Advances in Role and Reference Grammar*. Benjamins.

Van Valin, R. D. (1995). Toward a functionalist account of so-called extraction constraints. In Devriendt, B., Goossens, L., and van der Auwera, J., editors, *Complex Structures: A Functionalist Perspective*, 29–60. Walter de Gruyter.

Van Valin, R. D. (2001). *An Introduction to Syntax*. Cambridge University Press.

Van Valin, R. D. and LaPolla, R. J. (1997). *Syntax: Structure, Meaning, and Function*. Cambridge University Press.

Varley, R. A., Klessinger, N. J., Romanowski, C. A., and Siegal, M. (2005). Agrammatic but numerate. *Proceedings of the National Academy of Sciences*, 102(9):3519–3524.

Vasu, S. C. et al. (1897). *The Ashtadhyayi of Panini*, volume 6. Satyajnan Chaterji.

Vaswani, A., Shazeer, N., Parmar, N., Uszkoreit, J., Jones, L., Gomez, A. N., Kaiser, Ł., and Polosukhin, I. (2017). Attention is all you need. *Advances in Neural Information Processing Systems*, 30.

Vennemann, T. (1974). Theoretical word order studies: Results and problems. *Papiere zur Linguistik*, 7:5–25.

Vijay-Shanker, K. (1992). Using descriptions of trees in a tree adjoining grammar. *Computational Linguistics*, 18(4):481–518.

Vijay-Shanker, K. and Schabes, Y. (1992). Structure sharing in lexicalized tree-adjoining grammars. In *COLING 1992 Volume 1: The 14th International Conference on Computational Linguistics*.

Wagner, M. and Watson, D. G. (2010). Experimental and theoretical advances in prosody: A review. *Language and Cognitive Processes*, 25(7-9):905–945.

Wang, L., Hagoort, P., and Yang, Y. (2009). Semantic illusion depends on information structure: ERP evidence. *Brain Research*, 1282:50–56.

Wang, L., Uhrig, L., Jarraya, B., and Dehaene, S. (2015). Representation of numerical and sequential patterns in macaque and human brains. *Current Biology*, 25(15):1966–1974.

Warren, T. and Gibson, E. (2002). The influence of referential processing on sentence complexity. *Cognition*, 85(1):79–112.

Warstadt, A. and Bowman, S. R. (2022). What artificial neural networks can tell us about human language acquisition. *Algebraic Structures in Natural Language*, pages 17–60.

Warstadt, A., Singh, A., and Bowman, S. R. (2019). Neural network acceptability judgments. *Transactions of the Association for Computational Linguistics*, 7:625–641.

Wason, P. C. and Reich, S. S. (1979). A verbal illusion. *Quarterly Journal of Experimental Psychology*, 31(4):591–597.

Wasow, T. (1997). Remarks on grammatical weight. *Language Variation and Change*, 9(1):81–105.

Wasow, T. (2002). *Postverbal Behavior*. CSLI.

Wei, W., Li, X., and Pollatsek, A. (2013). Word properties of a fixated region affect outgoing saccade length in chinese reading. *Vision Research*, 80:1–6.

Weissweiler, L., He, T., Otani, N., Mortensen, D. R., Levin, L., and Schütze, H. (2023). Construction grammar provides unique insight into neural language models. *arXiv preprint arXiv:2302.02178*.

Wellwood, A., Pancheva, R., Hacquard, V., and Phillips, C. (2018). The anatomy of a comparative illusion. *Journal of Semantics*, 35(3):543–583.

Weskott, T. and Fanselow, G. (2011). On the informativity of different measures of linguistic acceptability. *Language*, 87(2):249–273.

Whorf, B. L. (1956). *Language, Thought, and Reality: Selected Writings of Benjamin Lee Whorf*. MIT Press.

Wilcox, E. G., Futrell, R., and Levy, R. (2023). Using computational models to test syntactic learnability. *Linguistic Inquiry*, 1–44.

Winawer, J., Witthoft, N., Frank, M. C., Wu, L., Wade, A. R., and Boroditsky, L. (2007). Russian blues reveal effects of language on color discrimination. *Proceedings of the National Academy of Sciences*, 104(19):7780–7785.

Wittgenstein, L. (1953). *Philosophical Investigations*. Blackwell.

Wnuk, E., Verkerk, A., Levinson, S. C., and Majid, A. (2022). Color technology is not necessary for rich and efficient color language. *Cognition*, 229:105223.

Wolf, F. and Gibson, E. (2005). Representing discourse coherence: A corpus-based study. *Computational Linguistics*, 31(2):249–287.

Yadav, H., Husain, S., and Futrell, R. (2021). Do dependency lengths explain constraints on crossing dependencies? *Linguistics Vanguard*, 7(s3).

Yamashita, H. and Chang, F. (2001). "Long before short" preference in the production of a head-final language. *Cognition*, 81(2):B45–B55.

Yang, Y. and Piantadosi, S. T. (2022). One model for the learning of language. *Proceedings of the National Academy of Sciences*, 119(5):e2021865119.

Yngve, V. H. (1960). A model and an hypothesis for language structure. *Proceedings of the American Philosophical Society*, 104(5):444–466.

Yudkowsky, E. (2017). A human's guide to words. https://www.lesswrong.com/s/SGB7Y5WERh4skwtnb.

Zaslavsky, N., Kemp, C., Tishby, N., and Regier, T. (2019). Communicative need in colour naming. *Cognitive Neuropsychology*, pages 1–13.

Zevin, J. D. and Seidenberg, M. S. (2002). Age of acquisition effects in word reading and other tasks. *Journal of Memory and Language*, 47(1):1–29.

Zhan, M., Chen, S., Lu, J., Levy, R., and Gibson, E. (2023). Rational sentence interpretation in Mandarin Chinese. *Cognitive Science*. 47:e13383

Zhang, Y., Kauf, C., and Gibson, E. (2023a). A noisy-channel explanation of the comparative illusion, talk presented at Architechtures and Mechanisms in Language Processing (AMLAP), San Sebastian, Spain.

Zhang, Y., Ryskin, R., and Gibson, E. (2023b). A noisy-channel approach to depth-charge illusions. *Cognition*. 232, https://doi.org/10.1016/j.cognition.2022.105346.

Index

Publisher contact:
The MIT Press
Massachusetts Institute of Technology
77 Massachusetts Avenue, Cambridge, MA 02139
mitpress.mit.edu

EU Authorised Representative:
Easy Access System Europe, Mustamäe tee 50,
10621 Tallinn, Estonia
gpsr.requests@easproject.com

Printed by Integrated Books International,
United States of America